Literature for Young Children

Custom Edition

Joan I. Glazer

Taken from:
Literature for Young Children, Fourth Edition
by Joan I. Glazer

Taken from:

Literature for Young Children, Fourth Edition
by Joan I. Glazer
Copyright © 2000, 1991 by Prentice-Hall, Inc.
A Pearson Education Company
Upper Saddle River, New Jersey 07458

This special edition published in cooperation with Pearson Custom Publishing.

Printed in the United States of America

10 9 8 7 6 5

ISBN 0-536-70466-X

2005220037

EM

Please visit our web site at *www.pearsoncustom.com*

PEARSON CUSTOM PUBLISHING
75 Arlington Street, Suite 300, Boston, MA 02116
A Pearson Education Company

PREFACE

Bringing children and books together is an exciting experience for parents and educators who care about children and who believe that well-written literature has much to offer the developing individual. This book is concerned with children and how they grow, with literature as an art form, and with the ways that literature supports children's development.

This fourth edition follows the structure used in earlier editions, but adds information about visual literacy, about national, regional, and local standards, and about the growing realm of technology and interactive books. There are new books mentioned throughout and updated research findings included. The first three chapters introduce the range of literature for children, demonstrate how standards of literary excellence can be applied, and provide suggestions for day-care professionals and teachers for working with parents as they select literature. Chapter 4 advocates grouping books for presentation so that children discern the interrelatedness of all literature. Chapters 5 through 9 focus on the opportunities books offer for supporting children's language, intellectual, personality, social and moral, aesthetic and creative development and indicate specific teaching strategies that will enhance growth in these areas. The final chapter shows the many options a day-care professional or teacher has in presenting books, using one book appropriate for preschoolers and one appropriate for primary-grade children as examples. It gives suggestions for determining appropriate approaches and guidelines for evaluating a literature program.

Literature for Children is designed to be used by both preservice and inservice teachers, by day-care professionals, and by all who work with preschool and primary age children. A brief introduction to each chapter reviews educational theory and research pertinent to the topic. Extensive examples of specific books and strategies follow each introduction. Charts at the end of chapters 4 through 9 give a quick review and age-level suggestions for the books presented. Experienced teachers and day-care professionals will find new titles discussed and will see familiar stories presented in a new light. Students preparing for a career in early childhood education will be introduced to both classic and contemporary books for children and will learn an approach to literature that allows them to select and share high quality books and poetry effectively.

The writer is indebted to the many colleagues who shared their experiences with books and with children, and to photographer Gordon Rowley, who captured on film the children, teachers, and day-care professionals at the Henry Barnard School as they went about their daily activities. Thanks to the reviewers of the manuscript for their comments and insights: Alice Denham, Texas Tech University; Maria Weiner, Medaille College; and Deborah W. Whaley, Fayetteville Technical Community College. Special thanks to Mary Evangelista of Prentice-Hall, always helpful, always cheerful. And, finally, thanks to and a kiss for my husband, Wes Miller, for his constant encouragement, pride in my work, and sense of humor about my working hours.

CONTENTS

LITERATURE FOR YOUNG CHILDREN
Fourth Edition

JOAN I. GLAZER
Rhode Island College

1

DEFINING LITERATURE FOR CHILDREN

The four-year-olds listened intently as a day-care professional read to them of Boris von der Borch, a pirate in search of buried treasure in *Tough Boris* (Fox, 1994). They chimed in on the refrain. Each time an adjective was applied to Boris, it was repeated in the statement that "All pirates are ____ ." All pirates are tough, and massive, and scruffy, and greedy, and fearless, and scary. The children looked at the illustrations, discovering that much of the story was being told through the pictures. They talked about times they had felt sad and cried, responding to the ending in which tough Boris cries when his parrot dies. Later that day, the children watched as trash haulers emptied a dumpster into their truck. "Wow," one little girl remarked. "That truck is massive."

It had been apparent during the reading that the children were enjoying the story. Their attention, their smiles, and their cheerful chorus on each refrain demonstrated that. Enjoyment, however, was not all that took place that afternoon. For at least one child, vocabulary enrichment had occurred. The regular sharing of literature with children frequently leads to vocabulary growth, increased reading comprehension, and concept development.

Children form attitudes about literature based on their individual experiences with books and with learning to read. One nine-year-old said that listening to stories was "like being there"; another child said that it was nice to have books when the classroom was noisy; a third simply said that books and reading were "punishment." Their encounters with literature had left them with very different opinions about books and reading.

The primary goal of a literature program in the preschool and primary years is the creation of a positive attitude toward literature. Children who enjoy and value literature will continue to read and experience it and will have found a lifelong source of emotional and intellectual enrichment. Teachers of young children, day-care providers, and parents are in an ideal position to help create such an attitude.

This book is designed to show the many ways in which literature can and does support the goals of early childhood education and how it can be presented so that children develop and maintain a positive attitude toward literary experiences. Before seeing how literature contributes to the achievement of developmental goals, however, it is essential that you first be aware of the wide range of stories and poems currently available for young children, and that you be able to select from these the best in terms of literary quality. Thus this first chapter is devoted to defining types of literature and the second chapter to describing criteria for selecting quality literature. In addition, there are sections on children's preferences and responses to literature, and suggestions for helping parents select books and book-related media.

THE RANGE OF LITERATURE

There are several categorization systems used to describe and classify books, and within each there are occasional differences of opinion among experts about the placement or labeling of books. Children's books frequently are classified in one of two ways, either by their format or by their genre.

Format

The format of a book is its general makeup. This includes its size, shape, binding, arrangement of illustrations, cover, paper, typography, and spacing. A description of the format of the picture book *Ox-Cart Man* (Hall, 1979) would include the fact that it is a hardcover book, wider than it is high. The dust jacket shows the New England farmer standing in front of his ox cart, ready to begin the journey to Portsmouth Market. The actual cover of the book depicts the farmer walking off, followed by ox and cart, with wife and child waving good-bye, all shown in silhouette. The end papers are white, with the first small illustration appearing on the title page. Most of the book utilizes full-page color illustrations facing a white page on which the text is centered. In a few cases the illustration blends over onto two pages or appears across the entire top half of a double-page spread. The text is printed in clear bold type, with ample space between lines. Heavy, high-quality paper and a sturdy binding make the book appear durable.

Many children's books are available in both hardcover and paperback editions. Paperbacks are less expensive, thus bringing quality literature within the economic reach of more families. However, they are not as durable as hardcover books. Sometimes a paperback edition of a picture book differs greatly from the original in size. This may be a factor in selecting a book to read to a group of children. A larger book will give the children a better view of the illustrations. Occasionally a paperback is published in black and white when the original is in color. In this case, the hardcover edition would be the better choice.

The effectiveness of the format is one criterion for assessing the quality of a book. For example, a book with an inadequate binding may resemble a looseleaf notebook after five readings. Poor paper can dull otherwise excellent illustrations. Even the placement of illustrations on the page is important. If eight Mother Goose rhymes are crowded together on a single page, with illustrations scattered randomly to fill the white spaces, young children may be confused about which illustration goes with which verse. The same is true for counting books, where placement on the page can help or hinder young children as they make the connection between the objects pictured and the numeral representing the objects.

Unusual Formats

Some books stand out because of their unusual format. In *The Very Busy Spider* (1984) by Eric Carle, each strand of the web is raised on the paper so we not only see but also feel the web as it develops from outer edge and spokes to its full pattern of concentric circles. In Carle's *The Very Quiet Cricket* (1990), the sound of cricket chirping is heard on the last page, thanks to a microchip embedded in the endpapers, as the little cricket finally is able to create sound by rubbing his wings together. The format and the repetitious text in both books encourage the child's active participation.

Robert Sabuda has illustrated Davol's *The Paper Dragon* (1997) using triple gate-fold illustrations. The reader sees an illustration on the left page and text on the right, and can then unfold the right page to reveal a broad three-page illustration, building on the Chinese scroll-maker's art. The format matches the content of this story of the humble artist, Mi Fei, who with paintings on paper scrolls is able to save his village from the great dragon of Lung Mountain.

Janet and Allan Ahlberg encourage participation through another unusual format. They have created two books that have pages constructed as envelopes, with letters inside. *The Jolly Postman or Other People's Letters* (1986) is the story of the postman who goes around on his bicycle delivering these letters; but the fun is in the letters themselves. They are all addressed to storybook characters and represent various types of mail. They include an advertisement from "Hobgoblin Supplies Ltd" that is addressed to the "Occupant" of the Gingerbread Bungalow; Baby Bear's invitation to Goldilocks' party; and a letter to the wolf received from the attorneys representing Red Riding Hood. *The Jolly Christmas Postman* (1991) has the same postman delivering Christmas gifts and messages, again to storybook characters but this time with small puzzles and games, even a fold-out peep show for the postman from Santa. Teachers using these books have found it helpful to take photocopies of the letters and games as insurance against loss or damage.

Format should be used to make the literature more effective. In *The Very Busy Spider,* the raised web reinforces the growing pattern of the web and complements the patterning of the language. In *Ox-Cart Man,* the basic format of placing illustrations on the page opposite the text is broken up three times by placing illustrations across the top half of double-page spreads. These three spreads depict the farmer's journey to and from the market. The long horizontal shape of the illustration creates a sense of the length of the journey and allows a panoramic view of the hills, valleys, streams, and farms that lie between the farmer's home and Portsmouth Market. Thus format is used to enhance the presentation of the story.

Format classifications are used regularly to identify types of books. The most common are toy and board books, wordless picture books, picture books, illustrated books, and chapter books.

Toy and Board Books

Toy books are books with some special device for involving readers. Some have portions that the children can touch to feel different textures. *The Touch Me Book* (Witts, n.d.), for example, includes sandpaper, a sponge, and a feather. The text includes adjectives describing how each feels, and, because of their active participation with the book, children will grasp the terms quickly. Van Fleet, in *Fuzzy Yellow Ducklings* (1995), uses this same technique but weaves in colors and shapes as well. Young listeners can touch the sticky pink frog tongue shaped like a line. Still other books have pop-up figures that come to life as the page is turned, or various flaps to be lifted or pulled. Eric Hill's stories about Spot (1980, 1982, 1984, 1986, 1990, 1996), a friendly and inquisitive puppy, are popular with toddlers who delight in answering the questions the text poses, then lifting the flap or pulling the tab to reveal the answers. Robert Sabuda's counting book, *Cookie Count* (1997), brings gasps of surprise and delight as his intricate paper engineering twists and twirls plate after plate of cookies, culminating in a gingerbread house with ten windows. Children can count the number of cookies and also search for the same number of mice, each wearing his baker's hat, as the numbers go from one to ten.

Toy books are generally best suited for use by individual children rather than groups. Many are not sturdy enough for repeated use, and even when durable they require that children take turns. Some, such as flip books, can be used by only one child at a time. In these, the reader must riffle through the pages rapidly to get the effect of animation and thus "see" the story. Only the person holding the book is positioned to see the full effect of changes in the drawings from page to page.

Board books are printed on heavy cardboard and are often laminated. They are designed for very young children who are just learning to handle books. Because of the stiffness of the pages, they can be grasped and turned more easily than paper pages, and they are less likely to tear. Some board books are cut in the shape of their "topic," often vehicles or animals.

Board books vary greatly in quality, from those with inaccurate information and overly cute language and characters, to those of moderate quality (the vast majority of books), to some very fine works by authors such as Eric Hill, Tana Hoban, Helen Oxenbury, Leo Lionni, Nancy Tafuri, John Burningham, Dick Bruna, and Rosemary Wells. Good board books give clear pictures for the child to use in naming, have simple direct plots, if there is a plot, are accurate in text and illustration, and are appropriate in content for children of one to three years of age. Helen Oxenbury's *All Fall Down* (1987) is an excellent example of a quality board book. The text is only four lines, with a catchy rhythm and rhyme. A group of toddlers is pictured running around, bouncing on the bed, then all tumbling down on the bed. The clear and uncluttered illustrations capture the action and enjoyment of the four youngsters, who seem to run and bounce in time with the text.

Many board books have been created from books originally published as picture books. They may use all the text and illustrations, or excerpt certain sections, or rewrite and simplify the text. Some make the transition well but others do not. Changing the size of the illustrations, say from 10 inches by 11 inches, to 4 inches by 5 inches, may cause the detail to be lost. The content that was written for a child eight or nine years old may not be understandable by a two year old. Lifting only portions of a text may eliminate the coherence and leave a somewhat confusing snapshot of a story. And, generally speaking, it is better to wait until a child can appreciate a particular story than to simplify it for a younger audience. When assessing a board book, look at it as a new publication and judge it for its own merit.

Some argue that toy and board books, and those printed on cloth or plastic—the latter float in the tub—are in fact not books at all. Dorothy Butler, in *Babies Need Books* (1982), acknowledges that for her something is a book only if it is printed on paper, and that she can accept board books uneasily at best. Nevertheless, board books are durable and can be handled successfully by very young children. Selecting such age-appropriate materials encourages a positive attitude toward books.

Wordless Picture Books

Wordless picture books are exactly what the name implies. They are books that have no text and present their message through pictures only. They are also called textless picture books and books without words. Raymond Brigg's *The Snowman* (1978) is a wordless picture book that tells the story in a sequence of pictures on each page, somewhat like a comic strip. Some pages have as many as twelve small illustrations, while others vary the size and number of pictures. At one point there is a single illustration covering two pages. The story opens with a little boy waking to a snowy morning, going outside, and building a snowman. During the night that follows, the boy wakes and goes outside to see his snowman. The snowman greets him with a tip of his hat. The two shake hands, and the boy invites the snowman into the house where they explore the marvels of indoor living. The fire in the fireplace is not to the snowman's liking, but he does enjoy cooling his hands before the open refrigerator door and playing with light switches and skateboards. The snowman returns the boy's hospitality by taking him by the hand and flying him to distant cities. They return before morning, and after a farewell hug and wave, the boy goes back to bed. Morning and the warm sunshine wake the boy, who runs eagerly to see his friend. Morning and the warm sunshine have also had an effect on the snowman. The boy finds a hat and scarf on a small pile of melting snow. *The Snowman* is simple enough to be understood by preschoolers, can still be enjoyed by second graders, and is appealing to an adult sharing the literary experience with a child.

The Snowman can provide a very interesting study in format and adaptation. It is available in the original hardcover 8½ × 11 inch size. It is also in paperback as well as in miniature edition, 3½ × 5 inches, with all of the original illustrations, just much smaller (1989). There is a board book series that uses segments of 12 illustrations for each book, but these illustrations are from the video based on the book, not the book itself. For example, *Raymond Briggs' The Snowman, Walking in the Air* (1985) has only parts showing the boy and the snowman flying, then landing in an area with pine trees and many other snowmen. The video, and also the film version, were produced by Weston Woods Studios and are available through Scholastic Publishers. The video adds animation and several new scenes, including one in which the snowman and boy come to a snowy Christmas celebration, and is known for the superb music on the soundtrack. There is even a version, titled *The Snowman Story Book* (1990), in which Briggs has written text to accompany illustrations selected from the original book for a shorter telling of the basic elements of the story.

Tabby (Aliki, 1995) is a simpler wordless picture book in terms of the structure of the illustrations and the directness of the story line. It has only one or two pictures on each page, plus five double-page spreads, easier to follow than a series of panels in various configurations. The narrative is straightforward. A little girl and her father select a kitten at the animal shelter, bring it home, and care for it. The kitten is shown lapping milk, sleeping quietly in its basket beside the girl's bed, and engaged in playing with the kitten from next door. The illustrations clearly portray the passage of time, with the seasons changing and a new baby ar-

Tabby is a wordless picture book with a straightforward narrative. (Copyright © 1995 by ALIKI. Used by permission of HarperCollins Publishers.)

riving in the household. The book ends with the little girl and the next-door twins celebrating Tabby's first birthday. Attention to details, such as the frog escaping from a watercan just over-turned by Tabby, give this wordless book added interest and humor.

Wordless books vary in complexity. Tana Hoban's *Just Look* (1996) focuses attention to detail as only a small portion of an object or animal shows through a circle cut out of every other page. The cut pages are black, making a clear frame for what is shown. When the cut page is turned, the full object shows. The black-and-white pattern, for example, is part of a penguin's neck. When the page with one penguin is turned, the back of it shows a group of penguins. The book can be used as a visual guessing game—what is it that we are seeing? Viewers begin paying attention to color and texture and pattern.

The predictable structure of *Just Look* gives it coherence. Another wordless book that involves guessing what is being seen is *Zoom* (1995) by Istvan Banyai. However, after the first illustration, a close-up of a cockscomb on a rooster, the game is not identifying what, but identifying where. Each illustration is from farther away, thus showing more of the context. Some are surprises. After going from rooster, to children watching it, to a full farmyard scene, the illustration shows that all of this is a toy farmyard being set up on a table. The toys turn out to be on the cover of a magazine about toys being read by a boy on an ocean liner. Eventually the view is of the earth, which fades into a tiny white dot on a double-page spread of black. There is a pattern, but one that requires a higher level of understanding than the pattern of *Just Look.* Not all wordless picture books are for very young children. You must evaluate the understanding level required for these books, just as you would for books with text.

Picture Books

Picture books are those books that rely on a combination of illustrations and narrative, with both being integral to the completed work. The author of *Hello Toes! Hello Feet!* (Paul, 1998) describes a day in the life of a very active little girl, beginning when she awakens, rubs her eyes, and looks down at her feet.

> "Good morning, toes,
>
> Good morning, feet,
>
> tangled up between my sheets."
>
> *Paul*

Her feet are the first part of her to touch the floor, the last part of her body she dries after her bedtime bath. In between she can clomp down the stairs, kick the kitchen table, point her toes to the sky as she swings, and jump across a creek. She can delight in the sensory awareness of mud between her toes or cool water splashing around her legs, the sound and feel of fallen leaves as she shuffles her way through them. The rhyming text is bouncy and upbeat, exuding energy and enthusiasm. The print appears in different places on different pages, always large and clear, often at a slightly jaunty angle.

The illustrations match the spirit of the text. They are filled with motion and humor, show the details of the action, and extend the story. The title page sets the stage with the letters of the title in different colors and patterns, the left page illustration showing just one hand and both feet, the hand carefully applying polish to the toenails, and the right page illustration showing the little girl bending over looking at the sandals on her feet—pink with pieces of fruit on top as decoration. When the girl wakes up, her dog is on the bed, and it is a part of all her adventures, from rather reluctantly crossing the stream after her, to tiptoeing with her past the sleeping baby. While the dog is not mentioned in the text, the illustrations make it an integral part of the events. Text and illustrations work together to convey both content and mood. When the text talks about the little girl kicking the table while she eats breakfast, the illustrations portray both the kick and the resulting action. Everything on the table bounces into the air, including the bowl of cereal. Some of the Happy O's cereal flies into the air, and the dog happily catches this unexpected reward. Her little brother slams his hand down on a piece of jam-covered toast and grins. Life is grand!

The illustrations in Hello Toes! Hello Feet! *by Ann Whitford Paul match the exuberant spirit of the text. (Copyright © 1998. Reprinted by permission of DK Publishing, Inc.)*

Picture Story Books.   Some authorities differentiate between the general term *picture book* and the more-specialized term *picture story book*. A picture story book is not simply a description of everyday events or a portrayal of how a character felt in a particular situation. It has a definite plot, a problem to be solved, and interrelatedness of events. For example, in *Grandmother Bryant's Pocket* (Martin, 1997), set in 1787, eight-year old Sarah has nightmares about fire and smoke after the family's barn burns down, and her dog Patches died in it. Her parents take her to spend time with her grandmother, who is "quiet and strong" and knows plants and herbs, and perhaps will have a cure for Sarah's bad dreams. Sarah drinks her grandmother's tea, enjoys her grandfather's stories and songs, and becomes friends with a stray cat. But there are, as her grandfather says, no quick cures. The dreams continue, and her grandmother gives Sarah a pocket that her own mother had made for her when she had bad dreams as a child. The pocket is linen, stitched with a tree and the words "Fear Not." Grandmother has used it for fifty years to carry herbs, bandages, and scissors she used in her healing, and two gold buttons. (A note at the beginning of the book explains that pockets were not sewn into women's skirts at that time, so women wore a pocket tied around their waists and hidden under their skirts.)

Sarah loses the pocket, and it is found by Beck Chadwick, a rather nasty neighbor, who keeps it. However, when Beck falls and needs Grandmother's help, she tells where the pocket is so that the scissors and bandages can be retrieved and she can be treated. Sarah learns how to get past the hissing geese that Beck owns, and by the time her grandparents' bean plants are full of blossoms, Sarah asks to go home. She takes her grandmother's pocket, filled with chamomile, rosemary, and comfrey seed, and a wooden box with a goose feather from her grandfather, and the cat with her.

The story's events are related through cause and effect and through the central problem—Sarah's fear and bad dreams after the fire. There is a definite chronology to the happenings. *Hello Toes! Hello Feet!* and *Grandmother Bryant's Pocket* are similar in that both have a young girl as the central character and both involve pets. Both are picture books but only *Grandmother Bryant's Pocket* is classified as a picture story book.

Concept Books.   Another specialized type of picture book is the concept book—a book that explicates a general idea or concept by presenting many specific examples of it. A book about colors will show an object or objects labeled with the color word. *Red, Blue, Yellow Shoe* (1986) by Tana Hoban is a board book that has a photograph of the object, a dot of that color, and the word printed in the color it names. The photographs are of familiar objects: an orange, a blue mitten, a black cat. The pictures have a clean and spacious look, good for use in naming activities as well as for color recognition.

Another book by Hoban, *Colors Everywhere* (1995), presents a visual matching game. Colors that are prominent in a photograph appear in a bar beside the photo. Thus the fuzzy ducklings have a bar showing yellow and gold; the city scene on a rainy day has yellow and red for the raincoats, blue for the jeans, gold that matches the boots the girl is wearing, green for the grass, and white for a parked car. Children can point to the matching colors, sometimes making gross discriminations, sometimes differentiating between two or more shades of the same hue.

Still other concept books combine ideas. *Chidi Only Likes Blue: An African Book of Colors* by Ifeoma Onyefulu (1997) introduces information about Chidi's Nigerian culture by describing selected objects in the village for each color. Black, for example, is the color used for decorating the outside of houses during the dry season. The color is derived from the juice of the seeds of the Uli tree.

Concept books often explain relationships. There are books that illustrate the concept of opposites, show the meanings of comparative terms, or match up parts of animals to the whole. *Step by Step* (1987) by Bruce McMillan looks at the relationship of age to motor skills by photographing the activities of a baby over a ten-month period, from age four months to age fourteen months. Footprints across the title page foreshadow the book's ending. The child goes from crawling, to kneeling and holding on, to standing up, and finally, to running home. The child in the photographs wears the same clothing for each photograph in the same age grouping, which helps the reader recognize the different age groups. Children can follow the chronology of the baby's growth, exploring the concepts that babies become more skilled as they get older, and that different abilities often are correlated with different ages.

Alphabet and counting books are two of the most popular types of concept books. As with other picture books, these come in many levels of sophistication. You cannot assume that the subject matter automatically makes them appropriate for children just learning to recognize letters or learning to count. Consider the child's level of development and your purpose for using the book as you begin looking over alphabet and counting books.

If you want children to recognize letters and see how they are formed, then you might select *Wildflower ABC: An Alphabet of Potato Prints* (1997) by Diana Pomeroy or *Flora McDonnell's ABC* (1997) by McDonnell. Initial letter recognition is best served by a book that shows both capital and lowercase letters, which both of these books do. *Wildflower ABC* shows an upper and a lower case letter beside the name of each flower and *Flora McDonnell's ABC* shows a large animal or object paired with a small one for each letter, with both upper-case and lower-case letters.

If you want children to explore the sounds that letters make, be particularly careful that the objects are those that give the usual sounds of the letters. For example, "C" should not be illustrated with a chicken, because even though the word begins with a "c," it is the sound of the "ch" blend that is heard. Check also that the pictures are not ones that could be given different names by young children—the rabbit for "R" being called a "bunny," for instance. *Alice and Aldo* (Lester, 1998) is good for sound/symbol correspondence because it gives several examples of words starting with a particular letter in the text. Alice and her stuffed donkey Aldo have "breakfast in bed" and "paint a pink picture." In addition, most pages have pictures of other items that begin with the letter shown around the framed central illustration. The repetition can help children make the connection between the letters and their sounds.

Sometimes an alphabet book will follow a theme, perhaps even weaving a story into the presentation of the letters. *Pigs from A to Z* (Geisert, 1986) opens with a depiction of some rather acrobatic pigs, who lean, bend, curve, and balance one another so that each letter is formed. Then the story begins: the pigs build a tree house, but take time out for recreation. "J is for juggling boards for the tree house joists," but "Q is for a quiet game of croquet before getting back to work." In addition, letters are hidden in various places throughout each illustration. This is a book for children with some knowledge of the alphabet, who are ready to play observational games.

For other books, the alphabet may be a way of organizing content; and it is the content, not the fact that it is an alphabet book, that determines its choice. Alma Flor Ada's *Gathering the Sun: An Alphabet in Spanish and English* (1997) is a collection of poetry about the lives of migrant farmworkers, with the Spanish text determining the placement. Thus "A" is represented by "arboles" (trees) and "Z" by "zanahoria" (carrot). You would choose to use this book for its outstanding short poems, for its depiction of the lives of the farmworkers and the honor in their work, or for its text in both Spanish and English more than for its usefulness as an alphabet book.

Choose alphabet books based on their special attributes and with an eye toward how children might use them. Shannon's *Tomorrow's Alphabet* (1996) makes the alphabet a guessing game about what comes next. The "B" is for "eggs," tomorrow's "birds," and "I" is for "water," tomorrow's "ice cubes." *Ah! Belle Cite! A Beautiful City ABC* (Poulin, 1985) uses the alphabet as the format for presenting a series of twenty-six paintings of Montreal, with both the French and the English words given. It encourages children to look at their own neighborhood, provides an opportunity to see similarities and differences between the two languages, and demonstrates that different peoples may speak different languages and that many speak more than one language.

All the alphabet books discussed present well-crafted illustrations using photography, painting, or graphic arts, and all of them may stimulate discussion between adult and child about the objects or scenes presented. Very young children may look at a single illustration and name it. Eight-year-olds may look at a page filled with action, with hidden letters or objects, and test their own observation skills.

Counting books often follow the same format as alphabet books. The numeral, the word, and a picture illustrating the number are shown, with one number per page. Books for toddlers concentrate on number recognition and matching a numeral or number word to the correct number of objects. Clarity of illustrations is essential, for these children are checking their skill at counting and their understanding of the concept. Children should be introduced to counting through the use of concrete objects, and this use of manipulatives should continue as they progress through the primary grades and as counting books and other materials are presented to them. George Lyon's *Counting on the Woods* (1998) uses color photographs of plants and animals, all identified in captions, to represent the numbers 1 through 10 clearly. Arlene Alda's *1 2 3: What Do You See?* (1998), focuses attention on the shape of the numeral, captured in photographs of natural and everyday objects. A stork's legs form a 4; a wisp of curly hair a 6; a conch shell a 9. Numerals from 1 to 10 show at the side or bottom of each page, with the numeral to be found in the photograph highlighted by its large size and its color. Children can look themselves for objects or parts of objects that form numerals.

Lois Ehlert's *Fish Eyes: A Book You Can Count On* (1990) adds several elements to basic counting. Using the premise that if the author were a fish, she'd swim far into the ocean and see, first, one green fish, then two jumping fish, and so on through ten, each page states that the number of fish seen, "plus me," makes ___ , and the next number is stated, thus introducing both the concept and the language of addition. The "me" is a tiny black fish on each double-page spread. The fish seen are in patterned neon colors shown on a deep blue background, with the eyes cut out so that colors from the previous and the next page show through. The endpapers, title page, and introductory and concluding pages have many fish, allowing for counting to higher numbers and counting by category—such as black fish or fish with blue eyes. Individual pages throughout the book can be used for categorization and counting also, using the number of dots or stripes on a fish, or the number of fins.

As with alphabet books, some counting books tell a story around the numbers or use the number format as an organizing theme. Hutchins's *1 Hunter* (1982) tells its story in the illustrations, as the one hunter, complete in safari outfit with pith helmet, stalks through the jungle, staring so intently ahead that he misses seeing all the animals—until he turns around, that is, and is so frightened seeing the entire menagerie that he runs off down the path.

Moja Means One (Feelings, 1971), subtitled *Swahili Counting Book*, organizes information about East African village life around the listing of a numeral and the Swahili word for it. The author writes in her introduction to the book that she hopes that boys and girls of African origin will learn both to count in Swahili and to know something of their heritage.

There are counting books that require a fair amount of counting competence and test, rather than teach, the concept. *When Sheep Cannot Sleep* (Kitamura, 1986) seldom mentions numbers, but tells what one sheep named Woody does when he cannot sleep. He goes for a walk and chases a butterfly; sees two ladybugs; notices "some" owls (there are three); and so forth. If you're wondering whether he ever does get to sleep, be assured that he does. This sheep that cannot sleep finally lies down in bed and thinks about his relatives. The child looking at this book must first identify the organizing scheme, then find and count the objects that are named in the context of the story.

Anno's Counting Book (Anno, 1977) is as much a book on categorizing as it is a counting book. The numeral is shown beside each double-page illustration, but within the illustration are objects that must be categorized into groups before they can be counted. Thus "four" has four buildings (three houses and a church), but eight trees (four evergreen and four deciduous). The illustrations, which also show seasonal changes, lend themselves to discussion about how objects might be categorized, what is happening in each illustration, and the need for a system of enumeration.

When you select counting books, keep in mind, once again, what you expect them to accomplish, and the child's level of comprehension. A group of kindergarten teachers looked at *26 Letters and 99 Cents* (Hoban, 1987), a book that combines teaching the alphabet and learning to count using money. The alphabet part is read in one direction, the counting part in the opposite direction. The teachers judged the illustrations to be outstanding, clear, and colorful. They considered the alphabet part to be extremely useful because the children could look at the letters and name the objects. The counting and coin part they saw as inappropriate for kindergartners. It begins with pennies and looks like a standard counting book; but beginning with number five, the illustration is divided into two blocks—one shows five pennies; the other, a nickel. The numbers 6 through 9 are shown with pennies and with a nickel and pennies. The block for the number ten is divided into thirds for pennies, nickels, and a dime; counting by ones, fives, and tens continues up to ninety-nine. This half of the book requires a knowledge of money that kindergartners do not usually have and that they would best learn through concrete experiences. Once children have learned the sets, the book would provide strong reinforcement.

Beginning-to-Read Books.   Publishers use labels such as "I Can Read," "Read Alone," "Step Into Reading," and "Easy-to-Read" to denote books that have a limited vocabulary and regulated sentence length, factors that contribute to the ease with which material can be read. They are designed for beginning readers. Attention is given to the number of difficult words, but the writing is not done from a standardized word list, as are some stories in basal readers. Beginning-to-read books are excellent choices for the independent reading of children just learning to read, and usually are used for this purpose rather than for reading aloud to children.

Skilled writers are able to work within the constraints of vocabulary and sentence-length restrictions to produce interesting and well-written stories. There is no need to limit the topics of easy-reading books. Young readers can explore traditional literature through books such as Patricia McKissack's *Monkey-Monkey's Trick* (1988), a story based on an African folktale. They can read about historical incidents in books like *The 18 Penny Goose* (Walker, 1998) in which young Letty and her family must leave their farm to escape approaching British soldiers during the Revolutionary War, or in a biography of Rosa Parks (Parks with Haskins, 1998) that explores the beginnings of the civil rights movement in the United States. They can laugh at and be challenged by the riddles, filled with language play and puns, in *Puppy Riddles* (Hall and Eisenberg, 1998). They can scare themselves with the tales in Alvin Schwartz's *In a Dark, Dark Room* (1984), a collection of classic ghost stories often told on Halloween or around a campfire at night.

There is no need, either, for writers to use an "Oh! Oh! Look! Look! Look!" style of writing. Arnold Lobel has captured the natural cadence of speech in *Frog and Toad Are Friends* (1970). Frog arrives at Toad's house and knocks on the door:

> "Toad, Toad," shouted Frog, "wake up. It is spring!"
>
> "Blah," said a voice from inside the house.
>
> "Toad, Toad!" cried Frog. "The sun is shining! The snow is melting. Wake up!"
>
> "I am not here," said the voice. (pp. 4–5)

The sentences are short and the vocabulary easy, but the humor shines through.

Young independent readers can begin to make friends with book characters such as Frog and Toad, getting to know them well through the several books that feature their adventures. Enjoying one book leads to reading another. Cynthia Rylant's series of easy-reading books about Henry and his dog Mudge (1998) and Edward and James Marshall's books about Fox (1988) are filled with natural-sounding dialogue, fast action, and humor. They capture children's imaginations by developing characters and themes effectively and by using language creatively.

Predictable Books.   Predictable books have a structure that allows children to predict with some accuracy what will happen next. Sometimes that structure is in the repetition of a refrain. *Busy Monday Morning* (Domanska, 1985) opens with "On a Monday morning, busy Monday morning, Father mowed hay, and so did I. We mowed hay together, he and I." Each day there is a different activity as they harvest the hay, and each day the refrain is the same. Even when heard for the first time, by "Thursday" children can respond with the second sentence once they hear the first. The words to this translated Polish folk song have rhyme and rhythm, and a pattern of following the days of the week that make it even more predictable.

Sometimes the predictability is in the structure of the story itself. Denise Fleming's *Mama Cat Has Three Kittens* (1998) shows Mama Cat engaged in many activities. When she washes her paws, or walks along a stone wall, or chases leaves, two of her kittens, Fluffy and Skinny, always do the same; but the third kitten, Boris, naps. The pattern of the language is always the same as well. However, when Mama, Fluffy, and Skinny curl up to nap, then Boris springs into action and pounces on all three of them. After that, of course, Boris once again naps.

Cumulative tales, such as *Bearsie Bear and the Surprise Sleepover Party* (Waber, 1997) are predictable because what has happened before is repeated with each new event. In this story, Bearsie Bear, in his nice warm bed, is snuggled down under the covers when one-by-one a series of animals come and ask for shelter from the snow and wind. Bearsie Bear admits each, finally sharing his bed with Goosie Goose, Foxie Fox, Piggie Pig, Cowsie Cow, and Moosie Moose. With each new animal, the whole line-up is repeated. The pattern is broken when Porkie Porcupine declares it a sleepover party and jumps into bed, causing all the others to leave. The problem is resolved first by Bearsie having Porkie sleep under the bed and inviting the others to return, and then, when Porkie expresses his loneliness, by allowing him back in as long as he doesn't "thrash about." This pattern allows children to participate in the reading or telling.

Predictable books are valuable for a variety of reasons. First, they encourage participation by children as they listen. *Busy Monday Morning* can be repeated or sung; *Bearsie Bear* can easily engage children in speaking the parts of the various animals. Second, they can stimulate children to begin learning to read naturally. Children learn the words easily, then begin to match the words they are saying with the words on the page. They can do this as they listen, and as they look at the book on their own. They gain quick control over a story and the words used to tell it, which gives them confidence in their ability to learn to read. Many of the current books published in large format and labeled "Big Books" are predictable stories. The large format allows the teacher to share the book with a group of children and lets each child see and follow the print. In this way, children are encouraged to learn first to "read" whole refrains, then sentences, then individual words. Daycare providers and parents provide the same stimulus for learning to read when they sit next to a child and share a book so that the child can see the print as the adult reads. In fact, it was from parents and other adults reading to children in this very natural way that educators came to realize the importance and potential of working with "Big Books."

Predictable books are also extremely useful in helping children for whom English is their second language learn the sounds, cadences, and meanings of English sentences and words. The emphasis on meaning, the use of context, and the enjoyment produced by good literature combine to provide both incentive and the tools needed for second language learning.

Illustrated Books

Illustrated books rely more heavily on text than on illustrations to convey the story. Generally, text takes up a greater portion of the page than do pictures. The illustrations can, and often do, enrich the narrative, but it's possible to comprehend the story fully without the illustrations. An example of an illustrated book is Ursula LeGuin's *Catwings* (1988). The story opens with Mrs. Jane Tabby thinking that maybe her kittens were born with wings because she had once dreamed of flying away from the neighborhood. Her concern about the poor neighborhood eventually prompts her to send her children flying off on their own to find a better place to live. They find such a place and also discover that some humans can be kind and gentle. The illustrations that accompany the text show the kittens, their old neighborhood, and the places they visit. The art adds interest and helps to establish setting and characters, but does not advance the plot. The illustrations do not carry equal weight with the text in the telling of the story.

Chapter Books

Chapter books, as the name indicates, are books with chapters. The format has importance for primary-grade children because they provide a transition between picture books and junior novels. The reading level is similar to that in many picture books, but the stories are longer and text predominates. Often the plot is episodic, with a character having a different adventure in each chapter. This is true in Ann Cameron's stories about Julian and about Huey. In *More Stories Huey Tells* (1997), the first chapter relates Huey's attempts to doctor his sunflowers when they begin to turn brown. He tries those things that seem reasonable to him—sugar because his father had told him that plants' leaves made sugar, coffee because that works for his father in the mornings, even vitamins. He borrows Julian's radio so the plants can have music. Although he is not successful in changing the looks of his sunflowers, he does learn that they are going to seed, and he can save some of the seeds and grow new sunflowers next spring. Chapter two has a completely new plot about Julian's birthday and the basketball he is to share, but once again involves both Huey and Julian.

Other chapter books have a continuous plot line, requiring the child to remember what has happened and who the characters are over several days of reading. Jackson Jones (*Jackson Jones and the Puddle of Thorns*, Quattlebaum, 1994) is also involved with plants, but only because for his birthday, his mother gives him a garden plot in Rooter's Community Garden. He had wanted a basketball, but his mother wanted him, a city boy, to know the joys of country living she had so much enjoyed when she was a girl. Jackson figures that he can grow flowers, sell them, and have enough money to buy the basketball he wants. The text tells of the trials he has with his project, including having to endure being called "Bouquet Jones." The thirteen chapters in this humorous book form a continuous story, more involved than the narratives in most picture books.

Format alone, however, is not a guide to the difficulty of a book. There are some picture books that are appropriate for toddlers and others that require the maturity of a sixth-grader for any real understanding to occur. Some beginning-to-read books are divided into chapters. Look carefully, not only at format, but also at content and writing style as you select books to share with children.

Literature Based Media

Many literature selections for children are now available through various media formats—audiocassette, video, film, CD-ROM. Children see stories animated on television, particularly the very popular *Arthur* series, using the books by Marc Brown featuring Arthur (an aardvark), Francine, his friend, and the energetic D. W., his little sister. They have traveled with *The Magic Schoolbus*, stories that combine fantasy and science education by Joanna Cole and Bruce Degan, joining Ms. Frizzle as she takes them on trips to the solar system or traveling through the bloodstream. They see iconographic techniques, in which the camera zooms in and out on various portions of an illustration, giving the sensation of motion, used for some of the sharing of books on Reading Rainbow. Flood and Lapp (1998, p. 300) note that "visual literacy, particularly in the form of viewing videotapes, is steadily on the rise. One reason is that numerous children's books have been adapted for television viewing." These videos are available for purchase also, so many children are viewing them at home or in libraries.

CD ROMs often add an interactive quality to the stories presented. In some presentations, the child clicks on to various objects in the story to see the motion and sound connected with them. In others, children make choices about the format before beginning the presentation, clicking on the language they prefer, or on whether they want words to be highlighted as a story is read, or if they want to view text at all. Some stories follow the "choose your own adventure" format in which the action stops at various points within the story, and the child selects which direction he or she would like the plot to turn. Children may make those choices by taking the role of one of the characters and manipulating that character through different settings. This is done particularly in mystery stories, where the viewer acts as detective.

The increasing popularity of media based on literature and the development of computer technology have vastly expanded the ways in which children may experience literature.

Genre

While *format* refers to the physical qualities of a book, *genre* refers to the content—what is said and how it is said. The major genre classifications are poetry and prose.

Poetry

This genre is better understood in practice than by definition. An attempt may be made to differentiate between poetry and prose by saying that poetry rhymes, but blank verse does not rhyme. It may be said that poetry has a depth of emotion and an imaginative quality, but so does some prose. It may be said that the sound of poetry is pleasing, and that the meaning often comes from the sound as well as the words; and certainly, rhythm plays an important role in poetry. Concrete poetry, however, which is shaped like its subject, needs to be seen rather than heard. It may be said that poetry relies on figurative language, yet there are narrative poems without a single simile or metaphor. The best that can be done is to list poetry's characteristics, recognizing that any one poem will not have all of them, and that almost any one of them may be present in prose, also.

A large part of young children's poetry experience will be with Mother Goose rhymes. Also in this genre will be books with collections of poems, and single poems illustrated in picture-book format. There will be verse as well; rhymed, but lacking the depth of emotion and compactness of language of quality poetry. Dorothy Aldis, Lucille Clifton, Beatrice Schenk deRegniers, Aileen Fisher, Eloise Greenfield, Lee Bennett Hopkins, Shirley Hughes, Karla Kuskin, Myra Cohn Livingston, David McCord, Eve Merriam, Lilian Moore, Laura Richards, and William Jay Smith are well-known poets whose writing is generally appropriate for young children.

Prose

Prose is divided into nonfiction and fiction, with nonfiction the factual work and fiction the invented work. Each of these is further subdivided.

Nonfiction.   Nonfiction includes informational books and biography. Informational books are designed to tell about a specific subject—such as stars, colonial times, or how to build a dollhouse. Sometimes the information is conveyed in story form, with child characters sharing their knowledge about a subject, or with the use of *you* and *we* to make it more personal. At other times the information is presented directly, organized by topic. Oz Charles begins his book *How Is a Crayon Made?* (1988) by noting that it would be hard to imagine not having crayons. He then guides the reader into wondering how crayons are made. The answer develops through a clear chronological presentation, aided by photographs. The melting, molding, stacking, and packing; the machinery and the people; the creation and the quality control—all are included in this text.

Concept books are related to informational books in that they, too, deal with facts as building blocks, but concept books tend to be simpler. The concept book *Colors Everywhere* (Hoban, 1995) gives examples of many colors, helping children learn or practice this basic classification. Color may be the first thing noticed about *How Is a Crayon Made?* but the book goes far beyond naming colors.

Biography is the story of a person's life or a segment of that person's life. Authentic biographies use only statements that the person is known to have made and base all incidents on recorded happenings. Fictionalized biographies may dramatize incidents and dialogue, having the person say what he or she is likely to have said, and filling in gaps in information with plausible events. Only probable dialogue and events may be added. Otherwise, the book ceases to be a biography and is classified instead as biographical fiction.

Fiction.   Fiction includes all stories that are created from an author's imagination, even though they may be based on real happenings. If the story could happen now, or could have happened in the past, it is called realism. If the setting is present day, the genre is contemporary realism; if the setting is in the past, it is historical fiction. *Henry and Mudge and the Starry Night* and *More Stories Huey Tells* are contemporary realism, since they have a present-day setting and could happen. *Ox-Cart Man* and *Grandmother Bryant's Pocket,* set in the past, are historical fiction.

If the story includes any actions that could not happen in the world as we know it today, the book is categorized as fantasy. *Frog and Toad Are Friends* and *Catwings* are fantasy because animals do not talk. *The Snowman* with its lively snowman who explores a house and gives a one-night flying tour of faraway places, is fantasy. Of course, if the little boy's adventures with the snowman are interpreted to be only a dream the boy is having, then this book could be classified as realism.

Traditional literature—folktales, epics, myths, and legends, which began in the oral tradition of storytelling—is a rich source of stories for children. The tales themselves were adapted by various storytellers to fit particular audiences. With their quick action and clear portrayal of good and evil, folktales have survived for generations in a number of versions. Some have been told in single picture book editions, while others appear in collections. The book's title page will often indicate that the tale is "retold by" or "adapted by" an author or illustrator, as the original authors are unknown. *Monkey-Monkey's Trick* is an easy-to-read version of an African folktale.

Genre and format are two separate systems for categorizing books. *The Snowman, Frog and Toad Are Friends,* and *Catwings* are all the same genre, fantasy, but they represent three different formats: wordless picture book, picture book, and illustrated book. *Grandmother*

Bryant's Pocket and *Hello Toes! Hello Feet!* are both in a picture-book format, but they are different genres—the first is historical fiction and the second is realism.

It is useful to know both ways of categorizing books so that you can provide a variety of format and of genre for your pupils or day-care children. Knowing these methods may also be useful as you look for books in a library. For example, folktales and poetry are sometimes classified by genre and appear in the nonfiction section of the library. At other times, folktales and poetry in picture-book format will be shelved with the picture books. You should check the card catalog or computer for the location of specific folktales and poetry books.

CHILDREN'S PREFERENCES IN LITERATURE

The topic of children's preferences in literature has been more fully researched for intermediate-grade children than for primary and preschool children. In looking at what is available, though, several cautions should be kept in mind. First, these research results, and others like them, tell what children as a group appear to like. They do not indicate what an individual child will like. They provide a starting point, a suggestion—not an answer. Second, while a survey of preferences helps educators judge the content and type of literature children may enjoy, it is not a guide to literary quality. Teachers must work both with what they know of children and with what they know of literature as they select books.

In general, sex differences in reading interest do not appear strongly until children are around eight or nine years of age (Purves & Beach, 1972). Primary school children, both boys and girls, enjoy stories about personified animals, about nature, about children their age or slightly older, and about daily life and familiar experiences (Purves & Beach, 1972; Monson & Sebesta, 1991). They prefer illustrations that adults would term *representational* as opposed to abstract when they are judging pictures apart from text (Watson, 1980). Although they generally prefer color illustrations over black and white, when a study was done with primary children choosing books in their own classroom, it was found that some books in black-and-white had special meaning for certain children (Kiefer, 1983). Any book, due a certain combination of content and type of illustration, may become a favorite.

Thus, isolating a single factor has not proved to be a reliable method of predicting children's responses to a specific book. You may want to observe the children you teach to see which books they prefer and what patterns of response they exhibit. Some teachers conduct interest surveys within their own classes, determining what interests the children have in common and finding individual interests that can be matched with appropriate literature. Many teachers find that books about monsters and books that are humorous are currently very popular with their classes.

You may also want to read each year's "Children's Choices" results. Under the direction of a joint committee of the International Reading Association and the Children's Book Council, a list of books is selected from those published during the current year. They are selected for literary quality and for diversity of types and subjects. The list is then sent to teams of educators, who share the books with children. The children vote on their favorites, and each year the list of winners is published in *The Reading Teacher* and is available as a reprint from the Children's Book Council.

Primary grade children, in a pilot study conducted by Carol Fisher and Margaret Natarella (1978), showed a favorable attitude toward both rhyming and unrhyming poetry but preferred the rhyming. Often, if they liked the topic of the poem, they liked the poem too. If they disliked the subject, they disliked the poem about it. The children had difficulty in comprehending figurative language, tending to interpret it literally for some rather strange conceptions of what the poem was about. Their favorite poems had strong rhythm and rhyme and frequently were narrative in form. These results were confirmed by a later study of primary grade children's poetry preferences (Kutiper & Wilson, 1993).

Perhaps one of the most consistent findings of all the studies is that preschool and primary grade children enjoy literature, both prose and poetry. Teachers and day-care providers have the opportunity to extend this enjoyment, to broaden children's taste in literature, and to plan literature experience in such a way that goals of early childhood education are supported.

Be aware also that there is a social dimension to children's literary preferences. Children will respond to the attitudes of other children and of the adults who are presenting books (Hickman, 1983). When a teacher shows that he or she enjoys a book and encourages children to look at or read it, the climate is set for a positive response. When a day-care provider makes the environment conducive to looking at and sharing books, children are more likely to do so. Even the way in which the book is presented may become associated with the book itself. Thus care should be taken that books are shared in ways that are enjoyable for children.

Whether adults or children, we bring our own expectations and backgrounds to whatever we read.

C H A P T E R   1

Individual Children and the Literary Experience

Each individual who reads or listens to a work of literature helps to create for himself or herself the meaning of that work. Whether adults or children, we bring our own expectations and backgrounds to whatever we read. Louise Rosenblatt (1978) describes experiencing literature as a transaction, a two-way process between a reader and a text. The reader comes to the work having made a decision, whether conscious or unconscious, about whether the reading is to be done primarily to gain information or primarily for enjoyment. Thus the reader may read a textbook or manual with the express purpose of learning certain facts or how to do something. The reading is a means to an end. At other times, the reader may approach a story or a poem simply for the pleasure of reading. There is no attempt during the reading to remember particular facts, no specific searching for information. Reading and responding are ends in themselves. The literary experience for young children is generally of this second type. They listen to stories and poems, responding to the rhythm of the language, the excitement of the plot, and the feelings evoked. They can express their responses later in art, in discussion, and in drama, but they are not listening in order to engage in the activities. Day-care professionals and teachers help reinforce the importance of responding to literature as a pleasurable experience by allowing children to share their interpretations and responses in open-ended activities and discussions. When very specific recall questions about facts within a story are employed regularly following story reading, children begin listening to stories as if they were for information gain only.

In addition to approaching reading material with a preconceived idea of its purpose, the reader also helps to create the meaning of the text by interacting with it. The author contributes the piece of literature, having selected a topic and developed it with conscious choice of style. The reader contributes meaning to that literature by making inferences and generalizations based on his or her own thoughts, feelings, and memories. A story may mean different things to different people or to the same person at different ages. In one day-care center the adults knew that the caterpillar in a book they read became the butterfly at the end because they understood the process of metamorphosis. The children said that the character was the same, but based their conclusion on the fact that the caterpillar and the butterfly had the same face in the illustrations.

An author may control some responses by using characters or words that generally evoke a particular reaction. Other responses, however, come from the individual. A child listening to *Dr. De Soto* (Steig, 1982), a story about a mouse who is a dentist and usually treats only small animals, may have heard enough stories about foxes to know immediately that the fox who appears begging for help will be dangerous. She may also expect the fox to try some clever trick. Thus the author's use of character matches the reader's expectation. One child may respond to the story with sympathy for Dr. De Soto, who is portrayed as a conscientious dentist who cares about his patients. Another child, perhaps having recently experienced pain in a dentist's office, may see Dr. De Soto as the antagonist and secretly hopes that the fox will have the dentist for dinner.

Choosing books for children means being aware of the child as reader or listener. Begin choosing books using what you know of children's preferences and of their developmental levels. The second half of the formula is selecting books of literary excellence, which is discussed in chapter 2.

Helping Parents Select Literature

As a day-care professional or teacher, it is likely that you will find yourself being asked many questions by parents who value your experience. One topic of concern for parents is the selection of books and media appropriate for their children. There are various ways that you individually, and the school or center where you work, can assist parents. It is helpful to describe for parents the type of books that are generally appropriate for particular developmental levels and to show them examples of such books. For infants and toddlers up to two years of age, toy and board books are often good choices. Board books are durable, and young hands can turn the pages. They allow the children, who are in a stage of exploring the world through the senses—they will taste as well as look at a book—to participate actively. The pictures should be clear and uncluttered, ones that can be identified by the child and discussed by parent and child together. Helen Oxenbury's set of *I Can, I Hear, I See,* and *I Touch* (1995) are good examples of board books that present clear illustrations of familiar objects and activities. Children of this age also respond to the sounds of language, and this is the time to introduce Mother Goose rhymes and books with patterned language.

Children from two to five can follow simple plots and are beginning to develop a sense of story. It is a good time to share books that have clear plots, such as *Hi!* (Scott, 1994) in which Margarita and her mother go to the post office to mail a package to Margarita's grandmother. Margarita waves and says "Hi!" to several people in line, but they all, very busy and loaded with packages, ignore her. Each "Hi" becomes a bit more subdued. Finally Margarita whispers her hello to the post office lady. This time she gets a reply, not just "Hi" but a smile as well. As Margarita and her mother leave, the post office lady says "Bye," and this prompts a happy Margarita to call "Bye! Bye! Bye!" and wave her way out the door. The story is clear, and it explores feelings and interactions that children of this age can understand.

Children from two to five years are in a period of rapid growth in language. They respond to rhythm and repetition in language. This is a time to present traditional literature that has refrains or cumulative plot structure, such as *The Three Little Pigs* and *The Three Billy Goats Gruff.* Children can repeat the refrains, clap to the rhythm of the words, and participate as they hear the story read or told.

Children from five to eight years are able to follow more complex stories that may have subplots. They are beginning to be able to distinguish between fantasy and reality, to generalize, to recognize different points of view, and to read for themselves. They notice details in both text and illustration. This is a time to present a wide variety of picture books, some that are fantasy, some that are realism. Traditional tales are still enjoyed, with ones such as *Snow White* and *Cinderella* being favorites. Beginning-to-read books such as the *Henry and Mudge* series (Rylant) give the new reader a chance to feel successful and to use his or her new skills. However, parents should be encouraged to continue reading aloud to their children during this period, for many of the books enjoyed by primary grade children are still above their reading level. In addition, the sharing of literature provides a period of closeness between parent and child.

You, as a teacher or day-care provider, will also be in a position to show the parents examples of what is being shared in the school or center. This can be done in a parent conference, where the parent is encouraged to browse through the room library, or by showing the parents books, videos, or CDs that have special appeal to their child. Children can be allowed to take books and media home to read or view with their parents, and some teachers send books home with suggestions of appropriate activities that parents might do with their children, or topics related to the book that they might discuss.

A school or center can provide ways for parents to see what literature is available, either through special workshops or through a book fair. If teachers or day-care professionals are present at these functions, they can talk with the parents at this time about appropriate literature. They may also have some input in the selection of which books will be discussed at a workshop or offered for sale at a book fair.

Schools or centers can also provide materials to parents that will aid them in selecting books and give suggestions for using books with their children. *Good Books to Grow On* (Cascardi, 1985) and *The Read-Aloud Handbook* (Trelease, 1995) include annotated lists of books appropriate for young children. *Family Storybook Reading* (Taylor and Strickland, 1986) and *Reading Begins at Home* (Butler and Clay, 1987) suggest ways parents may involve their children with books. Having these reference books available for parents to borrow would both build goodwill and encourage parents to select quality literature. The International Reading Association has a series of brochures for parents, including *How Can I Prepare My Young Child for Reading?* (Paula Grinnell, 1989), *Helping Your Child Become a Reader* (Nancy L. Roser, 1989), and *You Can Help Your Young Child with Writing* (Marcia Baghban, 1989), which give excellent advice in a very readable format.

Booklists could be made available to parents as well. Local children's bookstores can often help in providing booklists and brochures. Booklists are also available through the American Library Association. Lists of recommended wordless books, concept books, predictable books, alphabet, counting, and beginning-to-read books can be found at the end of this chapter. Internet sites that give book reviews include http://www.ucalgary.ca.˜dkbrown/index.html and http://www.crocker.com/ˉrebotis/.

Encourage parents to use their local libraries. They may find that story hours are presented on a regular basis. They can also find out what their children enjoy and provide a stimulus for reading if they take their children with them to the library and have the children select some books themselves. The parent also may select some books so that there is a variety of types of literature to be shared at home. Young children can learn to browse at bookstores, seeing what appeals to them and handling books carefully. One mother boasts that her four-year-old can occupy himself with books in a bookstore for thirty to forty minutes. Of course, this is a mother who likes to read herself, who is hooked on bookstores, and who has shared both her love of literature and her interest in seeing new books with her child. When the child becomes restless, they leave the store, so that it remains a pleasant experience for them both.

Let parents know the importance of children's owning books themselves. They might want to see which books are popular with their children, then buy these. They might also begin by purchasing books that are classics, such as Mother Goose and various fairy tales. A good collection of children's poetry is a necessity, too—*The Random House Book of Poetry for Children* (Prelutsky, 1986), *Sing a Song of Popcorn: Every Child's Book of Poems* (deRegniers et al., 1988) and *Read-Aloud Rhymes for the Very Young* (Prelutsky, 1997) are three good choices. Parents can designate a special place for the books, so that the child knows that these are his or her books, a private library. Paperbacks as well as hardcover books may be purchased. Parents might also look into magazine subscriptions or book clubs, so that new reading material would be arriving on a regular basis. Some parents buy cassettes or CDs so that their children can hear favorite stories read again and again. For families who have tape decks in their cars, listening to stories provides a valuable diversion during family trips.

Finally, talk with parents about techniques of reading aloud to children. Because they are reading to only one or two children at a time, they have the opportunity to listen to the children's responses during the story and to have the children point to objects and words and take part in the reading. They should set the stage for reading by finding a quiet place, helping the child get comfortable, and holding the book so that the child can see the illustrations. Parents should begin the reading by letting the child look at the cover of the book and make comments about the story within, and during the reading they should encourage the child to respond. The child should have some control over the reading, perhaps turning the pages so that it is the listener who determines when he or she is ready to continue. The child should also have the opportunity to select which books he or she would like to hear. If the child becomes restless, the parent should end the session. Children should be encouraged to talk about what they have heard and to participate as fully as possible in the sharing of books and poetry.

Parents who share literature with their children are providing a base of understanding about the reading process, about human relations, and about the enjoyment that books can bring. You should give them all the help and encouragement you can.

SUMMARY

This book is designed to show the many ways in which literature can and does support the goals of early childhood education. At the center of any literature program for children is the literature itself and its contribution to the development of children's imaginations. Beyond this, reading regularly to children and engaging them in active response to literature supports their language, intellectual, personality, social, moral, aesthetic, and creative development.

To plan a literature program, you need to know what literature is available for children. Books for children vary in format and in genre. *Format* refers both to the physical features of a book such as its paper, binding, and typography, and to the ratio and relationship of text and illustrations. *Genre* refers to the type of literature, whether prose or poetry, fiction or nonfiction, realism or fantasy. Teachers and day-care professionals may want to use research results about children's preferences in literature as a guide to the initial selection of literature to present, but need to keep in mind that any one book or poem is a combination of many elements and that preferences will vary from individual to individual. In addition, each individual helps to create the meaning of a work through his or her own background, which influences that person's interpretation of what the author has written. From the wide range of literature available, teachers and day-care providers will select for sharing only that which is of high literary merit.

You will be in a position to provide valuable assistance to parents in selecting books for their children. Information about which books are being used in the school or center, publications for parents, booklists, and techniques for sharing literature with the children will help parents give their children a rich literary background.

Extending Your Learning

1. Compare a hardcover and a paperback edition of the same book.

2. Go to both a bookstore and a drugstore or grocery store. Assess the range and quality of books for preschoolers in each of the settings.

3. Make a toy book for children that uses either the sense of touch or the sense of smell.

4. Rank five wordless picture books by level of difficulty. Tell why each one is placed as it is in your list.

5. Tell how you might use a specific alphabet, counting, or other concept book with a young child.

6. Read collections of poetry by at least three of the poets mentioned in the preceding chapter. Select two poems by each of the poets that you would enjoy sharing with children.

7. Suggest books and activities for three different age levels that parent and child might do together at home.

8. Develop a booklist for parents.

9. Do an Internet search under the names of three authors or illustrators of books for young children and report what you find.

RECOMMENDED WORDLESS BOOKS

Aliki. (1995). *Tabby, A Story in Pictures.* New York: HarperCollins.

Anno, Mitsumasa. *Anno's USA.* (1983). New York: Philomel.

Baker, Jeannie. (1991). *Window.* New York: Greenwillow.

Banyai, Istvan. (1997). *Rapid Eye Movement.* New York: Viking.

Bonners, Susan. *Just in Passing.* (1989). New York: Lothrop.

Briggs, Raymond. (1978). *The Snowman.* New York: Random House.

Collingwood, Peter. (1993). *The Midnight Circus.* New York: Knopf.

Collingwood, Peter. (1997). *A Small Miracle.* New York: Knopf.

Day, Alexandra. (1993). *Carl Goes to Daycare.* New York: Farrar.

Day, Alexandra. (1998). *Follow Carl.* New York: Farrar.

Hoban, Tana. (1997). *Look Book.* New York: Greenwillow.

Mayer, Mercer. (1974). *Frog Goes to Dinner.* New York: Dial.

Ormerod, Jan. (1982). *Moonlight.* New York: Kestrel.

Rikys, Bodel. (1992). *Red Bear.* New York: Dial.

Rohmann, Eric. (1994). *Time Flies.* New York: Crown.

Sara. (1991). *Across Town.* New York: Orchard.

Spier, Peter. (1982). *Rain.* Garden City, NY: Doubleday.

Tafuri, Nancy. (1988). *Junglewalk.* New York: Greenwillow.

Weisner, David. (1988). *Free Fall.* New York: Lothrop.

Weisner, David. (1991). *Tuesday.* New York: Clarion.

RECOMMENDED CONCEPT BOOKS

Barton, Byron. (1998, 1986). *Trucks.* New York: Crowell.

Baer, Gene. (1989). *THUMP, THUMP, Rat-a-Tat-Tat.* Ill. Lois Ehlert. New York: Harper-Festival.

Burningham, John. (1994). *First Steps: Letters, Numbers, Colors, Opposites.* Cambridge, MA: Candlewick.

Carl, Eric. (1977). *The Grouchy Ladybug.* New York: Crowell.

Crews, Donald. (1978). *Freight Train.* New York: Greenwillow.

Hoban, Tana. (1987). *Dots, Spots, Speckles, and Stripes.* New York: Greenwillow.

Hoban, Tana. (1998). *So Many Circles, So Many Squares.* New York: Greenwillow.

Kelley, True. (1989). *Let's Eat!* New York: Dutton.

MacDonald, Suse. (1994). *Sea Shapes.* New York: Gulliver.

MacKinnon, Debbie. (1995). *What Size?* Ill. Anthea Sieveking. New York: Dial.

McMillan, Bruce. (1987). *Step by Step.* New York: Lothrop.

Rockwell, Anne. (1987). *Bear Child's Book of Hours.* New York: Crowell.

Schwartz, David. (1985). *How Much is a Million?* Ill. Steven Kellogg. New York: Lothrop.

Skofield, James. (1993). *Round and Round.* Ill. James Hale. New York: HarperCollins

Tafuri, Nancy. (1997). *What the Sun Sees/What the Moon Sees.* New York: Greenwillow.

RECOMMENDED ALPHABET BOOKS

A Is for Artist: A Getty Museum Alphabet. (1997). Los Angeles: Getty.

Bourke, Linda. (1991). *Eye Spy: A Mysterious Alphabet.* San Francisco: Chronicle.

Bryan, Ashley. (1997). *Ashley Bryan's ABC of African American Poetry.* New York: Atheneum.

Chin-Lee, Cynthia. (1997). *A Is for Asia.* Ill. Yumi Heo. New York: Orchard.

Ford, Juwanda. (1997). *K Is for Kwanzaa: A Kwanzaa Alphabet Book.* Ill. Ken Wilson-Max. New York: Cartwheel.

Geisert, Arthur. (1986). *Pigs from A to Z.* Boston: Houghton Mifflin.

Lindbergh, Reeve. (1997). *The Awful Aardvarks Go to School.* New York: Viking.

McDonnell, Flora. (1997). *Flora McDonnell's ABC.* Cambridge, MA: Candlewick.

Pelletier, David. (1996). *The Graphic Alphabet.* New York: Orchard.

Pomeroy, Diana. (1997). *Wildflower ABC: An Alphabet of Potato Prints.* San Diego: Harcourt.

Poulin, Stephanie. (1985). *Ah! Belle Cite!/A Beautiful City ABC.* Montreal: Tundra.

Rankin, Laura. (1991). *The Handmade Alphabet.* New York: Dial.

Schick, Eleanor & Tapahonso, Luci. (1995). *Navaho ABC: A Dene Alphabet Book.* New York: Simon & Schuster.

Shannon, George. (1996). *Tomorrow's Alphabet.* New York: Greenwillow.

Van Allsburg, Chris. (1987). *The Z Was Zapped.* Boston: Houghton Mifflin.

RECOMMENDED COUNTING BOOKS

Alda, Arlene. (1998). *Arlene Alda's 1 2 3: What Do You See?* Berkeley, CA: Tricycle.

Anno, Mitsumasa. (1975). *Anno's Counting Book.* New York: Crowell.

Bang, Molly. (1983). *Ten, Nine, Eight.* New York: Greenwillow.

Cousins, Lucy. (1997). *Count with Maisy.* Cambridge, MA: Candlewick.

Ehlert, Lois. (1990). *Fish Eyes: A Book You Can Count On.* San Diego: Harcourt.

Enderle, Judith & Tessler, Stephanie. (1997). *Six Sandy Sheep.* Ill. John O'Brien. Honesdale, PA: Boyds Mills.

Feelings, Muriel. (1971). *Moja Means One, Swahili Counting Book.* Ill. Tom Feelings. New York: Dial.

French, Vivian. (1991). *One Ballerina Two.* Ill. Jan Ormerod. New York: Lothrop.

Garne, S. T. (1993). *One White Sail: A Caribbean Counting Book.* New York: Simon.

Hutchins, Pat. (1982). *1 Hunter.* New York: Greenwillow.

Jonas, Ann. (1995). *Splash.* New York: Greenwillow.

Moss, Lloyd. (1995). *Zin! Zin! Zin! A Violin.* Ill. Marjorie Priceman. New York: Simon.

Mullins, Patricia. (1998). *One Horse, Waiting for Me.* New York: Simon & Schuster.

Sis, Peter. (1989). *Going Up! A Color Counting Book.* New York: Greenwillow.

Tafuri, Nancy. (1986). *Who's Counting?* New York: Greenwillow.

RECOMMENDED PREDICTABLE BOOKS

RECOMMENDED BEGINNING-TO-READ BOOKS

Asch, Frank. (1981). *Just Like Daddy.* Upper Saddle River, NJ: Prentice-Hall.

Burningham, John. (1971). *Mr. Gumpy's Outing.* New York: Holt.

Carle, Eric. (1984). *The Very Busy Spider.* New York: Philomel.

Fleming, Denise. (1998). *Mama Cat Has Three Kittens.* New York: Holt.

Fox, Mem. (1987). *Hattie and the Fox.* Ill. Patricia Mullins. New York: Bradbury.

Ginsburg, Mirra. (1992). *Asleep, Asleep.* Ill. Nancy Tafuri. New York: Greenwillow.

Ginsburg, Mirra. (1972). *The Chick and the Duckling.* Ill. Jose Aruego & Ariane Dewey. New York: Macmillan.

Lewison, Wendy. (1992). *Going to Sleep on the Farm.* Ill. Juan Wijngaard. New York: Dial.

Lindbergh, Reeve. (1990). *The Day the Goose Got Loose.* Ill. Steven Kellogg. New York: Dial.

Mansell, Dom. (1992). *My Old Teddy.* Cambridge, MA: Candlewick.

Martin, Bill. (1983). *Brown Bear, Brown Bear, What Do You See?* Ill. Eric Carle. New York: Holt.

Neitzel, Shirley. (1989). *The Jacket I Wear in the Snow.* Ill. Nancy Winslow Parker. New York: Greenwillow.

Shannon, George. (1995). *April Showers.* Ill. Jose Aruego and Ariane Dewey. New York: Greenwillow.

Sheppard, Jeff. (1994). *Splash, Splash.* Ill. Dennis Panek. New York: Macmillan.

Ziefert, Harriet. (1998). *I Swapped My Dog.* Ill. Emily Bolam. Boston: Houghton Mifflin.

Avi. (1997). *Finding Providence: The Story of Roger Williams.* Ill. James Watling. New York: HarperCollins.

Byars, Betsy. (1998). *Ant Plays Bear.* Ill. Marc Simont. New York: Viking.

Cohen, Caron Lee. (1998). *How Many Fish?* Ill. S. D. Schindler. New York: HarperCollins.

Godwin, Laura. (1998). *Forest.* Ill. Stacey Schuett. New York: HarperCollins.

Hoban, Russell. (1970). *A Bargain for Frances.* Ill. Lillian Hoban. New York: Harper.

Hooks, William. (1998). *Mr. Baseball.* Ill. Paul Meisel. New York: Gareth.

Lobel, Arnold. (1970). *Frog and Toad Are Friends.* New York: Harper.

Madsen, Ross Martin. (1997). *Perrywinkle's Magic Match.* Ill. Dirk Zimmer. New York: Dial.

Marshall, Edward. (1988). *Fox on the Job.* Ill. James Marshall. New York: Dial.

McKissack, Patricia. (1988). *Monkey-Monkey's Trick: Based on an African Folk Tale.* Ill. Paul Meisel. New York: Random House.

Paterson, Katherine. (1997). *Marvin's Best Christmas Present Ever.* Ill. Jane Clark Brown. New York: HarperCollins.

Porte, Barbara Ann. (1997). *Harry's Pony.* Ill. Yossi Abolafia. New York: Greenwillow.

Rylant, Cynthia. (1998). *Henry and Mudge in the Family Trees: The Fifteenth Book of Their Adventures.* Ill. Sucie Stevenson. New York: Simon.

Schwartz, Alvin. (1984). *In a Dark, Dark Room.* Ill. Dirk Zimmer. New York: Harper.

Van Leeuwen, Jean. (1998). *Amanda Pig and Her Best Friend Lollipop.* New York: Dial.

PROFESSIONAL REFERENCES CITED

Baghban, M. (1989) *You Can Help Your Young Child with Writing.* Newark, DE: International Reading Association.

Butler, D. (1982). *Babies Need Books.* New York: Atheneum.

Butler, D. & Clay, M. (1987). *Reading Begins at Home.* Portsmouth, NH: Heinemann.

Cascardi, A. (1985). *Good Books to Grow On.* New York: Walker.

Fisher, C. (1978). *"Poetry Is: Questing."* Talk given at National Council of Teachers of English Preconference Workshop on Poetry, Kansas City, MO, November 22, 1978.

Flood, J. and Lapp, D. (1998). "Viewing: The Neglected Communication Process" or "When What You See Isn't What You Get" *The Reading Teacher 52:3,* 300–304.

Grinnell, P. (1989). *How Can I Prepare My Young Child for Reading?* Newark, DE: International Reading Association.

Hickman, J. (1983). "Everything Considered: Response to Literature in an Elementary School Setting." *Journal of Research and Development in Education 16,* 8–13.

Kiefer, B. (1983). "The Responses of Children in a Combination First/Second Grade Classroom to Picture Books in a Variety of Artistic Styles." *Journal of Research and Development in Education 13,* 14–20.

Kutiper, K. & Wilson, P. (1993). "Updating Poetry Preferences: A Look at the Poetry Children Really Like." *The Reading Teacher, 471(1),* 28–35.

Monson, D. & Sebesta, S. (1991). "Reading Preferences." *Handbook of Research on Teaching the English Language Arts,* edited by J. Floor, J. Jensen, D. Lapp, & J. Squire. New York: Macmillan, 664–673.

Purves, A. & Beach, R. (1972). *Literature and the Reader: Research in Response to Literature, Reading Interests, and the Teaching of Literature.* Urbana, IL: National Council of Teachers of English.

Rosenblatt, L. (1978). *The Reader The Text The Poem.* Carbondale: Southern Illinois University Press.

Roser, N. (1989). *Helping Your Child Become a Reader.*

Newark, DE: International Reading Association.

Taylor, D. & Strickland, D. (1986). *Family Storybook Reading.* Portsmouth, NH: Heinemann.

Trelease, J. (1995). *The Read Aloud Handbook.* New York: Penguin.

Watson, J. (1980). A Comparison of Picture Book Illustrations Preferred by Teachers and Children. *The Bulletin of the Children's Literature Assembly 6,* 13–15.

CHILDREN'S LITERATURE CITED

Ada, Alma Flor. (1997). *Gathering the Sun: An Alphabet in Spanish and English.* Ill. Simon Silva. English translation by Rosa Zubizarreta. New York: Lothrop.

Ahlberg, Janet & Allen. (1991). *The Jolly Christmas Postman.* Boston: Little Brown.

Ahlberg, Janet & Allen. (1986). *The Jolly Postman.* Boston: Little, Brown.

Alda, Arlene. (1998). *Arlene Alda's 1 2 3: What Do You See?* Berkeley, CA: Tricycle.

Aliki. (1995). *Tabby, A story in Pictures.* New York: HarperCollins.

Anno, Mitsumasa. (1977). *Anno's Counting Book.* New York: Crowell.

Banyai, Istvan. (1995). *Zoom.* New York: Viking.

Briggs, Raymond. (1978). *The Snowman.* New York: Random.

Briggs, Raymond. (1990). *The Snowman Story Book.* London: Hamilton Hamish.

Briggs, Raymond. (1985). *Raymond Briggs' The Snowman: Walking in the Air.* Boston: Little, Brown.

Cameron, Ann. (1997). *More Stories Huey Tells.* Ill. Lis Toft. New York: Farrar.

Carle, Eric. (1984). *The Very Busy Spider.* New York: Philomel.

Carle, Eric. (1990). *The Very Quiet Cricket.* New York: Philomel.

Charles, Oz. (1988). *How Is a Crayon Made?* New York: Simon & Schuster.

Davol, Marguerite. (1997). *The Paper Dragon.* Ill. Robert Sabuda. New York: Atheneum.

de Regniers, Beatrice Schenk, et al. (1988). *Sing a Song of Popcorn: Every Child's Book of Poems.* New York: Scholastic.

Domanska, Janina. (1985). *Busy Monday Morning.* New York: Greenwillow.

Ehlert, Lois. (1990). *Fish Eyes: A Book You Can Count On.* San Diego: Harcourt.

Feelings, Muriel. (1971). *Moja Means One.* Ill. Tom Feelings. New York: Dial.

Fleming, Denise. (1998). *Mama Cat Has Three Kittens.* New York: Holt.

Fox, Mem. (1994). *Tough Boris.* Ill. Kathryn Brown. San Diego: Harcourt.

Geisert, Arthur. (1986). *Pigs from A to Z.* Boston: Houghton Mifflin.

Hall, Donald. (1979). *Ox-Cart Man.* Ill. Barbara Cooney. New York: Viking.

Hall, Katy and Eisenberg, Lisa. (1998). *Puppy Riddles.* Ill. Thor Wickstrom. New York: Dial.

Hill, Eric. (1980). *Where's Spot?* New York: Putnam.

Hill, Eric. (1982). *Spot's Birthday Party.* New York: Putnam.

Hill, Eric. (1984). *Spot Goes to School.* New York: Putnam.

Hill, Eric. (1987). *Spot Goes to the Circus.* New York: Putnam.

Hill, Eric. (1990). *Spot Sleeps Over.* New York: Putnam.

Hill, Eric. (1991). *Spot Goes to the Park.* New York: Putnam.

Hill, Eric. (1996). *Spot Visits His Grandparents.* New York: Putnam.

Hoban, Tana. (1987). *Red Blue Yellow Shoe.* New York: Greenwillow.

Hoban, Tana. (1987). *26 Letters and 99 Cents.* New York: Greenwillow.

Hoban, Tana. (1995). *Colors Everywhere.* New York: Greenwillow.

Hoban, Tana. (1996). *Just Look.* New York: Greenwillow.

Hutchins, Pat. (1982). *1 Hunter.* New York: Greenwillow.

Kitamura, Satoshi. (1986). *When Sheep Cannot Sleep.* New York: Farrar.

LeGuin, Ursula K. (1988). *Catwings.* Ill. S.D. Schindler. New York: Orchard.

Lester, Alison. (1998). *Alice and Aldo.* Boston: Houghton Mifflin.

Lobel, Arnold. (1970). *Frog and Toad Are Friends.* New York: Harper.

Lyon, George. (1998). *Counting on the Woods.* Ill. Ann Olson. New York: DK Inc.

McDonnell, Flora. (1997). *Flora Mc Donnell's ABC.* Cambridge, MA: Candlewick.

McKissack, Patricia. (1988). *Monkey-Monkey's Trick: Based on an African Folk Tale.* Ill. Paul Meisel. New York: Random.

McMillan, Bruce. (1987). *Step by Step.* New York: Lothrop.

Marshall, Edward. (1988). *Fox on the Job.* Ill. James Marshall. New York: Dial.

Martin, Jacqueline Briggs. (1996). *Grandmother Bryant's Pocket.* Ill. Petra Mathers. Boston: Houghton Mifflin.

Onyefulu, Ifeoma. (1997). *Chidi Only Likes Blue: An African Book of Colors.* New York: Dutton.

Oxenbury, Helen. (1987). *All Fall Down.* New York: Aladdin.

Oxenbury, Helen. (1995). *I Can.* Reissue, 1986, Random House. Cambridge, MA: Candlewick.

Oxenbury, Helen. (1995). *I Hear.* Reissue, 1986, Random House. Cambridge, MA: Candlewick.

Oxenbury, Helen. (1995). *I See.* Reissue, 1986, Random House. Cambridge, MA: Candlewick.

Oxenbury, Helen. (1995). *I Touch.* Reissue, 1986, Random House. Cambridge, MA: Candlewick.

Parks, Rosa with Haskins, Jim. (1998). *I Am Rosa Parks.* Ill. Wil Clay. New York: Dial.

Paul, Ann Whitford. (1998). *Hello Toes! Hello Feet!.* Ill. Nadine Bernard Westcott. New York: DK Inc. Text and illustration used with permission.

Pomeroy, Diana. (1997). *Wildflower ABC: An Alphabet of Potato Prints.* San Diego: Harcourt.

Poulin, Stephanie. (1985). *Ah! Belle Cite!/A Beautiful City ABC.* Montreal: Tundra.

Prelutsky, Jack. (1983). *The Random House Book of Poetry.* Ill. Arnold Lobel. New York: Random House.

Prelutsky, Jack. (1997). *Read-Aloud Rhymes for the Very Young.* (Reissued, 1986). Ill. Marc Brown. New York: Knopf.

Quattlebaum, Mary. (1994). *Jackson Jones and the Puddle of Thorns.* Ill. Melodye Rosales. New York: Delacorte.

Rylant, Cynthia. (1998). *Henry and Mudge and the Starry Night: The Seventeenth Book of Their Adventures.* Ill. Sucie Stevenson. New York: Simon.

Sabuda, Robert. (1997). *Cookie Count: A Tasty Pop-Up.* New York: Simon & Schuster.

Schwartz, Alvin. (1984). *In a Dark, Dark Room.* Ill. Dirk Zimmer. New York: Harper.

Scott, Ann Herbert. (1994). *Hi.* Ill. Glo Coalson. New York: Philomel.

Shannon, George. (1996). *Tomorrow's Alphabet.* Ill. Donald Crews. New York: Greenwillow.

Steig, William. (1982). *Dr. De Soto.* New York: Farrar.

Van Fleet, Matthew. (1995). *Fuzzy Yellow Ducklings.* New York: Dial.

Waber, Bernard. (1997). *Bearsie Bear and the Surprise Sleepover Party.* Boston: Houghton Mifflin.

Walker, Sally. (1998). *The 18 Penny Goose.* Ill. Ellen Beier. New York: HarperCollins.

Witts, Pat & Eve. (n.d.) *The Touch Me Book.* Ill. Harlow Rockwell. Racine, WI: Western.

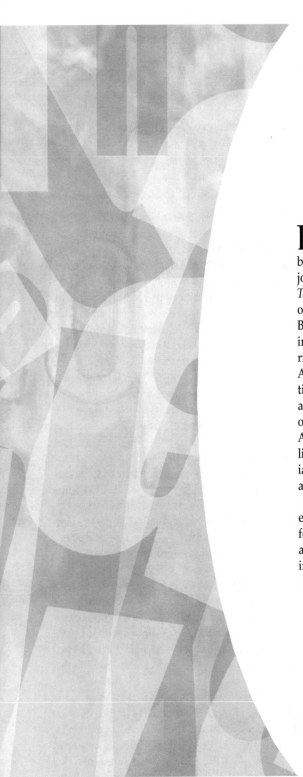

EVALUATING LITERATURE FOR CHILDREN

Books shared with children should represent the best by both literary and artistic standards. Some help in judging books can be found in reviews of new books that appear in journals such as *The Horn Book, Language Arts, The Reading Teacher, The New Advocate,* and *The Journal of Children's Literature* or in publications devoted entirely to book reviews, such as The Bulletin for the Center of Children's Books and Booklist. Reading these will let you see how some critics apply literary criteria. The Caldecott Award, given each year by a committee of the American Library Association to the illustrator of the most distinguished American picture book for children, records what another group considers to be outstanding illustrations. A list of the Caldecott winners and honor books can be found in the Appendix. Also, because libraries tend to purchase books that librarians judge to be of literary merit, talking with local librarians may help you discover how they apply standards of literary excellence.

But rather than rely totally on others' opinions, learn to evaluate children's books for yourself. This will enable you to feel secure using a book you haven't heard about from others, and is requisite for you to be able to help children develop taste in literature.

EVALUATING FICTION
Literary Elements

One way of analyzing fiction is to look at the literary elements that make up the selection. Strengths and weaknesses in plot, setting, characterization, theme, and style of writing can be identified.

Plot

The plot of a story is what happens in it. The plot of *Lilly's Purple Plastic Purse* (Henkes, 1996) is as follows. Lilly, a young mouse, loves school, everything about it, and especially her teacher, Mr. Slinger. She even thinks she might become a teacher when she grows up. One weekend her grandmother takes her shopping and buys Lilly a pair of movie star sunglasses and a new purple plastic purse that plays a tune when opened. Lilly brings them to school with her, eager to show her classmates. However, Mr. Slinger tells her she must wait until recess or sharing time and cautions her to be considerate of others as they listen to a story he is reading. Lilly tries to contain her enthusiasm, but finally interrupts to show everyone her new acquisitions. Mr. Slinger takes her purse and glasses to keep at his desk until school is over.

Lilly is sad and disappointed, but as she sits at the writing table thinking about it, she goes from sadness to anger. She draws a picture—and labels it—of "big, fat, mean, Mr. Stealing Teacher," and slips it into Mr. Slinger's bookbag. When school ends, Mr. Slinger returns her purse. On the way home she opens it and discovers that he has written her a note telling her that tomorrow will be a better day and included a bag of snacks. Now she again feels terrible.

Lilly tells her parents what she has done and voluntarily sits in the "uncooperative chair." They help, her mother by writing a note to Mr. Slinger and her father by baking some snacks for Lilly to take to school. Lilly writes a story in which she is very sorry and draws a new picture of her teacher, so great that he "could be principal." The next day she presents her offerings to Mr. Slinger. Together they decide that it would be a good idea to just throw the original drawing away, and during sharing time Lilly shows her sunglasses and purse, and does a dance to the music it plays. Mr. Slinger even joins in the dance. Lilly thinks that she really does want to be a teacher when she grows up.

A good plot is interesting. It builds suspense so that the reader will want to know what is going to happen next. This story builds: from the introduction, in which Lilly loves school and wants to be a teacher, to when she brings her gift of sunglasses and the purse to school, to the clash between her desire to do what Mr. Slinger says and her desire to show the purse. After that, there is the question of what each character will do in response to the actions of other characters. The climax has Lilly's peace offering accepted, the dance a kind of celebration that she and Mr. Slinger are once again on good terms.

A good plot builds logically. There are causal relationships that connect the events, and these are plausible within the context of the story. Although all the characters in this story are mice, they are personified, and the relationships among them and the plot have a very realistic feel. That a teacher would take something from a pupil who is distracting the class is hardly surprising. Nor is the reaction of the student to be angry and thus do something to express that anger. The clear cause and effect continues. Mr. Slinger's note makes Lilly sorry for her actions.

She finds a way to apologize. Mr. Slinger accepts Lilly's regret for what she has done and all is peaceful again.

Plots in picture books vary in complexity. There may be only one problem, or several, to be solved. There may be two characters or twenty. Occasionally there will be parallel plots, two story lines weaving together by the conclusion. However simple or complex the plot is, the events should be logically related to one another.

Setting

Setting, where and when a story takes place, should be an integral part of the story, not just a backdrop that could be changed without affecting the plot. The setting for *Lilly's Purple Plastic*

The plot, setting, characterization, and illustrations in a picture book should be mutually compatible. (Illustration from Lilly's Purple Plastic Purse *by Kevin Henkes. Copyright © 1996 by Kevin Henkes. Reprinted by permission of Greenwillow Books, a division of Wm. Morrow Company, Inc.)*

Purse is a contemporary school and home. In this case, the setting is such that it allows Lilly to go to a "Lightbulb Lab" writing center in the classroom and to have free time in school to be engaged in a writing activity of her own choosing. This table has been a place for students to express their opinions in writing and drawing, and Lilly certainly does so.

If the story has a specific setting, with the exact time and place identified, the description should be accurate. Other settings may be more generally depicted as being located in a town, or in the country, or "long ago in a faraway land." Even when location is not precisely spelled out, the reader should be given a taste of what life is like at the place and at that time.

Characterization

Characterization, how the author portrays each character in a book, is often what makes a book memorable. Children know Madeline, Petunia, George and Martha, and Curious George because these characters are clearly delineated. The reader knows what they like and dislike, how they will behave in a given situation, and what is special about them. They have more than one dimension, so the reader can respond to the many aspects of their personalities. There are some likable things they do or think, some not so likable. A good author lets the reader know about characters by showing what they do, what they think, what they say, and sometimes by showing what others say or think about them or how others treat them.

Many readers will know Lilly from earlier Henkes' books such as *Chester's Way* (Henkes, 1988), *Julius, the Baby of the World* (Henkes, 1990), and *Chrysanthemum* (Henkes, 1991). They recognize Lilly's exuberance, her assertive manner, and her vulnerability. In *Lilly's Purple Plastic Purse*, readers know how much Lilly really does like school by the many examples that are given—she stands in line even though she doesn't ride the bus and raises her hand even if she doesn't know the answer. They know her curiosity when she asks, in dialogue in the illustrations, what is in the note as her mother writes it and later as Mr. Slinger reads it. They know that she has friends from the first page when Chester and Wilson and Victor ask her to wait for them as she skips off to school.

Mr. Slinger is portrayed as a very popular and hip teacher. He greets his students with "Howdy;" he wears artistic shirts and sandals; he joins Lilly in her "interpretive dance." He lets his actions speak, taking Lilly's purse to keep for the day, but not reprimanding her verbally. He is kind and caring, writing her a note. All his students think that they too would like to be teachers.

In some stories the characters change, or develop, as a result of what has happened to them. It is difficult to have much character development in books for young children simply because the stories are fairly short. There is little time to delineate a character fully, then have a believable change take place.

Theme

The theme of a book is its underlying idea. It may be a general theme, such as friendship or courage, or be more specific and stated in sentence form such as "Even though persons seem alike, each one is unique," or "We should make our own decisions, and not let others make them for us." A story may have no theme, one theme, or more than one theme. One idea underlying *Lilly's Purple Plastic Purse* is that one can make amends for one's mistakes; another is that actions have consequences. Others might be that self control can be difficult, or that good teachers understand the feelings of their students, or that parents can be a source of help. None of these themes intrudes on the plot. If there is a theme, it should be an integral part of the story but should not overpower the story. There should be no need for closing comment by the author to make certain that the theme is understood clearly.

Style of Writing

The style of writing, which words are chosen and how they are arranged, helps create the mood of the story. Henkes sometimes uses short sentences in the same pattern to emphasize action and feeling. When Mr. Slinger takes her purse

> Lilly's stomach lurched.
>
> She felt like crying.
>
> Her glasses were gone.
>
> Her quarters were gone.
>
> Her purple plastic purse was gone.
>
> *Henkes, n.p.*

The vocabulary gives a full picture of what is happening in a succinct manner. The students are all ready to go home when they are "buttoned and zipped and snapped."

There is humor in the story, both in text and illustration. Mr. Slinger, a mouse as are all the characters, is reading *Stuart Little* to the class, and a picture on the classroom wall shows a rodent George Washington. The chalkboard has words that rhyme with "mice." Mr. Slinger is using a chart, with "Swiss, cheddar, romano, and provolone" on it as he teaches about types of cheese.

Henkes employs illustrations to clarify and advance the plot. It is in the illustrations only that readers learn exactly what is in Lilly's drawing of Mr. Slinger, or see from the expression on her face how very satisfied she is with the drawing.

Other authors may use descriptive passages, which achieve the same end of advancing the plot, but give a tale a slower pace. The style should be appropriate to the story being told. It should appear so natural that readers are not distracted by it and are scarcely aware of how it is functioning.

Plot, setting, characterization, theme, and style should be mutually compatible, each complementing the others. In addition to these marks of good writing, books for children should be free of stereotypes and of condescension in tone. Stereotypes generally indicate poor writing as well as being intellectually and socially offensive. They present a person not as an individual, but as a representative of a group, all of whose members are judged to possess the same characteristics. A condescending tone should be avoided because it is an insult to children.

Coherence

Another way of evaluating fiction is to look at the overall coherence of the story. There should be a sense of completeness when the book is finished. The author has taken or created an incident, developed it, structured it. The story will not have the lags, random happenings, or intrusions that characterize real life. It should flow in a meaningful way, with each part related to other parts and to the whole. Storytelling is recognized as one of the ways in which we make sense of our lives and the lives of others.

Coherence depends upon a carefully structured plot and compatibility between the individual elements of plot, setting, characterization, theme, and style of writing. *Lilly's Purple Plastic Purse* works because the plot revolves around the internal conflict Lilly has between what she wants to do and what she is being told to do, and how she can atone for a rash action.

The dialogue reinforces elements of characterization and advances the plot. The style of writing and the illustrations contribute to the understanding of the characters and to the mood of the entire story. The book presents a coherent whole.

Lilly's Purple Plastic Purse begins with a direct statement about Lilly, that she loves school. The author of *Owl Lake* (Tejima, 1987) begins the story of an owl's hunt for food by describing the setting.

> "Nestled deep in the mountains there lies a lake that shimmers in the evening sun. As the sun slips away, the sky darkens from gold to blue, and a gentle stillness settles upon the land. It is then that the owls come out." (n.p.)

The poetic language sets the mood of the story, and the large woodcut illustrations, with tones of first gold, then blue, reflect the serenity of the language. The text and illustrations depict Father Owl as he swoops over the lake, catches a fish, and returns to the family. After noting that Mother Owl will hunt next, the book concludes:

> "Nestled deep in the mountains there lies a lake that shimmers in the morning starlight. As the stars fade away, the sky brightens from black to blue and a gentle awakening settles upon the land. It is then that the owls go to sleep." (n.p.)

The repetition of the phrasing, with subtle changes to show the passage of time and the end of one segment in the life of the owls, gives a sense of closure to the story. It is almost as though the story were held in the author's hands, with the left hand gently opening the book to reveal the onset of night and the owls' coming adventure, and the right hand closing the book as dawn breaks and the story comes to an end.

Just Right Stew (English, 1998) uses a different but equally effective structure. Victoria, who tells the story, is sitting on the kitchen floor as Mama and Aunt Rose cook a special birthday dinner for her grandmother, Big Mama. They are discussing the pot of oxtail stew that needs something else to taste like the stew Big Mama makes. Rose suggests dill, so they send Victoria to get some from Cousin Shug. This begins the pattern. Rose and Mama think of spices that might be the missing ingredient and send Victoria to get them. Then, as other aunts arrive, each adds what she believes to be the needed spice. Finally, Big Mama herself slips into the kitchen and adds sugar, the secret ingredient that only she and Victoria know. The stew is a success, and all relax once Big Mama announces at the table that this is the best stew she's ever tasted. The structure is repetitive, with each unsuccessful attempt to fix the stew adding to the suspense, and to the humor, until Big Mama herself makes the stew perfect. The ending is particularly satisfying because of the surprise element that Victoria has known all along what needed to be added.

Literary elements reinforce one another. The repetition of the plot is echoed in the comments of the characters, as when one adds an ingredient, another always expresses doubt that the solution has been found. The variety in the comments adds interest, and the ways the statements are phrased fit with the delineation of the characters and the action of the story. Miss

Helena, the elderly neighbor who lives alone and always wants to give Victoria candy, ponders and says slowly that she doesn't think she's heard of lemmon pepper in oxtail stew. Mama, in contrast, shouts that it "ain't cumin" when her sister Violet, having arrived in a rush, insists that it is and wants to add cumin herself.

When you finish a book, first ask yourself if you have a sense of satisfaction, of a complete experience. Then go back and look at a book carefully to discern what it is that has given, or not given, coherence to the work as a whole.

Integrity

Good children's literature has a freshness and an honesty to it. It may touch children's emotions; it may light their imaginations. It may make them think about new ideas, or think about old ideas in new ways. The child's world is expanded through the inventiveness of the author and the illustrator. *Owl Lake* describes an event in nature with powerful yet quiet language. *Just Right Stew* takes a family gathering and builds it into a mystery to be solved and a study in human relations. *Lilly's Purple Plastic Purse* explores the frustration of not getting one's own way, and the possibility of making amends for rash actions. All bring a creative approach to their topics, an honest presentation of the story.

EVALUATING NONFICTION

Standards for nonfiction and biography should be applied as rigorously as are standards for fiction. Like fiction, nonfiction should be well-written and interesting.

Organization

Good writing in nonfiction is clear and informative. There is a careful and logical organization to the material being presented. The table of contents and index that are standard in nonfiction for older readers are often omitted in books for primary school children and the text may appear more like a story than a textbook. The organization, however, should follow a pattern that helps to make the content understandable to young readers.

Loreen Leedy, in *Tracks in the Sand* (1993), uses a straight forward, chronological approach with spare yet poetic language. She describes and illustrates sea turtles mating, the female laying eggs on the shore, the eggs developing and hatching, and the young turtles then heading out to the sea, where the cycle will be repeated. She carefully indicates the passage of time. Gail Gibbons, in *Marshes & Swamps* (1998), uses a pattern of general to specific and back to general. First she defines both marshes and swamps as forms of wetlands, then writes about freshwater marshes and saltwater marshes, then freshwater swamps and mangrove swamps. Each example is described in detail, with examples of the plants and animals that live in that ecosystem. She concludes by describing the importance of wetlands and how they can be protected. A flow chart of *Tracks in the Sand* would be a single line with items on it; a chart of *Marshes & Swamps* would have a single line (wetlands), branching into two lines (marshes and swamps), then these two branching again, each into freshwater and saltwater, and finally all joining into a single line at the conclusion. Both patterns or organization are clear and logical.

In books with more text, and without a table of contents, the pattern of organization may not be as immediately discernible. Yet a careful reading reveals that Seymour Simon in

Snakes (1992) is using a pattern of general topic with specific examples. Thus he writes about the general topics of number and location of snakes worldwide, then describes their body structure, their method of movement, how they grow, eat, sense, mate, what their skin is like, with examples of each, and concludes with a classification of families of snakes. Each topic fills one page, with the opposing page a color close-up photograph of the snake mentioned in the text. In contrast, Sandra Markle, in *Outside and Inside Snakes* (1995), focuses more on what the title says—what snakes are like both outside and inside. She writes about different kinds of scales and how the skin underneath the scales unfolds, allowing the snake to stretch enough to swallow animals that are wider than it is. She describes, and the photographs show, a snake's skeleton, its jaw bones, its windpipe when its mouth is wide open, and views of a snake's heart, lungs, and stomach. She gives more detail about the workings of a snake's body than Simon does, but she does not give the broad context about where snakes can be found and how they are classified. Where she describes what venom is and how it works, Simon tells about the kinds of poisonous snakes and where they live.

The Simon book would be a good introduction to snakes because it reads smoothly and gives an overall view of the topic. The Markle book, with its narrower focus and more complex information, might be used for research as well as enjoyment because it does have a glossary/index, making it easier for the reader to find specific information.

Accurate Presentation of Facts

Factual accuracy is one of the most important criteria to consider when choosing nonfiction books. Nonfiction for any age level should not contain misinformation nor oversimplify a topic to the point of inaccuracy. Look at concept books with the same critical eye that you use for all nonfiction. These beginning informational books should be accurate in the information they give and in the examples they use to illustrate a concept. A very simple book entitled *What's That Taste?* (Petty and Kopper, 1987) follows a little girl through the day, describing what she eats and how it tastes. A lemon tastes "sour" and the toothpaste tastes "minty." The apple she eats, however, tastes "crisp." Putting in a word that describes texture and using it to explain what something tastes like makes this a poor book to help children understand this concept.

Look for what is excluded as well as what is included. Although not a direct misstatement of fact, leaving out essential information can be just as misleading. Authors writing about broad topics must make choices, of course, and it is impossible to include everything. Seymour Simon and Sandra Markle, the two authors who wrote about snakes, had to select specific facts about snakes, and in some cases they chose different ones. However, neither chose to write about just poisonous or just nonpoisonous snakes, or just those that lay eggs or just those that bear living young. Had they done so, while still claiming that theirs was a book about snakes in general, they would have given readers an incomplete, and thus false, understanding of snakes.

Also, books of nonfiction should indicate when pertinent information about a topic is not known. Leonard Everett Fisher opens his book entitled *Anasazi* (1997) by explaining that these native peoples who once lived in the Four Corners region of the United States are known only through the archeological remains of their civilization. Throughout the text, his phrasing indicates what is supposition. In describing their petroglyphs, he says, "At times, the Anasazi included human figures in their designs—probably themselves.(n.p.)" When he talks about the

Anasazi leaving the area around 1300, after describing possible reasons for the move not supported by any evidence, he goes on to say, "There was one element, however, that could have played a large role in the Anasazi's move: drought.(n.p.)" He carefully develops the logic of what might have happened, but he is clear that no one knows for certain what did happen.

Nonfiction should be clear about when a statement is of a factual nature and when it is an opinion or a value position. The title *All Pigs Are Beautiful* (King-Smith, 1995) lets the reader know immediately that an opinion is being expressed. King-Smith opens by stating that he loves pigs, and his enthusiasm for them brings life to the book. Captions for the illustrations give factual information, such as noting that mud protects pigs from sunburn, while the basic text is King-Smith's personal descriptions of what pigs are like, particularly Monty, his favorite. Blended, the captioned illustrations and the text provide both information and appreciation.

The difficulty comes when an author gives an opinion as though it were fact. In one book, for example, an author writing about beavers tells that many have been killed for their fur, and then writes that this is sad, and continues to say that beaver dams help control floods, embedding her opinion among the facts and using the same tone and style of writing to express it. The reason for the sadness about beavers being killed is not stated. It might be implied from the text that the reason is that their dams are needed for flood control. Some people might agree with the sadness but base it on a value position that says that the killing of animals is wrong. Still others might worry that beavers might become extinct. Value positions related to nonfiction need to be included because they are a part of understanding a topic, but they should be identified.

Two other problems that sometimes occur in nonfiction are the inclusion of anthropomorphism and teleological explanations. Anthropomorphism is the giving of human feelings and thoughts to animals or to inanimate objects. Saying that snakes feel relieved after shedding their skins, for example, attributes human feeling to the snakes. While this would be appropriate in a book of fiction, it is not acceptable in a book of nonfiction. Teleological explanations assume that all of nature works according to one grand plan, often with "Mother Nature" guiding it. Whatever happens, it is because that is the way Mother Nature works. The snake sheds it skin because Mother Nature knows it needs room to grow. If you find yourself saying, "Isn't that cute?" about a nonfiction picture book, better reevaluate it.

Finally, be aware that fiction books may also be used to present factual information that you might expect to find only in a book of nonfiction. The books by Joanna Cole and Bruce Degan about a magic school bus delight children with their stories while presenting accurate and detailed information. In *The Magic School Bus Inside the Human Body* (Cole, 1989), the unflappable Ms. Frizzle take the class to an exhibit on the human body. While there, the bus shrinks in size, and one of the pupils who had not returned to the bus inadvertently eats it with his lunch. Thus the adventure begins. Ms. Frizzle and the children on the bus travel through the stomach and small intestine, abandon the bus for a ride through the bloodstream on red blood cells, and eventually, having climbed back aboard the bus, are sneezed back into the school parking lot. The humor of school life is portrayed in a cartoon format. One illustration depicts the children's awareness that a filmstrip is only the beginning of Ms. Frizzle's lessons. In *The Magic School Bus and the Electric Field Trip* (1998) Ms. Frizzle takes her class through high-voltage wires from a power plant to the library, to Jo's Diner and to Phoebe's house. They learn about electricity as a source of light and of heat, and how electricity powers motors. The fantasy of the trip and accurate science information are combined. This type of book almost demands a double evaluation—one for its effectiveness as a fiction story, and another for the accuracy of the facts presented.

Current Information

Books of nonfiction that you use should present current information. This means that you need to pay attention not only to the copyright date but also to the data themselves. Obviously some areas are changing more quickly than others, and so the topic itself may alert you. It is no surprise to find that a book on computers, *How to Talk to Your Computer* (Simon, 1985), is outdated in terms of today's computer usage. It is not factually inaccurate, but the emphasis is on computer languages and programming. A more contemporary book, *A True Book of E-Mail* (Brimner, 1997), focuses on electronic communications, e-mail, and the Internet. It not only shows how to use e-mail but also alerts the reader to safety features, from not giving out information about where you live, to netiquette, to even showing two pages of smileys. When a field is changing rapidly, it is particularly important to select recently published books and to alert children to the date of publication when you are using books that are older.

However, an "old" topic does not mean that new information is not being acquired, and that recent information is not necessary. Aliki Brandenberg has written many carefully researched books about dinosaurs. In *My Visit to the Dinosaurs* (1969), her protagonist describes seeing the skeleton of a brontosaurus. Later there is an illustration of how the brontosaurus is thought to have looked and accompanying text. In a 1981 book, *Digging Up Dinosaurs* (Brandenberg, 1981), the character is seeing a skeleton of a dinosaur in a museum and says that she has seen an apatosaurus. In one small drawing the dinosaur is labeled "apatosaurus" with "brontosaurus" in parentheses, and in a cartoon speech balloon, the character explains that while apatosaurus is its real name, some people call it a brontosaurus. By 1988, Aliki refers to it only as apatosaurus (*Dinosaur Bones,* Brandenberg, 1988). This alteration in terminology reflects new knowledge about a subject we many not think of as "changing," and demonstrates the need to be aware of when a nonfiction book was published no matter what the topic.

EVALUATING POETRY

A reliable choice of poetry for young children is Mother Goose rhymes. The rhythm and rhyme of these verses have lasting appeal. The narrative ones tell intriguing tales and the nonsense ones are filled with humor. A familiarity with Mother Goose, built by listening to and joining in as the rhymes are read, by dramatizing them, by knowing them, is a sound basis for later appreciation and enjoyment of poetry.

Poetry takes careful reading. There is a compactness of language—every word counts. The sound of the language as it is read aloud is vital. The rhythm should be strong and natural. Even free verse, with no rhyme, has a rhythm to it. The rhyme, if it is a rhyming poem, should have a pattern. There may be a steady beat, as in "The Little Turtle."

> There was a little turtle,
>
> He lived in a box,
>
> He swam in a puddle,
>
> He climbed on the rocks.

He snapped at a mosquito,
He snapped at a flea,
He snapped at a minnow,
And he snapped at me.

He caught the mosquito,
He caught the flea,
He caught the minnow,
But he didn't catch me.

Vachel Lindsay

Here the rhythm seems to sing. There may also be a more varied use of rhythm and rhyme, such as that found in "O Sliver of Liver."

O sliver of liver,
Get lost! Go away!
You tremble and quiver
O sliver of liver—
You set me a-shiver
And spoil my day—
O sliver of liver, Get lost! Go Away!

Myra Cohn Livingston

In both poems the authors have used language for its sound as well as for its meaning.

The rhyme in poems such as these should not take precedence over the meaning. That is, words should not be stated in awkward order just so the last words will rhyme. Nor should there be lines, included because they rhyme, that would not make sense if found in a prose selection.

Language should be fresh. It may show a new way of looking at something, or a new way of telling about it. Poetry often uses figurative language, makes comparisons. It relies heavily on imagery, describing how experiences are perceived by the senses. Read poems to see if the comparison and descriptions make sense, and if they are vivid.

Livingston has described liver with words that let the reader know not only how it looks but also how she feels about it. Children will know what she means when she says that it sets her "a-shiver." Some may wish that they, too, could tell liver to go away. The emotional content of poetry helps make contact between poet and reader.

The literary standards by which poetry for children is judged are no less demanding than those for adult poetry. A poem that is poor by adult standards is poor for children as well. Nor is there any need to talk down to children, to make poems cute or easy. To do so is to show a basic disrespect for the child reader or listener. Teachers have a responsibility to children to select poems that have literary merit.

EVALUATING ILLUSTRATIONS

Barbara Kiefer, in her book *The Potential of Picturebooks* (1995), writes that critics must begin with the verbal text of a picture book when they are judging it because that is where the artist usually begins. However, "Once we have some idea of the theme of the book, the motifs and moods, characters, setting, and events, we can evaluate how well the artist has chosen artistic elements, principles, and conventions to convey those meanings visually and how those artistic or stylistic choices have contributed to the overall aesthetic experience of the book." (p. 120) This is what you will be doing as you select picture books, looking at the overall effectiveness of the total book. And as you look at more books more carefully, you will become better at analyzing the art as well as the text.

Proximity to Text

Illustrations in a picture book should be near the text they depict, either on the same page or on the opposite page. Children look at the picture as the story is being read and, if they are reading the book by themselves, may use the pictures as clues to meanings. If the story is to be unified, then, text and illustrations must appear together. In books of poetry, the illustration should be tied to the poem by its placement on the page as well as by its content. This is particularly true if several poems appear on a single page.

Developing the Text

Illustrations should match both the description and the action in the text. When the text says that Lilly's teacher, Mr. Slinger, wore his glasses on a chain around his neck, and that he wore different-color ties on different days, and that he wore "artistic" shirts, that is exactly what should be shown. The reader sees Mr. Slinger with his glasses on a chain, several different ties, and several interpretations of what an "artistic" shirt might be. When the text says that Lilly used her purse and glasses as props for an "interpretive dance," and that Mr. Slinger joined in the dance, then if the scene is depicted, those elements must be shown. The illustrator, however, is free to add any actions or details that might extend the story, develop the setting, or enhance the characterization. We learn from the illustrations that Mr. Slinger wears sandals, quite in keeping with his artistic shirts. We see the drawing that Lilly made of Mr. Slinger in her anger, complete with descriptive words such as "thief." In a sequence of panels, Lilly opens her purse and finds the note and bag of snacks from Mr. Slinger, and in each panel the figure of Lilly gets smaller, clearly symbolic of how she is feeling.

The illustrator need not show everything that is mentioned in the text. The basic criterion is that there be no conflict between text and illustration. Sometimes illustrations can be confusing rather than helpful, even if there is no direct conflict. For example, illustrations that combine realism with fantasy when the text does not, or that portray elements of setting that are inconsistent with one another, make comprehension of the story more difficult.

Capturing the Emotional Link

Ian Wallace, a Canadian illustrator, has described the process he used to illustrate *The Very Last First Time* (Andrews, 1986), the story of an Inuit girl's first walk alone on the bottom of the sea. When the tide receded, it was possible to walk under the ice and gather mussels. At age 12, children of the village did this alone as a rite of passage to adulthood. The book tells about Eva Padlyat's walk. The challenge for Wallace was to capture the setting; but more important, to capture what he called the "emotional link" that ties the story to the reader. He explains:

> To discover the emotional link of a story, the illustrator must understand all levels on which the story functions: intellectual, physical, psychological, and spiritual. This link is then made by a variety of means: appropriate media, color, changing perspectives, shape of the illustrations, shape of the book, style of type, white space around the type and each of the drawings, and the position of each character in relation to one another. Nothing must be left to chance (1989, p. 7).

Wallace chose to use yellow as a dominant color for the scenes above the ice, and purple for those below. He noted that the Inuit call the land where they live the Land of Purple Twilight. He studied Inuit drawings and, realizing the importance of the spirit world in Inuit culture, included spirit images of wolf, bear, and seal sea monster in the under-ice scenes.

As you examine the art in children's books, consider those aspects of art that, according to Wallace, develop an emotional link between story and reader. That is, see if the media, colors, changing perspectives, style of illustration, use of white space, and shape of the book and illustrations help to tell the story well.

In materials developed by John Stewig for teaching children about illustrations (Stewig, 1988), children are frequently directed to look at a particular illustration and say what they notice about it. This is a good beginning for anyone assessing the art in a picture book. What stands out? What do you notice about the colors being used? Are they intense? Subdued? Natural? Arbitrary? What do you notice about lines? Are they thin or thick, straight or curved, harsh or soft? What about shapes? Do they overlap/Do some dominate? What is unique about the illustrations? Do they add humor? Imply action? What is the effect of the illustrations?

Look at the illustration reproduced from a double-page spread in *Owl Lake* (Tejima, 1987). The three panels and the owl are shown progressively larger, emphasizing the owl's approach. The diagonal cut at the bottom of the panels guides the eye and builds tension, as well as making room for the text, which also follows the diagonal pattern. The wingspread of the owl is so wide that it extends outside the border of the panel. As the text describes the movement and sound of the owl's wings, the illustrations capture the movement. The fish appear only in the last panel, when the owl sees them. The following page in *Owl Lake* shows the owl, even larger, catching the fish, with a V-shaped pattern repeated in the cut of the panels, the splash of the water, and in the upward thrust of the owl's wings.

These are woodcut illustrations, with sharp, clear edges. Tejima, as artist, has accentuated patterns in the trees on the hills surrounding the lake, in the ripples on the surface of the water, and in the reflections on the water. As author, he begins the story with a quiet tone in text that is matched by an illustration of a peaceful lake at sunset, in soft gold tones combined with black. As the story builds, the illustrations focus on the action. When the story concludes with the owls settling down for the day, the illustrations once again fade to a distant view of the lake. This time the color of accent is blue, as the light of dawn seeps in.

The illustrations are effective as art and in combination with the text. The style and the medium are appropriate. They give a sense of grandeur to the entire event in nature.

Other media might have been used, and used effectively. In another book about owls at night that creates a quiet mood, *Whoo-oo Is It?* (McDonald, 1992), the illustrator chose to use pastels. In this story, Mother Owl, sitting on her clutch of eggs in the barn, hears a mysterious

The artist has built movement and tension into this illustration. (From Owl Lake *by Keizaburo Tejima. Copyright © 1982 by Keizaburo Tejima, illustrations Copyright © 1987 by Philomel Books, translation. Used by permission of Philomel Books, a division of Penguin Putnam Inc..)*

"whhh, whhh, whhhhh"sound. She goes to investigate. It is not a puppy barking in the distance, nor a kitten, nor mice, nor the barn door, nor anything she can find outside when she flies out searching. When she returns to the nest, she finds the source—her first owlet hatching.

Look at the illustration from this book. It has a deep gray-blue border that fills the rest of the page, but the border serves to enclose and give a sense of security rather than to build tension. It, and the other illustrations within the book that are designed this way, all portray the mother owl and her eggs. Illustrations in which the mother owl is searching for the sound are double-page spreads that go to the edge of each page, giving a sense of freedom. The enclosed illustrations focus on the owl and her eggs; the full-page illustrations show the larger context, the expanded world in which the owls live. The pastels are soft edged and give an inky look to the night scenes; the white of the owl's underside and face seems to glow against this back-ground, phosphorescent. These illustrations capture both the apprehension caused by unrec-ognized sounds and the security of the nest.

Both books make the emotional link that Wallace describes. They are true to the mood and content of the text, blending words and pictures effectively. The cartoon-style illustrations of *Lilly's Purple Plastic Purse* (see illustration on page 35) are suited to that humorous story but would have been totally incongruous with either of these books. Illustrations must work as part of the whole.

Think for a minute of how you picture the character of Goldilocks and what you think the bears look like. Then look at the illustrations from two versions of *Goldilocks and the Three Bears*. Both show Goldilocks being discovered as she sleeps in Little Bear's bed. The first is by

This artist creates a quiet mood, with the border around the picture giving a sense of security. (From Whoo-oo Is It? *by Megan McDonald, copyright © 1992 by Orchard Press.) Ill. S.D. Schilder. Illustrations © by S.D. Schilder, Reprinted by permission.)*

Jan Brett (1987). Notice the details in the illustration, the use of a border, and the clothing and expressions of the characters. Then look at the second, by James Marshall (1988). Again, look at the details, the dress and expressions of the characters. You may want to read the two retellings. If you do, you will find that they differ in tone and language. The Brett version uses more traditional wording; Marshall's uses more contemporary wording. Brett's Goldilocks liked the porridge so much that she "ate" it all up; Marshall's "gobbled" it all up. Brett's bears go for a walk, rather matter-of-factly, while their porridge is cooling. Marshall's bears go after Papa Bear complains that the porridge is scalding, Baby Bear asserts that he's dying, and Mama Bear tells them they've both said "quite enough." Both sets of illustrations are compatible with the story as told, and both extend and enhance the text.

Appropriateness of Illustrations

The purpose for which the book was designed can help define criteria for evaluating the illustrations. In alphabet books, used with young children to name objects, the illustrations should be clear and uncluttered. If the alphabet book is designed to emphasize the sound or sounds made by each letter, then the illustrations must be accurate. That is, "s" should not be repre-

And then the little, small, wee bear came to look at his bed. There was Goldilocks—sleeping peacefully, her long shiny braids spread across his pillow. Little, small, wee bear just stared at her, for a moment, and didn't say anything.

But then he cried, "Somebody has been lying in my bed—and here she is!"

Notice the details included in this illustration. (Illustration by Jan Brett reprinted by permission of G.P. Putnam's Sons from GOLDILOCKS *and the Three Bears, © 1987 by Jan Brett.)*

sented by an object such as shoe, for although the word does begin with "s," it is the sound of the "sh" blend that is heard.

If the book is designed to help children learn to count and recognize numerals, then the illustrations must show the objects clearly. The child should know what is to be counted. There should be no confusing background, no questions about whether it is the bugs or the legs on the bugs to be counted.

In nonfiction, the illustrations must help convey the facts or concepts being presented. This means that diagrams must make a concept clearer; that photographs must convey information as well as beauty; that drawings that must help the reader understand.

Illustrations in nonfiction can be categorized by the degree of representationality (Kerper, 1988). Photographs, for example, are usually highly representational, showing the object's features as they appear naturally. Diagrams that combine pictures with labels are less representational and more abstract, and tables and charts are the least representational and the most abstract. Kerper writes that

> Nonfiction books for young children frequently contain visual displays such as photographs and pictures that fall at the high level of representationality end of the continuum. Their closer connection to the real world make them appropriate for the cognitive development of the intended audience. (Kerper, 1988, p. 64)

Think about the dialogue that might accompany this illustration. (Illustration by Jan Brett reprinted by permission of G. P. Putnam's Sons from GOLDILOCKS *and the Three Bears, © 1987 by Jan Brett.)*

Photographs should be of high technical quality. In addition, any information that will help in understanding them should be given. For example, the photographs in *Outside and Inside Snakes* (Markle, 1995) that have been taken using special heat-sensitive film, or that have been computer enhanced, are identified as such. Bruce McMillan explains in his forward to *Salmon Summer* (1998) that the pictures were taken in the Kodiak National Wildlife Refuge in the summer of 1996. He stayed at a fish camp with the family he photographed in this story of 9-year-old Alex, a native Aleut, as he and his family fished for salmon. Kate Waters' book *Tapenum's Day: A Wamponoag Indian Boy in Pilgrim Times* (1996) features photographs by Russ Kendall that were taken at Hobbamock's Homesite at Plimoth Plantation. The afterword explains that Hobbamock's Homesite is a place where the Wamponoag culture is shared with visitors by staff

In nonfiction, photographs should convey information and be of high technical quality. (Photograph from Salmon Summer. *Copyright © 1998 by Bruce McMillan. Reprinted by permission of Houghton Mifflin company. All rights reserved.)*

members who demonstrate how the Womponoag lived in the 1600s. The information in these books allows the reader to know that Alex is really living the life in the photographs, while Tapenum is a contemporary Womponoag boy portraying a boy and a lifestyle of the past.

Diagrams vary in complexity, from simple labeling of objects or parts of objects, to cutaway or cross-section drawings. They should clarify or extend the information in the text. Of particular interest in nonfiction is the way in which scale is shown, or whether it is shown at all. In *Poison Dart Frogs* (1998), Dewey gives the size of three different kinds of these frogs, then illustrates them above a ruler, with a notation that the scale is in inches. The frogs are thus shown life size. Often an artist will include in the illustration something whose size is known—such as a hand holding a baby mouse or a car parked next to a redwood tree—or may label the size of the object. The illustrations help the reader visualize not only the subject itself but also the subject in context.

Captions, while not essential, can make photographs, diagrams, maps, tables, and other ways of presenting data much clearer to the reader. They may also help to capture the reader's interest. Markle (1995) captions several photographs with questions and asks the reader to predict what will happen in the next photo. In one photograph, a snake is curled around a plant and a hummingbird is flying toward the plant. What will happen next? On the following page, the photo shows the snake uncoiled, mouth open, trying to catch the bird.

When you evaluate the illustrations in a nonfiction book, you may want to think of the ways you plan to use the book with children. Think about whether the book can help the children to become careful observers and interpreters of visual data.

Illustrations are central to the success of all picture books. They should be evaluated carefully, for they are a basic component of a young child's literary and artistic education.

EVALUATING INTERACTIVE LITERATURE ON CD-ROM

The National Association for the Education of Young Children has taken the position that computer software can enhance children's development, but note that it should not take the place of books, blocks, and other more traditional early childhood materials (Walter, 1997). This reflects the opinion of many early childhood educators, torn between excitement at the potential of the medium and concern that it not replace the warmth and sharing involved in the personal sharing of literature.

When looking at stories on CD-ROM, a first criterion is whether the content is age-appropriate. Look at the understanding level required just as you would in selecting a book. Look to see also if it can be run easily by a child if you are planning to have one or two children engaged with it on their own. Are the directions understandable? Can the children figure out how to go forward, go back, access special features? Assess the technical quality. Are voices clear and understandable, the animation smooth? Picture children viewing the story. Will they be engaged in thinking and feeling as they participate in the story, or just engaging in passive point-and-click activities?

One key criterion, however, is whether the CD makes good use of the special attributes of the medium. Terri Butler writes:

> Be aware, first of all, that this is a medium about doing. The most successful CD-ROMs are those that make the best use of the medium's potential for movement, action, sound, and music—a potential it shares with video. But unlike video, what you see is not all you get. At the click of a mouse, there are surprises just waiting to happen, whether it's a puzzle to put together in that famous Parisian house covered with vines, or discovering that French-fried fudge is the favorite food of Dr. Seuss's Fiffer-feffer-feffs.
>
> These surprises—the "hot buttons" built into the disk's program—are key to any good CD-ROM. They can summon a sound effect or a song, a problem to solve, or a game to play. When used well they broaden a story's potential to educate and entertain. And yes, they mean we've gone beyond a faithful rendering of the book— in some cases, way beyond.

Butler, p. 219

In the CD-ROM version of *Curious George ABC Adventure* (1996), there are games in which the child must identify the animal or object beginning with a certain letter, and the opportunity for the child to make choices about where George goes and how he gets there. The stories can be printed out. The style of illustration is faithful to the original illustrations. In the CDs based on the Arthur books by Marc Brown, such as *Arthur's Reading Roundup* (1998), the illustrations match the originals here as well. Animation moves the story along. However, if the child clicks on all the hot-button choices given, the story may be slowed down considerably. The buttons can keep the child very actively involved but can also dilute the force of the narrative.

When you are selecting a CD for a literary experience, you should assess the narrative flow of the story. Do the choices given enhance the story? That is, do they add interest, or give information, or provide entertainment in a way that is consistent with both the plot and the mood of the literature? A serious story interrupted with funny sounds loses its impact, while a humorous story with those same sounds could be very effective. Characterization may be augmented if the voice given the character fits, or confused if it doesn't. Hyperlinks may add depth to nonfiction by letting children select which aspects of a topic are of most interest to them or dilute the topic if they are only peripherally related.

Finally, look for CDs that may have special meaning for the children with whom you work. Many offer the text in both English and Spanish, for example, useful for many second-language learners. Some include word processing so that students can make notes as they interact. Some highlight text as it is read, encouraging reading development. Some allow a child to read, then play back his or her reading. In this rapidly developing field, there are likely to be more and more options, making evaluation more complex. A good CD, however, like a good book, should provide the child with both enjoyment and new understandings.

SUMMARY

Books shared with children should be the very best available based on literary and artistic standards. It is necessary, therefore, that day-care providers and teachers be able to judge the quality of children's books. Fiction can be evaluated by assessing the effectiveness of the literary elements of plot, setting, characterization, theme, and style of writing, as well as how the elements are integrated to provide a unified whole. Nonfiction should be judged for factual accuracy, current information, and clear differentiation between fact and opinion. The organization and choice of material affect the quality of nonfiction.

Poetry for children can be evaluated on freshness and compactness of language, use of rhythm and rhyme, and emotional content. Illustrations can be judged for appropriateness of style and medium to the mood and content of the text, for how well they extend the text, and for their artistic quality. Illustrations in nonfiction should present information clearly and accurately. Reading many picture books with a critical eye will help you to develop skill in assessing texts and illustrations. Books on CD-ROM should engage the child and use the medium to advantage, while still maintaining the narrative flow of the story.

Extending Your Learning

1. Compare two reviews of the same book. Reviews of children's books appear in journals such as *Language Arts, The Reading Teacher, The Horn Book, The New Advocate, The Bulletin of the Center for Children's Books, School Library Journal,* and *Booklist.*

2. Write your own book review. Then find a published review of the same book and compare the two. See if you and the other reviewer used the same criteria and saw the same qualities in the book.

3. Using the same criteria as were applied to *Lilly's Purple Plastic Purse,* evaluate a picture book of your choice.

4. Compare the illustrations in any two winners of the Caldecott Award. Look at the choice of media, the style of art, and the effectiveness of the illustrations in helping to tell the story.

5. Look at the book that won the Caldecott Award and the Honor Books for a single year. See if you agree with the committee's choice of the winner.

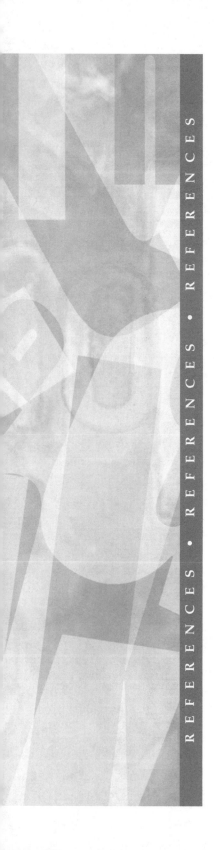

RECOMMENDED REFERENCES

Bader, B. (1976). *American Picturebooks from Noah's Ark to the Beast Within.* New York: Macmillan.

Bamford, R. & Kristo, J. (Eds.), (1998). *Making Facts Come Alive: Choosing Quality Non-fiction Literature K-8.* Norwood, MA: Christopher-Gordon.

Cameron, E. (1969). *The Green and Burning Tree.* Boston: Little, Brown.

Carr, J. (1982). *Beyond Fact: Nonfiction for Children and Young People.* Chicago: American Library Association.

Cullinan, B. & Galda, L. (1998). *Literature and the Child.* (4th ed.). New York: Harcourt.

Egoff, S., Stubbs, G., Ashley, R., & Sutton, E. (Eds.), (1996). *Only Connect: Readings on Children's Literature.* (3rd ed.) New York: Oxford.

Glazer, J. (1997). *Introduction to Children's Literature.* Columbus, OH: Merrill.

Horning, K. T. (1997), *From Cover to Cover: Evaluating and Reviewing Children's Books.* New York: HarperCollins.

Hunt, P. (1991). *Criticism, Theory, & Children's Literature.* Cambridge, MA: Basil Blackwell.

Kiefer, B. (1995). *The Potential of Picturebooks: From Visual Literacy to Aesthetic Understanding.* Columbus, OH: Merrill.

Lukens, R. (1999). *A Critical Handbook of Children's Literature.* (6th ed.). New York: Longman.

Lynch-Brown, C. & Tomlinson, C. (1999). *Essentials of Children's Literature.* (3rd ed.). Boston: Allyn and Bacon.

Marantz, S. (1994). *Multicultural Picture Books: Art for Understanding Others.* Worthington, OH: Linworth.

Marantz, S. S., & Marantz, K. A. (1995). *The Art of Children's Picture Books: A Selective Reference Guide.* (2nd ed.). New York: Garland.

May, J. (1995). *Children's Literature & Critical Theory.* New York: Oxford University Press.

Moline, R. (1995). *I See What You Mean: Children at Work with Visual Information.* York, ME: Stenhouse.

Nodelman, P. (1988). *Words About Pictures: The Narrative Art of Children's Picture Books.* Athens, GA: University of Georgia Press.

Norton, D. (1999). *Through the Eyes of a Child.* (5th ed.). Columbus, OH: Merrill.

Rudman, M. (1995). *Children's Literature: As Issues Approach.* (3rd ed.). White Plains, NY: Longman.

Sloan, G. (1991). *The Child as Critic.* (3rd ed.). New York: Teachers College Press.

Stewig, J. (1988). *Children & Literature.* (2nd ed.). Boston: Houghton Mifflin.

PROFESSIONAL REFERENCES CITED

Butler, T. (1997). "Tale-Spinning: Children's Books on CD-ROM." *The Horn Book, 2,* pp. 219–224.

Kerper, R. (1998). "Choosing Quality Nonfiction Literature: Features for Assessing and Visualizing Information." In R. Bamford & J. Kirsto (Eds.), *Making Facts Come Alive: Choosing Quality Nonfiction Literature K-8,* pp. 55–74. Norwood, MA: Christopher-Gordon.

Kiefer, B. (1995). *The Potential of Picturebooks: From Visual Literacy to Aesthetic Understanding.* Columbus, OH: Merrill.

Stewig, J. (1988). *Reading Pictures, Exploring Illustrations with Children.* New Berlin, WI: The Resourceful Educator.

Wallace, I. (1989) "The Emotional Link." *The New Advocate, 2,* pp. 75–82.

Walter, V. (1997). "Starting Early: Multimedia for the Tricycle Set." *Book Links, 5,* 26–33.

CHILDREN'S LITERATURE CITED

Andrews, Jan. Illustrations Ian (1986). *The Very Last First Time.* Wallace. New York: Atheneum.

Arthur's Reading Roundup, CD-ROM. Microsoft, 1998.

Brandenberg, Aliki. (1969). *My Visit to the Dinosaurs* New York: Crowell.

Brandenberg, Aliki. (1981). *Digging Up Dinosaurs* New York: Harper.

Brandenberg, Aliki. (1988). *Dinosaur Bones* New York: Crowell.

Brett, Jan. (1987). *Goldilocks and the Three Bears* New York: Dodd.

Brimner, Larry Dane. (1997). *A True Book of E-Mail* New York: Grolier.

Cole, Joanna. Illustrations Bruce Degan. (1989). *The Magic Schoolbus Inside the Human Body* New York: Scholastic.

Cole, Joanna. Illustrations Bruce Degan. (1998). *The Magic School Bus and the Electric Field Trip* New York: Scholastic.

Curious George ABC Adventure CD-ROM. Broderbund, 1995.

Dewey, Jennifer Owings. (1998). *Poison Dart Frogs* Honesdale, PA: Boyds Mills.

English, Karen. Illustrations Anna Rich. (1998). *Just Right Stew* Honesdale, PA: Boyds Mills.

Fisher, Leonard Everett. (1997). *Anasazi* New York: Atheneum.

Gibbons, Gail. (1998). *Marshes & Swamps* New York: Holiday.

Henkes, Kevin. (1988). *Chester's Way* New York: Greenwillow.

Henkes, Kevin. (1990). *Julius, the Baby of the World* New York: Greenwillow.

Henkes, Kevin. (1991). *Chrysanthemum* New York: Greenwillow.

Henkes, Kevin. (1996). *Lilly's Purple Plastic Purse* New York: Greenwillow. Illustration and text copyright © by Kevin Henkes. Used by permission of Greenwillow Books, a division of William Morrow and Company, Inc.

King-Smith, Dick. Illustrations Anita Jeram. (1995). *All Pigs Are Beautiful* Cambridge, MA: Candlewick.

Leedy, Loreen. (1993). *Tracks in the Sand* New York: Doubleday.

Lindsay, Vachel. (1920). *Collected Poems* New York: Macmillan. Used with permission.

Livingston, Myra Cohn. (1979) *O Sliver of Liver and Other Poems.* Copyright © Myra Cohn Livingston. Used by permission of Marion Reiner.

McDonald, Megan. Illustrations S. D. Schindler. (1992). *Whoo-oo Is It?* New York: Orchard.

Markle, Sandra. (1995). *Outside and Inside Snakes* New York: Simon & Schuster.

Marshall, James. (1988). *Goldilocks and the Three Bears* New York: Dial.

McMillan, Bruce. (1998). *Salmon Summer* Boston: Houghton Mifflin.

Petty, Kate, & Kopper, Lisa. (1987). *What's That Taste?* Los Angeles: Price Stern.

Simon, Seymour. Illustrations Barbara & Ed Emberley. (1985). *How to Talk to Your Computer* New York: Crowell.

Simon, Seymour. (1992). *Snakes* New York: HarperCollins.

Tejima, Keizaburo. (1987). *Owl Lake* New York: Philomel. From *Owl Lake* by Keizaburo Tejima. Copyright © 1982 by Keizaburo Tejima, illustrations. Copyright © 1987 by Philomel Books, translation. Used by permission of Philomel Books, a division of Penguin Putnam Inc.

Waters, Kate. Illustrations Russ Kendall. (1996). *Tapenum's Day* New York: Scholastic.

3

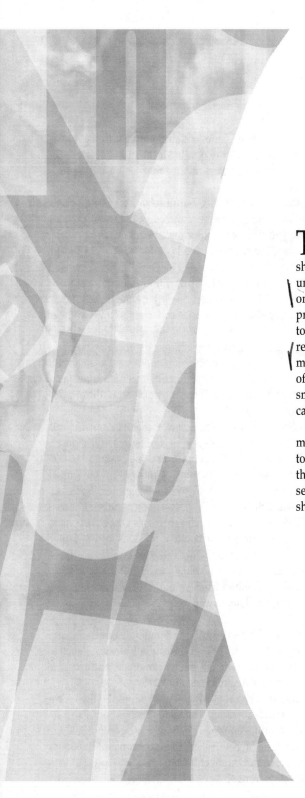

SHARING LITERATURE

The voice of a young child entreating an adult to "read it again" is proof of the pleasure that can come from literature shared aloud. Much of what children enjoy hearing they are unable to read themselves. Picture story books, usually written on a third grade or higher readability level, are inaccessible to preschool and many primary grade children without someone to present them. And poetry, even more than prose, needs to be read aloud by a skilled reader. Such a reader can emphasize the meaning and the rhythm of the words, having passed the stage of struggling simply to recognize and pronounce the words. A smooth presentation shows children the power that literature can have.

You may choose to read a story or tell it. If you tell it, you may want to let your voice alone carry the tale, or you may want to use a feltboard or other visual aid. You may share literature through CD-ROMs, records, films, filmstrips, or videocassettes. Throughout the year, you will have the opportunity to share literature in a variety of ways.

READING ALOUD

Finding the Right Book

As you begin looking through books or poems to choose one to share with children, you will want to consider several factors. One aspect, of course, is the quality of the material itself. Using the criteria presented in chapter 2, you will want to assess literary merit, eliminating from consideration any books that are of poor quality.

You will want to have in mind your purpose for reading. Suppose you are working with a group of three- and four-year-olds. It is the beginning of the year and you and the children are just getting to know one another. You decide you will begin story time by telling some stories you think they will have heard at home. You want the children to feel comfortable with you, and this will help you establish rapport. You also want this experience to lead into a sharing of similar stories that the children may not have heard. You decide to work with traditional literature.

The two stories that you will tell are *The Three Bears* and *The Three Little Pigs.* Both are folktales that use patterns of three and have a repetition of phrases and events. Now you need to select two or three similar folktales to share on succeeding days. These should also contain clear action, an appealing repetition of language, and only a few characters. You may begin by looking on the computer at the library and talking with the librarian about possible choices. You might look in texts or reference books about children's literature. *Children's Literature in the Elementary School* by Huck, Hepler, Hickman, and Kiefer (1997) has a section on traditional literature that groups tales by motif and by country of origin.

You might look in sources that list books for children. The *Subject Guide to Children's Books in Print* (1998), for instance, lists all of the children's books currently in print under subject headings. There are no annotations, so you would need to find the actual books to obtain further information about them. However, the titles alone may jog your memory about appropriate stories.

Other useful references are the *Children's Catalog* (1996) and the *Elementary School Library Collection* (Homa, 1998), both generally available in the children's section of public libraries as well as school libraries. *The Horn Book Guide,* issued twice each year, gives short, critical annotations for all hardcover trade children's and young adult books published in the United States during the preceding six-month period. They are listed within categories and are indexed by author, title, and subject. *The Horn Book Guide, Interactive* (1998), is a CD-ROM version that contains over 29,000 short reviews of the books published from 1990 to 1997. This database is searchable by author, title, subject, and bibliographic data, as well as by the rating given it in the original *Horn Book* review.

You may want to purchase reference books that categorize and annotate books for children. *Adventuring with Books,* edited by Wendy Sutton (1997), lists books under headings such as books for young children, traditional literature, modern fantasy, poetry, language, fine arts, and holidays. Age ranges and evaluative statements are listed for each book.

The Bank Street College Bookstore publishes a regularly updated pamphlet listing the books for sale at the store. Books are classified under headings such as concept books and relationships and feelings. It is a brief listing, with one-sentence descriptions of each book, but the list has been compiled by educators at the Bank Street College of Education and the books are recommended by them. Most of the books are for young children, from two- to four-year-olds to children in the kindergarten to grade three range.

If you check a variety of listings, you will have many book titles from which to choose. Some teachers keep a database or card file of books that they have used successfully. They add to it as they learn of new titles and explore new areas with their classes. In this way, they have personal listings readily available. New teachers sometimes find it helpful to talk with other teachers and librarians. They often find that colleagues are an abundant source of information.

Using these sources, you have selected titles and gathered books to read and preview. You have decided to share *The Little Red Hen* and found seven versions listed, four of which the library owns, and *The Three Billy Goats Gruff*, four versions to peruse. You are also going to look at *Who's in Rabbit's House?* (Aardema, 1977) and *Deep in the Forest* (Turkle, 1976). You read through the books, keeping in mind your purposes and assessing the literary and artistic quality of each selection. You choose *The Little Red Hen* illustrated by Paul Galdone (1973), and *The Three Billy Goats Gruff* (Asbjornsen, 1993), illustrated by Glen Rounds. Both are effective retellings of the tales, and both have uncluttered, expressive illustrations. You decide to wait until later in the year to read *Who's in Rabbit's House?* because, although it does have a repetition of phrases and of action, it has far more characters and is more complex than the other tales. It will be better appreciated by the children when they have had a little more experience with literature and are able to attend to a story for a longer period of time.

The next two books you select are *The Little Red Hen/Le pequena gallina roja* (1969) by Letty Williams and *Deep in the Forest* by Brinton Turkle (1976). You plan to read the second version of *The Little Red Hen* for two reasons. First, because it is told in both English and Spanish, you can mention to the children that it is written in two languages and tell them the title in both. If you have Spanish-speaking children in your group, you might read the entire story in both languages—assuming you read Spanish—but if you do not, you may introduce but not emphasize this aspect. Second, you will show how one tale maintains its structure but varies in details with different retellings. The Galdone version has a cat, a dog, and a mouse who watch while the Little Red Hen plants wheat and finally bakes a cake. The Williams version has a cat, a dog, and a pig who watch while the Little Red Hen plants corn and finally makes tortillas. In both, the Little Red Hen enjoys the fruits of her labor and eats what she has worked to produce.

Deep in the Forest is a wordless picture book in which a bear cub enters a cabin in the woods to find a table with three chairs and three bowls, in the standard small, medium, and large sizes of *Goldilocks and the Three Bears*. The story reverses the characters, for it is the young girl who returns to find a cub in her bed and her cabin in disarray. You choose this because you think the children will delight in grasping what has happened to the story, and because it will elicit discussion of the structure of the tale as the children point out the changes.

You also find versions of *Goldilocks and the Three Bears* by James Marshall (1988) and by Jan Brett (1987). You plan to bring them in together and tell the children that you have two books in which different artists have drawn pictures to go with a story they know. Can they tell from the covers what the story is? You will leave these books for the children to look at one their own, listen for their comments, and see if they ask for the stories to be read.

You have chosen carefully, keeping both your purposes and the children's needs and interests in mind. You have also noted that the books you are planning to share with the group are large enough for the children to see the illustrations clearly as you read. If they were not, you would need to share the books with only one or two children at a time, or perhaps use a filmstrip or video that would allow all of the children to see.

Of course, there are some instances when children may not need to see the illustrations as the story is being read. They may listen to familiar Mother Goose rhymes and only later look at the illustrations. In an illustrated book with few pictures, the teacher may decide to show the illustrations by walking around so that children get a closer view. With only a few pictures, this does not create much of an interruption in the story.

Creating a Positive Atmosphere

You will want to share the books in a way that invites children to enter into the experience wholeheartedly. Reading well orally is basic to this happening. It is often helpful to read the selection aloud yourself before sharing it with children.

Being familiar with the material will eliminate any stumbling over unusual words. It will give you a chance to rehearse any special voices you may want to use for different characters. If you are reading poetry, it will allow you to plan where the breaks should be so that you keep the meaning intact.

It may be useful to get feedback on your skill in reading aloud. One way of doing this is to record yourself. As you listen to the tape, ask several questions. Am I enunciating clearly? That is, are my words distinct? Is the volume pleasant, loud enough to be heard without straining, yet not uncomfortably loud? Am I reading at a speed that allows the listener to comprehend easily? Does the expression in my voice move the story along, make it more interesting? If the answer to any of these is "no," then perhaps you will want to practice the same story several times, concentrating on improving areas of weakness.

Whenever possible, hold the book so children can see the illustrations as you read.

Another way of getting feedback is to ask a friend to observe you as you read to a group of children. Ask the friend to answer the same questions you would ask of yourself if listening to a tape. In addition, ask the friend to tell you if you are looking up as you read, making eye contact with the children.

When you practice reading aloud, practice holding the books as you will with children. Try to hold it so that they can see the illustrations as you read. Some teachers accomplish this by holding the book to one side as they read. Others look down over the top of the book, reading the print upside down. If there is lengthy text, it may be easier to read the page, then show the illustrations. If you share pictures in this way, remind yourself to move the book slowly so that children have a chance to focus on the picture and see more than a blur of color flashing before them.

Being familiar with the content of the book through having read it aloud frees you to make more eye contact with the children and share in their enjoyment of the story. It allows you to see children's responses—what amuses them, for example, or if any of them are getting tired of listening.

After each reading, perhaps formally but usually informally, evaluate your sharing of the book. If all went well, remember what you did that contributed to that success. If there were problems, try to analyze why they occurred and what might be done to avoid them in the future. For example, if the fire bell rang in the middle of the story, there is little you could have done to have prevented it. But if the story was interrupted by one child kicking another, you might have seen the two poking at each other with increasing frequency if you had looked up more often. A look from you with a shake of your head, or separating the children as you showed illustrations in the book, might have prevented the incident.

Whether for a small group or the total class, plan the setting so that it will be as easy as possible for the children to pay attention. This means trying to find a quiet place to read. If there is going to be extraneous noise, move so that your voice and the noise are not coming from the same direction, competing with each other. Place yourself so that visual attention can be focused on you and on the book. Put the children's backs to any movement that may be distracting. If there is a strong light source, such as a window, have the children's backs to it also. Light shining on you and on the book will make both easily seen; light shining behind you and the book may have children squinting at a silhouette.

If you know the children are likely to be restless, plan how you will help them calm down. Perhaps it will be by saying a few poems together, having the children each tell one thing they heard on the playground, or doing two or three finger plays. Let children know what your expectations are. If story time is to be a quiet time for listening, praise such behavior. If you want children to hold their comments until the conclusion of a story, remind them of this when you begin.

A set time for story hour lets children know it is an important part of the day. It also gives them some control over the situation because they know what the pattern is. You may want to have a rule that says they may leave the story circle if they wish, but they are not to make noise, talk, or in any way distract those who are listening. Or you may want to establish a pattern in which all children stay for all of the story.

Think about the contingencies that may arise. A comment that you are certain to hear at least once is, "I've heard it before." You will want to be prepared to respond with a comment such as, " Don't tell how it ends," or "See if you notice anything in the story this time that you didn't when you heard it before." This acknowledges the child's remark, yet avoids a lengthy discussion about whether he or she wants to hear it again.

Plan how you will introduce the book. Some teachers give the title and author at the beginning, others do it at the end. At some time, however, children should be told the title, author, and illustrator. This helps to establish the idea that books are written by real people.

Helping Children Construct Meaning

There are many ways to build interest in, and enhance the comprehension of, a book you are about to read. You might ask children to make some guesses about the story from the title or from the picture on the cover. Before sharing *The Little Red Hen,* you might ask the children to look at the cover and tell what they think the Little Red Hen likes to do. For *The Three Billy Goats Gruff,* children might answer the question, "What differences do you see among the three goats shown here?" Introductory comments set the stage for the story and can be used to guide children's learning. Having them listen for special things encourages careful listening. Having them guess what will happen fosters logical thinking about cause and effect.

Narrative Structure

Children develop a sense of story, an idea of how events are sequenced and are interrelated. This comes in part with hearing many stories, but also with teachers and day-care providers who talk with them about what they have heard. Sipe (1998) found that the first and second graders who responded to picture books read aloud engaged in five conceptual categories of responses. They talked about the elements of literature, such as plot and characterization, and sequence, and how the illustrations influenced their understanding. They compared the story being read aloud with other stories they had heard. They connected the story to their own lives. They lost themselves in the story, and finally, they used it as a base for their own creative activities. This suggests that even young children can be part of a community that understands and responds to literature, even to fairly sophisticated techniques such as foreshadowing.

Sipe also noted that the teachers exhibited scaffolding behavior—that is, they engaged in practices that supported and encouraged the children's understanding. They mediated the stories for the children, pacing the reading appropriately and adding expression to their voices. They modeled how discussion could progress and managed it in ways the elicited more talk. They helped children make links between the literature and took a stance where they too wondered about event in the books. And finally, they were aware of and used the teachable moments, often taking children's comments to higher levels of abstraction.

Books read aloud provide the perfect time for talking about how stories are structured. This may well come during the story reading. For many children, it is helpful to make a visual representation of the structure of the story, a sort of flow chart of events, or arrows showing what caused what. These are usually most effective when constructed by the children and teacher together, so that explanation and conversation accompany the charting, and when not done too frequently.

Visual Literacy

Visual literacy is the ability to gain meaning from visual images. For children viewing picture books, this means interpreting the nontextual elements—the illustrations, the endpapers, the title page. John Stewig (1992) sees three steps in sharing books with children in a way that encourages the development of visual literacy. First, have children bring their own background to bear on what they see. Have them tell what they notice and how it compares with what they have experienced. Second, have them pay attention to individual units within the larger unit; perhaps look at the use of color in an illustration, or see how the endpapers relate to the text. Third, ask the children to make aesthetic judgments about the relative merits of one picture book over another, and give their reasons for their conclusions.

Your discussions about books will most likely involve both narrative structure and visual literacy, as both contribute to meaning. If you are going to discuss a book, questions should be developed and written down. If there are to be extension activities, you will need to have materials and directions ready. If there is to be no follow-up, then you may simply say, "And that's the story of Lilly and her new plastic purse," or "There are other books by Kevin Henkes. Would you like to hear another story by him?" If you do ask the children what they would like to hear, be prepared to honor their response. If they say yes, then plan to read what they want. If they say no, skip the book for now even though you may know it is excellent literature.

Many teachers have a special place where they put the book they have just finished reading. Children then know where to find it if they want to read it themselves or look at the pictures. This practice also gives the teacher a chance to judge the reaction of children to particular books. Some may sit unopened; others may be in constant demand.

Although reading aloud is probably the most frequently used method of sharing literature with children, other ways are effective also. One of these is storytelling.

STORYTELLING
Finding the Right Story

In selecting a story to tell, either with or without visuals, you will use many of the same criteria that you use to select books to read aloud. You want it to be good literature, and you want it to match the interest and understanding level of the audience. But there are other criteria to consider. The story should have a fairly compact plot, with much action. It should also have a strong beginning and a satisfying conclusion. Natural dialogue will keep the story moving and add interest, although having too many characters who speak can make a story difficult for both teller and listener to follow. Because folktales originated in oral, rather than written, form, they are excellent for telling. They are not the only "tellable" tales, of course, but they are a logical place to begin.

Some qualities may make a story better read than told. Examples are descriptive language that is an integral part of the story, or exact dialogue that is essential to the meaning or mood. The storyteller tells the tale in his or her own words; so if specific language is needed and it is more than can be memorized, the teller might be better off choosing another story.

The story should be one that you like. If you spend the time to learn it, you will want to tell it more than once. It should be a story that you think will appeal to many groups of children. You can build a repertoire of stories by learning three or four each year.

Briggs and Wagner (1979, p. 36) describe children ages three to six years old as being in the "age of repetition." They enjoy stories that have repetitive plots, such as *The Three Little Pigs* and *Chicken Little*. Repeated lines keep the children oriented to the sequence of the story. Children also enjoy taking part in the telling themselves, saying the refrain with the storyteller or engaging in motions to accompany the story. If you are working with preschool youngsters, you might want to learn a story like *Here We Go on a Lion Hunt,* (Wagner, 1970, pp. 74–75), which has motions for the children to perform as the tale is being told.

Children ages six to nine are described by Briggs and Wagner as being in the "age of fancy." From about age seven to nine is the period of peak interest in fairy tales. These children are able to distinguish fantasy from reality. They can tolerate the violence because they know the story is make-believe. They expect the evil characters to be punished and the good rewarded, a pattern of justice that exists in most fairy tales. You may find that you know many fairy tales already—in this case, a quick review and practice might be all the preparation you need.

A popular visual aid used by classroom and day-care storytellers is the feltboard. This is a board, usually masonite, plywood, or stiff cardboard, that is covered with cloth, usually felt. Characters and bits of setting are placed on the board as the story is told. To select stories for feltboard storytelling, keep in mind the space on the board and how much you can manipulate at one time. There will not be room for a cast of thousands. Even if there are only eight different characters, if they must be used in several different groupings, or appear in the story randomly rather than in a patterned sequence, you may end up giving all your attention to finding the right characters at the right time and be unable to concentrate on telling the story well.

Look for stories that have a fairly simple plot, perhaps either cumulative or repetitive. Think about what can be used to give the idea of the story. Neither setting nor characters need to be exact in detail. If you were to tell the story of *Red Hen and Sly Fox* (French, 1995) on the feltboard, you would need only two characters, the hen and the fox. Red Hen is known to her neighbors for her generosity in mending and sewing for them. She always wears her apron with needle, thread, and scissors in the pocket. Sly Fox has been thinking for some time that Red Hen would make an excellent chicken dinner. He awakens and decides that today is the day for his chicken dinner, so grabbing a pair of socks and a large sack, he heads off to her house. He explains that his socks need darning, and so, of course, kindly Red Hen invites him in. Once inside he lunges at her, but she flies up to the top of the cupboard. Sly Fox is indeed sly, though. He spins around, she watches and gets dizzy and falls down into his sack. But the fox is not the only clever one. When he stops for a nap, Red Hen cuts her way out of the sack—one should always carry scissors—and puts a stone in her place. Fox is home with the water boiling before he discovers the deception. Red Hen lives happily, helping her neighbors, and keeping needle, thread, and scissors at the ready.

The story itself is simple enough to work well. The plot is clear, there are only two characters, and it is through action rather than description that listeners learn in what ways both animals are both clever and deceitful. In addition to the characters, you would make Red Hen's apron with its pocket, perhaps even scissors; socks and a sack for Sly Fox; a large stone; and a pot with boiling water. You might want an outline of Red Hen's house, and several trees to place strategically as "the woods." You would then move the characters and objects around to match your telling of the story, covering the figure of Red Hen with the sack when she is captured, moving Sly Fox through the woods, placing the figure horizontally when he stops for a nap. The pattern makes the story easy for children to follow, and the few characters and props make it easy for you to tell.

Ed Young, in his book *The Lost Horse* (1998), provides the reader with puppets that can be used to tell the story. With colorful paper figures of the horse, the wise man Sai, and Sai's son, a day-care provider or teacher can tell about this man who lived in northern China, with few possessions other than his horse, the misfortunes that befell him, and his attitude. The figures can be moved to exhibit different postures and various motions because they are constructed with grommets connecting parts of the body. The "good news/bad news" pattern will be grasped quickly by listeners.

Creating a Positive Atmosphere

In storytelling, as in reading aloud, it is essential that the children be able to see the presenter. One of the rewards of storytelling is that you can maintain constant eye contact with the children. You can adapt the story to their reactions. You can show that you find the tale amusing, or sad, or quietly beautiful.

Some teachers use a puppet to introduce stories that they are going to tell. It may be a hand puppet that comes to the session with the teacher, hidden in a pocket or a bag. The teacher wakes the puppet, and the two may have a brief conversation about the story, or the puppet may talk directly to the children. It is a way of setting the stage for storytelling. The puppet is put away during the telling and perhaps recalled at the conclusion.

If you are going to use a feltboard, decide whether you want it to be propped up on an easel or a chair. Think about where it will be in relation to the children's eye level. Will they be able to see it comfortably? Plan also where you will stand or sit. It will need to be a place where you can reach the board, reach the characters, and see the children.

You can judge the reaction of your audience as you tell a story.

Preparing to tell a story usually takes more time than preparing to read a story. You may wonder where you will find the time to do this preparation, or whether you have the talent to tell a story well. It may help to keep in mind that your audience is not expecting a professional storyteller. You need not spend hours in getting ready, nor should you expect to always have a perfect presentation. Just do the best you can, improving as you gain experience.

It is useful to know how others learn a story, then adapt it to individual situations. Few storytellers memorize a story word for word. Most make note of the basic sequences of action—what happens when. They may memorize the opening sentence and the concluding sentence, and any refrains that are part of the story, but the rest they tell in their own words. They begin by reading the story over several times, getting a sense of the story as a whole. Then they may list the action on a sheet of paper or on note cards. Storytellers use these lists to set the action in their minds and to refresh their memories when they have not told that particular story for awhile. These lists are not used during the storytelling itself.

Some storytellers visualize the story, picturing in their minds the setting, characters, and how the action progresses. This picture helps them remember, and is also useful as they begin to describe the scene or tell about a character.

Suppose you have decided to learn the story of *The Cat's Purr* as told by Ashley Bryan (1985). First, read the tale several times. Picture in your mind how Cat and Rat were best friends, how they lived near one another, visited one another's huts, and worked together in the fields. Then make a series of note cards denoting the basic action of the story. The cards might look something like this.

Card 1: Cat and Rat are good friends, do everything together. Examples; hoe fields, Cat lets Rat play his bamboo flute, decide to have a feast when the vegetables are ready.

Card 2: Cat's uncle visits and gives Cat a tiny drum. It has been in the family and only Cat is to play it. He must stroke it gently, never beat it or poke it. When he does stroke it gently, it goes *purrum, purrum.*

Card 3: When Rat arrives, he first hears Cat playing, then dances to Cat's playing, then wants a turn playing himself. Cat refuses.

Card 4: Rat tries to stall, saying he is hungry. Cat fixes him breakfast, then is concerned that he will eat so much he will be sick. Rat seizes on the idea, feigns sickness.

Card 5: Cat goes to the fields alone. Rat picks up the drum, by chance plays it correctly.

Card 6: Cat hears the sound, returns. Asks Rat, who has jumped back in bed, who was playing the drum. Rat says he doesn't know—and he's still sick.

Card 7: Cat goes back to the field. Rat again plays the drum.

Card 8: Cat returns. Rat acts innocent again.

Card 9: Cat heads for the field, but sneaks back in through the window and hides under a table. He sees Rat play the drum and emerges, telling him to drop it.

Card 10: Rat sees Cat's open mouth and sharp teeth, throws the drum into Cat's mouth and runs.

Card 11: Cat swallows the drum, sits down to stroke his stomach to settle the drum, and sound of drum is heard softly—*purrum, purrum.*

Card 12: That's why cats chase rats. And ever since then Cat has carried his drum safely within, and only he can decide who will play it. But you must not beat it—you must stroke it gently. Then you will hear the cat's drum. *Purrum, purrum, purrum.*

The cards give the sequence of action, but they don't give the flavor of the story. Reading it over and over does this. Keep in mind that the story is enhanced by sound and refrains. The Rat squeaks; the phrase about the drum—"Don't rap it or beat it or tap it or poke it, or you won't get a good sound. Just stroke it gently and listen"(Bryan, p. 7)—figures prominently each time the drum is played; and both Rat and Cat use "Pit-tap-a-la-pat," as in Rat's gleeful

> Pit-tap-a-la-pat
>
> Pit-tap-a-la-ping
>
> Eat off Cat's food
>
> And don't pay a thing
>
> *Bryan, p. 20*

as he plays Cat's drum. It's a good idea to memorize several of the refrains.

Now practice saying the story aloud. You will be able to identify any rough spots in the telling. Some teachers practice telling stories as they drive or do chores around the house. Once you have mastered the story, you can recall it by going over your note cards quickly and perhaps saying it once or twice to yourself.

Using a feltboard to tell a story shortens one part of the preparation and lengthens another. Learning the story will probably take less time, for by stacking the figures in the order they appear you give yourself clues to the story's sequence. If you were telling *Red Hen and Sly Fox* with a feltboard, you would see each object in order. Some day-care providers keep the figures face up in a pile; others put them face down so the numbers that mark sequence will show on the back. A brief synopsis of the story can be kept in a folder with the figures. This provides a quick review before each telling.

The preparation would be lengthened by the making of the figures themselves. They can be cut from felt, or made from paper with sandpaper or felt pieces glued to the back so that they will adhere to the board. Velcro is also used for sticking figures to the board. Many storytellers make characters from pellon, a type of interfacing available at fabric stores. Figures can be traced onto it, then colored in with crayon, felt-tip markers, or liquid embroidery. Pellon figures tend to be more durable than those constructed from paper. The feltboard itself is covered with cloth, generally a dark, solid color that provides a background for many stories. Ramon Ross (1972) describes using indoor-outdoor carpeting for this purpose. You can experiment with different backings and methods of making characters to find the ones that suit you best.

It is necessary to practice using the figures as you rehearse the story. Set the board up exactly as you plan to use it with children. Find out ahead of time if the angle of the board is such that the characters will fall to the floor every minute-and-a-half. Adjust the board or add more backing to the figures so that the story can proceed smoothly when you tell it to the children. If necessary, rough up the back of the characters with an emery board or fine sandpaper. Decide where to put the characters so the children will not see them before they are placed on the feltboard. You may want to keep them in a box or behind the board.

When you have completed the story, take a minute to evaluate your presentation. After you have told three or four stories to a group of children, you might ask them to tell which stories they liked best and why. Putting their impressions into words will help children to compare stories to see how tales are alike and different. It may also give you some insight into your own presentations. If they tell you that they liked *The Three Billy Goats Gruff* because the troll's voice was scary, you know your expression and voice quality were effective. If they cannot remember any of the events in *The Cat's Purr,* then there was a problem either with the presentation or with the selection of the tale for those children. Perhaps there were distractions during the telling of the story. The children may be able to tell about the fight on the playground outside the window instead of the story. Perhaps the story was too complicated or too long for that group. They simply may have lost interest and been unable to follow what was happening from the beginning. Analyzing past presentations will help you improve future storytelling.

Helping Children Construct Meaning

Telling stories well is a key to helping children develop understanding. There are many similarities, obviously, between reading a story and telling a story, but some differences also.

Narrative Structure

The requirements of storytelling to young children, especially when using a feltboard, mean that sequence is a prime concern. Thus it makes sense to focus on this area of story structure. Stories can be retold, having children come up and select the figure that should go next on the feltboard and adding the appropriate text, or moving figures around. You might also have them listen to a story, then decide what characters would be needed to tell it as a feltboard story. Children would thus be identifying the key characters.

Some stories may be told twice, allowing the children to become familiar with the sequence and to master any refrains so that they can say them with the teacher. The same is true as children learn motions to accompany the telling or if they sing during the telling as a part of the story. If the children are taking turns participating, or retelling the story, let them know when the session is about to be ended. Comments such as "Let's hear from two more people before we stop," or "Teddy, we'll let you be the last one to tell our story for today," give children a sense of conclusion rather than interruption.

Visual Literacy

As with looking at illustrations in picture books, children will look at how the teacher or daycare provider has represented elements of the story visually if a feltboard is being used. Often it will be in less detail, so that rather than looking at the subtleties, as in an illustration, they will look at the symbolic nature of the representation. The children themselves might suggest what objects are central to the plot and thus necessary for the retelling, or how the setting could be suggested with only a few objects. If they were telling a cumulative tale, such as *The Jacket I Wear in the Snow* (Neitzel, 1989), the objects are clear—each piece of clothing that the child puts on. If they were telling *Red Hen and Sly Fox,* they would have to decide the importance of the houses, the cupboard, the cooking pot, the stone. They will be addressing the question of how visual elements contribute to understanding.

SHARING LITERATURE THROUGH MEDIA
Finding the Right Media

The number and range of audiovisual materials, particularly CD-ROMs, is expanding rapidly. Some companies have been in the business of producing filmstrips, videos, and audiocassettes based on children's books for many years. Among these are Weston Woods Studios, Recorded Books, Inc., Spoken Arts, and Live Oak Media. Sending for their, and other companies' catalogs may give you an idea of what is currently available. Also, Reading Rainbow sells its programs on videocassettes. *Parents Guide: A Review of Children's Media* is published by the nonprofit corporation Parents Guide to Media and has reviews of the media (as well as books and toys) that its experts and the children who have participated recommend. Information about books in media format is also readily available in publisher's book catalogs and on their internet sites. A useful reference book is *Bowker's Complete Video Directory* (1996).

The proliferation of CD-ROMs that are literature related means that it is necessary first to read how the company describes the material on its package or in advertising, and then to actually preview the material. It is more likely that an electronic version of *Stellaluna* (Living Books, 1996) will have more literary merit than Teletubbie's or Hasbro's *Mr. Potato Head Saves Veggie Valley* (1995), though that is not guaranteed. However, a package that tells you that beginning readers will love filling in the blanks and "learning about adjectives, nouns, and verbs" because the exercises are based on a popular children's book is no more than an electronic workbook.

Sound and action and, with CDs, interaction, should engage the viewer in a literary experience, bringing the narrative to life. Your purpose should also guide you in the selection of media. Perhaps you want to share a book with the total class, but it is so small that they could not see the illustrations. A filmstrip will overcome this problem. If you have been introducing the work of several poets, your class could listen to recordings of these poets reading some of their own poetry. It may be that you want a cassette that the children can play themselves, that you can leave in the listening center. Children can then elect to hear their favorite stories or poems again and again. If you want to encourage children to follow along in a book while listening to the text being read, then you will probably want a recording that has a sound to mark the turning of each page. This will help beginning readers keep their place. Another option would be to select CDs that show the text as it is read. Being clear in your own mind about the purpose for using the media will help you select the most appropriate type.

Preview the material before you share it with the children. Assess the quality of the audiovisual material just as you do print materials. Generally speaking, media or an interactive format cannot rescue a book that was of poor quality originally. If you know that the book version is of literary merit, you will still need to evaluate the media version. The medium should be appropriate to the story. A recording may fit very well with a story that has many descriptive passages, for children can visualize the picture in their minds as they listen to the words. On the other hand, a recording may prove confusing to children if several speakers utter dialogue from a book and the voices are difficult to distinguish.

Check the technical quality of the production. Voices should be clear and easily understood. In live action films or videos, lips and voices should be synchronized. Prints and pictures should be distinct, in focus. Sound effects and music should help establish the mood of the story, not overpower the story.

Check also for authenticity. If there is a dialect, it should be spoken accurately. If the story has a specific setting, it should be realistically portrayed. Note whether a film or filmstrip based on a children's book has the original artwork. If it does not, you will need to judge the quality of the art as well as the technical quality of the filming.

Creating a Positive Atmosphere

When you order nonprint materials, note the type of equipment that will be needed to share it. When selecting CD-ROMs, note the system requirements. If possible, set up the equipment either before the children arrive or while they are engaged in other activities. They can become restless as they wait for a program to load or a video to be set at the desired starting place. It is also more difficult to concentrate on equipment if you must simultaneously attend to twenty-five children.

Let the children get settled before beginning a video or filmstrip. They can be asked to be sure they can see the screen before the lights are turned out. You may want to tell them a little about what they are going to see to set the mood, or ask them to watch for specific happenings.

Think about the length of the presentation in relation to the attention span of the children who will be experiencing it. Weston Woods Studios has made a motion picture and a video of *The Snowman*, a wordless picture book by Raymond Briggs. It is exquisitely produced, with smooth animation and a beautiful orchestral score. The story is easier to follow

For both books and book related media, build on children's social nature.

in this format than in the original because only one scene appears on the screen at a time, rather than the progression of small scenes that appear on a single page in the book. A few scenes have been omitted and several sequences added. It is a superb production, yet it runs for 26 minutes—a long time for preschool or primary children, particularly because the film is rather slow-paced. To retain the attention of young children, you may want to show the movie in two segments. Decide where to make the break during your preview session.

Adapting a story to a new medium does not necessarily change the level of difficulty of comprehension. If five-year-olds are baffled by the four parallel stories that comprise David Macaulay's *Black and White* (1990), it is likely that they will have the same difficulty whether they encounter the story as a picture book, a video, a record, or a CD. If the content or presentation is too sophisticated for your group, make another selection, even though the work itself and the translation into audiovisual format may be outstanding.

Think also about the children's reactions to the presentation. The Children's Film Theatre tested films with children ages three to twelve. In their second report, a book listing recommended films titled *More Films Kids Like,* they sometimes list suggestions for preparing children. For the film *Hansel and Gretel, An Appalachian Version,* they write:

> Some adults were reluctant to use it; they thought it would frighten kids. But it was one of our most successful films—most groups ask for it again and again (perhaps in part to time it). It does require discussion, particularly with young and middle groups, and before we showed it to these children we told them it was a scary film and suggested they sit near someone they like or hold hands if they got scared. (Gaffney, 1977)

This sort of preparation could make the difference between children's enjoyment of a film and their dislike of a film they find frightening.

Helping Children Construct Meaning

Children are very accustomed to taking in information visually. They see advertisements, Web TV, videos, animated cartoons. Flood and Lapp noted that "From a very early age, children see and respond to images shifting approximately every 7 seconds on the television screen with the background 'noise' of musical and verbal messages" (1998, p. 343). While they may not understand all these messages, they do come to expect many of the accompanying features. Teachers and day-care providers can help children make sense of what they are seeing and hearing by encouraging them to talk about the meaning they are getting and how they have arrived at it. There may be elements to which they are responding, but that they have never identified. For example, the musical background while a title and credits are showing often sets the mood of a video or film.

Narrative Structure

A pivotal element that sets interactive media apart from books or videos is that is often nonlinear in construction. That is, the viewer can move back and forth in a retelling, can decide to take a side trip as it were. Things are happening simultaneously. They are not in the neat, sequentially organized, planned recounting of events. The author has less control in the construction of meaning, and the reader/viewer more, than in books. The author no longer determines the sequence in which a story will be experienced. This may be "good news/bad news" for the viewer. The good news is the opportunities it opens, such as the possibility of finding new meanings by clicking on a icon, and new ways of understanding how a story is put together. The bad news is that the side trips may block out the main path, with children remembering the animation but having no idea of what the story actually was.

Visual Literacy

It is helpful to have children explain orally what they are seeing or have seen, how they have interpreted visual action and symbols. Media can be played and replayed so that children can check on their observations. Teachers have also found that with media, as with books, it is important to set, or have the children set, purposes for viewing and listening.

The ways in which meaning is created visually can be explored by children using programs, such as Hyperstudio, with which they are manipulating the visual elements, in combination with text, to create meaning themselves. And viewing a video or CD, or listening to a cassette, several times encourages more attention to detail and form.

Teachers have a wide selection of literature they may share with children, and ways in which to share it. Guided by their purposes, their knowledge of children, and their evaluation of the literature itself, they can bring children and books together in ways that will make the relationship a lasting one.

HELPING OTHERS SHARE LITERATURE

It is likely that you will have either professional or volunteer aides at least part of the time to assist you in your classroom or center work. Some day-care centers have a regular schedule of "grandparents" who come once a week to work with the children. Some actually are the grandparents of the children in the program, but many others are older community residents who enjoy being with children and want to contribute their time and skills to a meaningful activity.

Having these people share literature with children is an excellent use of their time. They can read to one or two youngsters, letting them select their favorite stories. It is important that children hear some stories over and over, for this helps them gain the concept that print holds a story constant, and that whoever reads the story will use the same words. The words are in the book, not in the adult's head. The story that one child wants to hear again, however, may not be the favorite of others. Thus individual and small group sharing of literature is vital.

In addition, when reading to only one or two children, the adult can allow the child to point to objects and to discuss the book in the midst of the reading. This practice can become distracting when done with a large group, for as one child discusses, others may become confused about the story line or lose interest in hearing the book. The adult can focus on left-to-right progression of words, point to certain words and tell what they say, have the child find words that he or she can recognize, and in general engage in practices that set the stage for the child to learn to read. Those children who can read already might read every other page themselves, or perhaps even read the whole story with the adult as the listener.

When the adult is reading to just one child, he or she can talk with the child about the child's reaction to the story, or let the child retell the story, either from memory or by looking at the illustrations. It is an ideal time for communication and for maximum involvement of the child.

You may need to be very direct in suggesting to the aide those behaviors that contribute to effective oral reading. In a study that compared the oral reading skills of teachers with those of aides, Lamme (1977) found that the aides were not as effective as the teachers in oral reading, and that there was no relationship between the way the teacher read and the way the aide read. Even aides who indicated that they read regularly to their own children at home were not necessarily skilled readers. Be certain that aides know what is expected of them. They should practice so that they read with expression, using appropriate volume and speed. They should show the illustrations and involve children with the reading. They should maintain eye contact as much as possible.

If you have an aide who is skilled as a storyteller, by all means make use of him or her in this capacity. Find out if your aide speaks and reads in the language or languages spoken by your bilingual students. This opens up more possibilities for the sharing of literature, as many public libraries have sections of children's books in other languages. Train your aides in the skills they need to work effectively, and build on the unique skills they bring to the center or classroom.

SUMMARY

To involve children with literature, whether by reading, telling, or using audiovisual materials, it is necessary to prepare carefully. One way of thinking about this is to focus first on finding the right book to read, or story to tell, or media version to experience.

During the selection process, you find the literature you may share, using selection guides when necessary. Apply the standards of good literature to any story or poem under consideration, with added criteria applied to stories for telling or in audiovisual format. The selection is done with a specific group of children in mind.

The next step is to create a positive classroom atmosphere for enjoying literature. Decide how you will share the literature and how you will involve the children. Plan so that distractions are kept at a minimum. A regular time and procedure for the sharing of literature help establish a pattern and demonstrate that you consider literature an important activity. Know how you are going to introduce the literature, perhaps having children describe what they think the story may be about as they look at the book cover and hear the title, or setting the stage by working with a hand puppet. Know also what concluding statements, questions, or activities will follow the actual sharing of the literature.

Read aloud the stories and poems you plan to share; make cards to help you recall the sequence of action in a story you plan to tell; stack the figures for a feltboard story in the order in which you will use them; preview audiovisual materials both for the content and to make certain you know how to use the equipment.

If you have aides to assist you, have them read to one or two children at a time. Teach them to read skillfully. Careful preparation by you and your aides will help bring children and books together not only for the 15 minutes it takes to read a story, but for the rest of their lives.

Extending Your Learning

1. Ask a friend or classmate to listen as you read a picture book orally, and to evaluate your reading based on appropriate speed and volume, enunciation, expression, and eye contact.

2. Make a tape recording of yourself reading a book for children and evaluate your oral reading skill.

3. Plan how you would introduce three different picture books to a group of children.

4. Read five folktales that are in picture-book format. For each, assess whether it would be good for telling as well as reading.

5. Make feltboard characters and use them to tell a story. You may want to use the list of books recommended for feltboard stories at the end of this chapter to help you find an appropriate book.

6. Read a folktale and divide it into units of action for telling.

7. Preview a video based on a children's book. Assess the quality of the production and describe a potential audience for the material.

8. Preview a CD-ROM based on a children's book. Describe the interactive features and assess their merit in terms of developing literary understanding.

9. Compare a children's book with an audiovisual or CD-ROM adaptation of it.

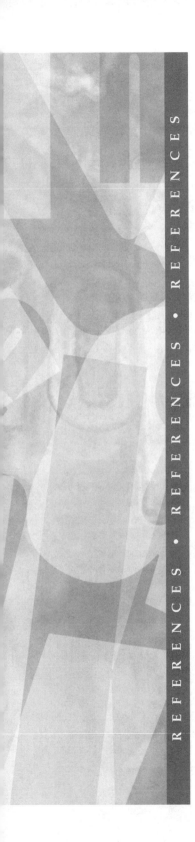

RECOMMENDED REFERENCES

Baker, A., Greene, E. (1987). *Storytelling: Art and Technique.* (2nd ed.) New York: R. R. Bowker.

Barton, B. (1986). *Tell Me Another: Storytelling and Reading Aloud at Home, at School, and in the Community* Portsmouth, NH: Heinemann.

Bauer, C. (1993). *Caroline Feller Bauer's New Handbook for Storytellers* Chicago: American Library Association.

Bauer, C. (1997). *Leading Kids to Books Through PUPPETS* Chicago: American Library Association.

Chaplin, C. (1998). *Storytelling With Puppets* (2nd ed.). Chicago: American Library Association.

Gaffney, M. (1981). *What to Do When the Lights Come on* Phoenix, AZ: Oryx Press.

Hicks, D. (1997). *Flannelboard Classic Tales* Chicago: American Library Association.

Nichols, J. (1998). *Storytimes for Two-Year-Olds* (2nd ed) Chicago: American Library Association.

Pellowski, A. , (1987). *The Family Story-Telling Handbook* New York: Macmillan.

Pellowski, A. (1984). *The Story Vine* New York: Macmillan.

Roe, B., Alfred, S., Smith, S. (1998). *Teaching Through Stories: Yours, Mine, and Theirs* Norwood, MA: Christopher-Gordon.

Sawyer, R. (1945). *The Way of the Storyteller* New York: Viking.

RECOMMENDED TITLES FOR STORYTELLING

Aylesworth, Jim. (1998). Illustrations, Barbara McClintock. *The Gingerbread Man.* New York: Scholastic.

Brown, Marcia. (1974). *Stone Soup* New York: Scribner's.

Bruchac, Joseph. (1995). Illustrations, Christine Shrader. *Gluskabe and the Four Wishes* New York: Cobblehill.

dePaola, Tomie. (1983). *The Legend of the Bluebonnet* New York: Putnam.

Farley, Carol. (1997). Illustrations Benrei Huang. *Mr. Pak Buys a Story* Morton Grove, IL: Whitman.

Ginsburg, Mirra. (1997). Illustrations, Jos. A. Smith. *Clay Boy.* New York: Greenwillow.

Grimm, Jacob, Grimm, Wilhelm. (1998). Illustrations, Hans Fischer. *The Bremen Town Musicians* New York: North-South.

Lelooska, Chief. (1997). *Echoes of the Elders: The Stories and Paintings of Chief Lelooska* New York: DK Ink.

Lobel, Arnold. (1982). *Ming Lo Moves the Mountain* New York: Greenwillow.

Mollel, Tololwa. (1991). Illustrations, Barbara Spurll. *Rhinos for Lunch and Elephants for Supper.* New York: Clarion.

Root, Phyllis. (1986). Illustrations Sue Truesdall. *Soup for Supper* New York: Harper.

Steptoe, John, (1984). *The Story of Jumping Mouse* New York: Lothrop.

Wolkstein, Diane. (1997). Illustrations Jesse Sweetwater. *Bouki Dances the Kokioko: A Comical Tale from Haiti* New York: Gulliver.

Zelinsky, Paul. (1986). *Rumpelstiltskin,* New York: Dutton.

Zemach, Harve. (1971). Illustrations, Margot Zemach. *A Penny a Look* New York: Farrar.

RECOMMENDED TITLES FOR FELTBOARD STORIES

Birdseye, Tom. Illustrations, Andrew Glass. *Soap! Soap! Don't Forget the Soap: An Appalachian Folktale* (New York: Holiday, 1993).

Brett, Jan. *The Mitten* (New York: Putnam, 1989).

Ehlert, Lois. *Moon Rope: A Peruvian Folktale/Un lazo a la luna: Una leyenda peruana* (New York: Harcourt, 1993).

French, Vivian. Illustrations Sally Hobson. *Red Hen and Sly Fox* (New York: Simon & Schuster, 1994).

Galdone, Paul. *What's in Fox's Sack?* (Boston: Houghton Mifflin, 1982).

Ginsburg, Mirra. Illustrations, Jose Aruego and Ariene Dewey. *Mushroom in the Rain* (New York: Macmillan, 1974).

Hobson, Sally. *Chicken Little* (New York: Simon & Schuster, 1994).

Hogrorian, Nonny. (1988). *The Cat Who Loved to Sing* New York: Knopf.

Lionni, Leo. (1959). *Little Blue and Little Yellow* New York: Astor-Honor.

Martin, Rafe. (1985). *Foolish Rabbit's Big Mistake* New York: Putnam.

Mollel, Tololwa M. (1997). Illustrations, Andrew Glass. *Ananse's Feast* New York: Clarion.

Peck, Jan. (1998). Illustrations, Barry Root. *The Giant Carrot* New York: Dial.

Stevens, Janet. (1995). *Tops and Bottoms* New York: Harcourt.

Summers, Kate. (1997). Illustrations, Maggie Kneen. *Milly and Tilly: The Story of a Town Mouse and a Country Mouse.* New York: Dutton.

Young, Ed. (1992). *Seven Blind Mice* (New York: Philomel.

Zemach, Margot. (1977). *It Could Always Be Worse* (New York: Farrar.

PROFESSIONAL REFERENCES CITED

Bank Street College Bookstore, 610 West 112th Street, New York NY, 10025.

Bowker's Complete Video Directory (New Providence, NJ: R. R. Bowker, 1996).

Briggs, N., Wagner, J. *Children's Literature Through Storytelling and Drama* (Dubuque, IA: Wm. C Brown, 1979).

Children's Catalog. (New York: H. W. Wilson, 1996). (Also annual softcover supplements.)

Homa, L. L. (Ed.) *Elementary School Library Collection: A Guide to Books and Other Media* (Williamsport, PA: Brodart, 1998).

Flood, J., Lapp, D. Conceptualizations of Literacy: The Visual and Communicative Arts, *The Reading Teacher* 51:4, 1998, 342–344.

Horn Book Guide, The. Published spring and fall by The Horn Book, Inc., 56 Roland Street, Suite 200, Boston MA, 02129.

Horn Book Guide, Interactive, The. (1998) Published by The Horn Book, Inc., 56 Roland Street, Suite 200, Boston MA, 02129.

Huck, C., Hepler, S., Hickman, J., Keifer, B. *Children's Literature in the Elementary School* (Dubuque, IA: Brown & Benchmark, 1997).

Lamme, L. *Reading Aloud to Children: A Comparative Study of Teachers and Aides.* Unpublished research report (University of Florida, 1977).

Live Oak Media. P. O. Box 652, Pine Plains, NY 12567.

Parents Guide. (1998). Parent's Guide to Children's Media. Shenandoah University, 186 N. Loudoun Street, Winchester, VA 22601.

Recorded Books, Inc., 270 Skipjack Road, Prince Frederick, MD 20678. (www.recordedbooks.com)

Reading Rainbow. GPN. P. O. Box 80669, Lincoln, NE 68501–0669.

Ross, R. *Storyteller* (Columbus, OH: Merrill, 1972).

Sipe, L. The Construction of Literary Understanding by First and Second Graders in Response to Picture Storybook Read-alouds. *Reading Research Quarterly 33:4,* 1998, 376–378.

Spoken Arts, 801 94th Avenue North, St. Petersburg, FL 33702.

Stewig, J. Reading Pictures, Reading Texts: Some Similarities. *The New Advocate 5:1,* 1992, 11–22.

Subject Guide to Children's Books in Print (annual). (New Providence, NJ: R. R. Bowker, 1998).

Sutton, W. (Ed.). *Adventuring with Books* (Urbana, IL: National Council of Teachers of English, 1997).

Wagner. Children's Literature Through Storytelling. (Dubuque, IA: William C. Brown, 1970).

Weston Woods, P. O. Box 2193, Norwalk, CT 06852–2193.

CHILDREN'S LITERATURE CITED

Aardema, Verna. (1977). Ill., Leo & Diane Dillon. *Who's in Rabbit's House?* New York: Dial.

Asbjornsen, P. C. (1993). Ill., Glen Rounds. *The Three Billy Goats Gruff* New York: Holiday.

Brett, Jan. (1987). *Goldilocks and the Three Bears.* New York: Dodd.

Briggs, Raymond. (1980). *The Snowman* (video) Weston, CT: Weston Woods.

Bryan, Ashley. (1985). *The Cat's Purr.* New York: Atheneum. Reprinted with the permission of Atheneum Books for young Readers, an imprint of Simon and Schuster Children's Publishing Division.

French, Vivian. (1995). Ill., Sally Hobson. *Red Hen and Sly Fox.* New York: Simon & Schuster.

Marshall, James. (1988). *Goldilocks and the Three Bears.* New York: Dial.

Macaulay, David. (1990). *Black and White.* Boston: Houghton - Mifflin.

Neitzel, Shirley. (1989). Ill., Nancy Winslow Parker. *The Jacket I Wear in the Snow.* New York: Greenwillow.

Turkle, Brinton. (1976). *Deep in the Forest.* New York: Dutton.

Williams, Letty. (1969). Ill., Herb Williams. *The Little Red Hen/Le pequena gallina roja.* Upper Saddle River, NJ: Prentice-Hall.

Young, Ed. (1998). *The Lost Horse.* San Diego: Harcourt.

4

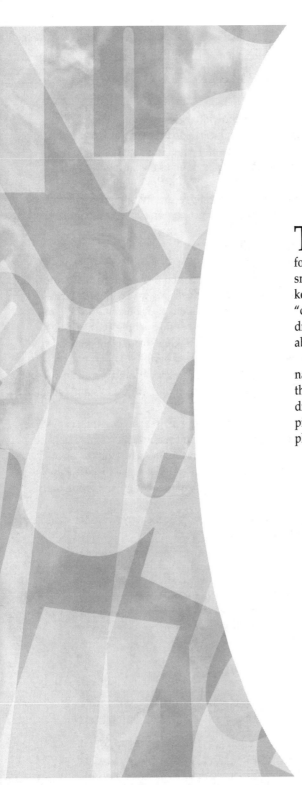

THE LITERATURE CURRICULUM

The kindergarten teacher looked around her classroom after the children had gone home. She visualized the church four youngsters had constructed in the block corner; she smiled at her remembrance of the dramatic play in the housekeeping corner, and "mother" Darice's insistence that the "children" take a nap; she looked at the four paintings still drying on the easels and decided to display them on the wall above the bookshelves.

The teacher was actively engaged in using her imagination. She was forming mental images, some based on events that had happened, others on projections of ideas. The children, too, had been using their imaginations as they created pictures and buildings and as they took the roles of other people in dramatic play.

CHAPTER 4

DEVELOPING THE IMAGINATION

Imagination is central to the competent functioning of independent individuals and of free societies. The ability to construct mental images allows individuals to weigh evidence and explore the possible consequences of particular actions. It allows them to create, and to evaluate, new ideas. Northrop Frye (1964) writes that "The fundamental job of the imagination in ordinary life is to produce, out of the society we have to live in, a vision of the society we want to live in" (p. 140). Without an educated imagination, one can only adjust to society as it is. With an educated imagination, one can evaluate and attempt to change society, and exercise what Frye sees as free speech, the capability of using language effectively and having thoughts of one's own to express with that language.

Literature contributes to the development of the imagination. Participating in the literary experience is itself an imaginative endeavor, for readers are projecting themselves into a story. Often they are seeing worlds that they could not, or would not choose to, experience themselves. The confrontation with lives both better and worse than their own and with experience quite different from their own refines their sensibilities and broadens their perspectives.

Literature exposes for readers the basic wants and needs of other people, the problems they have, the values and attitudes that underlie their decision making. Readers are forced to look at their own values, and their own prejudices, more objectively. Frye (1964) writes that as readers experience literature, they gain a kind of detachment in viewing others and themselves. This detachment leads to an ability to accept the existence of differing beliefs and thus to the development of tolerance.

Literature presents readers with a more structured picture of life than does real experience. Authors select for presentation those events that have the most relevance to characters' actions and those feelings that most epitomize the characters' personalities. They impose an order or mode of presentation designed to help the reader grasp the significance of the total happening. Literature thus aids readers in their ability to interpret experiences by narrowing the range of events discussed.

The development of the imagination through literature is particularly vital for children. Aiden Chambers writes in *Introducing Books to Children:*

> All of these different ways in which literature functions have enormous value for children, as for adults. Children are forming attitudes, finding points of reference, building concepts, forming images to think with, all of which interact to form a basis for decision-making judgment, for understanding, for sympathy with the human condition. Literary experience feeds the imagination, that faculty by which we come to grips with the astonishing amount of data which assails our everyday lives, and find patterns of meaning in it (1983, p. 28).

Glenna Davis Sloan, author of *The Child as Critic,* concurs.

> The structures of literature are self-contained; the reality they present is an imaginative reality. Contemplating these structures critically and reflectively can help us to develop the capacity to view with detachment other verbal structures that surround us. A well-developed imagination, educated on literature, is protection against social mythology in all its forms: entertainment, advertising, propaganda, the language of cliché and stereotype, the abstractions of jargon and gobbledegook. In an irrational world the trained reason is important, but an educated imagination is fundamental to the survival of a same society. (1991, p. 14)

A basic goal, then, of a literature curriculum is the education of children's imaginations. By listening to a broad spectrum of literature, children participate in the imaginative experiences of many authors and begin to see that all literature is part of a body of interrelated works. Day-care professionals and teachers of young children contribute to this basic goal by involving children with literature in ways that establish positive attitudes toward it and by grouping books and structuring presentations so that children begin to perceive the interrelatedness of literature.

PROMOTING POSITIVE ATTITUDES

Because literature is more experienced than taught, if children are to become deeply involved with it, they must choose to do so. This will happen if literature is a satisfying experience for them. You can help children become involved and develop positive attitudes toward literature through regular reading and careful selection of stories and poetry, and through involving children in activities that extend books in a pleasurable manner.

Regular Sharing of Literature

Obviously, for prereaders to experience literature it must be read to them or presented through dramatic or audiovisual means. Even after children have begun to read themselves, however, literature should be shared orally by the teacher on a daily basis. Many books and poems that are appropriate for young children are still too difficult for them to read themselves. Most are more enjoyable when presented by a skilled reader than when deciphered on a word-by-word basis. The teacher has the opportunity to show children how effectively language can be used and what enjoyment it can bring.

Literature Selection

As suggested in Chapter 1, you need to know the children and their backgrounds as you select books to read to them. Most young children like humor, with slapstick being very popular and the verbal humor of puns and riddles becoming more and more appreciated. Young children respond to exaggeration in words and illustrations and enjoy being in on pranks and jokes that are played on fictional characters. Humorous books should be a basic part of your literature curriculum. So, too, should books whose contents appeal to many young children: books about everyday events, animals, and the world of "once upon a time."

In a study of the poetry preferences of first, second, and third graders, Fisher and Natarella (1979) found that the children liked the poetry presented to them, with 76% of the responses to each poem being positive (either "all right" or "great" as a rating). There were strong patterns of preference, but the researchers noted that every poem read had some students who gave it a star as outstanding and some who did not like it at all. For teachers, this means that a wide selection of poetry is recommended. Knowing the types of poetry that were most popular, however, will allow you to make certain that you include poems with a high probability of being well received. The children like narrative poetry best, with free verse, lyric poetry, and haiku the least-popular forms; they liked rhymed, metered poetry, but disliked poetry that was heavily dependent on metaphorical language, even though care was taken to use poems with metaphors children were expected to understand; they liked poems about familiar experiences involving children and animals, and rated humorous poetry as their favorite kind. There was evidence that the children tended to like poems they had heard before. Fisher and Natarella conclude their report with the following statement:

> Since the focus for selecting poems is two-fold, extending children's taste and maintaining a positive attitude toward poetry, teachers and publishers should be clear about their purpose for each choice. We do not want to turn off children by too many poems that are not apt to be popular, and yet we should expand the range of well-liked poetry (1979, p. 385).

Keeping in mind the general preferences of young children, you will also need to assess the difficulty of the poem or book you are considering. Children, and adults too, often dislike what they do not understand. If the literature is beyond the children's comprehension, you are likely to be wasting both your time and theirs by reading it. The following is an excellent poem that builds on a knowledge of *The Three Little Pigs*, and that might make it seem a reasonable choice for young children. However, it uses the characters and situation to express in subtle fashion an emotion more familiar to adolescents and adults than preschool or primary children.

The Builders

I told them a thousand times if I told them once:
Stop fooling around, I said, with straw and sticks;
They won't hold up, you're taking an awful chance.
Brick is the stuff to build with, solid bricks.

You want to be impractical, go ahead.
But just remember, I told them; wait and see.
You're making a big mistake. Awright, I said,
But when the wolf comes, don't come running to me.

The funny thing is, they didn't. There they sat,
One in his crummy yellow shack, and one
Under his roof of twigs, and the wolf ate
Them, hair and hide. Well, what is done is done.
But I'd been willing to help them, all along,
If only they'd once admitted they were wrong.

Sara Henderson Hay

There are no hard-and-fast rules for determining *exactly* which book is appropriate for exactly which child, nor for saying exactly how much of a book a child should understand for the literary experience to be a legitimate one. Still, you will get an idea of the difficulty of a book if you assess the style of writing, the approach to the content, and the complexity of the theme.

Style of writing includes, among other aspects, the choice of vocabulary and the sentence length and structure. Reading and listening comprehension are related to these items. Here are excerpts from two picture books. The first is from *The Wall* (Bunting, 1990), a story in which a young boy and his father visit The Vietnam Veterans Memorial to look for his grandfather's name.

This is the wall, my grandfather's wall. On it are the names of those killed in a war, long ago.

"Where is Grandpa's name?" I ask.

"We have to find it," Dad says.

He and I have come a long way for this and we walk slowly, searching. (n.p.)

The second passage is from *Pink and Say*, the story of Sheldon Russell Curtis, Say, and Pinkus Aylee, Pink, boys fighting for the north in the Civil War. Pink finds Say wounded in the leg and helps him to his home in Georgia, where Pink's mother, Moe Moe Bay, cares for him.

"Bein' here, boy, means you gotta be dead," the voice said as he gave me drink from his kit. "Where you hit?" "Cause if it's a belly hit, I gotta leave you here," he said.

I had never seen a man like him so close before. His skin was the color of polished mahogany. He was flyin' Union colors like me. My age, maybe. His voice was soothin' and his help was good.

"Hit in the leg," I told him. "Not bad if it don't go green."

"Can you put weight on it?" he asked as he pulled me to my feet. "We gotta keep movin'. If we stay in one spot, marauders will find us. They're ridin' drag and lookin' for wounded." (n.p.)

Some picture books are more appropriate for second and third graders, or even older children, than for preschoolers. (From Pink and Say *by Patricia Polacco. Copyright © 1994 by Babushka, Inc. Used by permission of Philomel Books, a division of Penguin Putnam, Inc.)*

The vocabulary in the second passage is far more advanced than that of the first. Not only are more difficult words used—"marauders" for example,—but there are also idiomatic expressions, such as "flyin' Union colors," "ridin' drag" and "go green." Neither passage has inordinately complex sentence structures, which would make comprehension difficult for young children.

There is a similarity of content, in that both books are about the effects of war on the boy who tells the story. In *The Wall,* the effect is of the child wishing the grandfather were with him, not just a name carved in marble. He also observes the many other visitors to the wall and their reactions to the loss of members of their own families. It is a straightforward presentation of the experience, with a situation understandable to young children. The death itself is in the past and is not described. What is clear is the emotional impact the loss of this person has had on the boy's father and on him.

Pink and Say has older characters, the boys about fifteen, and direct experience of the death that war can bring. Marauders arrive at Moe Moe Bay's home, and she sends both boys to the root cellar to hide. When they emerge, they find that she has been killed. They hold her hand until the body is no longer warm, then bury it. Eventually Pink and Say are captured by Confederate troops and taken to Andersonville Prison, where they are separated. Say is freed at the end of the war, but Pink is hung within hours of his arrival. Both books are about the effects of war, but the second is more graphic and detailed.

Both books share a theme of remembering those who died in wars, one through the memorial and through the rubbings that the boy and his Dad make of his grandfather's name, as well as the photographs and flowers left at the wall itself, and the other with an afterward stating directly that this book is a memorial to Pinkus Aylee. However, *Pink and Say* has more complex themes and content than *The Wall.* Within the story is the role of race, that former slaves were not trusted with guns when they first became part of the Union army; that the black soldier was hung immediately while the white one was not; that slaves were not supposed to be taught to read. Among themes woven into the context are that bravery doesn't mean not being afraid; that there are things worse than death; that once you can read, you become your own person; that friendship and caring are not dependent on skin color.

Thus, writing style, approach to content, and theme all make *Pink and Say* a book appropriate for children eight or older, while *The Wall* can be shared with children as young as four or five. There are, however, books that are enjoyed by both age groups. Use your judgment about the difficulty of a book, then watch the children's reactions as you read and listen to their comments. Use their responses to determine how well you are matching their level of comprehension.

Activities for Response to Books

In addition to careful selection, you can maintain and enhance positive attitudes toward literature by suggesting activities for extending the books that are enjoyable and satisfying for the children. Activities should be such that they encourage further involvement with literature. If second-graders must fill in book report forms for each book they complete, they may decide to stop reading. If they are asked to draw their favorite part of every book they hear, they may begin to dread story time. If, however, they are engaged in a variety of creative responses as suggested in chapters 4 through 9 and have the opportunity to work both with others and by themselves and make choices about their activities, they are likely to want to hear and read more literature.

Activities serve many purposes. They help children explore the structure of literature. They encourage comparisons of stories, leading to a concept of what a story is. They support growth in many areas of development. They give teachers a measure of their students' comprehension.

Glenna Sloan writes:

> The child's response to the literature is a central aspect of criticism. The response may come in the form of a question or comment; it may involve sharing a favorite poem or retelling a familiar story; it may be an original composition in words, a drawing, a dramatization, a puppet play, a dance drama, or the story board for a film or a video. . . . Response is both free and guided, the teacher building upon initial response to guide young critics to a greater insight and appreciation of literary works and literature as a whole. (1991, pp.39–40)

Here, criticism means the study of literature in which children learn the verbal trappings for talking about prose and poetry. They learn these in a context in which the terms arise naturally, and they build a foundation for a later, more formal analysis of literature. It is one more reason for encouraging creative responses to literature.

GROUPING BOOKS FOR INSTRUCTION

Children should be guided to perceive literature as a body of work rather than as separate and unrelated stories and poems. If you group books for presentation, you set the stage for children to see the relationships among books, to notice the recurring structural patterns of literature. You give children a database from which they can make their own generalizations about literature.

Arthur Applebee (1978) analyzed the patterns children used in telling stories and the responses they gave when asked about fiction and fictional characters to determine the concept of story held by children ages two through seventeen. He assumed that young children, who might not say directly what they expected to find in a story, would reveal their expectations in the stories they told. He found that even two-year-olds distinguished some conventions of a story. They told stories having formal openings or titles:

> "Once upon a time . . ."; having formal closings: ". . . and they lived happily ever after" or "the end"; and which were consistently in the past tense. Seventy percent of the two-year-olds included at least one of these conventions in the stories they told. The use of the three devices rose with age until by age five, ninety-three percent of the children used at least one of them and forty-seven percent used all three (pp. 36–38).

Applebee noted that many of the stories read to young children are based on the oral tradition and employ these conventions.

The data also showed that as the children matured, they told stories that became more and more removed from the immediate setting of home and family. They also used the conventions of story to explore behaviors unacceptable in terms of general social norms. As the unacceptable behaviors were included, the use of realistic settings dropped. The threat of exploring bad actions was lessened by the distance from reality.

Young children often see stories more as histories than as fictions. At age six, nearly three-fourths of the children studied were still uncertain about whether stories were real; but by age nine, all of the children classified stories as make-believe. This interview with Joseph, age six years and three months, shows a process that occurs often. Children combine the events of the story with the rest of their knowledge about the world.

> Is Cinderella a real person? No
> Was she ever a real person? Nope, she died.
> Did she used to be alive? Yes.
> When did she live? A long time ago, when I was one years old.
> Are stories always about things that really happened? Yes.
> When did the things in Little Red Riding Hood happen? A long time ago when I was a baby, they happened. There was witches and that, a long time ago. So when they started witch . . . they say two good people and they made some more good people, so did the more horrible people. And they made more good people and the bad people got drowned.
>   Are there still people like that? Nope, they were all killed, the police got them. (Applebee, 1978, p. 44)

Joseph's knowledge of police is combined with characters from folktales and with the biblical story of Noah and the flood.

Applebee reasons that "It is only after the story has emerged as a fiction that it can begin a new journey toward a role in the exploration of the world not as it is but as it might be, a world which poses alternatives rather than declares certainties." (p. 41)

One role of the preschool and primary teacher is to guide this emerging realization that fiction presents possible alternatives, that it is of the imaginative world. Children develop a sense of story as they mature intellectually. Realizing that the world of literature is not factual, but an imaginative way of learning and knowing, is a gradual process. Applebee found that many children of six said that stories in general did not have to be about real happenings, but they nonetheless contended that certain fictional characters special to them were real. Stories might be make-believe, but yes, they could visit Snow White if only she did not live so far away.

As you share books with children, tell them the names of the authors and illustrators. This gives them the information that stories were created by people, information that will take on meaning for them when they are ready to fit it into their schemata for organizing their world. Present examples of many types of stories, with diverse settings and varied characters, so that children have the data to generalize broadly about the conventions of story. Group stories to help children see that certain events, images, or story shapes occur repeatedly. They can observe how two stories, with differing characters, settings, and plots, may still offer the same theme. They can see that one animal character and one human character may occupy the same role in different stories as each leaves home for an adventure, is successful, and returns home. There are many ways of grouping books. During any one school year, you will want to vary your approach to grouping. At times you will group only two books for comparison, while at other times you may use either the unit or the web approach to larger groupings.

Book Comparisons

Questions in any discussion about books usually focus attention on only a few of the many responses to literature. Some questions help children identify with the characters; others stimulate creative thought. Still others guide children in their literary understandings. It is particularly useful to discuss more than one book at a time if the goal of the discussion is sharpening children's awareness of the interrelatedness of literature. Book comparisons demonstrate that certain patterns, themes, and types of characters appear in many stories. They show that the elements of literature work together in any one story, and that these same elements are the core of all literature.

Suppose you read *I Wish I Were a Butterfly* (Howe, 1987) to a group of second-graders. In this book, a little cricket is convinced that he's ugly because a fog at Swampswallow Pond has told him that he is the ugliest creature he's ever seen. The cricket meets a series of other insects, each of which responds with some piece of advice to his laments about being ugly and his wish to be a butterfly. The glowworm says there's no use in making impossible wishes; the ladybug, that he must learn to accept himself; and so on. All seem to agree that he should not listen to the frog. Finally the Old One, a spider, tells him that he is beautiful, but the cricket doesn't believe it; whereupon the Old One takes him to the water, where they look at their reflections. The cricket sees a beautiful spider and an ugly cricket. The spider sees "two beautiful friends" and tells the cricket that he is more beautiful than any butterfly. The cricket sees his ugliness begin to fade. Then, to help the time go more quickly for the spider as she spins, the cricket begins to fiddle. Hearing the sound, a passing butterfly thinks the music is beautiful and wishes it were a cricket.

There are many possibilities for extending this book. Children might draw pictures using the "insect level" view that the illustrator, Ed Young, has used in the book. They might explore making pictures with chalk after noting Young's soft-edged leaves and grass. They might make leaf patterns, either using a collage technique or doing leaf rubbings. Certainly the story lends itself to dramatization.

To help children develop literary understandings, however, you need to ask questions or suggest activities that focus on the structure of the story. These should be questions that explore the relationship of one part of the story to another or describe how the author and illustrator create a mood or tone for the tale. Here is a series of questions for discussion of *I Wish I Were a Butterfly.*

1. Why did the cricket pay more attention to what the frog said than to what the other insects told him?

2. How did what the spider said make a difference in how the cricket felt about himself?

3. Were you surprised that the cricket finally listened to someone? Why or why not?

4. What did the cricket learn? What else did he learn?

5. If this story were about you, how would the sentence "I wish I were . . ." be completed? What might someone else envy about you?

6. How might the story have been different if the cricket had met and talked with the spider at the very beginning?

When children tell how a story might be different if one thing were changed, whether it be a happening, a character, or a setting, they are seeing how that element fits into the total story, the impact it has on every other part. When they tell what one of the major characters "learned," they frequently are identifying the theme of the story. When they tell whether they were surprised by an event, they are demonstrating their expectations about the story—expectations that are founded on characterizations and plot development. And when they tell why a character may have acted as he or she did, they are looking at motivation and characterization.

Questions should be phrased so that they allow children to explain, in their own words, their understanding of the story. If children answer with only "yes" or "no," they miss the opportunity to develop their own ideas, and the adult and the other children miss the opportunity to see how the child is reasoning. If a child has difficulty with a question, it can be rephrased in such a way that the response requires less information or fewer inferences, but still allows the child to explain fully. For example, if children had trouble responding to the second question above, it could be changed to two questions. First, "How was what the spider said different from what the other creatures said?" and then, after the children have responded, "Why do you think the cricket listened to and believed the spider?"

Reading a second book on a similar theme, about a similar situation, or of the same genre, or contrasting a second book sharply with the first, provides more information for children to process—information about how literature works. After reading *I Wish I Were a Butterfly,* you could share *The Mountains of Tibet* (Gerstein, 1987), another book that presents the idea of accepting and appreciating oneself. It describes a little boy in Tibet who, as he grows up and lives his life as a woodcutter, thinks about other countries, other worlds, believing that he will someday go and see them. But he is busy, and never leaves his valley. When he dies, he hears a voice speaking to him. The voice gives him the choice of becoming part of heaven or living another life. He remembers that he had wanted to see more of the world and chooses another life. He is then presented a series of choices—what galaxy, what planet, what creature, what country; and eventually, which sex. He selects everything just as it had been before, except that this time he wants to be a girl. The book ends with a little girl being born in the mountains of Tibet, a little girl who loves to fly kites, just as the woodcutter had when he was a small boy.

The illustrations show the life on Earth in rectangles at the center of each page, with the opening picture showing the boy flying a kite. In the scenes where the old woodcutter is making choices about his next life, he is shown on the left-hand page in a small blue circle. On the right-hand page we first see swirling galaxies; then the Milky Way; then the planets in orbit around the sun; and finally, each choice in a circle surrounded by blue. The last page, showing the final choice, shows a square surrounded by white, and in it is a little girl flying a kite.

Children could follow this story with activities such as writing a paragraph about themselves, describing what they love to do, or showing it in an illustration. Children could share their projects with the class. Afterward, you could lead a discussion about the book that would encompass its literary aspects as well as its content. Here are some questions you might use.

1. Watch as I show the illustrations in the book again. Why are some illustrations in squares and others in circles? Why does the galaxy spread over both pages?

2. The woodcutter decided to be a girl in his next life. If you were going to change one thing about yourself, what would it be, and why? What would you want to be sure stayed the same? Why?

Children can interpret and extend ideas in books through art.

3. Why do you think the woodcutter made the choices he did?

4. If the cricket from *I Wish I Were a Butterfly* were given choices, would he be a cricket again? Why do you think this?

5. How are the stories *I Wish I Were a Butterfly* and *The Mountains of Tibet* alike? How are they different?

6. How is the way in which the stories are told alike? How is it different?

The questions help children explore the structure of the story. They see that the illustrations work with and extend the stories. They see that two seemingly different stories may have much in common. Question 5 lets children explore similarities and differences in content and theme. They can identify the idea of accepting oneself, contrasting the cricket's unhappiness over one frog's comment with the woodcutter's vague memory that made him like his life well enough to live it over in almost exactly the same way. Question 6 leads children to explore the patterns within the stories and the use of repetition in plot. Just as the cricket meets a series of insects, the woodcutter makes a series of choices. The cricket's are basically equal encounters, whereas the woodcutter makes a finer distinction each time.

Having compared books under the guidance of their teacher, children can then begin to compare them on their own, working within a framework that includes literary comparisons. Jean Karl, an editor and writer of children's books, has said that "A good children's book is an experience of events and also an experience of ideas that lie deeper than events. Such a book is a means by which a sensitive adult can give a child an opportunity to deepen as well as broaden his vision of life" (1970, p. 6). Children should have these sorts of books and should have the chance to talk about that deeper vision.

Units

Books with characteristics in common can be grouped together into units that focus on a single item, describe similar content, or represent literature of a particular genre or by a particular author or illustrator. When you plan a unit, consider a variety of titles but narrow the selection to those books that best fit your purposes and include only those that you actually plan to use. The sequence of books and activities is usually planned in advance, although modifications may be made based on children's reactions or new information.

Suppose you are working with five- or six-year-olds. You think about their interests and needs about the literature you know. You might do a unit on making friends, being afraid, or stories about animals that talk. You decide to do a unit on books in which the characters use their imaginations in ways that are understandable to young children. You want the children to recognize that people use their imaginations in a variety of ways and for a variety of purposes. You hope to engage the children in activities that stimulate their own imaginations, and you want the children to discern techniques used by authors and illustrators to indicate the imaginative life of the characters.

You list books with which you are familiar, and use the book selection guides available in the library to make a general list. Then you decide on the four or five books or poems to share with the children. You choose the following books:

Burningham, John. (1977). *Come Away from the Water, Shirley.* New York: Thomas Y. Crowell.
> Shirley and her parents go to the beach, where her parents set up their beach chairs and get comfortable. Shirley stands at the water's edge. While her parents, shown on the left page throughout the book, make comments to her about not petting the dog and being careful not to get tar on her shoes, Shirley imagines all sorts of adventures for herself, all shown on the right-hand pages.

Kroll, Virginia. (1998). *Faraway Drums.* Ill. Floyd Cooper. Boston: Little Brown.
> Jamila is left in charge of her little sister after school when her mother must leave for work. Her mother tells her to stay locked into their apartment and to remember that their neighbor will check on them periodically. But as it gets dark, and the noises of the building and in the hallways are heard, both girls are frightened. Jamila tells her sister to imagine drums and various animals in Africa making those noises, remembering the stories about "where her people, my people, began" told to her by their great grandmother.

Dorros, Arthur. (1991). *Abuela.* Ill. Elisa Kleven. New York: Dutton.
> Rosalba and her abuela go to the park, where Rosalba sees birds and begins imagining herself and her grandmother flying over the city, New York, and all the things and people they would see. The book concludes with her fantasy being interrupted by her grandmother asking if she would like to take a boat ride. Spanish words are integrated into the text.

Marzollo, Jean. (1990). *Pretend You're a Cat.* Ill. Jerry Pinkney. New York: Dial.

    This collection of thirteen riddle poems about animals describes what each animal does with the question of whether the child can do that too. Illustrations portray the animal and a child or group of children imitating it. The poems are short and action-filled.

Morgan, Michaela. (1987) *Visitors for Edward.* Ill. by Sue Porter. New York: Dutton.

    Edward overheard his parents talking, and for each sentence or phrase, he imagines the meaning. For "they have such a long way to come . . ." he imagines aliens from space. The next morning, when they arrive, "they" are his grandparents. The illustrations show what was really meant by each statement.

Sendak, Maurice. (1963) *Where the Wild Things Are.* New York: Harper & Row.

    Max, wearing his wolf suit and making mischief, is called a wild thing and sent to bed without his supper. He fantasizes a forest in his room and sails to where the wild things are. They make him king and at his command take part in the "rumpus," and although they beg Max to stay, he sails home. He wants to be where someone cares for him, and when he returns his supper is waiting for him.

    To determine the sequence of presentation, you look for ways the books relate to one another and for natural progressions. You plan discussion questions and activities that will help children explore the relationships among the books and support their growth in other areas.

    You want to begin the unit with the children's experience so you engage them in guided fantasy. They sit comfortably in a group and you tell them that they will have the chance to play an imagination game. They are to close their eyes and make a picture in their minds of what you tell them. Your description goes something like this.

    "Picture yourself inside your house looking out your front window. Are you standing or sitting? Stretch so that you can see as much as possible. Move drapes or curtains if you need to. What can you see? Keep looking. In the distance a visitor is approaching your house. You can just begin to make out a little about the visitor. Can you tell who it is? This visitor has come a long way. Keep watching. It looks like the visitor has presents. Can you tell what they are? Why is this visitor coming to your house? The visitor is at your front door now. Decide what you are going to do, and then open your eyes."

    You ask each child to describe the visitor, and what they plan to do. After the children have finished talking, you introduce *Visitors for Edward* by telling them that this is a story about a boy who also used his imagination. You read the book, showing the illustrations as you read. When it is finished, you show several of the pictures and ask the children why some of the pictures are encircled with a blue, wavy line. They recognize that this is the technique used to show the fantasy part of the story, what Edward imagines. You place the book on a special table, and on the wall behind it you post a large sheet of paper that has many spaces encircled with blue wavy lines like those used in the book. The children illustrate the visitors they saw in their imaginations, placing them within the "borders of imagination."

    The next day you continue with the idea of imagination and imaginative activities by reading *Abuela.* You have children think of places they'd like to be able to "fly" over as Rosalba imagines herself and her abuela doing, then make a class list of places they'd go and special relatives or friends who would travel with them. You ask the children to tell how they know what is real and what is imagined in this story.

    Later in the day you introduce *Pretend You're a Cat* by reading three of the riddle poems, having children first guess what the animal might be, and then each acting out the verses as you read them. For the next two days, you will read a few of the poems each day.

On a trip to the park with her abuela, Rosalba imagines her grandmother and herself flying over the city. (From Abuela *by Arthur Dorros, illustrated by Elisa Kleven. Illustrations copyright © 1991 by Elisa Kleven. Used by permission of Dutton Children's Books, a division of Penguin Putnam, Inc.)*

The third day you read *Come Away from the Water, Shirley.* The children have heard two stories in which the characters use their imaginations. In the discussion that follows your reading, you concentrate on the artist's technique for differentiating the fantasy from the realism of the story.

1. If Shirley's parents told about their day at the beach, what might they say? (Show the illustrations again here.)
2. If Shirley told about her day, what might she say? (Again, show the pictures.)
3. Do Shirley's parents know what she is doing? What makes you think this?
4. How does the artist let you know what is going on?
5. Would you rather have Shirley's day or her parent's day? Why?

You call the children's attention to the fact that Shirley figures prominently in the stories she imagines. She rows herself out to the pirate ship, engages in battle with the pirates, and discovers buried treasure. Then you let two or three children tell an adventure with themselves in the key position, recording their stories for transcription later. The stories will be put with the books and the wall drawings. You encourage the other children to dictate stories about themselves in an adventure to you or to classroom aides, or to write it themselves, so that the collection grows and each child has the opportunity to tell a story.

Now you read *Where the Wild Things Are.* You lead a brief discussion, asking questions designed to stimulate the children to think about Max's feelings as related to his fantasy, and to see the illustrator's use of increasingly larger pictures to build a climax. You ask:

1. How did a forest grow in Max's room?
2. Why do you think Max went to visit the wild things?
3. Do you think the wild things are scary? Why or why not?
4. Watch as I show the pictures again. What do you notice about them? Why do you think the illustrator made them that way?
5. How do you think Max was feeling at the end of the story? What made him feel this way?

You and the children look again at the rumpus scenes. The children try to imagine the sounds the wild things are making. Then you ask, "What kind of music could the wild things hear as they danced?" Using rhythm instruments, the children develop music for the rumpus. Once the rhythm is established, other children dance to it, having their own "rumpus."

You conclude the unit with *Faraway Drums.* You have all five books handy for the discussion that follows the reading, first asking a few questions about the book just completed.

1. Why is the book titled *Faraway Drums?*
2. Why is the idea of listening so important to Jamila and Zakita in this story?
3. If you were going to think of things that might make you less afraid, what would you think of? Why might this help you?
4. Do you think it's easier to imagine with someone else or by yourself? What makes you think this?

Then you guide the children in a comparison of the books, holding up the books as you mention them. Begin by asking the children what they remember about each book. Call on several children to respond to each question.

1. As I hold up each book, tell me one thing you remember about it.
2. In what ways are these books like each other?
3. What are some of the ways characters in these books used their imaginations? Why did they use their imaginations?

With the children dictating, you make a chart that lists all the ways they use their imaginations.

You place the books, chart, drawings, and dictations in the same area. You listen to the children's comments during the week, and after a few days, ask the children to select one of the five books for you to reread. Moving the books back to the regular bookshelves, you inform the children of what you are doing as you prepare the space for a new display and new work.

When the unit has been completed, you look at your purposes to evaluate whether they have been fulfilled. Did the children recognize that imagination was being used for differing reasons, sometimes for the enjoyment of it, other times for escaping fear, boredom, or frustration? Were the children stimulated to use their own imaginations? Did they participate in the guided fantasy, tell a story in which they had fantastic adventures, create and move to a "wild thing" rhythm, and contribute to a listing of ways the imagination can be used? Did they notice how the illustrator showed fantasy within a story, using techniques such as placing the fantasy within a frame, or placing reality on one page and fantasy on another? Your purposes should be sufficiently clear for you to assess the effectiveness of specific lessons.

If you are working with three- or four-year-olds, the literature you select will of course be simpler than that you would choose for six-year-olds. You will plan to involve the children in the language, content, and feelings of the stories, but will spend less time analyzing the literature itself. You will, however, be aware yourself of the types of literature you are choosing, and will plan to expose children to a variety of genres.

Suppose you are working with three-year-olds in a day-care center. You decide that you will select books with a single kind of animal as the main character. You begin looking at pigs, dogs, and bears, and settle on bears because the children have enjoyed *Brown Bear, Brown Bear, What Do You See?* (Martin, 1983). Then you realize that you will probably need to choose between bears as animals or bears as toys. There are ample stories in each category. Because you have been talking about seasons, you decide to choose bears as animals and integrate some discussion about hibernation and seasonal changes. You select the following five books as the core of your unit.

Allen, Pamela. (1983) *Bertie and the Bear.* New York: Coward-McCann.

> This story opens with Bertie being chased by a bear. The queen sees what is happening, chases after the bear shouting "shoo," and then a series of other characters join the chase, all making noise. The bear suddenly stops, amazed that it is all for him. He takes a bow, does some cartwheels, and begins to dance. The other characters then dance along with him.

Asch, Frank. (1981) *Just Like Daddy.* Upper Saddle River, N.J.: Prentice-Hall.

> This story is told in first person by a little bear who wakes up and yawns "just like Daddy." Throughout the morning he does everything "just like Daddy" as the family has breakfast and heads out for a fishing trip. On the last page he catches a large fish, "just like Mommy."

Dabcovich, Lydia. (1982) *Sleepy Bear.* New York: Dutton.

> This is a very simple story in which fall activities, such as leaves falling and birds flying south, are noted. Bear goes into his cave and sleeps through the winter. When spring comes he awakens and emerges, unfortunately to bugs, but also to bees and the pleasant thought of honey.

McCloskey, Robert. *Blueberries for Sal.* New York: Viking.

> Little Sal and her mother go blueberry picking, while on the other side of the hill a mother bear and her cub are also seeking berries. Sal follows her mother, listening to the sound of the berries hitting the bottom of her pail, then eating them, until she finally sits down in a large clump of bushes.

The bear cub, tired of trying to keep up with his mother, also stops in a clump of bushes. The two little ones hear sounds ahead, but each ends up following the wrong mother. The two mothers are able to set matters straight, and the two families head for home, Sal and her mother with blueberries to can for winter, and Little Bear and his mother full of food stored up for the winter.

Walters, Catherine. (1998). *When Will It Be Spring?* New York: Dutton.

A bear cub and his mother are hibernating, but the cub keeps waking up, thinking he is seeing the signs of spring his mother has described. When spring finally comes, the cub falls asleep in a meadow of flowers.

With these five books you expose children to both nonfiction, *Sleepy Bear,* and fiction. They will hear several types of plot construction. *When Will It Be Spring?* and *Just Like Daddy* have progressive plots that advance toward a single climax. *Blueberries for Sal* has parallel plots, with two sets of action occurring simultaneously. *Bertie and the Bear* has a cumulative plot, with repetition and the addition of character after character to the chase. The children are also introduced to the idea of a surprise ending in *Just Like Daddy.*

You begin the unit with *Sleepy Bear.* As the children listen to the story and see the pictures, you draw their attention to the bear's contented look in the title page illustration and ask why they think he is so happy. Some may note the bees and the honey he is eating. At the end of the story, it is the memory of honey that entices him to leave his cave. Although it is not used in the book, you introduce the word *hibernate* and encourage the children to describe what happens in fall, winter, and spring.

Next you share *Blueberries for Sal.* When the text has the mother bear telling her cub that they must eat berries so they will grow big and fat for the long winter, you mention the similarity to *Sleepy Bear,* but then continue reading. Talk about the sounds in the story: the berries hitting the bottom of the pail, the rustling in the bushes, the noises that both mothers recognized as belonging to their children. You might use an activity that another teacher has done successfully with her group. Each child takes a handful of fresh blueberries and drops them one by one into a pail, listening to the sound and describing it either as was done in the book—"kuplink, kuplank, kuplunk"—or making up his or her own words for the sounds. Then the children eat the blueberries.

The third book used in this unit is *Bertie and the Bear.* Because each character makes a sound as he or she joins the chase, read a page once, introducing the sound, then again, allowing the children to make the sound with you. After you have finished the book, ask them what they think the author meant when he said that all those characters made an "IN-CRED-IBLE" noise. You tell the children, "This story is make-believe," and ask, "What parts do you think couldn't really happen?" Then, looking at the illustrations of the bear, the children first assume some of his poses, then show how they think the bear walked. Put a record on and encourage the children to dance, follow-the-leader style, just as Bertie danced after the bear.

When you read *Just Like Daddy,* the children quickly catch on to the pattern and begin chiming in with "Just like Daddy" at the appropriate times. When the story is over, ask them if they were surprised at the ending. Then discuss things they do just like their mothers, fathers, grandparents, or siblings. Finally, ask each child to draw something he or she does just like someone else in his or her family.

As you prepare to read the last book, *When Will It Be Spring?,* ask the children to tell you what they think will happen in the story and why. After reading it, reread *Sleepy Bear* and ask the children how the two bears are alike. See if any remember the term *hibernate* and use it in their descriptions of both bears sleeping. Notice if they talk about what the bears liked to eat. Tell them that one of these two stories is make-believe. Which one do they think it is and why? Then have the children look at the covers of the other books about bears that you have read, and decide if each is make-believe or could really happen.

You then put all the books together on a "Books About Bears" shelf. You also create book bags for two of the books and begin having them circulate. Children bring in books they have about bears, and although some are about bears as toys, you add these to the shelf. You notice that the children are looking at these books regularly, and you hear one little girl whispering, "kuplink, kuplank, kuplunk" as she drops crayons into a box. From these responses, you know that your literature presentation has been successful.

Webs

A web is a diagram that charts either the potential within a single book or the possible ways of developing a single topic through literature. Webs differ from units in that they show far more ideas than will be actually used, and they do not show sequence. They are a form of brainstorming. Think of all the possible extensions of a book or all the aspects of a topic. Jot them down around the main heading, categorizing as you go. When you have finished you have many ideas you might pursue with children. Webs can help teachers remain flexible in their use of books because they encourage an exploration of many facets of a book or topic. A teacher may then emphasize one aspect of the book or topic with one group of children, another aspect with a second group.

Figure 4–1 shows a web on the topic of rain. Stories, poems, and activities are grouped around topics related to rain. If you were using this web, you would select those items from it that seemed appropriate for your group of children, developing the ideas more fully before you presented them. For example, if you were talking about feelings you might use all the books and activities under the heading *Experiences,* for all these relate to children's reactions to rain and storms. With another class, you might compare the different retellings of the story of Noah. Webs are most often used, however, to provide a spectrum of books and activities rather than to concentrate on a single aspect of a topic. Thus, you would be most likely to use the web by selecting one or two books, poems, or activities from each heading.

USING LITERATURE ACROSS THE CURRICULUM

Literature and other curricular areas can be integrated in a variety of patterns. Often literature is combined with other sources of knowledge to broaden the study of a topic in science or social studies, mathematics or the arts, or the language arts. Trade books are selected because they give up-to-date information, give a broader view of a topic, and provide for the interests and capabilities of a diverse group of children. The key concepts come from the subject area.

For example, a teacher might read *The Doorbell Rang* (Hutchins, 1986) as part of a study of division. In this book, Ma places a plate of cookies between Victoria and Sam, and tells them they can share. Sam quickly figures that they will each get six. Then the doorbell rings and Tom and

STORMS

The Sleeping Porch—Ackerman
Down Comes the Rain—Branley
The Washout—Carrick
Sing Sophie!—Dodds
Rain Song—Evans
Harry's Stormy Night—Leavy
Storm in the Night—Stolz
—Compare fiction and nonfiction
  books about storms
—Make mural of a rainstorm

POETRY

"Tornado!"—Adoff
"Roof Dancers"—Esbensen
"April Rain Song"—Hughes
"Storm"—O'Connell
"Galoshes"—Bacmeister
"Rain"—Livingston
"The Little Rain"—Thurman
"Rain Rivers"—Moore
"Rain Rain Go Away"—Mother Goose
"Bella had a New Umbrella"—Merriam
"Wet"—Hughes

TALES

Mushroom in the Rain—Ginsburg
It All Began With a Drip Drip Drip . . .—Lexau
How Thunder and Lightning Came to Be—Harrell
The Gullywasher—Rossi
The Rain Puddle—Holl
—Use cartoon strip format to tell a rain tale in
  pictures

NOAH

Noah's Ark—Spier
Noah's Ark—Haley
Noah's Ark—Janisch
The Boat of Many Rooms—Lewis
One Wide River to Cross—Emberley
Noah's Ark—Hogrogian
Prayers From the Ark—DeGasztold
—Dictate own prayers "from the ark"
—Compare versions of the ark story

EXPERIENCES

Umbrella—Yashima
One Monday Morning—Shulevitz
James and the Rain—Kuskin
Bump Rumpus and the Rainy Day—Reay
Rain—Spier
All Wet! All Wet!—Skofield
Rainy Day Magic—Gay
—Measure rainfall
—Role play helping someone afraid of thunder
—Make catalog of rainy day activities

SENSORY AWARENESS

Rain Drop Splash—Tresselt
Rain—Crews
Rain Rain Rivers—Schulevitz
Where Does the Butterfly Go When It Rains?
  —Garelick
Rabbits and Raindrops—Arnosky
Outside, Inside—Cumi
The Rain—Laser
Riddles—London
Listen to the Rain—Martin
Taste the Raindrops—Hines
—Listen to and tape record sounds of rain
—Make onomatopoetic words for rain
—List words that describe different kinds of
  rain—"drizzle" "shower"
—Make rain song using rhythm instruments
  and tone bars
—Take walk following rain—note smells, sights

RAIN

RAINBOWS

The Gold at the End of the Rainbow—Hazel
Theodoric's Rainbow—Keaner
A Rainbow of My Own—Freeman
Annie's Rainbow—Brooks
—Make rainbow picture using chalk

HUMOR

Mr. Gumpy's Motor Car—Burningham
Heat Wave at Mud Flat—Stevenson
Is There Room on the Feather Bed?—Gray
It's Raining Said John Twaining—Bodecker
Cloudy With a Chance of Meatballs—Barrett
We Hate Rain—Stevenson
—Dramatize Mr. Gumpy or John Twaining nursery rhyme
—Dictate story of a rainy day "disaster"

FIGURE 4–1

Hannah drop by, and when they are to share the cookies, the number for each child is down to three. The doorbell keeps ringing, more children keep arriving, and the number of cookies per person keeps dropping. When they each have only one cookie and the doorbell rings, there is hesitation about answering it. But it is grandma, with a big plate of cookies. The teacher might engage children in dramatization, with cookies, or manipulatives that would represent the cookies, that they would try to distribute evenly, perhaps changing the number of cookies and the number of children. He or she might have children respond to the story, perhaps sharing how they would feel in the same situation, or comparing the book to other stories with repetitive patterns.

The books selected match the topic at hand and the understanding level of the children. *One Grain of Rice* (Demi, 1997) might be shared with slightly older children. It is a folktale set in India. The raja refuses to give rice to his people in a time of famine, even though he collected it from them with the promise that it would be used to see that no one went hungry. A small village girl returns some spilled rice to him, and he says he will give her anything she wants. She wants only one grain of rice the first day, but the raja is for the next twenty-nine days to give her double the rice given her the day before. The raja readily agrees, realizing too late the effect of the mathematical progression. On day thirty, she gets 536,870,912 grains of rice. Children can do further activity with the mathematics involved as well as discuss the raja's development into a fair and wise ruler.

Another pattern for integrating literature and other content areas is that of the literature based curriculum, in which the literature is the focal point for the study of all other content areas. *One Grain of Rice* might be the focal point for a study of folktales in language arts, of India in social studies, of the concept of fairness and of the rights and responsibilities of rulers in social studies, of style of painting and the use of objects drawn partly outside the borders of a picture in art, of the need for water and the causes of drought in science. Other books might be combined with it for each of the topics.

In this textbook the organizing principle is how books can stimulate and support children's growth in five different areas of development. These areas cut across the preschool and primary years and are important in themselves. However, some of these goals correlate with the goals of particular academic areas. For example, observing and classifying as part of intellectual development are goals of science and of art education. Learning to see from the viewpoint of another, a goal for social and moral development, is also a goal of many social studies programs. And certainly, language development addresses the goals of many areas of the language arts. If you are working with preschool children, you will focus on the goals as stated. If you are working with primary grade children, you may want to think of the goals as both developmental for the child and as a way of looking at curriculum goals.

SUMMARY

A basic goal of a literature curriculum is the education of children's imaginations. Teachers of young children and day-care professionals contribute to this goal by involving children with literature in ways that establish positive attitudes toward it, and by grouping books and structuring presentations so that children begin to perceive the interrelatedness of literature.

Positive attitudes are developed through the regular sharing of literature; careful selection of high-quality literature, so that it matches children's interests and understanding; and activities that allow children to respond to books in a stimulating and satisfying manner.

Children begin to perceive the interrelatedness of literature when books are grouped, either in pairs for comparison, or in units or webs. When books are paired, questions should focus on the structure of the stories so that children see how each is like or different from the other. Books may also be grouped into units that focus on a single theme, describe similar content, or that represent literature of a particular genre or by a particular author or illustrator. Generally the books, the sequence in which they will be presented, and the accompanying activities are planned in advance, although modifications may be made.

A web is a diagram that charts either the potential within a single book or the possible ways of developing a single topic through literature. Webs differ from units in that they show far more ideas that will be actually used, and they do not show sequence. Both units and webs present literature so that children see the relationships among several works.

Literature is a basic part of the curriculum in itself, but can also be used across the curriculum in conjunction with other content areas. Sometimes the literature is the core around which the content area concepts are developed, and at other times it serves as a source of information supplementing other approaches to content area instruction. The growth in children that literature supports, as explored in chapters 5 through 9, often relates to processes and skills utilized in the study of various content areas.

Extending Your Learning

1. Interview a child between the ages of three and five about whether a particular story or book character is real or not.

2. Develop and sequence a set of questions to guide a discussion about a book. Design questions that will help the child develop literary understanding.

3. Read any two books that are similar in content or theme. Develop and sequence a set of questions that will engage a child in comparing the books.

4. Develop a unit using books on a single topic or theme.

5. Develop a web on a topic of interest to young children.

6. Select a book from the list of recommended references by Beaty, Bromley, Harris, Hickman, Holland, McClure, Moss, Roser, or Short. Apply one of the suggestions given to a book of your own choosing, or read a book they've suggested and develop your own ideas for its use.

7. Look at two or three of the bibliographies listed in the recommended references. Describe the criteria that were used for selecting the books and how this might influence your use of the list.

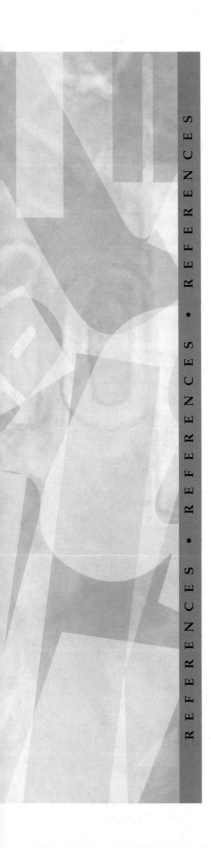

WEB LISTINGS

EXPERIENCES

Kuskin, Karla. (1995). *James and the Rain.* (New ed.) Ill. Reg Cartwright. New York: Simon & Schuster.

Gay, Marie-Louise. (1987). *Rainy Day Magic.* Montreal: Stoddart.

Reay, Joanne. (1995). *Bumpa Rumpus and the Rainy Day.* Ill. Adriano Gon. Boston: Houghton Mifflin.

Shulevitz, Uri. (1967). *One Monday Morning.* New York: Scribner's.

Skofield, James. (1984). *All Wet! All Wet!* New York: Harper.

Spier, Peter. (1982). *Rain.* New York: Doubleday.

Yashima, Taro. (1958). *Umbrella.* New York: Viking.

SENSORY AWARENESS

Arnosky, Jim. (1997). *Rabbits and Raindrops.* New York: Putnam.

Crimi, Carolyn. (1995). *Outside, Inside.* Ill. Linnea Asplind Riley. New York: Simon & Schuster.

Crews, Donald. (1978). *Rain.* New York: Greenwillow.

Hines, Anna Grossnickle. (1983). *Taste the Raindrops.* New York: Greenwillow.

Laser, Michael. (1997). *The Rain.* Ill. Jeffrey Greene. New York: Simon & Schuster.

London, Jonathan. (1997). *Riddles.* Ill. G. Brian Karas. New York: Viking.

Martin, Bill, Archambault, John. (1988). *Listen to the Rain.* Ill. James Endicott. New York: Holt.

Shulevitz, Uri. *Rain Rain Rivers.* New York: Farrar.

STORMS

Ackerman, Karen. (1995). *The Sleeping Porch.* Ill. Elizabeth Sayles. New York: Morrow.

Branley, Franklyn. (1997). *Down Comes the Rain.* New York: HarperCollins.

Carrick, Carol. (1978). *The Washout.* Ill. Donald Carrick. New York: Seabury.

Dodds, Dayle Ann. (1997). *Sing Sophie!* Ill. Rosanne Litzinger. Cambridge, MA: Candlewick.

Evans, Lezlie. (1995). *Rain Song.* Ill. Cynthia Jabar. Boston: Houghton Mifflin.

Leavy, Una. (1995). *Harry's Stormy Night.* Ill. Peter Utton. New York: McElderry.

Lyon, George Ella. (1990). *Come a Tide.* Ill. Stephen Gammell. New York: Orchard.

Stolz, Mary. (1988). *Storm in the Night.* Ill. Pat Cummings. New York: Harper.

RAINBOWS

Brooks, Ron. (1975). *Annie's Rainbow.* Cleveland: CollinsWorld.

Freeman, Don. (1966). *A Rainbow of My Own.* New York: Viking.

Hanel, Wolfram. (1997). *The Gold at the End of the Rainbow.* Trans. Anthea Bell. Ill. Loek Koopmans. New York: North/South.

Kramer, Stephen. (1998). *Theodoric's Rainbow.* Ill. Daniel Mark Duffy. New York: Scientific.

N O A H

De Gaztold, Carmen. (1967). *Prayers from the Ark.* Trans. Rumor Godden. Ill. Jean Primrose. London: Macmillan.

Emberley, Barbara. (1966). *One Wide River to Cross.* Ill. Ed Emberley. Upper Saddle River, NJ: Prentice-Hall.

Haley, Gail. (1971). *Noah's Ark.* New York: Atheneum.

Hogrogian, Nonny. (1986). *Noah's Ark.* New York: Knopf.

Janisch, Heinz. (Adapter). (1997). *Noah's Ark.* Trans. Rosemary Lanning. Ill. Lisbeth Zwerger. New York: North/South.

Lewis, J. Patrick. (1997). *The Boat of Many Rooms: The Story of Noah in Verse.* Ill. Reg Cartwright. New York: Atheneum.

Spier, Peter. (1977). *Noah's Ark.* New York: Doubleday.

P O E T R Y

Adoff, Arnold. (1977). *Tornado.* Ill. Ron Himler. New York: Delacorte.

Bacmeister, Rhoda. "Galoshes" (1940). *Stories to Begin On.* New York: Dutton.

Esbensen, Barbara. "Roof Dancers" (1995). *Dance With Me.* Ill. Megan Lloyd. New York: HarperCollins.

George, Kristine O'Connell. "Storm" (1998). *Old Elm Speaks.* Ill. Kate Kiesler. New York: Clarion.

Hughes, Langston. "April Rain Song" (1932). *The Dream Keeper.* New York: Knopf.

Hughes, Shirley. "Wet" (1988). *Out and About.* New York: Lothrop, Lee & Shepard.

Merriam, Eve. "Bella Had a New Umbrella" (1985). *Blackberry Ink.* New York: Morrow.

Moore, Lilian. "Rain Rivers" (1967). *I Feel the Same Way.* New York: Atheneum.

Thurman, Judith. "The Little Rain" (1976). *Flashlight and Other Poems.* New York: Atheneum.

T A L E S

Ginsburg, Mirra. (1974). *Mushroom in the Rain.* New York: Macmillan.

Harrell, Beatrice Orcutt. (1995). *How Thunder and Lightning Came to Be: A Choctow Legend.* Ill. Susan Roth. New York: Dial.

Holl, Adelaide. (1965). *The Rain Puddle.* Ill. Roger Duvoisin. New York: Lothrop, Lee & Shepard.

Lexau, Joan. (1970). *It All Began with a Drip Drip Drip...* Ill. Joan Sandin. New York: McCall.

Rossi, Joyce. (1995). *The Gullywasher.* Flagstaff, AZ: Northland.

H U M O R

Barrett, Judi. (1978). *Cloudy with a Chance of Meatballs.* Ill. Ron Barrett. New York: Atheneum.

Bodecker, N.M. (1973). *It's Raining Said John Twaining.* New York: Atheneum.

Burningham, John. (1973). *Mr. Gumpy's Motor Car.* London: Jonathan Cape.

Gray, Libba Moore. (1997). *Is There Room on the Feather Bed?* Ill. Nadine Bernard Westcott. New York: Orchard.

Stevenson, James. (1997). *Heat Wave At Mud Flat.* New York: Greenwillow.

Stevenson, James. (1988). *We Hate Rain.* New York: Greenwillow.

RECOMMENDED REFERENCES

Applebee, A. (1978). *The Child's Concept of Story.* Chicago: University of Chicago Press.

Barton, B. and Booth, D. (1990). *Stories in the Classroom.* Markham, Ontario: Pembroke.

Bettleheim, B. (1976). *The Uses of Enchantment.* New York: Knopf.

Butler, D. (1980). *Cushla and Her Books,* Boston: The Horn Book.

Chambers, A. (1996). *The Reading Environment: How Adults Help Children Enjoy Books.* York, ME: Stenhouse.

Duff, A. (1944). *Bequest of Wings.* New York: Viking.

Favat, A. (1977). *Child and Tale: The Origins of Interest.* Urbana, IL: National Council of Teachers of English.

Frye, N. (1964). *The Educated Imagination.* Bloomington, IN: Indiana University Press.

Hazard, P. (1985). (5th ed.). *Books, Children and Men.* Trans. Marguerite Mitchell. Boston: The Horn Book.

Langer, J. (1995). *Envisioning Literature: Literary Understanding and Literature Instruction.* Newark, DE: International Reading Association.

Nodelman, P. (1996). *The Pleasures of Children's Literature.* (2nd ed.). White Plains, NY: Longman.

Raphael, T. and Au, K. (Eds.) (1998). *Literature-Based Instruction: Resharing the Curriculum.* Norwood, MA: Christopher-Gordon.

Rosenblatt, L. (1976). (3rd ed.). *Literature as Exploration.* New York: Noble & Noble.

Rosenblatt, L. (1978). *The Reader, The Text, The Poem.* Carbondale, IL: Southern Illinois University Press.

Short, K. (1997). *Literature as a Way of Knowing.* York, ME: Stenhouse.

RECOMMENDED REFERENCES— TEACHING IDEAS AND BOOKLISTS

Barreras, R. (Ed.) (1997). *Kaleidoscope: A Multicultural Booklist for Grades K-8.* (2nd ed.). Urbana, IL: National Council of Teachers of English.

Barstow, B. and Riggle, J. (1995). *Beyond Picture Books: A Guide for First Readers.* (2nd ed.). New York: Bowker.

Beaty, J. (1997). *Building Bridges with Multicultural Picture Books.* Upper Saddle River, NJ: Prentice-Hall.

Beaty, J. (1994). *Picture Book Storytelling: Literature Activities for Young children.* San Diego: Harcourt.

Bromley, K. (1996). *Webbing With Literature: Creating Story Maps with Children's Books.* (2nd ed.). Needham Heights, MA: Allyn & Bacon.

Diamond, B. and Moore, M. (1995). *Multicultural Literacy: Mirroring the Reality of the Classroom.* White Plains, NY: Longman.

Dreyer, S. (1997). *The Bookfinder: A Guide to Children's Literature about the Needs and Problems of Youth Aged 2–15.* Circle Pines, MN: American Guidance Service.

Harris, V. (Ed.) (1997). *Using Multiethnic Literature in the K–8 Classroom.* Norwood, MA: Christopher-Gordon.

Hickman, J., Cullinan, B., and Hepler, S. (Eds.) (1994). *Children's Literature in the Classroom: Extending Charlotte's Web.* Norwood, MA: Christopher-Gordon.

Holland, K, Hungerford, R., and Ernst, S. (Eds.) (1993). *Journeying: Children Responding to Literature.* Portsmouth, NH: Heinemann.

Johnson, T. and Louis, D. (1990). *Bringing It All Together: A Program for Literacy.* Porthsouth, NH: Heinemann.

Kobrin, B. (1995). *Eyeopeners II! How to Choose and Use Children's Books about Real People, Places, and Things.* New York: Penguin.

Lima, C. and Lima, J. (1998). *A to Zoo: Subject Access to Children's Picture Books.* (5th ed.). New York: Bowker.

McClure, A., and Kristo, J. (Eds.) (1996). *Books That Invite Talk, Wonder, and Play.* Urbana, IL: National Council of Teachers of English.

McClure, A., and Kristo, J. (Eds.) (1994). *Inviting Children's Responses to Literature.* Urbana, IL: National Council of Teachers of English.

Moss, J. (1990). *Focus on Literature: A Context for Literacy Learning.* Katonah, NH: Richard C. Owen.

Roser, N. and Martinez, M. (Eds.). (1995). *Book Talk and Beyond: Children and Teachers Respond to Literature.* Newark, DE: International Reading Association.

Short, K, and Pierce, K. (Eds.) (1990). *Talking About Books: Creating Literate Communities.* Portsmouth, NH: Heinemann.

Stott, J. (1995). *Native Americans in Children's Literature.* Phoenix, AZ: Oryx.

Sutton, W. (1997). *Adventuring with Books: A Booklist for Pre-K-Grade 6.* (11th ed.). Urbana, IL: National Council of Teachers of English.

Tomlinson, C. (Ed.) (1998). *Children's Books from Other Countries.* Lanham, MD: Scarecrow Press.

Trelease, J. (1995). *The Read-Aloud Handbook.* (4th Ed.). New York: Penguin.

PROFESSIONAL REFERENCES CITED

Applebee, A. (1978). *The Child's Concept of Story.* Chicago: University of Chicago Press.

Chambers, A. (1983). *Introducing Books to Children.* Boston: The Horn Book.

Fisher, C. and Natarella, M. (1979). Of Cabbages and Kings: or What Kinds of Poetry Young Children Like, *Language Arts, 56,* 380–385.

Frye, N. (1964). *The Educated Imagination.* Bloomington, IN: Indiana University Press.

Karl, J. (1970). *From Childhood to Childhood.* New York: John Day.

Sloan, G. (1991). *The Child as Critic.* (3rd ed.). New York: Teachers College Press.

Children's Literature Cited

Bunting, Eve. (1990). *The Wall.* Ill. Ronald Himler. New York: Clarion. Text copyright by Eve Bunting. Reprinted by permission of Clarion Books/Houghton Mifflin Co. All rights reserved.

Demi. (1997). *One Grain of Rice.* New York: Scholastic.

Gerstein, Mordicai. (1987). *The Mountains of Tibet.* New York: Harper.

Hay, Sara Henderson. (1982). The Builders. *The Story Hour.* Fayetteville, AK: The University of Arkansas Press. Used by permission of the author.

Howe, James. (1987). *I Wish I Were a Butterfly.* Ill. Ed Young. San Diego: Harcourt.

Hutchins, Pat. (1986). *The Doorbell Rang.* New York: Scholastic.

Martin, Bill. (1983). *Brown Bear, Brown Bear, What Do You See?* Ill. Eric Carle. New York: Holt.

Polacco, Patricia. (1994). *Pink and Say.* New York: Philomel.

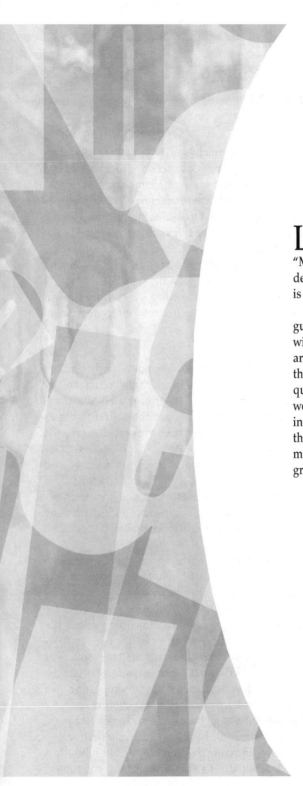

SUPPORTING CHILDREN'S LANGUAGE DEVELOPMENT

Linguists have listened to the utterances of children as eagerly as new parents awaiting the first "Da Da" or "Mama." They have identified certain patterns in children's development of language and attempted to explain just what is happening.

Although linguists do not agree on all aspects of language acquisition, there is a consensus that children are born with a natural capacity for oral language and that youngsters are influenced by the language environment in which they find themselves. Children also go through predictable stages in acquiring the phonology, or sound system, and the syntax, or word order, of their native tongues. Their semantic knowledge increases as they both learn new words and clarify and refine their concepts of words already familiar to them. In a similar manner, their knowledge of the meaning and function of print grows out of their experiences with it.

C H A P T E R   5

LANGUAGE DEVELOPMENT IN YOUNG CHILDREN
How Children Learn Language

The process by which children learn language is one in which they construct for themselves the grammar, or rules, of the language they are hearing. This construction of the rules is not a conscious effort, however; a four-year-old could not state the rule for making a verb past tense. Yet the same four-year-old could use the rule to tell about yesterday's trip to the dentist. "I played in the waiting room until it was time to go in. I looked at all the things on the tray. Dr. Carroll cleaned my teeth." It is because she knows the rules subconsciously that she is able to create new sentences and not simply repeat the exact sentences she has heard someone else say. It is because she is using rules that she will overgeneralize on occasion, applying the rule when the example at hand is irregular and does not follow the rule. She may say, "I runned all the way home," or "That one's yours and this one's mines." As she matures she will include the exceptions as well as the rule-based word formations in her language repertoire.

How Children Become Literate

Marilyn Cochran-Smith, in *The Making of a Reader* (1984) looked at the way adults help children understand and develop the ability to read and write. The process by which children figure out how print works grows out of their experiences with adults in print-related situations. Cochran-Smith describes these literacy events as being with "contextualized print," such as street signs or labels, where much of the meaning can be derived from the context in which it occurs, and "decontextualized print," such as books, where the meaning of the language is independent of the environmental context. Children in the nursery school she observed had many opportunities to interact with print in the environment, learning in social situations where adults acted as "intermediaries" between the children and the print, performing tasks children were unable to do themselves. The children also had wide experiences with story reading, learning how to use their own knowledge of the world to make sense of the text and illustration in books.

Adults sharing books with toddlers can see children's growing concept of print as the child listener no longer covers the words with his or her hand, and stops turning pages rapidly when there is print but no picture. These actions show that the child knows that it is the print that is carrying the message. The child may engage in "reading-like" behavior, providing some of the text of stories he or she has heard before, or repeating a phrase immediately after it has been read. Many toddlers absorb a story so thoroughly that they can "read" the book by looking at the illustrations, often maintaining most of the story language, but at times using their own language while retaining the meaning (Doake, 1985). As children begin to associate the print with the exact word, they go through a time when the number of words appearing on a page does not match the number of words they are using, particularly if they think of each syllable as a word. Knowing a story by heart allows them to go back again and again to a page, work on the problem, and teach themselves that long words have more than one syllable.

Careful observation of and conversations with young children have demonstrated to a series of researchers that children know more about writing than had once been assumed.

Harste, Woodward, and Burke (1984) contend that adults often confuse product with process and thus overlook what children know. They point out that if children's writing doesn't look like adult writing, this does not mean that the children do not know about writing. If their spelling differs from standard spelling, that does not mean that the children do not know about spelling. These researchers noted that the children they observed could produce writing when asked to, and could tell what their writing said, even though it might appear to be a "scribble" to the adult observer.

> We have found that by the age of 3 all children in our study could, under certain conditions, distinguish art from writing. Their decisions in writing, as in art, are systematic and organized. We found further that all 3-year-olds have developed a marking which to them symbolized their name. This marking acted as any symbol acts, serving to placehold meaning during writing, and to reconstruct that meaning during reading (p. 18).

Children refine their writing over time, learning to make the letters in standard form. However, their initial understanding of what print is, and how writing functions, comes from their experiences with print and with writing in their everyday lives. Living in a literate society, they expect that reading and writing will be part of their lives.

There are two basic ways in which adults can nurture the language learning of young children. The first is to provide rich, varied, and abundant samples of both oral and written language. The second is to give children regular opportunities to use their language.

The Need to Hear Rich Language

It is important that children hear rich samples of language, for this is the data base from which they generalize rules for how the language works. It is also their source of vocabulary items. Adults are of more help to children's language growth if they use mature syntax than if they limit their speech to what they perceive to be the child's level and if they respond to the content of children's telegraphic speech with mature language of their own (Cazden, 1972). Other researchers have reached the same conclusion, finding that adults are most effective in aiding children's language development if they respond with new information or if they encourage the child to add to his or her previous comments (Genishi, 1984).

Literature provides another source of mature and expressive language. Children listening to stories read aloud are being exposed to language which is often more complex than that which they hear in ordinary conversation. They hear new sentence patterns and new words. Chomsky (1972) found that there was a positive correlation between the linguistic development of the children in her study and the average complexity level of the books each had encountered, the number of books each named as familiar, and the numerical score each received based on factors such as having been read to during the early years. This positive relationship between linguistic development and exposure to literature was true for prereaders who had listened to books as well as for older children who had read the books themselves. The prereaders in the high linguistic stages had heard more books each week, were read to by more people, and had heard more books at higher complexity levels than had those children at lower linguistic stages.

Hearing books read aloud increased children's competence in other areas of language as well. Cohen (1968) tested the reading ability of a group of second graders at the beginning, and again at the end, of the school year. Some of the children were in an experimental group that heard literature every day. After hearing the stories, the children engaged in follow-up activities. The other group heard stories, occasionally, but with no specific plan or follow-up. The children in the experimental group showed an improvement in vocabulary, word knowledge, and reading comprehension that was significantly greater than that of the group only randomly exposed to literature.

These studies demonstrate the positive results of presenting children with examples of effective language. Note that, in all of these studies, the language was used in context. Adults responded to children in light of the situation and with regard to the children's comments. The books described experiences or thoughts as wholes, giving vocabulary and sentence patterns within the total story setting. It is essential that language be tied to experience and that it be presented in context if it is to have optimal meaning for children.

The Need to Use Language

In addition to presenting abundant samples of language, adults can nurture children's language growth by providing opportunities for them to use language. Children form hypotheses about grammar and must then test their hypotheses. This testing by using language themselves provides direct feedback. Children can judge whether or not they have communicated effectively. They may also refine their definitions of particular words as they gather more information about the concept named by the word. "Car" is no longer used for any four-wheeled vehicle but is narrowed down to one type of vehicle.

It seems logical that correcting children's speech would accelerate their grasp of adult language patterns. This is not the case, however. Only when children are ready to assimilate a new pattern will it have meaning for them. McNeill cites the following example of a conversation between a parent and child.

Child:	Nobody don't like me.
Parent:	No, say "Nobody likes me."
Child:	Nobody don't like me.
Parent:	No, "Nobody likes me."
Child:	Nobody don't like me. (seven more repetitions of this)
Parent:	No! Now listen carefully. Say "Nobody likes me."
Child:	Oh! Nobody don't likes me.

McNeill, 1966, p. 69

The form the parent is attempting to teach is not within the child's current rule system; therefore, the child is not able to assimilate this new information. You, as a day-care professional or teacher, will want to give children opportunities to use their language in conversations, discussions, spontaneous dramatics, and writing. Efforts to encourage extensive use of language will prove far more productive than attempts to "correct" children's grammar or their handwriting and spelling. Overcorrecting a child's grammar may result in that child's refusal to talk, the exact opposite of the desired behavior. Overcorrecting the mechanical aspects of writing may result in the child's avoidance of composition. Jane Hansen, in discussing writing conferences with children, says:

> Adults respond to the messages young children try to communicate, not to the errors they make in their attempts. Toddlers' early words confuse us, but we concentrate on trying to figure out their intent as we listen to their tone and watch their body language. We respond to what we think they are trying to tell us. If we respond to children in an encouraging way, they try again. The more supportive we are, the more likely it is that they will want to experiment with language, both oral and written. The bottom line in the writing conference is, "The writer wants to write again."
>
> *Hansen, p. 13*

Structure your program so that children become more skilled in all areas of language. Work in one area is likely to have a strong influence on other areas. Children who are experimenting with writing are also learning about reading. Comprehension taught through listening is an aid to comprehension in reading, as Cohen's study demonstrates. In addition, children who have been exposed to literature are familiar with the patterns of written language—patterns they will encounter when they read by themselves.

Morrow, Strickland, and Woo, in their application of research findings to the design of effective kindergarten literacy programs, concluded the following:

> Research also suggests the concurrent learning of reading, writing, oral language, and listening in a meaningful way through the integration of these skills into play and into content-area teaching such as art, music, math, science, and social studies. This integration can be done through the use of themes that bring meaning and purpose to learning and provide a reason to read, write, listen and speak. Children's literature should be a major source of these themes.
>
> *Morrow, Strickland, Woo, pp. 69–70*

Immersion in literature, which helps children make sense of written language, also helps create a positive attitude toward learning to read. Reading becomes desirable because there are things to be learned and tales to be enjoyed in books. Children are also intrigued by the sounds of language, from its poetic beauty to its light-hearted nonsense. Chukovsky (1978, p. 25) observed the speech of three-year-olds and found that they repeated pairs of rhymed words and played games with repetition and rhyme. Literature builds upon and expands this fascination with language.

Children should be encouraged to experiment individually with print. The child who has used scribbles symbolically, knowing how writing functions if not how letters are formed, moves into more standard writing while maintaining the view of writing as a purposeful activity. Regular writing times in the primary grades, where children know that they will write and that they will usually choose the topic themselves, lets them know that writing is a personal and effective way of communicating.

To summarize, children's language develops best in an environment where mature language is heard, where children have many opportunities to communicate with others, and where language is presented in context.

GOALS FOR TEACHING AND LEARNING

Teaching and learning goals for language growth can be categorized into long-term developmental goals, into general goals for each grade or age level, and into specific goals for individual children. Long-term goals describe behaviors or competencies that are developed over time and are thought of as desired patterns of behavior. One long-term goal for language development is that children will enjoy the creative and aesthetic use of language. They will become lifelong readers and appreciators of literature.

General goals for each grade level are often listed in curriculum guides. At other times they are developed by the teacher or day-care professional as he or she plans an outline for the year's learning. A general goal for the preschool level is that children will listen attentively and follow simple directions.

Goals for specific children are more individualized. Teachers develop these as they come to know each child. A specific goal for a second-grader might be, "Roberta will read one book by herself and tell her classmates one incident from the story." The goal reflects Roberta's need, a need that may not be shared by other members of the class. Goals of this type are referred to as "objectives" in some planning schemes.

Your use of books can aid in the achievement of many types of goals and standards. This chapter focuses on long-term developmental goals common to the preschool and primary years. Literature offers opportunities for you to help children toward the following goals for language development:

> Children will understand and use the mature syntax of their language.
>
> Children will expand their vocabularies.
>
> Children will enjoy the creative and aesthetic use of language.
>
> Children will become skilled listeners.
>
> Children will learn to read.
>
> Children will communicate effectively in oral, written, and visual formats.

As with other areas, these goals can be correlated with national and regional standards. For example, the goal that children will communicate effectively in oral, written, and visual formats correlates with Standard 4 of the International Reading Association/National Council of Teachers of English *Standards for the English Language Arts*. That standard states that "Students adjust their use of spoken, written, and visual language (e.g., conventions, style, vocabulary) to communicate effectively with a variety of audiences and for different purposes" (1996, p. 25). As you look at national standards, or those for your region or school district, look for ways in which these goals and the specific standards mesh.

OPPORTUNITIES BOOKS OFFER
Exposing Children to Mature Language

Children need to hear many examples of mature language if they are to develop an understanding of the more complex syntactic structures of the language and if they are to become users of those structures themselves. Read to children every day, perhaps twice each day. Encourage parents and guardians to share literature with their children at home. Become aware of the kind of language being used in a book.

Listening to Varied Syntax

Language varies. This is one of the reasons that literature is so beguiling. Some authors present material in a direct manner, yet use more compound and complex sentences than one would hear in normal conversation. This passage is from *The Divide* (Bedard, 1997):

> The road was lined with sunflowers now. Father said they sprang from seeds the first settlers had dropped from their wagons as they crossed this land, to mark the way for those who followed. She followed it now and found a pond where ducks came, a solitary elm that grew from a deep cleft in the ground. It had fought so hard to grow; she would visit it as if it were a friend. She sat within its shade and played her music box and watched a hawk turn circles in the blazing sun. In this flat land these were precious things.
>
> *Bedard, n.p.*

Children hearing this passage are being given data about standard word order in English, and about ways that several pieces of information can be combined into a single sentence.

Other authors may invert word order and use more poetic language. Theo Gilchrist opens *Halfway up the Mountain* with:

> Over the green hill and across the blue river, in a shack halfway up the mountain, there lived an old man and an old woman. Though the old man was slow of movement, the old woman didn't mind. Though the old woman was almost blind, the old man didn't mind. Hand in hand they greeted the sunrise. Hand in hand they greeted the sunset.
>
> *Gilchrist, n.p.*

Children learn that changing the word order maintains the meaning but gives a different mood to a story. "Hand in hand they greeted the sunrise" gives the same information as "They greeted the sunrise hand in hand," but the tone is more gentle. Hearing patterns which occur far more frequently in writing than in speech prepares children to cope with written language when they begin reading themselves.

Enjoying Figurative Language

Authors often use expressive language, with carefully chosen words and figurative language fitting naturally into the text. The girl in Joanne Ryder's *A Wet and Sandy Day* was standing on the beach in her bathing suit when it began to rain. She describes what happened:

> The warm drops trickled down my nose and chin. I had to squint to keep them out of my eyes. "I'm wrinkling up," I said, looking at my pruney fingers. But my arms and legs were wet and shiny like a big slippery fish. "I am a rainy thing now," I

thought. There were a million raindrops on me. And I felt cleaner than if I'd taken a
hundred baths.

Ryder, n.p.

Listening to this story, children are exposed to the flexibility of language and its creative possibilities. If a prune has wrinkled skin, then "pruney" could describe human skin wrinkled from having been wet over a period of time. If one feels thoroughly clean, it is as though
one had "taken a hundred baths."

Listening to *Saving Sweetness* (Stanley, 1996), children can appreciate that figurative
language can be used to add humor. These are the opening two lines that describe the woman
who runs the orphanage where Little Sweetness lives.

> Out in the hottest, dustiest part of town is an orphanage run by a female person
> nasty enough to scare night into day. She goes by the name of Mrs. Sump, though I
> doubt there ever was a Mr. Sump on accounta she looks like somethin' the cat drug
> in and the dog wouldn't eat.
>
> *Stanley, n.p.*

Children need to hear the language of books such as that contained in these books.
They do not need to discuss it, for word order and writing style are topics that are too abstract
to be appropriate for young children. Your task as teacher is to select books that the children
will enjoy and that will, in the process, give them exposure to the mature and effective use of
language.

Hearing Different Dialects

You will find that books give you the opportunity to let children hear a variety of different dialects. Some may give a feel for the language but not follow all the rules of the specific dialect.
The books about Obadiah by Brinton Turkle (1965) do this by using "thee" and "thou" to help
establish that the characters are Quakers.

Patricia McKissack has several books in which some of the characters speak a dialect
other than standard English. In *Flossie and the Fox* (1986), Flossie's soft and rhythmic speech, and
that of the narrator, contrast with the formal speech of the fox. Flossie has been sent to deliver
a basket of eggs to neighbors and is told to watch out for the fox. When he appears, sitting by
the side of the road, he greets her with, "Top of the morning to you, Little Missy . . . And what
is your name?" She responds with "I be Flossie Finley. . . I reckon I don't know who you be either." He tells her that he is a fox, but Flossie says she just "purely don't believe it" (n.p.). This
begins a series of efforts on the part of the fox to prove his identity to her, while Flossie continues to insist that he is not a fox. When they come upon a kitten, the fox declares, "Since you
won't believe me when I tell you I am a fox, perhaps you will believe that fine feline creature,
toward whom you seem to have some measure of respect." Flossie looks at the cat, winks, and
says, "He sho' use a heap o' words" (n.p.). Only when the neighbor's house is in sight and Flossie
is certain she can deliver the eggs does she admit that she knows he is a fox.

In her introduction to the book, McKissack explains how much she enjoyed stories her
grandfather told, and that she has retold this one in the same "rich and colorful language" that

he used. Listeners have the opportunity to hear this language and to begin building an appreciation for the variety of speech patterns within the English language.

In general, the books currently available in dialects other than standard English are for children of school age. Books for three- and four-year-olds are direct, simple, and in standard English. *Flossie and the Fox* would be more appropriate for children in kindergarten or first grade than for toddlers. Five- and six-year-olds recognize when a dialect differs from their own, although they may not be able to tell how it differs. Let children begin early to hear various dialects and to appreciate the many ways in which English is spoken and written.

Introducing New Vocabulary in Context

Vocabulary expands as children learn new concepts and the words that denote them, and as new words are presented for concepts already known. When new words are presented in context, children often can determine the meanings themselves. If they do, they are less likely to forget the word than they would be if its meaning had been explained to them in isolation. Thus, teachers of young children introduce new words as they arise in the course of ongoing activities.

Presenting New Words

Literature presents new words to children in the context of a complete story or poem. When you call attention to a particular word, look carefully at the section where it appears to determine if the context needed is the entire story, one or two paragraphs, or just one sentence. For example, in the book *The Storytellers* (Lewin, 1998), Abdul and his grandfather are walking through a town in Morocco on their way to work. At one point the text describes the noise at the copper and brass "souk"; two pages later Abdul and his grandfather pass through the date souk. The following page begins, "The souks go on and on—streets of spice sellers and chicken vendors and saddle makers." Later they pass the carpet souk.

In this story, "souk" is explained in the text that follows its initial appearance (as well as in a glossary of Arab words). After reading the entire story, you could return to several of the pages that refer to a souk. Show the illustrations, read the references again, and then ask the children what they think a souk is. Let them tell you what they think and also how they know. They might rely on the several examples that are given, or they might key into the page that incorporates the definition into the text. It is important to read the story through so that the children have the full context, and to reread the sections under discussion so that they are fresh in the children's memories.

Sometimes the explanation for a word is developed through many examples. In *The Cut-Ups Cut Loose* (Marshall, 1987) a "cut-up" is not defined, and many children have not heard that term. On the first page, Spud and Joe are described as "a couple of real cut-ups." The next pages show some of their antics—from time, as babies, they crawled from their bassinets out onto a window ledge, to their preschool adventure of driving the car with their mother running frantically after the moving vehicle. Children can figure out what a cut-up is from the behavior of characters described as cut-ups.

If you plan to ask children to use context to hypothesize about the meaning of a word, make certain that there is indeed context that is explanatory. At one point in *A Birthday for Blue* (Lydon, 1989), about a family traveling on the Cumberland Road around 1816, the wagon loses a wheel. One of the boys announces that the linchpin is missing. Another boy finds it among the rocks and the family fixes the wheel. There is no explanation, and the illustration shows neither the lost linchpin nor any wheels with linchpins in place. Thus this would not be a valid example for using context to determine word meaning.

There are opportunities to evaluate and to reinforce children's comprehension of words that may be new to them. You can ask them to tell what happened in the story, or use phrases from the story to elicit personal responses from the children. There are five short stories in *George and Martha Round and Round*. This is the beginning of the story titled, "The Artist."

> George was painting in oils.
>
> "That ocean doesn't look right," said Martha.
>
> "Add some more blue.
>
> And that sand looks all wrong. Add a bit more yellow."
>
> "Please," said George.
>
> "Artists don't like interference."
>
> But Martha just couldn't help herself.
>
> "Those palm trees look funny," she said.
>
> *Marshall, n.p.*

Martha begins her "interference" with George's painting. (From George and Martha Round and Round *by James Marshall. Copyright © 1988 by James Marshall. Reprinted by permission of Houghton Mifflin Company.)*

George goes off in a huff, telling Martha to see if she can do any better. She notes that some artists are "touchy" and then makes "improvements" in the painting. When George returns, he thinks she has ruined the picture. Martha just says she's sorry he feels that way, but that she likes it. She is not a touchy artist.

Children might be asked to tell the class about, or draw pictures of, times when they interfered with someone else or when someone interfered with what they were doing. They could list things that others might be "touchy" about. After the children have been introduced to words in one context, activities such as these help them apply those words to other contexts.

Unless you are certain that the story will be misunderstood without fully discussing the meaning of a word or phrase, wait until the book is completed before talking with children about it or give only a brief explanation and continue reading. If it is necessary to explain a number of words in order for the children to make sense of the selection, the book is probably too difficult for that group of children and should not be shared with them until they are older.

Sharing Books That Emphasize Word Meanings

Most books will present the vocabulary as part of the story, as a tool needed to convey the content. There are some books, however, that work directly with vocabulary. An example is *I See* by Helen Oxenbury (1995). This board book shows a drawing on the left page, with a caption identifying the object, and then a toddler interacting with the object or person on the facing page. *Daddy and Me* (Ricklen, 1997) and *Mommy and Me* (Ricklen, 1997) label everyday activities of parent and child.

Sometimes the books are concept books, exploring the qualities of the concept as well as the word that names it. Shirley Hughes, in *Giving,* illustrates the meaning of the concept by showing that the child can give a hug, her dad can give her a ride on his shoulders, a man can give his seat on a bus to a woman carrying a small child and a shopping bag, her grandparents can give her a birthday present (Hughes, 1993). The illustrations reinforce the text with a clear visual representation of the action, and the endpapers show a toddler in many other activities—kicking, writing, washing, dancing, yawning.

Involving Children with New Vocabulary

Whether you are working with vocabulary within a story or as part of a book emphasizing new words, involve children as actively as possible with the meanings of the words. You may do this by having them act out the meanings. Suppose you read "Jump or Jiggle" by Evelyn Beyer.

> Frogs jump
> Caterpillars hump
>
> Worms wiggle
> Bugs jiggle
>
> Rabbits hop
> Horses clop

Snakes slide
Sea gulls glide

Mice creep
Deer leap

Puppies bounce
Kittens pounce

Lions stalk—
But—
I walk!

Beyer, in Poetry Place Anthology

Children can listen to the poem, then on the second reading show how each animal moves. There is the fun of the movement, the enjoyment of the rhyming language, and also the learning of new words for some of the children.

You might involve them by having them tell about experiences they have had that are similar to those you are reading about. In *The Blushful Hippopotamus* (Raschka, 1996), a young hippo is told by his sister that he is a blushful hippopotamus, and she asks him if he is blushing whenever she sees him do something awkward, like losing the ice cream off the cone or falling off his bike or being unable to remember the right word. His friend Lombard assures him that he is hopeful, mindful, and skillful. The pink background on these pages indicates that he blushes at Lombard's kind words just as he did at his sister's derisive words. Children might describe times when they have felt like blushing; what they are able to do skillfully; when they have been thoughtful. Using the vocabulary to describe their own experiences makes it part of their repertoire.

Several Books on a Single Topic

You can reinforce vocabulary by reading several books on the same topic. If you had been discussing baby animals with a group of three- and four-year-olds, you might want to read *Whose Baby?* (Yabuuchi, 1985) a book that begins by naming the baby animal then asking whose baby it is. The book gives the answer, with clear illustrations of the baby and its parents. You might then introduce *The Chick and the Duckling* (Ginsburg, 1972) by asking the children what kind of animals they expect to see in the book. After their guesses, you could read this book about a chick who attempts everything the duckling does and succeeds—until the duckling decides to go for a swim! Your reading of the story would reinforce the terms. You might also choose to have the children join in the book's "Me too" refrain or in some other oral activity, rather than once again asking about "chick" and "duckling." Books about specific baby animals such as *The Chick and the Duckling,* or *Little Lions* (1998) by Arnosky, or *Bashi, Elephant Baby* (1998) by Radcliff develop full stories with what will be new words for some children used in context.

Encouraging Language Play and Demonstrating How Others Have Used Language Creatively

If you listen to young children as they play, you will find that they seem to have a natural enjoyment of language. They repeat nonsense words just for the fun of listening to the sounds; they use jump rope rhymes and other chants in their games; they tell riddles. Literature that exudes this same delight in language appeals to them, and often their favorite books are those that capitalize on the sound of language.

Playing with Language

Using literature that demonstrates how others have played with language has several benefits for children. First, of course, they enjoy it and thus develop positive attitudes toward literature. It sets the stage for continued enjoyment of poetry, with its reliance on the rhythm, rhyme, and the patterns in language. It shows them that the tone and feeling of a word contribute to its meaning, that words connote as well as denote. It stimulates them to reflect upon the language itself, not just the message being conveyed. Linguists refer to this ability to attend to the forms of language as "metalinguistic awareness," and suggest that it may be critically important in both reading and writing (Heller, 1991, p. 18).

Language play takes on a variety of forms. Some center on the sound of the language, some on the patterns within the language, some on the appearance of written language, and others on the meanings of words or phrases. Children's books can stimulate children to engage in word play themselves.

One nursery school teacher suggested to her group of three- and four-year-olds that they make their own goodnight poem after listening to *Goodnight Moon*. The children followed the book's short couplet format naturally. Here is their poem:

> Goodnight toys,
> Goodnight boys,
> Goodnight book,
> And goodnight hook.
> Goodnight fire,
> And goodnight tire.
> Goodnight flowers,
> And goodnight powers.
> Goodnight rocks,
> And goodnight box.
> Goodnight cradle,
> Goodnight dreydl.
> Goodnight dolls,
> And goodnight balls.
> Goodnight berries,
> Goodnight cherries.

Goodnight koala bear,

Goodnight little chair.

Goodnight Daddy,

Goodnight Matty.

Goodnight Mummy,

Goodnight tummy.

Goodnight bee,

Goodnight flea.

Goodnight everything,

And goodnight me.

Kaplan, n.d.

The children explained as they dictated that the "powers" in line eight were space heroes. They also changed the position of the last two lines from the middle to the end after hearing their poem reread.

Playing with the Sounds of Language

Playing with the sounds of language may take many forms, but those appearing most frequently in books for children are rhythm, rhyme, alliteration, and onomatopoeia. Preschoolers respond to the toe-tapping rhythm and rhyme of *Chicken Soup With Rice* (Sendak, 1962). By the time the narrator has told of the joys of chicken soup in each month of the year, the listener is ready to join in extolling its virtues. The rollicking rhythm and rhyme in *Chicka Chicka Boom Boom* (Martin and Archambault, 1989) capture children as they see the letters of the alphabet race to the top of the coconut tree, only to weigh it down so much that they all tumble to the ground.

A contrasting rhythm in *Grandfather's Love Song* (Lindbergh, 1993) has its own appeal, the softness and warmth of a lullaby:

I love you high

Like the top of the sky

Where the sun and moon

Go floating by

I love you low

Like the world below

Where parents watch

Their children grow.

Lindbergh, pp. 4,7

This book sets a quiet mood as each verse of the poem expresses the grandfather's love, throughout the seasons, and each illustration shows grandfather and child enjoying the natural surroundings together. The last verse provides a satisfying conclusion.

I love you strong
Like the sparrow's song
That sings in my heart
Your whole life long.

Lindbergh

Some authors write narratives in rhyme. Their work may be lighthearted and humorous or of a serious and thoughtful mood. If you are working with children in the preschool and kindergarten years, look for the books of Rosemary Wells, Denise Fleming, Ludwig Bemelmans, Margaret Wise Brown, and Janina Domanska. If you are working with primary grade children, look for the works of Jack Prelutsky, Virginia Kahl, Theodor Geisel (Dr. Seuss), Lucille Clifton, Byrd Baylor, and Aileen Fisher. These will give you a standard of good writing by which you can measure other poetic narratives for children.

Look also at the works of poets Clyde Watson, David McCord, and Eve Merriam. All three have poems that play with the language in various ways. You will need to select poems from their collections that are appropriate for the age of your students.

Alliteration is a technique of writing in which initial consonant sounds are repeated at close intervals. The little snake who awakens in the spring and begins looking for the Snake Alley band is at first not impressed by the other animals musical noises, but comes to appreciate them. "I want a sky-skipping, hip-hopping, splish-splashing, flip-flapping, stamp-stomping, wig-wagging Snake Alley band" (Nygaard, 1998, n.p.), he declares. The alliteration makes his wish memorable and fun to say.

Tongue twisters are based on alliteration. They intrigue children all through the preschool and primary years. Read aloud some of the selections from *A Twister of Twists, a Tangler of Tongues* (Schwartz, 1972). After reading several to the children, ask them to make up their own. Kindergartners can work as a group, dictating their twisters for the teacher to write down. Primary children can work individually, spelling words using their best guesses based on the sounds they hear. All can try saying the tongue twisters, then repeating them as fast as they can.

They might also illustrate their twister. In *Santa's Short Suit Shrunk: And Other Christmas Tongue Twisters* (Buck, 1997), the holiday happenings feature the same characters throughout. There are many ways to bring unity to a class book of tongue twisters. One group of thirdgraders made their own counting book, with each child responsible for providing the tongue twister and illustration for one numeral. Their book went to twenty-two. The class favorite was the illustration that accompanied "Fifteen frisbees flying forward" showing members of the class engaged in a frisbee-throwing contest.

Preschoolers enjoy the slapstick action and the word play in *Thump and Plunk* (Udry, 1981), a tale of a bother and sister pair of mice and their two dolls, named Thumpit and Plunkit, who manage to "thump" and "plunk" their way through an entire story. The repetition of sounds delights the young listener.

Onomatopoeia, the use of words whose sound suggests their meaning, is another element of writing that is popular with children. David McCord's poem "The Pickety Fence" (1952) is built on a technique of using words so that they make the sound and the rhythm of a stick being run along a picket fence. Denise Fleming's short rhymes in *In the Tall, Tall Grass* (1991) capture animal sounds, as in the "ritch, ratch" as moles scratch. In *Umbrella*, Moma listens to the sound of the raindrops on her umbrella.

> Bon polo
>
> bon polo
>
> ponpolo ponpolo
>
> ponpolo ponpolo
>
> bolo bolo ponpolo
>
> bolo bolo ponpolo
>
> boto boto ponpolo
>
> boto boto
>
> ponpolo
>
> *Yashima*

Children hear how others have used language to describe sounds. They can listen to sounds on the playground, in the boiler room, or in their own classroom. What word could they make up for each sound? Try having children listen to machines in their homes or in the neighborhood, then make their own words for those sounds. What sound does a vacuum cleaner make? A washing machine? A hair dryer?

As children play with the sounds of the language, they can appreciate when a book character has trouble with those sounds. *The Surprise Party* (1969) by Pat Hutchins opens with Rabbit whispering to Owl that he is having a party. Owl repeats the news to Squirrel, explaining that Rabbit is going to be hoeing the parsley. Squirrel repeats it as Rabbit going to sea, and the message continues to be garbled as it passes from animal to animal. The game of Telephone, where each child whispers a message to the next person, saying it only once, would be a natural follow-up to this book.

Playing with the Patterns of Language

Authors may play with the pattern of language as well as with the sound. *The Little Engine That Could* (Piper, 1930) has remained a favorite with children for over fifty years. Some of its popularity may be attributed to the story itself—that of getting the toys to the children on the other side of the mountain—but equally important is the author's use of onomatopoeia in the sounds of the engine and the patterning of the language. The engine's pep talk to herself, where she keeps repeating "I think I can," sounds like the rotation of the train wheels, getting faster and faster as she picks up speed. The pattern is established on the way up the mountain and continues after she has made it to the top and started down. The refrain is then "I thought I could."

The use of refrains invites children to join in with the teacher as the story is being read. The little old man and little old woman in *Millions of Cats,* who must contend with

> Hundreds of cats
>
> Thousands of cats
>
> Millions and billions and trillions of cats
>
> *Gag*

in order to find the one cat to be their own, are remembered both for their plight and for the language that tells about it.

Cumulative tales have a patterning of language that is part of the story. As each new event or character is added, all the earlier ones are repeated. *I Know an Old Lady* (Karas, 1995) can be read or sung and intrigues children as the old lady, who first swallowed a fly, keeps swallowing larger and larger animals in order to catch the animal before. All the while the spider, which she swallowed to catch the fly, just keeps wiggling and jiggling and tickling inside her. And after they have experienced this song, they will particularly enjoy *I Know an Old Lady Who Swallowed a Pie* (Jackson, 1997), a clever take-off in which an old lady swallows an entire Thanksgiving meal.

The patterning may consist of positive versus negative, real versus imaginative, or other opposites. In *Fortunately* (Charlip, 1993), first something good happens, fortunately, and then something bad, unfortunately. Children in the primary grades generally see the pattern after four or five pages and are then thoroughly captivated by the humor. In the story, Ned has been invited to a surprise party, but has to get from New York to Florida.

> Fortunately, a friend lent him an airplane.
>
> Unfortunately, the motor exploded.
>
> Fortunately, there was a parachute in the airplane.
>
> Unfortunately, there was a hole in the parachute.
>
> *Charlip, n.p.*

Ask the children what they notice about the pages to see if they recognize the use of color on the "fortunately" pages and black and white on the "unfortunately" pages. Let them do short sequences themselves, perhaps giving them the opening statement. This is the sort of composing which could be made into a roll story, where each phrase and a picture illustrating it is drawn on a roll of shelf paper, so that the story unwinds as the paper unwinds.

Playing with the Appearance of Language

Authors can play visual games with language. Rebus writing is one such game. It is a combination of words and pictures, in sentence form. To read it, one must name the object in the order in which it appears and read the words or parts of words attached to it. *Who Stole the Apples?* (Hueck, 1986) introduces the idea of rebus writing by starting on the first page with a single sentence, with one picture. The next page has a longer sentence and several pictures. The story then builds until there are several sentences on each page. *The Rebus Bears* (Reit, 1989), designed to encourage children to read, gives the rebus picture but has the word printed over it. Children may respond to either picture or print, and will begin to associate the two for the nouns pictured. *From A to Z: The Collected Letters of Irene and Hallie Coletta* (1979) is an alphabet of rebus rhymes. It might best be presented to several children at once, who could work together to decipher the poems. This book is appropriate only for children who are reading and who have a grasp of phonic skills. They must work out combinations of syllable and picture such as no plus a picture of a bull to get *noble,* and a picture of a slipper plus *y* for *slippery.* Context clues play a part in successfully reading the poems, for some pictures could have several different names—*steps* or *stairs,* for instance. Children who enjoy it could make puzzles of re-bus writing to be solved by their classmates.

Another visual game with language is to print the word in a way that signifies its mean-ing. In *Barnyard Lullaby* (Asch, 1998), the farmer is trying to sleep but keeps hearing the sounds of the animals. The cow, for example, is "moo, moo, mooing." The intensity of the noise is shown as the letters get larger and the color of the words gets stronger. In *So Say the Little Monkeys* (Van Laan, 1998), the words curve around, mirroring the actions of the monkeys. Children need to see the illustrations closely to appreciate what is being done with the print.

Playing with the Meanings of Language

One last broad area of language play is based on the meaning of words. This includes puns, riddles, nonsense words that sound as though they have meaning, idioms, and figurative lan-guage. The books about Amelia Bedelia take a look at the literal interpretation of idioms. Amelia is a maid who believes in interpreting language literally. In the first of the series, *Amelia Bedelia* (Parish, 1963), she does what Mrs. Rogers has told her to do in a list of instructions. When the list says to dust the furniture, she sprinkles dusting powder all over the sofas and ta-bles. When it says to change the towels, she does so by cutting them into a different shape. Amelia is not totally unknowing, however. When Mrs. Rogers returns to find all of the mistakes and is about to fire Amelia, she gets a taste of the lemon-meringue pie that Amelia has baked even without instructions to do so. The job is saved, and Mrs. Rogers learns to say things such as "undust" the furniture. Children delight in Amelia's interpretation of idioms they under-stand and often can think of other examples themselves.

There are many Amelia Bedelia books, the last of which is *Amelia Bedelia's Family Al-bum* (Parish, 1988). Amelia shows pictures in the album and tells the occupation of each family member; but once again, the terms are used literally. Aunt Mary, a bank teller, doesn't work with money—she tells everyone in the bank where to go.

A similar approach to language play is used by Fred Gwynn in books such as *A Little Pigeon Toad* (1988) and *A Chocolate Moose for Dinner* (1976). In the latter, a little girl repeats some of the things her parents have said, with her interpretation of the meaning shown by the illus-trations. Some are idioms, such as her father playing the piano by ear. He is shown banging away on the keys with—yes—his ear. Others are plays on homophones, such as the title pic-ture, which shows a brown moose sitting at the table with a napkin tied carefully around its neck. This is the "chocolate moose" they had for dinner. The spellings given are for the words as interpreted by the girl. If the book is to be enjoyed by children, they must understand the correct meaning for the phrases. Seeing men in seashells rowing with oars is not funny unless they know what is really meant by "rowing in shells." Thus, this book and others like it are most appropriate for second- and third-graders, and even older children. They might even make up full stories based on one of the homophones, seeing how the author of *Truman's Ant Farm* (Rat-tigan, 1994) plays on the difference between "ant" and "aunt." Truman gets hundreds of "aunts," all ready to be kind and attentive to their new nephew.

Preschoolers and kindergartners enjoy Naomi Bossom's *A Scale Full of Fish and Other Turnabouts* (1979). The book is a collection of language turnabouts illustrated with woodcuts. The examples face each other. On one page is "race for a train," with passengers hurrying along; opposite it is "train for a race," with three runners. Once children catch onto the pattern they can be shown the first illustration and asked to guess what the second one will be.

Children of all ages delight in riddles. There is a vast supply of books with riddles available. Select one or two, let children guess the answers, then let them tell what they think makes a good riddle. They can make up one of their own to try on their classmates. Having them tell you several riddles themselves will give you some insight on how complex the riddles should be in books you select for them. Here are riddles several children offered when asked simply, "Can you tell me a riddle?" You may remember some of these from your own childhood.

Three-year-old: Why did the bunny cross the road?
To get to the other side.

Four-year-old: What has two eyes and a sheet over it?
A ghost.

Four-year-old: Knock, knock.
Who's there?
Lettuce.
Lettuce who?
Lettuce in, it's cold out here.

Six-year-old: What is black and white, black and white, black and white and green?
Two skunks fighting over a pickle.

Six-year-old: What time is it when an elephant sits on a fence?
Time to get a new fence.

Eight-year-old: What can jump higher than a house?
Anything—houses can't jump.

Eight-year-old: What is a vampire's favorite holiday?
Fangsgiving.

Understanding Figurative Language

Riddles are similar to figurative language in that new meanings are often attached to words, and differences and similarities are emphasized. Young children sometimes have difficulty understanding the figurative language that others use even though they may use metaphors that seem very inventive themselves. To see the similarity between a psychological state and a physical entity, as in phrases such as "heart of stone," requires a high level of abstract thinking.

Fisher and Natarella, in their study of primary children's poetry preferences, found that none of the children's favorite poems contains metaphors, while the least-preferred poems were heavily dependent on metaphorical language. They conclude that it may be because the children did not understand the poems with metaphors, or because the poems with metaphors tended to be descriptive rather than narrative (Fisher & Natarella, 1979). They note, however, that every poem in the study was given the top rating by some pupils.

It would seem that figurative language can best be presented in a context that provides other clues to the meaning and should not be singled out for "study." If children are to hear the full range of language, they must be exposed to the use of metaphor. It is central to much literature, both poetry and prose. Effective use of metaphor gives the reader new insight into ideas being expressed as well as new ways of looking at old ideas. Yet it is illogical to stress the discussion of topics that do not appear to be compatible with the developmental level of young children. The inclusion of well-written stories in a literature curriculum will ensure that children hear metaphorical language. Children hearing Lyle's reaction to a birthday party for Joshua will identify with his feelings and will at the same time hear figurative language such as, "Suddenly, like storm clouds coming down upon a lovely day, Lyle was jealous. . . ." (Waber, 1966, p. 6).

Enjoying Mother Goose Rhymes

For encouraging language play, the key source of material for young children is Mother Goose. The verses are catchy, often humorous, and display the range of kinds of play with language. For those children who have heard the rhymes at home, hearing you read them provides a link between home and school that fosters a feeling of security. For the increasing number of children who are not read to at home and are not familiar with Mother Goose, it brings to them a part of their literary heritage that nearly all enjoy. Here is just a quick sampling of the kinds of language that appear in Mother Goose.

Rhythm and rhyme—

Tom, Tom, the piper's son,
Stole a pig, and away he run.
The pig was eat, and Tom was beat,
And Tom went roaring down the street.

Pease-porridge hot,
Pease-porridge cold,
Pease-porridge in the pot,
Nine days old.
Some like it hot,
Some like it cold,
Some like it in the pot,
Nine days old.

Alliteration—

Peter Piper picked a peck of pickled peppers,
A peck of pickled peppers Peter Piper picked;
If Peter Piper picked a peck of pickled peppers,
Where's the peck of pickled peppers Peter Piper picked?

Onomatopoeia—

This is the way the ladies ride,
Tri, tre, tre, tree,
Tri, tre, tre, tree;
This is the way the ladies ride,
Tri, tre, tre, tre, tri-tre-tre-tree!
This is the way the gentlemen ride,
Gallop-a-trot,
Gallop-a-trot;
This is the way the gentlemen ride,
Gallop-a-gallop-a-trot!
This is the way the farmers ride,
Hobbledy-hoy,
Hobbledy-hoy;
This is the way the farmers ride,
Hobbledy hobbledy-hoy!

Patterning of language—

There was a crooked man, and he went a crooked mile,
He found a crooked sixpence against a crooked stile;
He bought a crooked cat, which caught a crooked mouse,
And they all lived together in a little crooked house.

Nonsense—

Hey diddle diddle,
The cat and the fiddle,
The cow jumped over the moon;
The little dog laughed
To see such sport,
And the dish ran away with the spoon.

Riddles—

Humpty Dumpty sat on a wall;

Humpty Dumpty had a great fall.

All the king's horses and all the king's men

Couldn't put Humpty Dumpty together again.

"A Candle"

Little Nanny Etticoat

In a white petticoat,

And a red nose;

The longer she stands

The shorter she grows.

Look through collections of Mother Goose yourself. Plan to read the verses to children on a regular basis. Look also for ways that children can be involved with the rhymes. Which ones lend themselves to dramatization? Which have games that accompany them? Which could children clap to, sway to, move to? Which have refrains that could be repeated? Which can be sung? Look for and build upon the strengths of these rhymes, which have enthralled children for generations.

Select rhymes from various cultures. *Diez Deditos: Ten Little Fingers and Other Play Rhymes and Action Songs from Latin America* (Orozco, 1997) gives the music, the motions, and the text in both Spanish and English for over thirty rhymes. *Dragon Kites and Dragonflies* (Demi, 1986) gives many short Chinese nursery rhymes. The illustrations in both books depict a style of art frequently used in the culture.

Exploring Other Languages

The increasing number of bilingual books being published, and of familiar stories translated into languages other than English, give teachers and day-care providers a wide selection of literature from which to choose. Many of these books introduce children to aspects of a culture where the language is spoken, though not all do.

Vocabulary items from other languages may be introduced in context, either with or without explanation. In *Abuela's Weave* (Castaneda, 1993), the meaning is given in apposition, noting that "Esperanza's grandmother, her Abuela," was kneeling in front of a loom. In *The Day Gogo Went to Vote* (Sisulu, 1996), the reader must ascertain on his or her own that "gogo" means grandmother, for the text has Thembi talking about her gogo and the illustrations picture the old woman, but no specific information is given within the story. A glossary, however, does explain that "gogo" is "grandmother" in both Xhosa and Zulu.

Other books work vocabulary from other languages into English text. *In the Park* (Lee, 1998) has Xiao Ming's mother showing him how to draw several Chinese characters, and as he does so, he notices how some of the characters resemble the objects they represent. *The Iguana Brothers* (Johnston, 1995) has Dom and Tom, two iguanas, interspersing Spanish with English. When Tom tells Dom that he really does not like to eat bugs, the following conversation ensues.

Dom said, "You will get thin, Tom. You will get *flaco, flaco, flaco.*"

"I would rather be *flaco* than eat bugs."

"You will get pale, Tom," said Dom. "You will get *palido, palido, palido.*"

"Bugs make me pale already."

(Johnston, 1995, n.p.)

Still other books will give the complete text in both English and another language. Spanish is the most common language for bilingual books at present. With short text, as in Pat Mora's poetic text *Listen to the Desert/Oye al desierto 1994*, children can repeat the phrases after you and it is very easy for them to compare the writing in the two languages. In more complex books, such as *A Gift for Abuelita/Un regalo para Abuelita* (Luenn, 1998), you might want to have children just listen as you read first in one language and then another, or as you and a reader of the other language take turns reading the text. You might also want to ask a native speaker of the language to make a tape of himself or herself reading so that you can use it several times.

Using such books introduces your English-speaking students to the concept of the many languages that are spoken around the world, and supports the native language of your students for whom English is their second language. Just as for many children, hearing stories or rhymes in school that they have heard at home helps ease the transition into a new environment, so hearing their native language can help make students feel at home in school and feel pride in their heritage.

Giving Children Practice in Attentive, Critical, and Appreciative Listening Skills

Educators use a variety of terms to describe and categorize types of listening skills. One such system classifies listening as marginal, attentive, critical, or appreciative. The sort of listening that occurs when one is not really paying attention, but does respond if his or her name is called or if a sound such as a siren intrudes, is often termed *marginal* or *passive* listening. Sharing literature with children is seldom concerned with this type of listening.

Building Attentive Listening Skills

Attentive listening occurs when the listener can decipher the literal meaning of what is heard, recall sequence, and follow directions. It requires that the listener attend to what is being presented and understand the meaning directly conveyed by the words. One way in which literature can build skill in attentive listening is for the teacher to involve the children with the story during the reading. This can be done by having children repeat refrains in cumulative stories. They must listen to the story and be ready when it is time to say "Hundreds of cats, millions of cats . . ." or "I think I can."

Children can be given special parts in the telling of a story so that they must listen for their time to participate. You could read a story such as *Good-Night, Owl!* (Hutchins, 1972) in which the owl is trying to sleep but all the other animals are alert and noisy. The pattern of the book is such that as each animal is named, the sound it makes follows. Thus, the bees "buzz buzz," and the jays scream, "ark ark." Read it through once so that the children see the pattern.

Then have two or three children take the part of each animal. When you read that the bees buzzed, the two or three will respond "buzz buzz." The story reading becomes a joint project in which the children provide the sound effects. There is the possibility of expanding upon this, perhaps having all the children make the sounds together to hear what owl heard as he tried to sleep. Many teachers find it useful to have a hand signal that the children recognize when sound effects or musical instruments are being used. For example, teach the children that when you lift your hand in the air, the sound is to begin, and when you lower it to the top of the book, the sound is to end. The higher your hand, the louder the sound; the lower your hand, the softer the sound. This allows you to orchestrate the effects and lets you and the children work together rather than having to stop their continued buzzing and barking in a voice that rings of reprimand.

A second technique for helping children become attentive listeners is to give them or have them decide upon a specific purpose for listening. Most people listen more carefully when they need or want to know the information being given. Before reading an informational book, ask children to listen for the answer to specific questions, or for what they hope to find out, or to listen for one new bit of information. Second- and third-graders can dictate to the teacher what they already know about the topic, or what they would like to find out. This helps focus their listening. Sometimes teachers will give each child a different question to answer. Sometimes they will ask children to raise their hands when they hear a specific piece of information. All of these set a purpose for listening.

Building Critical Listening Skills

The kinds of questions you ask about a book determine the kind of listening children are likely to do. If you ask only questions that require direct recall, then children are going to form the habit of listening for detail only. To encourage critical listening, you will need to develop a pattern of asking questions and providing activities that go beyond memory. Critical listening, sometimes called analytical listening, requires the listener to go beyond the data as stated directly. The facts are interpreted, generalizations and inferences are made, and the material is evaluated. The listener engages in critical thinking about what has been heard.

Respond to *Good-Night Owl!* with the sounds is an activity that promotes attentive listening. If, following the reading, you were to ask, "What did the woodpecker do?" or "What did owl want to do?" you would be reinforcing habits of attentive listening. To encourage critical listening, you would need to plan activities and questions that require thinking that goes beyond the memory level. You might ask questions such as "Do you think the other animals will behave any differently toward owl in the future? Why or why not?" or "How do you think owl felt about the other animals? What makes you think this?" You could have children draw a picture showing one solution to owl's problem of not being able to get his daytime sleep.

In general, memory-type questions and activities do not lead children to explore the more important aspects of literature. Thus, you will want to go beyond this level and engage children in critical listening and thinking. Chapter 6 has a more detailed discussion of questioning and of types of activities that encourage children to interpret, compare, and evaluate literature.

Building Appreciative Listening Skills _____

The fourth type of listening, appreciative, is listening that leads to aesthetic enjoyment. This is the sort of listening one engages in when hearing a symphony—or a rock concert—hearing poetry, or enjoying the humor in a story. You can encourage appreciative listening by showing that you value it. This means that you listen to a poet read several of her poems on a record as the children listen, and do not succumb to the temptation to fill out the attendance while the children are listening.

You can encourage the children to make mental images as they listen. How did they picture the dog in the poem? Did they imagine themselves when they had an ice-cream cone melt in their hand? They might later transfer some of their mental images to paper.

For all types of listening, you can help children develop skill by occasionally rereading a story after a discussion. Children can check their own impressions as they hear once again what the author said.

Leading Naturally Into Reading

The best preparation for reading is no doubt the desire to read. Literature shared orally helps instill this desire, for children learn that books give interesting information and contain good stories and poems. In addition, those who have listened to a variety of stories have been introduced to many new words and sentence patterns that they will encounter when they read themselves.

Observing the Reading Process _____

The oral sharing of literature can be structured in such a way that it helps children understand the process of reading. Simply from watching the adult look at the page, turn the pages, and "tell" a story from it, children begin to realize that the print on the page carries a message. When they hear the same story several times, they learn that somehow the book keeps the story constant. If they watch the print as the adult reads, they begin to associate certain segments of print with segments of speech. At first this may be the entire sentence or phrase, later separate words, and eventually the correspondence between letters and sounds.

To help children gain these understandings it is essential that you provide ways for children to hear a story more than once. This may be accomplished by your reading it to a group when many of them request it again, but more often it should be a rereading for the individual who requests it. Have parents who are willing to help or classroom aides set up an area for reading, where a child can come to have his or her special book read again and again. It is through this repetition that children can begin to generalize about print and speech. The adult can point to words as they are read, reinforce the left to right progression that you have demonstrated in your reading to the entire class, can let the child read any words that he or she knows, can let the child turn the page, can talk about ideas or words with the child.

Big Books, published in a format large enough for children to see the print clearly when they are sitting in a group, serve this purpose well. Children watch as the print is read; and because so many of these books have predictable story and language patterns, children can begin to read the book with the teacher often after hearing only part of the story.

Some teachers invite fifth- and sixth-graders to their kindergarten and primary classes to read to individual children. This can be a valuable experience for the older as well as the younger child. Older children have a chance to improve their own oral reading skills, and they get feedback on how well they are doing. Younger ones get attention and individual help with reading. It may be necessary, however, for you to provide some instruction on oral reading not only for older children but for parents and aides as well. This is especially true if you want them to involve children in the story through discussion and pointing out words and phrases.

Set up a listening or computer center where children can listen to tapes or view CD-ROMs of stories and poems. For a listening center, have the books there so that children can follow the story as they hear it, seeing the illustrations and the print as well. Several companies, including Weston Woods, Spoken Arts, Miller-Brody, and Scholastic, sell media packages that include a copy of the book and a tape of the text. For children who are not yet reading or are just beginning, a bell or beep on the soundtrack that indicates that a page is to be turned helps children follow accurately. If you are making the tape yourself, consider using a sound to tell children to turn the page, or simply say "Turn the page." When children are viewing CD-ROM versions of stories, encourage them to go through the story at least once watching as the print is bolded to show the words being read. A listening or computer center can be a regular option for children as they make work choices or as you assign tasks.

Sharing Familiar Texts in Writing

Let children see in writing rhymes, chants, or poems which they know. If they can repeat "Mary Had a Little Lamb," or "Rime de chocolate," make a wall chart of that rhyme and point to the words as they say or "read" it. You could make copies of the rhyme and let them create the illustration. If you did this for several rhymes, they could make a booklet. Your regular sharing of Mother Goose and other nursery rhymes should ensure that the children will have a repertoire of rhymes, even those children who did not know any when they first came to preschool or school. Select and display for the children's perusal several books of Mother Goose rhymes that have only one rhyme per page and have illustrations that will help children identify the rhyme. Two good editions are *Tomie dePaola's Mother Goose* (dePaola, 1985) and *The Baby's Lap Book* (Chorao, 1990).

All of these procedures are designed to help children move into reading naturally by letting them observe for themselves the uses of written language. The process is one in which they see enough examples to begin making generalizations for themselves.

Give children opportunities to read words they see regularly in their environment. Three books by Tana Hoban, *I Walk and Read* (1984) *I Read Signs* (1983) and *I Read Symbols* (1983) have clear and colorful photographs of common signs and symbols. There is no text. Children will readily recognize and read words such as "stop," "exit," and "don't walk." Because the books show photographs, children see the print exactly as it appears, which helps in recognition and demonstrates that there are many different styles of print.

Providing Time for Reading

Depending on whether you are working in a day-care center, a kindergarten, or the primary grades, you will have different expectations for the children, and the day may be structured differently. You will, however, want to provide time on a regular basis for the children to read and to look at books. This may be done through a period of sustained silent reading, as a work choice for the children, or while others are working in small groups with the teacher.

Children should select some books themselves. Begin early to help them become responsible for their own choices and let them know that much reading is for personal enjoyment. They need not read every story aloud nor discuss every story with an adult. Particularly in sustained silent reading, children choose books freely and are not responsible for reporting on their reading. Children who are not yet reading also need the opportunity to look at books, enjoy the illustrations, and think of themselves as "book people" right from the start.

Encouraging Children to Respond to Books Orally

Activities frequently involve more than one aspect of language development, even though only one may be emphasized. While some children are speaking, others are listening. What one child writes, another reads. Oral activities for children can help both the speakers and the listeners: speakers to become more fluent and lucid, listeners to become more attentive and analytical. For example, a child opens a picture book and describes one of the illustrations without showing it to other members of the class. Another child is then given the closed book and asked to find the illustration just described. The speaker needs to be detailed in describing the illustration; the listener needs to be attentive so that the description can be compared with each picture until a match is found. Most oral activities either naturally involve listening activities or can be structured so that they do. The discussion that follows will focus on oral presentation, but there is a listening component as well.

Dramatizing a Story

Literature offers many opportunities for creative dramatics, both interpreting and improvising. Children interpret a story when they dramatize it following the plot closely; they are improvising when they create their own plot. A story that has long been a favorite with young children is *Caps for Sale* (Slobodkina, 1940). In this story a peddler who sells caps walks along with his merchandise stacked on his head. After a morning of calling out "Caps for sale," and having made no sales, he walks out into the country and sits beneath a tree to take a nap, still carefully balancing the caps. When he awakens, he finds only his own hat on his head and looking up discovers that the tree is filled with monkeys, and on the head of each monkey is one of his caps. He shakes his finger at them and demands that they return his caps. They shake their fingers at him. With each action emphasizing his pleas to return his caps, the monkeys only mimic him. In disgust he throws his hat on the ground—and all the monkeys follow suit. Picking up his caps, the peddler returns to the village to try once again to sell his wares.

Another approach would be for you to narrate parts of the story, but have the children speak the dialogue. You would tell about the peddler, then the "peddler" would call out his pitch of caps for sale. As you prepare for this, children could take turns saying the peddler's words and trying to make their voices sound the way they thought his might have. They do not memorize lines, but rather say what fits with the progression of the story. The "monkeys" could work to make their voices reflect a teasing mood.

You might have the children dramatize the story, providing all of the dialogue themselves and adding words or phrases that would help move the story along. The peddler, for instance, might mutter to himself about feeling hungry or make some exclamation upon discovering that his hats were gone. The monkeys could talk among themselves as they picked up the hats from the head of the sleeping peddler.

For any of these three approaches you could use simple props, such as hats for the peddler, or you could have children pantomime. You would not want to get involved in the extensive use of props, which is more appropriate to a production than to a classroom story interpretation.

Role-Playing and Improvising

Literature can provide a stimulus for drama that does not follow the content of the story, but builds upon themes, characters, or ideas within it. Role-play and improvisation both fit into this category. In role-play, the child takes on the role of one of the characters and then reacts to a new situation as he or she thinks the character would. A child role-playing the peddler might be told that it is the next day and the peddler is once more at the tree where he had rested previously. He must decide what to do. Will he take off the caps to protect them? Will he keep going? The monkeys also must decide what to do. Will they follow the peddler? Will they grab for the caps even if the peddler does not go to sleep?

Role-play involves being able to understand the viewpoint of another. For this reason, it is more appropriate for children who are in the primary grades than for three- and four-year-olds. Often children will be themselves in the situation, giving their own reactions and not those that they think the character might have. Even so, role-play encourages children to listen to others and express ideas clearly in speech.

Improvisation builds an entirely new story but may use the characters or a problem from literature as its source. Using an idea from *Caps for Sale,* children could be asked to pretend that they are in the painting area, then go out for recess or stop for snack time. When they go back to finish their painting, the paints and paper are gone. The improvisation begins at the point where they go back to the painting area. They discover their paints missing and must decide what to do. When the improvisation is completed, children talk about what happened and how they felt. They often repeat role-plays or improvisations, exploring different actions and solutions to problems.

Using Masks and Puppets

Children who are somewhat reticent to speak sometimes are more verbal if they use a mask or puppets in the interpretation of literature. It becomes less them and more the characters who are speaking. Masks can be made by the children to represent characters and are held in front of the face as they speak. Some have a space cut out for the child's face, some just for the eyes. Puppets, too, can be constructed from various objects that are then attached to a stick or dowel of some kind and manipulated by moving the rod. Paper plates, pictures cut from magazines and mounted on heavy cardboard, figures drawn on heavy paper, and paper cups are all commonly used as puppet heads or bodies. The important thing to remember in helping children make puppets is that the youngsters should be able to manipulate them easily. The children can then concentrate on the action and dialogue of the puppets and the interaction among the characters. If you are interested in more information about mask and puppet construction, check the Recommended References at the end of this chapter for reading on the topic.

Talking About and Telling Stories

In addition to leading to dramatization, books can also lead to other oral activities. Children can tell parts of stories they liked to classmates, with a period in which they can be asked questions. They can record their opinion as to particular books and put the tapes in the book area for other children to hear. These same tapes can be played for the speakers to listen to, not to evaluate but to hear how they sound. They can retell a story using the feltboard. They can engage in book discussions. They can explain art activities based on books as they share their creations.

Wordless picture books offer many opportunities for children to tell a story. First-graders looking at *Pancakes for Breakfast* (dePaola, 1978) can add to the text by looking at the pictures and giving a sentence or two for each illustration. They would describe the woman who awoke thinking of pancakes, got out her recipe book, began gathering the ingredients for the pancakes, and after collecting eggs from the hen house and milking the cow, still needed maple syrup. They would describe how she returned home with the syrup to discover that her cat and dog had knocked over the batter and ruined her breakfast plans. And finally, they would end by telling how she smelled pancakes from the house next door, went over, and ate her neighbor's breakfast.

They might tell the story by passing the book around a group of four children, each telling about a page when it was his or her turn. One child might tell the story by making a recording of it and seeing if other children could understand the book from the tape alone. They might tell the story as if they were the old woman, beginning with "When I woke up . . ." instead of narrating it in third person. As you listen to the descriptions children give, you will learn about their understanding of the story itself and gain some insight into their language development.

As you preview books and poems, look for those that lend themselves to choral speaking. Books with refrains, such as *Millions of Cats* (Gag, 1928) or with sounds, such as *Good-Night, Owl!* (Hutchins, 1972) invite class participation. Short poems can be spoken in unison or divided so that groups within the class say different lines. All might recite "Jack Be Nimble" as they act out the rhyme and jump over an imaginary candlestick. "Jack Sprat" is divided easily. The first line is said by one group; "Jack Sprat could eat no fat"—the second, by a second group; "His wife could eat no lean"—and the last two by the entire group; "And so between them, they licked the platter clean." Find opportunities where you can lead children in echo reading, where you say the phrase first, with them repeating it. *Listen to the Rain* (Martin & Archambault, 1988) allows for the teacher to model, and have children follow, volume, speed, and phrasing as the different aspects of rain, from fierce thunder to the quiet time after a rainstorm, are described poetically.

Finally, give children the opportunity to talk with one another as they work on projects that are book-related. This informal conversation provides language practice in a natural situation and gives many children the opportunity to speak if they are working in pairs or small groups. Their turn to talk comes often, and they actively engage in listening.

If two or three children work on the same project, then their conversation can be focused. They must also use group interaction skills. If the class had heard and repeated the short couplets that make up *Greetings, Sun* (Gershator, 1998), a book that opens at sunrise as two children greet the morning, and the many things they see throughout the day until they return home and get ready for bed, they might create a class big book using the text but creating their own illustrations. In groups of three, children could select which page they wished to illustrate. Then they would need to present their ideas to one another and plan just how the illustration would be drawn. When completed, each illustration could be shared with the other groups, then combined into a single book for repeated reading.

Engaging Children in a Variety of Writing Activities

In a discussion of writing activities, it is necessary to remember that there is a strong connection between reading and writing. Oral and written aspects of language develop simultaneously and are linked in that both engage the child in actively making meaning of the world (Fletcher, 1993; Schwartz, 1988). Talking about their topic, both before they write and while they write, helps some children to write in a more focused manner. They may share their writing while the piece is in progress, getting feedback from an audience of their peers.

Children will be selecting their own topics to write about and may record thoughts and feelings in a daily response journal. There are times, however, when you may want to provide an idea, or prompt, for their writing. Sometimes books seem to lead directly into writing activities. *Only the Cat Saw* (Wolff, 1985), for instance, alternates between pages having text and those with illustration only. The text tells what the family was doing, so busy that "only the cat saw . . ." what is shown in the double-page spread that follows. Children can create a piece of descriptive writing by looking at the illustration and adding the text for what the cat saw, which are all night scenes. In the morning, when the family is at breakfast, the cat has curled up and gone to sleep. So "only Amy saw. . . ."

The Mysteries of Harris Burdick (1984) by Chris Van Allsburg contains fourteen illustrations, each accompanied by a title and one sentence. The premise of the book is that an author, Harris Burdick, had come to a children's publisher with the pictures, promising to return the next day with the stories if the publisher was interested. The publisher was, but Burdick never returned. Thus the drawings remained, and one can only imagine the stories they were meant to illustrate. And that is the fascination of the book—what is the story for each picture? Children can select an illustration that interests them and create the story. Perhaps they will complete the story for "Under the Rug," deciding just what it is that is creating the bump between the carpet and floor. Or they might decide what the little girl will do with the two caterpillars that she knows she should "send back," and who are spelling "good-bye" in her hand. Some of the illustrations are fairly sophisticated, but primary grade children will be able to select those with meaning for them.

At times both the content of a book and its format will suggest writing activities. *Farm Boy's Year* (McPhail, 1992) has one diary entry per month as though written by a boy living on a New England farm in the 1800s. Children might keep a book during the school year, deciding at the end of each month what stood out for them and making a diary entry. Another possibility would be to have them remember back and create a year's diary based on events from the previous, or earlier, year. The book shows that regular parts of our lives, as well as unique events, make good subjects for writing.

Children can be engaged in a variety of types of writing based on literature.

Yuck! (Stevenson, 1984) is told in cartoon format, with characters' dialogue appearing above them in "balloons." This is a format many children know from looking at comics in newspapers, and one they can manipulate to tell stories in a combination of art and writing. The story itself appeals to children both for the terrible sounding—and smelling—potions that the witches Emma and Lavinia brew, and for the poetic justice as the little witch, Emma, outwits these two after they have refused to let her help. The book encourages children to play with language, perhaps making their own recipes for potions, and to explore storywriting in cartoon format.

Stringbean's Trip to the Shining Sea (Williams, 1988) is about a boy's trip from Kansas to the Pacific Ocean with his older brother, told through the postcards he sends home. His messages reveal his feelings and his relationship with his brother as well as the experience he has. Children could explore the whole world of postcards—the messages, pictures, descriptions, special stamps—all first explored through this book.

Building Ideas from Types of Writing

At other times, it may be helpful to use a category system as a stimulus to find writing activities that will extend children's responses to literature. One such category system is based on the type of writing: narrative, expository, persuasive, or descriptive. Narrative writing tells a story and has a plot. Children can listen to the first part of a story and then write an ending for it, or they could listen to the actual ending first, then write a new one. They could use a character from a book—Curious George, for instance—and create a new adventure for him. They might look at the structure of a specific kind of narrative, such as a folktale with wise and foolish beasts, and write a story in that mode.

Expository writing explains how something is done. Children who have heard how the characters in a book spend their holidays might then write how their own family decides where to go on vacation. They might try writing their own recipe for stone soup after hearing how the soldiers in the book of that title made soup with the help of the villagers.

Persuasive writing is designed to influence people, to be convincing. Children can write commercials for their favorite books, using language that highlights all the good points of the book and makes it sound appealing to others. They might write a letter in a defense of a book character.

Descriptive writing portrays a character or situation. It describes how an object appears to the senses, how someone feels, or what a scene was like. Children can write descriptions of book characters without including the names of the characters. The descriptions can be put on a bulletin board as part of a riddle game. Children read the descriptions and try to guess who the characters are.

After reading *Winnie-the-Pooh* (Milne, 1926) orally, one third-grade teacher brought in a stuffed Winnie-the-Pooh toy and let a different child take it home each evening along with Pooh's diary. During the evening, the child, as Pooh, would write an entry telling what he had seen and done that night. Children were eager to take Pooh home and equally eager to share his diary the next day.

Being Flexible in Amount of Writing

A second way of thinking about writing is to consider the quantity of writing. Some responses to books may take the form of lists or one-word answers. Children might be asked to list four places they think a cricket could hide in their classroom, or look out the window and list all the things they see that they think Crow Boy would be interested in watching. Often the written response may be just one sentence. First-graders answered the question at the end of *Clifford's Halloween* (Bridwell, 1986) "What would Clifford be for Halloween?" with these responses: "He could be Santa Claus"; "He could be a big red bird"; "He could be a red witch"; "He could be Superman." Because Clifford is a huge red dog, disguising him is somewhat of a problem. The children drew pictures to accompany their answers. Both the pictures and the sentences kept the bigness and the redness of Clifford in mind. Only one of the students used a suggestion that had appeared in the book.

Children may write a paragraph or more, developing an idea fully. A special writing corner, a writer's club, and access to a computer for word processing often encourage children to write. So too will writing and illustrating their own books, which can be sewn together and bound in cardboard covered with cloth. These are then placed in the classroom library where other children may read them. Several companies are now producing books with cloth covers and blank pages. You might suggest these books to parents as a way of encouraging their children to write at home.

Helping Children Write Well

As you plan writing activities related to literature, you will want to do all that you can to make the writing experience a successful one for the children. Generally this means that you will engage children in a discussion period before they begin writing. During this time, children can exchange ideas and think through their own responses so that when they begin to compose they have some notion of what they want to say. A good writing program will have children writing daily, taking responsibility for choosing most of their own topics, and having regular conferences with the teacher during the writing process. These procedures will carry over when children write about literature.

According to recent research, children's approaches to writing change as they mature. Children of five or six put thoughts on paper with little preplanning. Writing is like play in that the children put on paper whatever comes to mind and are not concerned with the product or potential readers. They develop a sense of audience gradually. Children become aware of others' reactions to their stories and the need for the conventions of punctuation, capitalization, and correct spelling. By the end of first grade, many children are able to postpone the immediate task of writing to do preliminary tasks such as checking the spelling of a word.

Once children begin to plan, they frequently go through a period of overplanning, wanting everything decided before they begin so that there will be no "mistakes." The period of spontaneity has given way to a period of deliberatness. Before children begin composing as a professional writer does, they must rediscover the playful aspects of writing (Calkins, 1980). They must combine initial personal response with their awareness of audience, compose, and then edit.

Thus your task as a primary grade teacher is not only to encourage and support the concept of planning but also to work with children as they write, helping them clarify thoughts and consider whether they are writing for an audience or just for themselves. You will introduce the ideas of proofreading and editing, both in stories dictated by a group and in the writing of individuals. In this way, children learn that the first draft may or may not say exactly what they want, and that changes and corrections are not only permissible but desirable. If you are working with preschoolers, your task is to encourage the children to tell stories, to engage in oral composition, and to experiment with print, writing their stories and telling you what each says.

Try to vary the writing activities that you suggest to children. This will help maintain their interest in writing and will give breadth to their concept of content and style. Structure writing activities so that they are challenging but not overwhelming, allowing the children to see growth in their own skill.

Incorporating Visual Literacy

Visual literacy, the ability to discriminate and interpret images, has taken on new importance as children both view and create images on computer programs, and as more information and entertainment are presented through visual means. Just as we help children become more knowledgable and more skilled in their use of verbal communication, so too we can help them gain skill in using and understanding visual images. Illustrator studies, in which children compare several works of a single artist, let children explore the techniques that person uses and show children that there are choices being made. The artist often thinks of audience just as a writer does.

Because books capture selected events within a story, children can describe what else might have been shown and think about why the artist chose to illustrate particular portions of a story. Comparing the book format with an animated format of the same story can enhance this strategy. The books and CDs and television programs based on the Arthur stories of Marc Brown are numerous and easily purchased and so make an easy place to start.

Creating stories in cartoon format, as mentioned earlier, lets children combine art and writing. *The Adventures of Sparrowboy* (Pinkney, 1998) incorporates both style and content of the superhero comic book. Many of the conventions of showing motion, of sound, of explanatory comment can be identified by children reading this book. They might then want to compare it with the hero-style computer programs that they use.

How people use visual images to learn about other cultures is clearly shown in George Ancona's *Mayeros* (1997). Using photographs of a contemporary Yucatan Maya family, he shows how some of their activities appear in ancient artifacts. A Mayan dish shows a woman using a metate, for example, and a carving from a stone monument shows a figure using a tumpline to carry objects. Children can look at photographs from many books, both fiction and nonfiction, and tell what they learn from the visual elements.

SUMMARY

Children learn language by constructing for themselves the grammar of the language they hear. To develop mature syntax and vocabulary they need to be exposed to rich, varied, and abundant samples of language, for this is the data base from which they generalize. They need to hear stories and see print in their daily environments. They also need the opportunity to use their language for a variety of purposes and in a variety of settings.

The following long-term developmental goals are appropriate for the language growth of young children:

Children will understand and use the mature syntax of their language.

Children will expand their vocabularies.

Children will enjoy the creative and aesthetic use of language.

Children will become skilled listeners.

Children will learn to read.

Children will communicate effectively in oral, written, and visual formats.

Books offer opportunities for helping children achieve these goals. Table 5–1 suggests appropriate teaching strategies. Children can be exposed to mature language in literature, hearing varied and complex syntactical structures, figurative language, and a variety of English dialects. They can be introduced to new vocabulary in context, sometimes as part of a story and at other times in concept books that focus on language. Children should be involved in using the new words they are learning.

Children can be encouraged to enjoy the ways others use language and to play with it themselves. Some "play" is with the sound of language, rhythm, rhyme, and repetition; some with patterns, refrains in books, and songs. Still other play involves both the visual aspect of language and the meaning. As children listen to and recite Mother Goose rhymes, they are being introduced to the flexibility and fun of language.

As they listen to literature children can practice attentive, critical, and appreciative listening skills. They can be guided to think analytically about what they have heard through carefully structured questions and activities. They also develop a concept of the reading process as they observe how adults use the printed page and how verses they recite orally can be preserved in print.

Table 5–1. Supporting Children's Language Development

Developmental Goals	Teaching Suggestions	Recommended Literature	
Children will understand and use the mature syntax of their language.	Provide rich and varied samples of mature language. Respond to the content of children's telegraphic speech with mature language. Read regularly to children. Encourage primary caregivers to read to the children. Encourage children to read on their own. Expose children to a variety of writing styles and dialects.	Ages 3–5: Gilchrist Ryder Turkle Ages 5–8: Bedard McKissack Stanley	*Halfway Up the Mountain* *A Wet and Sandy Day* *Thy Friend, Obadiah* *The Divide* *Flossie and the Fox* *Saving Sweetness*
Children will expand their vocabularies.	Introduce new words in the context of a story. Let children explain the meaning from the context. Let children retell a story in their own words. Use phrases from a story to elicit personal responses from children. Share concept books that present vocabulary items. Have children create sentences or stories from the words and pictures given. Let children respond physically to words in a story or poem. Read several books on the same topic to reinforce vocabulary. Have children use accurate vocabulary to tell personal experiences similar to ones presented in literature. Guide children to dramatize stories so they will use the vocabulary they have heard.	Ages 3–5: Arnoski Beyer Ginsberg Hughes Marshall Oxenbury Ricklen Ricklen Yabuuchi Ages 5–8: Lewin Marshall Raschka	*Little Lions* "Jump or Jiggle" *The Chick and the Duckling* *Giving* *George and Martha Round and Round* *I See* *Daddy and Me* *Mommy and Me* *Whose Baby?* *The Storytellers* *The Cut-Ups Cut Loose* *The Blushful Hippopotamus*

Table 5–1. *(continued)*

Developmental Goals	Teaching Suggestions	Recommended Literature	
Children will enjoy the creative and aesthetic use of language.	Read literature that emphasizes language play and follow up by engaging children in word play themselves.	Ages 3–5: Bossom	*A Scale Full of Fish*
		Demi	*Dragon Kites and Dragonflies*
	Read poetry regularly to the children.	Emberley	*Drummer Hoff*
		Fleming	*In the Tall, Tall Grass*
	Let children listen to and write tongue twisters.	Gag	*Millions of Cats*
		Hutchins	*The Surprise Party*
	Encourage children to say refrains in books with you as you read.	Johnston	*The Iguana Brothers*
		Karas	*I Know an Old Lady*
		Lindbergh	*Grandfather's Love Song*
	Share literature in which there is a patterning of language. Let children create short sequences themselves.	Martin	*Chicka Chicka Boom Boom*
		Mora	*Listen to the Desert*
		Orozco	*Diez Deditos*
	Present cumulative folktales.	Piper	*The Little Engine That Could*
	Show visual games with language such as rebus writing.	Sendak	*Chicken Soup with Rice*
		Udry	*Thump and Plunk*
		Van Laan	*So Say the Little Monkeys*
		Yashima	*Umbrella*
Children will enjoy the creative and aesthetic use of language.	Encourage riddles and other play on the meanings of words.	Ages 5–8: Buck	*Santa's Short Suit Shrunk*
		Charlip	*Fortunately*
	Read or recite a wide selection of Mother Goose rhymes.	Colette	*From A to Z*
		Gwynn	*A Chocolate Moose for Dinner*
		Gwynn	*A Little Pigeon Toad*
		Hueck	*Who Stole the Apples?*
		Luenn	*A Gift for Abuelita*
		McCord	*"The Pickety Fence"*
		Nygaard	*Snake Alley Band*
		Parish	*Amelia Bedelia*
		Parish	*Amelia Bedelia's Family Album*
		Rattigan	*Truman's Ant Farm*
		Schwartz	*A Twister of Twists A Tangler of Tongues*

Table 5–1. *(continued)*

Developmental Goals	Teaching Suggestions		Recommended Literature
Children will become skilled listeners.	Give children a specific purpose for listening.	Ages 3–5: Hutchins	*Good-Night Owl!*
	Have children participate in telling a story.		
	Set a pattern of asking questions that require critical thinking.		
	Model appropriate listening behavior.		
	Suggest that children create mental images as they listen.		
	Reread stories occasionally for children to check their original impression.		
Children will learn to read.	Share literature so that children hear language patterns which occur more frequently in writing than in speech.	Ages 3–5: Chorao dePaola	*The Baby's Lap Book* *Tomie dePaola's Mother Goose*
	Present whole stories, giving children a broad context for comprehending meaning.	Hoban	*I Read Signs*
		Hoban	*I Read Symbols*
	Hold books so that children observe the process of reading—looking at print, turning pages.	Hoban	*I Walk and Read*
	Use "Big Books."		
Children will learn to read.	Reread children's favorite stories and poems.		
	Plan for an aide or parent to read to children individually.		
	Reinforce left to right progression in reading.		
	Present books in such a way that reading becomes desirable.		
	Set up listening centers where children can hear a story while looking at the book.		

Table 5–1. *(continued)*

Developmental Goals	Teaching Suggestions	Recommended Literature	
	Make charts or individual booklets of rhymes children know.		
	Display books that contain rhymes children know.		
	Provide time for reading.		
Children will communicate effectively in oral, written, and visual formats.	Transcribe stories that children dictate.	Ages 3–5:	
	Let children tell about stories they like.	Bridwell	*Clifford's Halloween*
		Gag	*Millions of Cats*
	Have children retell a story using a feltboard.	Gershator	*Greetings, Sun*
		Slobodkina	*Caps for Sale*
	Let children interpret stories dramatically.	Wolff	*Only the Cat Saw*
	Encourage use of masks and puppets for dramatization.		
	Have children provide the text for wordless picture books.		
	Tape-record children telling plot of wordless books.		
	Engage children in choral speaking.	Ages 5–8:	
		Ancona	*Mayeros*
	Pair children for game in which one describes a picture in a book and the other tries to locate it.	dePaola	*Pancakes for Breakfast*
		Martin	*Listen to the Rain*
		McPhail	*Farm Boy's Year*
		Pinkney	*The Adventures of Sparrowboy*
	Allow informal conversation as children work on projects.	Stevenson	*Yuck!*
	Suggest activities that require group interaction and discussion.	Van Allsburg	*The Mysteries of Harris Burdick*
	Conference with children as they write.	Williams	*Stringbean's Trip to the Shining Sea*
	Encourage varied types of writing.		

Finally, literature provides myriad opportunities for children to engage in both oral, written, and visual language. Story interpretations and improvisations, role-play, the use of masks and puppets, written responses to books, character studies, diaries, making one's own book, comparing a story in several different formats—all enhance children's appreciation of literature and strengthen children's communication skills.

Extending Your Learning

1. Have a child retell a story after you have read it orally, first without the book and then looking at the illustrations. Describe and analyze the retellings.

2. Assess the language strengths of any three of the recommended children's books listed at the end of this chapter.

3. Make a list of possible book topics for young children. Tell what vocabulary you would expect to be introduced in the books.

4. Begin a collection of riddles children tell. Classify them by the age of the teller. See if you can identify any patterns.

5. Read through a collection of Mother Goose rhymes. Select five rhymes and identify the poetic elements present in them.

6. Again looking through a collection of Mother Goose rhymes, find ones that lend themselves to dramatization, movement, singing, or game-playing.

7. Tell how you might get a child to participate in the reading or telling of any three books mentioned in the preceding chapter.

8. Read a picture book of your own choosing to a group of classmates or friends without showing the illustrations. Have them create "mental images" as they listen. After the reading compare the images first with one another, and then with the illustrations in the book.

9. Plan an activity in response to a book for children that will require thinking above the memory level.

10. Select a book that you feel has potential for use in a dramatic activity. Suggest three different approaches for its use.

11. Have children add narration or dialogue to a wordless picture book. You might want to do the narration twice, once in first person and once in third person.

12. Suggest two writing activities that vary in difficulty but are based on the same book.

RECOMMENDED REFERENCES

Au, K. (1993). *Literacy Instruction in Multicultural Settings.* San Diego: Harcourt.

Ballenger, C. (1999). *Teaching Other People's Children: Literacy and Learning in a Bilingual Classroom.* New York: Teachers College Press.

Bruner, J. (1983). *Child's Talk: Learning to Use the Language.* New York: Norton.

Cary, S. (1997). *Second Language Learners.* York, ME: Stenhouse.

Cazden, C. (1988). *Classroom Discourse, The Language of Teaching and Learning.* Portsmouth, NH: Heinemann.

Chaney, A. and Burk, T. (1998). *Teaching Oral Communication in Grades K-8.* Boston: Allyn & Bacon.

Chukovsky, K. (1971, 1925). *From Two to Five.* Trans. Miriam Morton. Berkeley: University of California Press.

Clay, M. (1998). *By Different Paths to Common Outcomes.* York, ME: Stenhouse.

Cochran-Smith, M. (1984). *The Making of a Reader.* Norwood, NJ: Ablex.

Diamond B. and Moore, M. (1995). *Multicultural Literacy: Mirroring the Reality of the Classroom.* White Plains, NY: Longman.

Dyson, A. and Genishi, C. (1994). *The Need for Story: Cultural Diversity in Classroom and Community.* Urbana, IL: National Council of Teachers of English.

Faltis, C. (1993). *Joinfostering: Adapting Teaching Strategies for the Multilingual Classroom.* New York: Macmillan.

Fox, M. (1987). *Teaching Drama to Young Children.* Portsmouth, NH: Heinemann.

Genishi, C. and Dyson, A. (1984). *Language Assessment in the Early Years.* Norwood, NJ: Ablex.

Grabe, M. and Grade, C. (1998). *Integrating Technology for Meaningful Learning.* 2nd ed. Boston: Houghton Mifflin.

Graves, D. (1983). *Writing: Teachers and Children at Work.* Portsmouth, NH: Heinemann.

Harste, J., Woodward, V. and Burke, C. (1984). *Language Stories and Literacy Lessons.* Portsmouth, NH: Heinemann.

Heard, G. (1989). *For the Good of the Earth and Sun, Teaching Poetry.* Portsmouth, NH: Heinemann.

Heath, S. and Mangiola, L. (1991). *Children of Promise: Literate Activity in Linguistically and Culturally Diverse Classrooms.* Washington, DC: National Education Association.

Holland, K., Hungerford, R., and Ernst, S. Eds. (1993). *Journeying: Children Responding to Literature.* Portsmouth, NH: Heinemann.

Jagger, A. and Smith-Burke, M. Eds. (1985). *Observing the Language Learner.* Newark, DE: International Reading Association.

Lamme, L. (1984). *Growing Up Writing.* Washington, DC: Acropolis.

Loughlin, C. and Martin M. (1987). *Supporting Literacy, Developing Effective Learning Environments.* New York: Teachers College Press.

McCaslin, N. (1996). *Creative Drama in the Classroom.* 6th ed. White Plains, NY: Longman.

MacLennan, J. (1988). *Simple Puppets You Can Make.* New York: Sterling.

Morrow, L. (1997). *Literacy Development in the Early Years: Helping Children Read and Write.* 2nd ed. Upper Saddle River, NJ: Prentice-Hall.

Morrow, L., Strickland, D., and Woo, D. (1998). *Literacy Instruction in Half- and Whole-Day Kindergarten: Research to Practice.* Newark, DE: International Reading Association.

Morrow, L. (1996). *Motivating Reading and Writing in Diverse Classrooms.* Urbana, IL: National Council of Teachers of English.

Nelson, O. and Linek, W. (1999). *Practical Classroom Applications of Language Experience.* Boston: Allyn and Bacon.

Schwartz, J. (1988). *Encouraging Early Literacy: An Integrated Approach to Reading and Writing in N-3.* Portsmouth, NH: Heinemann.

Short, K. (1997). *Literature as a Way of Knowing.* York, ME: Stenhouse.

Stewig, J. and Cuege, C. (1994). *Dramatizing Literature in Whole Language Classrooms.* 2nd ed. New York: Teachers College Press.

Taylor, D. and Dorsey-Gaines, C. (1988). *Growing Up Literate: Learning from Inner-City Families.* Portsmouth, NH: Heinemann.

Wagner, B. Ed. (1998). *Educational Drama and Language Arts: What Research Shows.* Portsmouth, NH: Heinemann.

Way, B. (1967). *Development Through Drama.* London: Longman.

Wells, G. (1986). *The Meaning Makers.* Portsmouth, NH: Heinemann.

RECOMMENDED CHILDREN'S BOOKS

Aardema, Verna. (1998). *Anansi Does the Impossible!* Ill. Lisa Desimini. New York: Antheneum.

Baer, Gene. (1989). *THUMP, THUMP, Rat-a-Tat-Tat.* Ill. Lois Ehlert. New York: Harper.

Domanska, Janina. (1976). *Spring Is.* New York: Greenwillow.

Dunrea, Oliver. (1998). *The Trow-Wife's Treasure.* New York: Farrar.

Fleming, Denise. (1994). *Barnyard Banter.* New York: Holt.

Hoguet, Susan Ramsay. (1983). *I Unpacked My Grandmother's Trunk.* New York: Dutton.

Kellogg, Steven. (1979). *Pinkerton, Behave!* New York: Dial.

Kipling, Rudyard. (1983). *The Elephant's Child.* Ill. Lorinda Bryan Cauley. New York: Harcourt.

Lindbergh, Reeve. (1987). *The Midnight Farm.* Ill. Susan Jeffers. New York: Dial.

Lindgren, Astrid. (1961). *The Tomten.* Ill. Harold Wiberg. New York: Coward.

Lobel, Arnold. (1985). *Whiskers and Rhymes.* New York: Greenwillow.

McCloskey, Robert. (1957). *Time of Wonder.* New York: Viking.

McGee, Marni. (1991). *The Quiet Farmer.* Ill. Lynne Dennis. New York: Atheneum.

Meddaugh, Susan. (1998). *Martha Walks the Dog.* Boston: Houghton Mifflin.

Schotter, Roni. (1997). *Nothing Ever Happens on 90th Street.* Ill. Krysten Brooker. New York: Orchard.

Shulevitz, Uri. (1969). *Rain, Rain, Rivers.* New York: Farrar.

Swann, Brian. (1998). *The House with No Door: African Riddle Poems.* Ill. Ashley Bryan. San Diego: Harcourt.

Tresselt, Alvin. (1947). *White Snow, Bright Snow.* Ill. Roger Duvoisin. New York: Lothrop.

Westcott, Nadine Bernard. (1987). *Peanut Butter and Jelly.* New York: Dutton.

Williams, Linda. (1986). *The Little Old Lady Who Was Not Afraid of Anything.* Ill. Megan Lloyd. New York: Crowell.

RECOMMENDED POETRY

Adoff, Arnold. (1988). *Greens.* Ill. Betty Lewin. New York: Lothrop.

Cullinan, Bernice, Ed. (1996). *A Jar of Tiny Stars: Poems by NCTE Award-Winning Poets.* Honesdale, PA: Boyds Mills.

Degan, Bruce. (1983). *Jamberry.* New York: Harper.

deRegniers, Beatrice Schenck et al. (1988). *Sing a Song of Popcorn: Every Child's Book of Poems.* New York: Scholastic.

Dotlich, Rebecca Kai. (1998). *Lemonade Sun: And Other Summer Poems.* Ill. Jan Spivey Gilchrist. Honesdale, PA: Boyds Mills.

Florian, Douglas. (1994). *Beast Feast.* San Diego: Harcourt.

Gunning, Monica. (1993). *Not a Copper Penny in Me House.* Ill. Fran Lessac. Honesdale, PA: Boyds Mills.

Hoberman, Mary Ann. (1998). *The Llama Who Had No Pajama: 100 Favorite Poems.* Ill. Betty Fraser. San Diego: Harcourt.

Hughes, Shirley. (1988). *Out and About.* New York: Lothrop.

Kuskin, Karla. (1998). *The Sky is Always in the Sky.* Ill. Isabelle Dervaux. New York: HarperCollins.

Lobel, Arnold. (1985). *Whiskers and Rhymes.* New York: Greenwillow.

McCord, David. (1986). *All Small: Poems by David McCord.* Ill. Madelaine Gill Linden. Boston: Little, Brown.

Mado, Michio. (1998). *The Magic Pocket.* Translated by The Empress Michiko of Japan. Ill. Mitsumasa Anno. New York: McElderry.

Moore, Lilian. (1992). *Sunflakes: Poems for Children.* Ill. Jan Ormerod. New York: Clarion.

Mora, Pat. (1998). *This Big Sky.* Ill. Steve Jenkins. New York: Scholastic.

Prelutsky, Jack. (1983). *The Random House Book of Poetry for Children.* Ill. Arnold Lobel. New York: Random House.

Prelutsky, Jack. (1998, 1986). *Read-Aloud Rhymes for the Very Young.* Ill. Marc Brown. New York: Knopf.

Siler, Deborah. Ed. (1991). *Make a Joyful Sound: Poems for Children by African-American Poets.* Ill. Cornelium Van Wright and Ying-Hwa Hu. New York: Checkerboard Press.

Worth, Valerie. (1987). *All the Small Poems.* Ill. Natalie Babbitt. New York: Farrar.

Yolen, Jane. (1987). *The Three Bears Rhyme Book.* Ill. Jane Dyer. San Diego: Harcourt.

PROFESSIONAL REFERENCES CITED

Calkins, L. (1980). Children Learn the Writer's Craft. *Language Arts, 57,* 207–213.

Cazden, C. (1972). *Child Language and Education.* New York: Holt.

Chomsky, C. (1972). Stages in Language Development and Reading Exposure. *Harvard Educational Review, 42,* pp. 124–28.

Chukovsky, K. (1978, 1925). *From Two to Five.* Translated by Miriam Merton. Berkeley: University of California Press.

Cochran-Smith, M. (1984). *The Making of a Reader.* Norwood, NJ: Ablex.

Cohen, D. (1968). The Effect of Literature on Vocabulary and Reading Achievement. *Elementary English, 45,* pp. 209–213.

Doake, D. (1985). Reading-Like Behavior: Its Role in Learning to Read. Jagger, A. and Smith-Burke, M.T., Eds. *Observing the Language Learner.* Newark, DE: International Reading Association.

Fisher, C. and Natarella, M. (1979). Of Cabbages and Kings: On What Kind of Poetry Young Children Like. *Language Arts, 56,* pp. 380–385.

Fletcher, R. (1993). "Roots and Wings: Literature and Children's Writing" in Cullinan, B. Ed. *Pen in Hand: Children Become Writers.* Newark, DE: International Reading Association.

Genishi, C. and Dyson, A. (1984). *Language Assessment in the Early Years.* Norwood, NJ: Ablex.

Hansen, J. (1987). *When Writers Read.* Portsmouth, NH: Heinemann.

Harste, J., Woodward, V., and Burke, C. (1984). *Language Stories and Literacy Lessons.* Portsmouth, NH: Heinemann.

Heller, M. (1991). *Reading-Writing Connections.* New York: Longman.

Kaplan, N. Nursery School Teacher at Jewish Community Center, Providence, RI.

McNeill, D. (1966). Developmental Psycholinguistics. Smith, F. and Miller, G., Eds. *The Genesis of Language: A Psycholinguistic Approach.* Cambridge, MA: Massachusetts Institute of Technology Press.

Morrow, L., Strickland, D., and Woo, D. (1998). *Literacy Instruction in Half- and Whole-Day Kindergarten: Research to Practice.* Newark, DE: International Reading Association.

Schwartz, J. (1988). *Encouraging Early Literacy: An Integrated Approach to Reading and Writing.* Portsmouth, NH: Heinemann.

Standards for the English Language Arts. (1996). Newark, DE: International Reading Association.

CHILDREN'S LITERATURE CITED

Ancona, George. (1997). *Mayeros.* New York: Lothrop.

Arnosky, Jim. (1998). *Little Lions.* New York: Putnam.

Asch, Frank. (1998). *Barnyard Lullaby.* New York: Simon.

Bedard, Michael. (1997). *The Divide.* Ill. Emily Arnold Mc-Cully. New York: Doubleday. Reprinted by permission of Doubleday, a division of Random House, Inc.

Beyer, Evelyn. (1983). "Jump or Jiggle." *Poetry Place Anthology.* NY: Scholastic, p. 131.

Bossom, Naomi. (1979). *A Scale Full of Fish and Other Turnabouts.* New York: Greenwillow.

Bridwell, Norman. (1986). *Clifford's Halloween.* New York: Scholastic.

Buck, Nola. (1997). *Santa's Short Suit Shrunk: And Other Christmas Tongue Twisters.* Ill. Sue Truesdell. New York: Harper-Collins.

Castaneda, Omar. (1993). *Abuela's Weave.* Ill. Enrique Sanchez. New York: Lee & Low.

Charlip, Remy. (1993, 1964). *Fortunately.* New York: Aladdin.

Chorao, Kay. (1990). *The Baby's Lap Book.* New York: Dutton.

Colette, Irene and Hallie. (1979). *From A to Z: The Collected Letters of Irene and Hallie Coletta.* Upper Saddle River, NJ: Prentice-Hall.

Demi. (1986). *Dragon Kites and Dragonflies.* San Diego: Harcourt.

dePaola, Tomie. (1978). *Pancakes for Breakfast.* New York: Harcourt.

dePaola, Tomie. (1985). *Tomie dePaola's Mother Goose.* New York: Putnam.

Fleming, Denise. (1991). *In the Tall, Tall Grass.* New York: Holt.

Gag, Wanda. (Reissue 1996). *Millions of Cats.* New York: Coward-McCann. Copyright © 1928 by Coward-McCann; renewed 1956 by Robert Janssen. Reprinted by permission of Coward, McCann & Geoghegan, Inc.

Gershator, Phyllis and David. (1998). *Greetings, Sun.* Ill. Cynthia Saint James. New York: DK.

Gilchrist, Theo. (1978). *Halfway Up the Mountain.* New York: Harper & Row. Text copyright © 1978 by Theo Gilchrist. Used by permission of HarperCollins Publishers

Ginsburg, Mirra. (1972). *The Chick and the Duckling.* Ill. Ariane Dewey and Jose Aruego. New York: Macmillan.

Gwynn, Fred. (1976). *A Chocolate Moose for Dinner.* New York: Dutton.

Gwynn, Fred. (1988). *A Little Pigeon Toad.* New York: Simon.

Hoban, Tana. (1983). *I Read Signs.* New York: Greenwillow.

Hoban, Tana. (1983). *I Read Symbols.* New York: Greenwillow.

Hoban, Tana. (1984). *I Walk and Read.* New York: Greenwillow.

Hueck, Sigrid. (1986). *Who Stole the Apples?* New York: Knopf.

Hughes, Shirley. (1993). *Giving.* Cambridge, MA: Candlewick.

Hutchins, Pat. (1972). *Good-Night Owl!* New York: Macmillan.

Hutchins, Pat. (1969). *The Surprise Party.* New York: Macmillan.

Jackson, Alison. (1997). *I Know an Old Lady Who Swallowed a Pie.* Ill. Judith Schachner. New York: Dutton.

Johnston, Tony. (1995). *The Iguana Brothers.* Ill. Mark Teague. New York: Scholastic. Reprinted by permission of Scholastic, Inc.

Karas, G. Brian. (1995). *I Know an Old Lady.* New York: Scholastic.

Lee, Huy Voun. (1998). *In the Park.* New York: Holt.

Lewin, Ted. (1998). *The Storytellers.* New York: Lothrop.

Lindbergh, Reeve. (1993). *Grandfather's Love Song.* Ill. Rachel Isadora. New York: Viking. Copyright © 1993 by Reeve Lindbergh. Used by permission of Viking Penguin, a division of Penguin Putnam, Inc.

Luenn, Nancy. (1998). *A Gift for Abuelita/Un regalo para Abuelita.* Ill. Robert Chapman. Phoenix, AZ: Rising Moon.

Lydon, Kerry Raines. (1989). *A Birthday for Blue.* Ill. Michael Hays. Niles, IL: Whitman.

McCord, David. (1952). "The Pickety Fence" in McCord, David. *Far and Few.* Ill. Henry B. Kane. Boston: Little, Brown.

McKissack, Patricia. (1986). *Flossie and the Fox.* Ill. Rachel Isadora. New York: Dial. Copyright © 1986 by Patricia C. McKissack. Used by permission of Dial Books for Young Readers, a division of Penguin Putnam, Inc.

McPhail, David. (1992). *Farm Boy's Year.*

Marshall, James. (1987). *The Cut-Ups Cut Loose.* New York: Viking.

Marshall, James. (1988). *George and Martha Round and Round.* Boston: Houghton Mifflin.

Martin, Bill and Archambault, John. (1989). *Chicka Chicka Boom Boom.* Ill. Lois Ehlert. New York: Simon.

Martin, Bill and Archambault, John. (1988). *Listen to the Rain.* Ill. James Endicott. New York: Holt.

Milne, A. A. (1926). *Winnie-the-Pooh.* Ill. Ernest Shepard. New York: Dutton.

Mora, Pat. (1994). *Listen to the Desert/Oye al desierto.* Ill. Francisco Mora. New York: Clarion.

Nygaard, Elizabeth. (1998). *Snake Alley Band.* Ill. Betsy Lewin. New York: Doubleday.

Orozco, Jose-Luis. (1997). *Diez Deditos: Ten Little Fingers and Other Play Rhymes and Action Songs from Latin America.* Ill. Elisa Kleven. New York: Dutton.

Oxenbury, Helen. (1995). *I See.* Cambridge, MA: Candlewick.

Parish, Peggy. (1963). *Amelia Bedelia.* Ill. Fritz Siebel. New York: Harper & Row.

Parish, Peggy. (1988). *Amelia Bedelia's Family Album.* Ill. Lynn Sweat. New York: Greenwillow.

Pinkney, Brian. (1998). *The Adventures of Sparrowboy.* New York: Simon.

Piper, Watty. (1930). *The Little Engine That Could.* Ill. George and Doris Hauman. New York: Platt & Munk.

Poetry Place Anthology. (1983). New York: Scholastic.

Radcliff, Theresa. (1998). *Bashi, Elephant Baby.* Ill. John Butler. New York: Viking.

Raschka, Chris. (1996). *The Blushful Hippopotamus.* New York: Orchard.

Rattigan, Jama Kim. (1994). *Truman's Ant Farm.* Ill. G. Brian Karas. Boston: Houghton Mifflin.

Reit, Seymour. (1989). *The Rebus Bears.* Ill. Kenneth Smith. New York: Bantam.

Ricklen, Neil. (1997). *Daddy and Me.* New York: Simon.

Ricklen, Neil. (1997). *Mommy and Me.* New York: Simon.

Ryder, Joanne. (1977). *A Wet and Sandy Day.* Ill. Donald Carrick. New York: Harper & Row. Text excerpt copyright © 1977 by Joanne Ryder. Reprinted by permission of Harper & Row, Publishers, Inc.

Schwartz, Alvin. (1972). *A Twister of Twists, A Tangler of Tongues.* Ill. Glen Rounds. Philadelphia: Lippincott.

Sendak, Maurice. (1962, 1991). *Chicken Soup with Rice.* New York: HarperCollins.

Sisulu, Elinor Batezat. (1996). *The Day Gogo Went to Vote.* Ill. Sharon Wilson. Boston: Little, Brown.

Slobodkina, Esphyr. (1940). *Caps for Sale.* Reading, MA: Addison-Wesley.

Stanley, Diane. (1996). *Saving Sweetness.* Ill. G. Brian Karas. New York: Putnam's. Copyright © 1996 by Diane Stanley. Used by permission of G. P. Putnam's Sons, a division of Penguin Putnam, Inc.

Stevenson, James. (1984). *Yuck!* New York: Greenwillow.

Turkle, Brinton. (1965). *Obadiah the Bold.* New York: Viking.

Udry, Janice. (1981). *Thump and Plunk.* Ill. Ann Schweninger. New York: Harper.

Van Allsburg, Chris. (1984). *The Mysteries of Harris Burdick.* Boston: Houghton Mifflin.

Van Laan, Nancy. (1998). *So Say the Little Monkeys.* Ill. Yumi Heo. New York: Atheneum.

Waber, Bernard. (1966). *Lyle and the Birthday Party.* Boston: Houghton Mifflin.

Williams, Vera. (1988). *Stringbean's Trip to the Shining Sea.* New York: Greenwillow.

Wolff, Ashley. (1985). *Only the Cat Saw.* New York: Dodd.

Yabuuchi, Masayuki. (1985). *Whose Baby?* New York: Philomel.

Yashima, Taro. (1958). *Umbrella.* New York: Viking, p. 20.

6

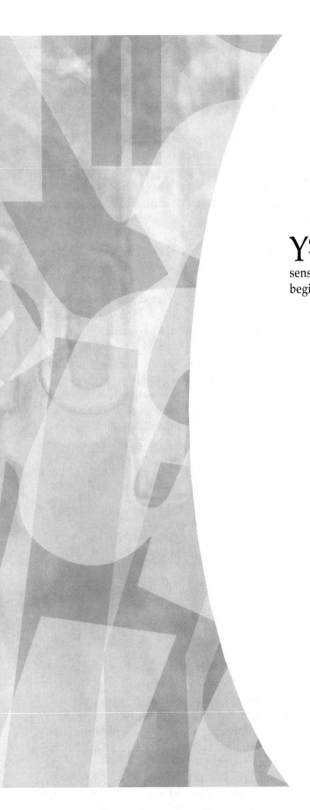

SUPPORTING CHILDREN'S INTELLECTUAL DEVELOPMENT

Young children come to school with a wealth of information. They are attempting to organize that information, make sense of their world, and integrate their experiences. They are beginning to form concepts from isolated pieces of knowledge.

INTELLECTUAL DEVELOPMENT IN YOUNG CHILDREN

A concept is "an idea that represents a class of objects or events" (Coon, 1989, p. 260). It embodies many images and memories that blend to make a meaningful whole. The advantage of developing a system of concepts is that it allows one to process new information by fitting it into a framework. Each impression, object, or event need not be assessed and remembered separately. When children have seen several round objects and have been told that each is a ball, they generalize so that new examples fit into their concept of ball. When they hear the term *heavy* used to describe a box that is difficult to lift, a desk their father cannot move, and an overweight neighbor, they begin to develop a concept of heavy. This learning of concepts is termed concept formation and "refers to the discernment of the properties common to a class of objects or ideas" (Sousa, 1998, p. 421).

Adults are often more aware of young children's ability to conceptualize when they are inaccurate than when they conform to expected perspectives. A four-year-old was told that her grandfather was in the hospital. She asked each day when he would be coming home. After nearly two weeks of frustration, she announced that she wished he could get out of the hospital soon because "I want to see the baby." This child's experiences with hospitals had been limited to expectant mothers making the trip. Her concept of hospital was that of a place where people went to have babies. If Grandpa had gone there, he should be returning with a baby. The problem with the generalization is not with the reasoning, but that it was made on the basis of insufficient examples. When the parent explained that Grandpa was in the hospital because he was sick and that doctors there were trying to help him get well, the child's concept of hospital was enlarged. The changing and enlarging of concepts as new events are experienced and new insights are gained is a continual process.

One task of the day-care professional or teacher is to help young children form accurate concepts. Teachers help by providing materials for the children to manipulate, bringing information to the classroom or center, taking children on trips, and encouraging children to discuss what they have seen. In other words, they provide the raw data from which the children can construct their own concepts. Through questioning, teachers guide children to think about and order what they have experienced.

Simply telling children the concepts you would like them to acquire is seldom effective. It may result in rote learning, but not in real understanding. "Concepts are constructions that must be made by each person for herself. Words, of course, can be given to others" (1983, p. 34) writes Helen Robison, a specialist in early childhood education. Thus the adult may provide the conventional name, but the child must build the concept.

Young children engage in thinking processes that are fundamental in concept formation. They associate ideas, classify, generalize, and reach logical conclusions (Papalia, Olds, and Felman, 1998). Until they are seven or eight years of age, however, children rely more on sensory data than on logic to reach conclusions regarding physical objects. Almost all four-year-olds will look at two short, wide glasses of water equally filled and report that both glasses have the same amount of water. After watching the water from one of these glasses poured into a tall, narrow container, the children will report that the tall glass has more water than the short one or vice versa. The logic that no water has been added or taken away is secondary to the sensory data that after the water is poured from one glass into a taller container, it looks as if the amounts are different. Around the age of seven, children begin to rely on the logic of the situation and will report that the quantities of water remain equal. At this time they are also able to keep more than one attribute in mind, to look at both the height and the width of the containers.

After the age of seven, children are also more likely to use the standard forms of logical reasoning. They will use deductive reasoning, which goes from the general to the particular. "All collies are dogs. This is a collie. Therefore it is a dog." They will use inductive reasoning, which goes from the particular to the general. "Collies, spaniels, boxers, beagles, and terriers all have hair, four legs, and make a barking sound. They are dogs. It is likely that all dogs have hair, four legs, and make a barking sound."

Four- and five-year-olds sometimes use what is termed transductive reasoning (Papalia, Olds, and Felman, 1998, p. 199). They go from particular to particular, without any reference to the general. This often results in faulty conclusions. The child may connect two events in a cause-and-effect relationship simply because they occur together. "The dog ran away. My Daddy was late getting home from work. The dog ran away because Daddy was late."

One four-year-old, reasoning from particular to particular, was not concerned that Santa Claus appeared in three department stores she and her mother went into, nor that he was also stationed in the center of the shopping mall. It did not occur to her that there might be more than one. For her seven-year-old brother, however, the generalization that a man cannot be in two places at the same time led to a questioning of the ever-present Santa and the conclusion that there had to be more than one.

The Swiss psychologist Piaget has concluded that the order in which children's thinking matures is the same for all children, but that the pace varies from child to child (Piaget and Inhelder, 1969). Particularly if you are teaching seven- and eight-year-olds, who are in a period of transition from one stage of intellectual development to another, you may find great variety in the logic children use as they explain what they observe.

Young children engage in intuitive and associative thought as well as rational. An essential aspect of cognitive development is the development of the imagination. Many young children have imaginary playmates. They talk to them, play with them, reserve space for them at the table. The fantasy world may seem real to four- and five-year-olds, and at times they may have difficulty distinguishing between fantasy and reality. The teacher or day-care professional helps them as they develop the ability to differentiate, but at the same time encourages them to use their imaginations.

Children develop their cognitive abilities through interactions with other people. Lev Vygotsky, a Russian psychologist, looked at tasks children could perform independently and at tasks they could perform with assistance but not on their own. He described what he called the Zone of Proximal Development (Vygotsky, 1978), the range beyond the independent level but within the child's potential. Working with guidance from others helps children reach this potential. Teachers provide support, or scaffolding, for children to encourage intellectual growth.

GOALS FOR TEACHING

As in other areas, teaching goals for intellectual growth can be categorized as long-term developmental goals, general goals for an age or grade level, and specific goals for individual children. The long-term goals are those behaviors or competencies that are developed over time and are considered desired patterns of behavior. A long-term goal for intellectual development is that children will continue to acquire new concepts and to refine old ones. Teachers and day-care professionals will be helping children attain this goal throughout the preschool and primary years.

General goals for each grade level are often listed in curriculum guides. At other times they are developed by the teacher as he or she plans an outline for the year's learning. A general goal for the first-grade level is that children will verbalize the criteria they use to classify various sets of objects.

At times you will have specific goals for individual children. An example for a four-year-old might be "Katanya will place the scissors and crayons in the appropriate boxes when she is finished using them." It is an intellectual goal because it requires classification, putting scissors with scissors and crayons with crayons. While most of the children may be doing this, it is a goal for Katanya because she is not yet cognizant of the categorization system being used.

Literature contributes to the achievement of all three types of goals. This chapter focuses on selected long-term developmental goals common to the preschool and primary years. Literature offers opportunities for you to help children grow toward the following goals for intellectual development:

> Children will continue to acquire new concepts and to refine concepts already held.
>
> Children will develop skill in a variety of thinking processes.
>
> Children will expand their powers of logical reasoning.
>
> Children will utilize critical-thinking skills.
>
> Children will engage successfully in problem solving.

As with other areas, these goals can be correlated with national and regional standards. For example, the goal that children will develop skill in a variety of thinking processes fits with Standard 9 of the Standards for School Mathematics (National Council of Teachers of Mathematics, 1989). That standard addresses geometry and spatial sense, and suggests that in grades K-4, the curriculum should be such that students can "describe, model, draw, and classify shapes." Classifying is one of the thinking skills within that goal, and many concept books for children focus on the identifying and classifying of shapes. As you look at standards, look at how these goals and the specific standards mesh.

OPPORTUNITIES BOOKS OFFER
Assisting in the Acquisition and Refinement of Concepts

Young children have many concrete experiences that aid them in the process of developing and refining concepts. Books, both fiction and nonfiction, are another source of information from which children gather data necessary for generalizing, and through which they assess the accuracy of concepts already held.

Giving Information

Literature often provides information that children could not discover through their own manipulations and observations of the environment. Some is in the form of naming what they have observed. Children may know that there are three different kinds of fish in the aquarium, but no amount of watching will teach them what the fish are called. You may want to read books to the children that will provide this information, or you may want to leave the books for them to use themselves. If the children are working with wood, *The Toolbox* (1971) by Anne and Harlow Rockwell is a useful book to have. The premise is a child looking at the tools in a toolbox. Each tool is clearly illustrated, its name given, and its use described. Children can learn the names of the tools they are using and see some other tools as well.

Books may also explain a process. Aliki's *How a Book Is Made* (1986) begins with the question, "Who made this book?" and then proceeds to show all the people involved and what each one does. The combination of text, and cartoon illustrations in which the characters speak, gives both basic information and a feel for the effort and the occasional frustration that go into the preparation of a book. As children write and publish their own books they will find that Aliki's explication of the copy editor's work, the finding of mistakes in typesetting, and the care that goes into the artwork have a very real connection to the writing and publishing that they are doing. They may also relate to the final pages in which a father buys a book as a birthday gift for his child, who is delighted to have a book to read, to smell, and to keep forever.

Many times books will give information about a topic that is familiar to the children but will present new facets of that topic. Children know about television heroes and heroines from having watched their fantastic exploits week after week. *The Bionic Bunny Show* (Brown, 1984) has as its protagonist a rabbit named Wilbur, the star of a television series about a bionic bunny. The story tells about the filming of one episode of the show—from Wilbur's arrival at the studio with only 10 minutes to get his costume and makeup on and finish learning his lines, to his capturing the Robber Rats on film. In the course of the story children see the use of a storyboard, the props used to simulate Wilbur's bionic powers, retakes when he muffs his lines, and various camera angles. At one point the director instructs Wilbur to pose for three shots to be used for the bionic leap, and tells him that the editor will put the shots together so that they look like he had made the leap himself. The book is good fiction as well as being informative. Wilbur, at home after his "bionic" day, is unable to remove a stuck jar lid.

Children can compare shows they watch on television to Wilbur's "Bionic Bunny Show." They can categorize what is real and what is make-believe on the shows they watch; they can create storyboards, composing their own television stories.

With other books, you can present ideas about people, places, and events far removed from the children's own situations. Young children have ideas about different peoples and places from television and from the conversation of the adults around them. Even though their concept of distance is vague, they can learn about different places and people. There should, however, be some point of reference between the children's experiences and those presented in the book. Often this reference point is in the characters' emotions. Most American children listening to *Ali, Child of the Desert* (London, 1997) have never experienced anything like the blinding desert sandstorm that leaves Ali alone, lost from his father and the others traveling to the Moroccan market town of Rissani. They would not know what it is like to ride on a camel, to spend the night at the camp of a goatherd, or to fire a musket to identify their whereabouts. However, they could relate to Ali's fear, and to the comfort he finds in listening to the goatherd's story told before the fire. They may know how it feels to be lost, or to have to decide whether to take a chance or to play it safe. Teachers and day-care professionals presenting such a book would talk with the children about the differences in the ways people live, but stress the similarities of needs and feelings.

Books can help children learn to appreciate cultural diversity. (Illustration from Ali Child of the Desert *by Jonathan London. Illustrations copyright © by Ted Lewin. Used by permission of Lothrop, Lee and Shepard Books, a division of William Morrow and Company, Inc.)*

As you choose books about different peoples, look for those that consider the characters' emotions and motivations. Books that emphasize only "strange" customs or lifestyles may influence children to have negative reactions to people who are different from themselves, rather than to appreciate cultural diversity. *How My Parents Learned to Eat* (Friedman, 1984) does a superb job of presenting different customs, in this case contrasting American and Japanese eating habits. The little girl who tells the story explains that some days her family eats with chopsticks and other days with knives and forks. She goes on to tell about her parents' courtship when her father was an American sailor and her mother a Japanese schoolgirl. Both attempted to learn about the culture and customs of the other. Her father learned to use chopsticks by going to a Japanese restaurant and having the waiter show him. Her mother learned to use a knife and fork from a great-uncle who had visited England. She learned to hold the utensils British style, and then had to change to American style. Both parents felt insecure with their newly acquired skills, but both cared about the other and accepted the cultural differences. The book focuses on the parallel experiences and feelings of the parents.

Past events can be introduced with emphasis being placed on what happened and why it was interesting or important. As children listen to *The Bobbin Girl* (McCully, 1996), a story based on the memoirs of a mill girl in Lowell, Massachusetts, in the 1830s, they can imagine what life was like for the mill workers, many of them children. They can learn about early protests of working conditions and options open to workers who felt they were being treated unfairly. They need not be concerned with understanding fully the period in which the event took place nor the exact location of the place.

You may want to share with children books that represent a variety of American settings. As a beginning step, look at the books of Robert McCloskey, Donald Carrick, Natalie Kinsey-Warnock, and Donald Hall for settings on the Northeast Coast; at those of Byrd Baylor or Pat Mora, or the publications of Rising Moon Press for a Southwest setting; and at the work of Ezra Jack Keats, Lucille Clifton, and John Steptoe for urban settings.

Using Books as Teaching Aids

Some books have qualities that make them visual aids in themselves. This is true of many alphabet, counting, and concept books. *What's Inside?* (Daughtry, 1984) for example, shows pairs of photographs to illustrate "inside" and "outside," with the outside of familiar objects being shown, then what's inside them appearing when the page is turned. Three-year-olds can look at a photograph of socks, for example, and tell "what's inside." The book suggests questions an adult might use with children to encourage them to tell not only what they expect to see, but to describe the object inside, how it got there, and why it is there.

Often a group of books can be used. Suppose you were working on color names with a small group of children. You could begin by showing Hoban's *Of Colors and Things* (1989). Each page has a grid. A different object is shown in each rectangle, except for one rectangle that holds several objects. The single objects are the same color. The objects in the collection are of different colors. Children could identify the objects and the color being featured. They could do a variety of classification activities: objects by color; objects by shape; objects that move; objects that are alive. They might tell which of the objects pictured they have at home. There are opportunities to describe the pictures and to make up stories about them. You might use the book for classifying colors with one group, and for language experience in storytelling with another.

Some teachers help children with color names by having them cut pictures of a certain color from magazines; some have them draw pictures using different shades of the same color; some have days when everyone wears something of a certain color, or when the snack is food of that color; some reinforce color concepts by daily reminders such as calling children to a table by the colors they are wearing.

If you had used some of these ideas, you might then want to use another book that includes color concepts, *Freight Train* (Crews, 1978). This book shows a train with each car a different color. The print matches the color of the car. Reading almost like a poem, the story names the cars, then shows the train traveling.

The last illustration shows only smoke. There are strong possibilities for vocabulary development and for information about trains as well as for color. If you were using the book for the color aspects, you might read it several times. After they had heard it once, the children could supply the name of the color as each appeared. Then they could say as much as they remembered while you read. Finally, you could have them repeating the phrases in choral speaking, capturing the rhythm of a train. There is reinforcement of the color aspect while at the same time giving enjoyment in the sound of language.

You might further involve children with books and with color by sharing books that play with and build on the concept. *My Box of Colors* (Siomades, 1998) asks in rhyme if particular objects and animals would either act or be considered differently if their color were changed. Would spiders still be scary if they were bright colors? The illustrations show the changed colors. The book concludes with a page of inchworms of many different colors and asks if "I" were not the color I am, would "you" still be my friend?

If you find several books on the same topic, you will have more opportunities for approaching that subject from a variety of perspectives and for involving children in a variety of ways.

Look at books for ways in which they can be used by the children themselves. Alphabet books can be shared by two children learning to recognize letter sounds. They take turns opening the book, seeing the letter, naming its sound or sounds, and naming the objects pictured. Counting books can be used by having a child open the book randomly, see the numeral, select that many counters, then place one counter on each object to see if he or she counted correctly. *Anno's Counting House* (Anno, 1982), although it requires an introduction by an adult, can be used by pairs of children to count and categorize as different numbers of people appear in the cutout windows of two houses.

Books need not be used in their entirety. Select those portions that fit your goals. In the preceding section a book was mentioned for naming tools. If you had used it, and were using tools in the classroom, you might share just one page from *Crash! Bang! Boom!* (Spier, 1972) a book about sounds. Each double page has 15 to 20 objects and the sounds they make, classified by where the sounds occur. You would use only the page that shows tools and the sounds they make. Children could try naming the tools and could listen for the sounds to see if they would describe them as the author does. It might lead to their wanting to look at other pages, but if not, it would still have met your original goal.

Sharing Books That Stimulate Projects

Books can be used as direct models for further work. Children who had seen and listened to *Crinkleroot's Guide to Walking in Wild Places* (Arnosky, 1990) would know what it was like to observe carefully on a walk and keep a record of those observations. Pages with sketches and descriptions of the things Crinkleroot sees are interspersed with the narrative of Crinkleroot's walk. Children can observe on a walk of their own, perhaps just touring the school grounds. They can make notes and sketches of what they observe. At the end of the day, they can go back and read what they have said and see what they have noticed. This would be an opportunity for them to summarize what they learned through their own observation.

Another project could be modeled after *Where Does My Cat Sleep?* (1982) by Norma Simon. Illustrated with pencil drawings, this book shows the various places the family cat sleeps. Children might watch their own pets for a short period of time, carefully noticing their behavior. Later, they can dictate or write short descriptive passages, or show through illustration what they've discovered.

You may choose books to introduce an area of study or a new learning center. In one third grade in New England, the teacher set up a display with books about prairie life. *My Prairie Year* (1986) by Brett Harvey told of the everyday life in the Dakota Territory in the late 1800s; *Dakota Dugout* (Turner, 1985), with its poetic language, told of the same period; *Christmas on the Prairie* (Anderson, 1985) with its slightly earlier setting, described the holiday customs; *A Prairie Boy's Winter* (Kurelek, 1973) set on the prairie in the 1930s, captured the imagination with its paintings by William Kurelek, and *Prairie Town* (Geisert, 1998), showed a thriving contemporary midwestern town throughout the course of a year. The children were asked to look at the illustrations and to compare them with their own homes and the contemporary New England countryside.

When the teacher then read *Sarah, Plain and Tall* (MacLachlan, 1985), about Anna and Caleb and their hopes that Sarah, who was visiting from Maine, would stay and marry their father, the children had an idea of how the land might have looked, and why Sarah would have

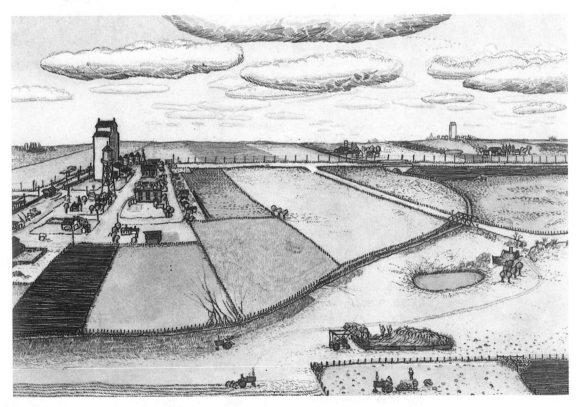

Children can look at a region presented in illustrations and compare it to where they live. (From Prairie Town *by Bonnie and Arthur Geisert. Illustrations copyright © 1998 by Arthur Geisert. Reprinted by permission of Houghton Mifflin Company. All rights reserved.)*

missed the coast and the blues and grays of the ocean. The presentation of effective and var-ied art—two books illustrated with black-and-white drawings, one with detailed colored drawings, one with photographs, and one with colorful paintings—and the reading of a well-written story set the stage for a unit of study on the prairie and provided ideas for the many activities that followed.

Sometimes a book will catch the children's fancy even if you have not planned it as an introduction to further work. Be open to children's responses so that you can take advantage of what some have termed the *teachable moment,* that unplanned yet perfect opportunity to ex-tend children's knowledge and thinking skills. Remember also that fiction can be as effective as nonfiction in providing a stimulus for study.

Reinforcing Concepts

Just as some books can be used to introduce ideas, others serve to reinforce concepts, or to add further information to a topic children have already explored through direct experience. The concept book *Over, Under & Through* (Hoban, 1973) is excellent for reinforcing children's un-derstanding of these terms and the other prepositions demonstrated in the book. Only the word is given, with photographs illustrating the concepts. For *in* and *on* the pictures show a cat sitting *in* the window, *on* the sill; strawberries *in* a basket; a child putting a letter *in* a mailbox; a chick perched *on* a child's hand; a bird *on* its perch *in* a cage; two boys *in* a telephone booth. Children can look at the pictures and describe what is happening.

Reinforcement may be simply reading a book. If you read *Rosie's Walk* (Hutchins, 1968), you would also be reinforcing these same concepts of *in, or, under,* and *through* because they are used to describe Rosie's walk around the barnyard. You would choose to read the book with no further work, knowing that children are hearing the terms used in context.

You can use books to answer questions that have been raised, or to give further infor-mation. If the children are fascinated by dinosaurs, you might want to extend their knowledge by bringing in books that show how scientists piece together information to learn about topics they cannot observe directly. *Digging Up Dinosaurs* (Aliki, 1981) and *Dinosaur Bones* (Aliki, 1988) both show how paleontologists discover, retrieve, and analyze fossils. They show the mistakes as well as the successes as the scientists attempt to make sense of what has been found. You might also share *Big Old Bones: A Dinosaur Tale* (Carrick, 1989), a fiction story in which Profes-sor Potts attempts to reconstruct a dinosaur from the bones he has found, with some astonish-ingly inaccurate results.

Often you will find books that describe experiences similar to those children in your group have had. Read some of these so that they can see how others have reacted, and com-pare their feelings and their knowledge with those of characters in books. *The New Baby at Your House* (Cole, 1998) has a warm and loving tone as it welcomes a new baby and describes both positive and negative feelings of older siblings. This is an appropriate book if one or more of the children have new brothers or sisters. Children can describe what they have noticed about the baby in their family and how it compares to what the book says.

Clarifying Misconceptions

One of the ways people learn is by expressing their ideas to others and listening to the com-ments and reactions that result. Teachers who listen to what children are saying will find that children's talk often reveals misconceptions they may have. The teacher is then in a position to help the children clarify their thinking.

There are times when books are very helpful in this endeavor. There are other times when direct experience makes far more sense. One first-grader commented to her teacher that "Mr. Gaddis and Mrs. Crabtree sure are good singers." The teacher was puzzled at first over the child's assessment of the musical abilities of the principal and the school secretary. Her pause was filled by further comment from the child. "I like the way they sing those songs at noon." Then she knew. As a special project, music was being played on the intercom system during the lunch hour. The only voices that the child had heard on the intercom were those of the principal and the secretary. Therefore, if there was singing at noon, they must be the ones doing it. This was one of those times when direct experience was far better than a book. The teacher explained that the singing was coming from the office, but that the secretary was playing a tape, not singing herself. Then that afternoon, the teacher and several of the children went to the office to see just how it was done.

Other times, however, a book may be the better aid for clarifying concepts. A five-year-old came to school telling about an old movie he had seen on television. The cars were funny, he said, and nobody dressed like that. Earlier the class had been talking about *real* and *make-believe* stories. He gave his judgment of the film, saying it had to be make-believe.

There are several concepts involved in his statement. There is the distinction between realism and fantasy. He is including in realism only that which he has experienced himself and knows to be possible. Everything else is fantasy. The teacher will help him define other criteria for deciding the differences between realism and fantasy, perhaps emphasizing the aspect of impossibility within fantasy. Also involved in his statement is a lack of realization that changes are occurring continually, in cars, in clothing, in people, in himself.

Both of these involve more than a single experience, and both can be explored through books. In the regular period for literature, the teacher might read a book of historical fiction, perhaps one of the Obadiah books by Brinton Turkle (1965, 1969). She could introduce it by saying, "This story is about people who lived long ago." After comparing their lives and feelings with those of Obadiah, the children could be asked if they thought there was anything make-believe about the story.

On another day, the teacher could look for a book that deals specifically with changes over time. One such book is *Maisie* (Schertle, 1995). The book opens with Maisie's birth and shows her growing up on the farm, attending school where desks have inkwells and the boys wear knickers. Maisie marries, moves to a suburb where she and her husband raise their children. A sign at the train station gives the year as 1942 when Maisie waves to one of her children, now grown and leaving home. When Maisie's grandchildren arrive to visit, they are wearing bell-bottom pants, fringed jackets, and headbands. The book closes as the whole family, including the great-grandchildren, celebrate Maisie's ninetieth birthday. Maisie and her youngest great-granddaughter walk to the stream, where they catch, then release, a frog, just as Maisie had done when she was a child so many years earlier.

Children can be encouraged to talk with their parents and grandparents about what they wore and what they liked to do when they were five- and six-year-olds. Parents and grandparents could be invited to come to the class and tell the children about their childhoods. Children might bring family snapshots to school, comparing them. Another project might be for the children to bring in pictures of themselves as babies and as toddlers, seeing how they have changed already. Many classrooms keep charts of children's growth during the year. This could be a time for seeing what growth had occurred thus far in the year.

When you hear children making comments that indicate misconceptions, you will have several decisions to make. First is whether to approach it directly, such as the teacher did with the singing on the intercom, or to make notes to provide experiences at a later time, as was suggested for the comments about the old movie. You will also have to decide how to go about giving the child some feedback. Generally speaking, it is better if you can provide firsthand experience for the children. Not all concepts, however, lend themselves to this approach. Sometimes, also, you will need preparation time to do a good job. Literature can be particularly useful for giving information and for providing a starting point for discussions and projects.

If you are just beginning to work with young children, books that are written for them may give you some help in gearing your expectations to the children's level of understanding. *Maisie,* for instance, does not require any real concept of how much time has passed, only that as time passes, things change. This is in keeping with young children's concept of time, which is not clearly developed. Look at several books on the same topic, plan your presentation to be on what seems a reasonable level in terms of the books and what you know of your class, then listen carefully to the children's reactions.

Developing Skill in a Variety of Thinking Processes

Books provide the opportunity for children to engage in many thinking processes. Obviously, almost any picture book you select could be used to help children improve in their observational skills. Some, however, are better than others.

Observing

If you want children to become aware of detail, you might select a book by Peter Spier. His illustrations are filled with action and rich detail. In *Noah's Ark* (1977) the front endpaper begins the story, with Noah tending his vineyard while armies fight and cities burn. The building of the ark continues through the title page. Then the text appears, a translation of "The Flood" by Jacobus Revius. The illustrations continue the saga, with no further text. Children can look at the story once, then go back and pick out the details. Do they notice the one owl that stays awake during the day? They might do a matching game. Can they find the pairs of animals? Guide questions from you can direct their attention to patterns within the detail. For example, ask them if they can find the work that Noah is doing on each page, or have them tell what things they see outside the ark.

The color illustrations in *What Color is Camouflage?* (Otto, 1996) stimulate attention to detail in a different way. The text describes the protective coloration and strategies of both prey and predators. Children looking at the photos will want to both find the animal and identify the protective device.

If you are using a book such as this, you will want to be certain that the children can see the illustrations easily. This will mean working with a few children at a time or using a filmstrip. Filmstrips can make it easier for children to see, and any single frame can be shown for as long as necessary.

Some books are observational guessing games. For children four to six, *Each Peach Pear Plum* (Ahlberg, 1978) challenges them to find a storybook or nursery rhyme character hidden in each of the illustrations. A couplet tells about one character, then says "I spy" another one. Children can look for Bo Peep, Mother Hubbard, Jack and Jill, and others. If you have shared it with one child, you might then ask the child to choose a friend and play the game again with the friend doing the guessing. The "I spy" technique can be applied to other books. One child can look at an illustration and tell something he or she spies in the picture, and another then finds the object. This and similar guessing games can be played with *1 Hunter* (Hutchins, 1982) the counting book in which a lone hunter walks through the jungle unaware of the many partially hidden animals, and *Pigs in Hiding* (Dubanevich, 1983) a story of trickery in which the hidden pigs are found only when food lures them into the open.

For the sheer challenge of it, for you as well as for children of any age, try finding Waldo in the books *Where's Waldo?* (1987), *Find Waldo Now* (1988) and the many other Waldo books by Martin Handford. Waldo, in his red and white striped shirt and stocking cap, travels to highly populated places, with nearly all the population in evidence. The task is to find Waldo in the crowd of people, all engaged in activities appropriate to the place and time. In the first book, Waldo goes on a worldwide hike, visiting beaches, ski slopes, and other vacation spots; and in the second, he travels back to various periods in history, such as ancient Egypt or "On Tour with the Vikings." The Waldo books can be used in a variety of ways. First, of course, is finding Waldo in each illustration. After that, children can look for the things Waldo mentions in his postcards or notes, then for things listed at the end of the book. Children could make their own lists of things to look for, perhaps trading lists with others in the group. They could write about some of the small dramas played out on each page. In one railway scene, there is a car stopped on the railroad tracks because of engine trouble. In the middle of the gold rush days there is a clown on a unicycle. There is humor in text and illustration that makes these books appealing to a wide range of ages. Waldo explains, for instance, that the Crusaders finally returned home because they ran out of clean T-shirts. Young children concentrate on finding Waldo and seeing all the activity, while older viewers may respond more to much of the humor.

Another book that requires careful observation and involves guessing is *Look Book* (Hoban, 1997). Readers open the book to find that they are seeing part of something through a square hole that has been cut from a black page covering a photograph. They try to guess what they are seeing. When they turn the white page, the whole photograph shows, and they can see how accurate their guesses were. Seven- and eight-year-olds, as well as intermediate-grade children, can play the game. They might tell why they guess what they do before they turn the page. Some might want to make their own Look Books, cutting pictures from magazines and making cover sheets with windows showing only a portion of the picture.

Also using the technique of a hole in one page for viewing the pages before and after it is *Peek-A-Boo!* (Ahlberg, 1997), appropriate for three- and four-year-olds. It adds the element of perspective—for example, the left page will show a baby, with what the baby sees showing through the hole in the page on the right. When the page with the hole is turned, the viewer is now the character on the right, and it is the baby being seen.

Children who enjoy this will also enjoy *Look Closer!* (Ziebel, 1989) where they can see the close-up photograph of an everyday object. A question about the object provides a clue to its identity. Thus they are asked about what keeps their teeth clean as they see the photograph of the bristles on a toothbrush. A turn of the page answers the question and presents a new one.

Perspective plays a role in *Round Trip* (Jonas, 1983) and in *The Look Again . . . and Again, and Again, Book* (Gardner, 1984). For both, as the book is turned, and perspective altered, the illustrations also change. In *Round Trip,* the black-and-white illustrations show a trip from a small town, through the country, to the city. When reversed and read backwards, the story is of the trip home. The now upside-down illustrations reverse foreground and background to create new images. *The Look Again . . . Book* asks the reader to turn each page so that illustrations are viewed from all four sides. A caption tells what the graphic could be from each of the angles. Both books are intriguing and both encourage careful and flexible observation. Older children might want to create some graphics of their own.

You may want children to observe the action in a story, or the reactions of characters. Wordless picture books are excellent for this purpose, for the entire story is told through illustrations. Children can describe what is happening. In books such as *A Boy, A Dog, A Frog, and a Friend* (Mayer, 1971) in which facial expressions play a prominent part, children could tell how a character feels. The body language of a finger in front of a closed mouth could be explained, or the boy's reaction when he falls in the water.

Keep in mind the maturity level and the experience of the children as you select books for practice in observing. The four-year-old will need less complex books with clearer illustrations than the seven-year-old. Alphabet and counting books can be used with very young children just for looking at the objects pictured. Books such as *Anno's Journey* (Anno, 1978), with more detail and a somewhat unfamiliar setting (Europe), would be better used with slightly older children, who can make sense of the journey through the countryside, villages, and cities, and who may recognize some familiar characters in the background. There will still be detail they will miss. In one illustration, among the many activities around the farm, three characters are attempting to pull a huge turnip out of the ground, and a rider, accompanied by a man on foot, is headed, spear in hand, for the windmill. Some but not all will know the folktale about the enormous turnip, but doubtless it will be only the teacher who recognizes Don Quixote.

Hypothesizing

Children can be guided to hypothesize about any book being shared with them. They can look at the cover or listen to the title and make reasonable guesses about the book's possible content. They can tell what they think a character will do next, or what might happen next. Children should be taught that hypothesizing means taking into account the information one already has in order to make predictions and should be encouraged to give reasons for their conjectures. They should be taught that hypothesizing is a logical process and is not simply telling what one would like to happen, or what one thinks would be interesting. Their guess may prove to be exactly what the author has done with plot, but it may turn out to be quite different though still reasonable. The object is to suggest logical possibilities, not to match exactly the author's choice.

Some books have plots that naturally invite hypothesizing. *Bub, or the Very Best Thing* (1994) by Natalie Babbitt opens with the King and Queen arguing about what is really the best thing for the young Prince, whom the King thinks has too many toys and the Queen thinks is given too many lessons. Since both want what is best for him, the King begins to seek the answer in books and the Queen and the Prince go around the castle asking. The Prince says only "bub." Children can see the pattern developing as each character sees the best thing is something related to him or her. The gardener says that the best thing is sunshine. They can make guesses about what each character will advise, and make their own hypotheses about what the Prince is saying and what really would be best. If you are wondering, the best thing is love.

Other books have such strong characterization that this becomes the basis for children's hypotheses about what will happen next. They see the character's feelings and reactions and use these, as well as their own understanding of the emotions, for anticipating actions. After hearing any one of the George and Martha books by James Marshall (1997), children will know that neither George nor Martha will do anything knowingly that might hurt the other, and that both are tolerant of the other's foibles.

Still other books will have an identifiable pattern to the actions within them. *It's Just Me, Emily* (Hines, 1987) has the pattern of something being done or heard, and each time it is Emily who is teasing and playing games with her mother. Folktales, also, often have cumulative or repetitive plots. Children thus may use the generalizations they make about the literary form itself to suggest what will happen.

Comparing

Literature offers the opportunity for children to engage in structured comparisons. As noted in chapter 4, when you group books in pairs, units, or webs, you are setting the stage for the children to compare and contrast one work of literature with another.

Suppose you have been talking with the children about city life and country life. The time would be ideal to have children compare books about the topics as well as the topics themselves. *Town & Country* (Provensen, 1987) gives many specific examples of everyday experiences in a large city and in a rural area. The color illustrations add even more detail. Experiences a child might have, such as attending school, are compared and contrasted. After looking carefully at the book and listening to the text, children might compare their own lifestyles with the two described in the book. Are they living in a rural or urban area? If neither fits, how is their home like the country? How is it like the city? What sounds do they hear at night? What do they do for fun during bad weather?

The next day, you might share a much shorter and simpler book, *Tall City, Wide Country* (Chwast, 1983). The illustrations are uncluttered, and the text consists of only one phrase per page. The book can be read forwards or backwards, for the phrases string together in a long sentence either way. When reading about the "wide country," you hold the book horizontally, and the pictures spread out like the flat farmland, with a wide expanse of land and sky. When reading about the "tall city," you hold the book vertically, and the pictures rise like the skyscrapers and elevators they depict. This book presents one basic contrast between country and city. The country is wide; the city, tall.

Then you put both books side by side and ask the children how the two books are alike and how they are different. They respond immediately that both are about city and country life, and that both compare the two. They note the detail in *Town & Country* and the format of *Tall City, Wide Country*. You ask them what they think each author wanted the reader to know about country life and city life. Then you ask if the pictures for each book help the author get his or her point across. You show the illustrations for both books again, and ask what they now notice about the format in *Town & Country*, which also uses vertical versus horizontal to symbolize the difference between city and country, but does so by the placement of text as well as by the shape of illustration. The city section has vertical illustrations with the text running down the side. The country section has horizontal illustrations with the text running beneath the pictures. You close by showing the end papers for *Tall City, Wide Country*. In the front is a horizontal double-page spread of farmland, and in the back is a vertical double-page spread of tall buildings. Ask the children to design endpapers for *Town & Country* that would show another contrast between city and country.

Think about what topics your class is exploring, or what areas you plan to introduce. When you have several books on that topic, read through them for possibilities of activities or questions that will lead children to compare them. There should be some points of similarity. For example, *North Country Night* (San Souci, 1990) and *A South African Night* (Isadora, 1998) both focus on animal life at night, so children can compare the types of animals, the settings, and how each illustrator conveyed a feeling of place.

Occasionally there are companion books that are excellent for children to compare. Such a set is *City in the Summer* (1969) and *City in the Winter* (1970) both by Eleanor Schick. Chil-

In Johannesburg, stores close for the night, but in the Kruger National Park, the animals are stirring. (Illustration by Rachel Isadora from her A South African Night. *Copyright © 1998 by Rachel Isadora. Used by permission of Greenwillow, a division of William Morrow, Inc.)*

dren can tell how the city looks different, how people's dress is different, and what sort of activities go on in the city in the summer and in the winter as pictured in the books. They can compare the days of the boy in each story, one who spends the day with an elderly neighbor at the beach, and the other who spends the day inside with his grandmother. They might draw or paint what their house and yard look like in the summer and in winter, or dictate a story telling one thing they do only in the summer and another that they do only in winter. Another interesting set of books that can be compared in this same manner is *Island Winter* (Martin, 1984) and *Summer Business* (Martin, 1984). The same protagonist, Heather, appears in both books. *Island Winter* shows what happens on the island in winter when all the visitors have gone home, while *Summer Business* shows the activities of Heather and her friends in the summer when the island is filled with tourists.

Sometimes changes are pictured within a single book. The role of the teacher in this case is to draw attention to the changes and to the qualities that remain the same. In *The Story of an English Village* (1979) John Goodall shows in watercolor illustrations the changes that take place in a village in England in each century from the 14th to the 20th. He shows an outdoor scene and an indoor scene for each century, and two for the 20th. Third-grade children can flip the pages back and forth to see what has changed from one picture to the next. They might be directed to name as many changes as they see from the 14th to the 15th centuries, with the teacher listing the changes on the board. Then as they look at the illustrations for the 16th century, they can follow their list and see what is happening and continue this procedure for each set of pictures. They might be directed to look only at clothing, or transportation, or the food shown, and tell what is happening on that one subject as the time passes. Skill in comparing both builds on and strengthens skill in observing.

Classifying

Some books lend themselves readily to experiences in classification. *Shapes and Things* (Hoban, 1970) is one that does. The book is a collection of photograms, photographs made by placing objects directly on photographic paper and exposing them to sunlight. When the paper is processed, the result is a series of silhouettes. In this book, which has no text, the objects have been grouped by the author. Children looking at a page might first try to identify the objects—on one page, a hammer, a nail, three screws, a screwdriver, and a wrench—and then tell what the objects have in common. In doing this they are recognizing the class to which the objects belong and naming it. They might also be asked to tell one other object that would fit with those pictured. Children can be encouraged to do some classification of their own by collecting items that they think would fit together for another page of the book. For books such as this one, the teacher should feel free to select only those pages that will have meaning for the class. There is no need to "do" every page. The teacher will also want to work with small groups of children, so that all will be involved in the thinking and discussion.

Other books have the potential if the teacher sees it. One teacher had read *Frog and Toad Are Friends* (Lobel, 1970) to her kindergarten class. At one point in the book Toad and Frog return home from a walk and Toad discovers that he has lost a button off his jacket. He and Frog go back over all the places they have walked in an attempt to find it. Frog and several other animals find buttons, but none matches the one Toad lost. They find a black one but his was white. They find one with two holes but his had four. Attribute by attribute, it is narrowed to a white, four-holed, big, round, thick button. They cannot find it, and an angry Toad returns home to find the button on the floor of his living room. Concerned about the trouble he has caused his friend, he sews on the button, and also sews on all the other buttons that they have found. The next day he gives his button-covered jacket to Frog.

After the children had heard the story, the teacher produced a large box of buttons. Each child decided what kind of button he or she would look for. They used the classifications Toad used, such as thick or white, but chose others as well. They tried to see how many they could find that would fit their classification, then compared their collections of buttons. Later some of the children made pictures of Frog wearing Toad's jacket. They used fabric from the scrap box to make jackets, then pasted buttons all over the jackets for decoration. It was an enjoyable experience for the children, in part because of the story, and in part because the teacher selected a classification activity that was challenging but not overwhelming for the children. They pasted the buttons on their pictures because the teacher knew that attempting to sew small buttons onto cloth would have been frustrating for them.

Children might be asked to classify some of the stories they have heard. If the categories are not given, children can begin to develop their own. They might divide stories into those they liked and those they did not like; they might divide them into stories that could happen and stories that were make-believe; it might be stories about animals and stories about people. The teacher guides the children to think about the content of the stories, and perhaps the format, and to find a variety of ways of classifying them.

Organizing

Another thinking skill is that of organizing. Young children can be helped to organize by learning to sequence events. Cumulative folktales, as well as many contemporary stories, are a rich source of material. Reconstructing the sequence of events in some tales, however, is a difficult task because knowing the order of events is a matter of straight recall. For example, the little boy in *In the Forest* (Ets, 1944) is followed by a series of animals who join him for his walk before his father arrives. That he happens across the elephants before the bears is of no consequence. Likewise, the animals whom the little chicken in *Chicken Forgets* (Miles, 1976) meets on his way to pick blackberries could be met at any time, for each distracts him with new advice. It is necessary only that the robin be the last he meets, for the robin shows him the blackberries, and he is successful in getting the basket of wild berries that his mother has requested.

Other tales have a patterned order to the events. The goats in *The Three Billy Goats Gruff* (Rounds, 1993) get progressively larger, until the third and largest is able to crush the ugly troll. The poor villager whose house is too small with his mother, his wife, and his six children follows the rabbi's advice in *It Could Always Be Worse* (Zemach, 1976). He brings larger and larger animals into the house with them, from chickens to the cow. When the largest has been there for a week and the man can stand it no longer, the rabbi advises him to put all the animals out. Suddenly the house is larger and quieter, and life is sweeter. Again a pattern of increase in size makes the sequence of events easier to remember.

Sometimes the pattern is that of chronological order. In *Charlie Needs a Cloak* (dePaola, 1973) Charlie first shears his sheep, then washes the wool, then cards it. From spring to fall Charlie proceeds with the preparation of his cloak: dying the yarn, weaving the cloth, sewing the pieces of fabric. When winter comes, he has completed his new cloak. In *The Little Red Hen* (Galdone, 1973) the hen gets no help from the cat, the dog, or the mouse from the time she finds the grains of wheat until she has planted them, harvested them, had them ground into flour, and used the flour to bake a cake. The others are willing to help her eat the cake, but having done all the work by herself, the hen decides to eat the cake by herself. The sequence in these books reflects the way something is made. Children repeating the sequence can infer as well as recall what comes next.

Children can be given the need to sequence the events in a story by making plans to interpret it dramatically. After talking about the characters in the story, they can review what happened first, second, and so on. They may tell how they know when each event in the story happened.

You might encourage children to work with sequencing by telling the story on a felt-board, then letting children retell it. Put all the figures in random order on a table beside the feltboard. Children can take turns selecting the piece that should go up next and telling that part of the story.

Another technique to engage children in sequencing is to have the children draw a picture of one thing that happened in the story. Working with only three or four children, ask each to tell what is happening in his or her picture. Then ask them which of the pictures would come first in the story, which next, and so on until all are ordered. Work with small groups, in part because the more pictures there are the more complex the task becomes, and in part because children tire of listening to many children describing their pictures.

Sequencing should allow the children to be active participants, doing something that requires them to use the sequence, not just answering the question, "Then what happened?"

Applying

Books that describe "how to do it" can be used to give children the opportunity to apply what they are hearing or reading. The directions need to be clear and the project within the capabilities of the children. Roche's *Loo-Loo, Boo, and Art You Can Do* (1996) gives clear and careful directions for a variety of art projects including face masks, potato prints, and collages. The materials are easily available. Directions are accompanied by paintings of the bespectacled Loo-Loo and her dog Boo. A teacher might read one project from this already clear book to a small group of first- or second-graders, then give it to them to follow the directions for a different project. They should be able to make the projects on their own.

A teacher of kindergarten children might read the directions, then work with the children, reading each direction again as the children complete each step. A book such as this might also be used as a model for children to dictate or write their own directions for making something. Can they describe the procedure clearly enough for another child to follow the directions? They can find out by trying it.

Expanding the Ability to Reason Logically

For young children, basic experiences with logical thinking involve working with *if . . . then* propositions. If it rains, then we will stay inside all day. If she forgets to return the permission slip, then she cannot go on the picnic. Certainly much literature involves such cause-and-effect relationships. Letting children predict what will happen next in a story is one technique for encouraging them to think about causality and to determine when connections between events appear reasonable.

David Macaulay's *Why the Chicken Crossed the Road* (1987) takes the cause and effect to delightful extremes. It opens by stating that one day a chicken ran across the road, but in doing so startled some cows, who then ran across a bridge, which collapsed onto a train. The series of events comes full circle eventually to answer the question, with the final two pages showing the same illustrations as the first two—the chicken is crossing the road, the cows are stampeding across the bridge.

There are also books for children that center on errors in logical reasoning, on trickery, or on the humor of exaggeration. Reading them gives children a chance to feel superior to the book characters because they know what is going on. They recognize the absurdity and enjoy their own mastery of the situation. Young children know that it is an alligator that has hatched, not a chicken, in Lionni's *An Extraordinary Egg* (1994), even though the confident frog Marilyn insists that she knows what it is because there are some things you "just know."

Then there is Mr. Higgins in *Clocks and More Clocks* (Hutchins, 1970). When he finds a clock in the attic he wants to know if it tells the correct time. He buys another clock to check, but when he walks from clock to clock, he notices that they always read about 1 minute different. After buying several more clocks and having the problem continue, Mr. Higgins invites the Clockmaker to check the clocks. As the Clockmaker goes from clock to clock and compares their time to that on his watch, he finds that they are all correct. Mr. Higgins is so impressed that he buys the watch. And, of course, there is Cully Cully, the hunter who, in *Cully Cully and the* Bear (Gage, 1983), shoots at a bear but only nicks its nose. A chase begins that eventually culminates with hunter and bear circling a tree, each convinced that there are several of the other.

Some books depend on the illustrations to show the absurdity of what the characters are saying. In *Nothing Ever Happens on My Block* (Raskin, 1971), Chester Filbert sits on the curb and complains about how dull his block is. Readers looking at the illustrations see a neighborhood alive with action. A witch appears in different windows, a robber is chased by a policeman, children play, fires burn, houses are rebuilt. Still Chester sits, oblivious to the excitement around him. In *Treed by a Pride of Irate Lions* (Zimelman, 1990), readers can see that father's reports of his attempts to find the one animal that likes him are rather understated, considering that even the family dog is generally seen biting father's leg.

Some books show cleverness in the form of trickery. The Haitian tale *Bouki Dances the Kokioko* (Wolkstein, 1997) shows first the king's plan to enjoy dancing, free of any expense, every evening by announcing that anyone who can dance the Kokioko will be given five thousand gourdes. Only the king knows the steps to this dance he has invented, but many come to try. Then Malice, the gardener, sees the king dancing, learns the steps, and goes to his friend Bouki with a proposition. He will teach Bouki the steps and Bouki can win the prize. The plan works, even though Bouki has never trusted Malice. As he returns home with the sack full of money, Bouki meets Malice, who teaches him another dance, this one to words that say if he had no sense, he will put his sack down and dance. Not listening to the words, Bouki puts the sack down, closes his eyes, and performs the new steps, allowing Malice's wife to slip quietly away with the sack. Malice assures Bouki that he tried to warn him not to put the sack down.

Topsy-Turvies (Anno, 1970) subtitled "Pictures to Stretch the Imagination," makes a direct challenge to the reader. Each illustration in this wordless picture book in some way plays with perspective. Second- or third-graders might look at the illustrations and try to see what is strange about them. Some may be able to verbalize the impossibilities, such as a maze where people enter right side up but exit upside down, or a building where the inside and the outside walls seem to shift positions.

For each of these books, the children's responses during the reading may give you an indication of whether or not they understand the twists of logic that the authors employ. You may want to ask children, "If you could tell Mr. Higgins (or another character) one thing that you think would help him, what would it be?" Children can then demonstrate their command of the situation.

Encouraging Critical Thinking

The term *critical thinking* is being used in this text to indicate thought that involves seeing relationships between events, inferring what is not stated directly, analyzing events within a story, synthesizing evidence, and evaluating both the content and the quality of literature. It is thinking that goes beyond the literal level. Two strategies for encouraging children to think critically are the asking of higher level questions and the planning of questions and activities that will elicit divergent responses.

Asking Higher Level Questions

One widely used system for categorizing questions is that of Sanders (1966). Based on the work of Benjamin Bloom (1956), this system categorizes questions by the kind of thinking required to answer them. Thus a question that asks for information directly stated in a reading is a *memory* question because it requires recall, or memory, to answer.

The other types of questions described by Sanders and applied to literature are as follows:

Translation—These questions ask children to translate an idea in a book into a different form, such as telling part of the plot in one's own words, or drawing a picture of a scene that has been described.

Interpretation—These questions ask children to draw inferences, explain cause-and-effect relationships, or compare facts. Children must process the information presented in a book.

Application—These questions ask children to apply ideas from literature to new situations.

Analysis—These questions ask children to respond based on a knowledge of logical reasoning processes or knowledge of literary forms.

Synthesis—These questions ask children to combine pieces of information in a new way.

Evaluation—These questions ask children to both develop and apply standards for judging a work.

Discussion is one means of exploring ideas within books.

Thinking about questions in this way is useful because it helps a teacher provide variety in the kinds of thinking he or she asks children to do and because it emphasizes forms of critical thinking.

To plan a series of questions for a discussion with young children, decide first on the focus of your questions. Then devise questions that will develop this focus and that will engage children in such processes as interpretation or synthesis or evaluation. For each of your higher level questions, think of what memory level information it encompasses. You may need to ask several memory questions to establish the children's base of literal understanding before progressing with your key questions.

Suppose you had read *Dark and Full of Secrets* (Carrick, 1984) to a group of children. In the story, Christopher and his father are canoeing, and Christopher doesn't want to swim because he can't see what is in the water nor what might be on the bottom. He has enjoyed swimming in the ocean, but the pond is dark and full of secrets. His father laughs at first, but then brings a mask and snorkel for each of them so that Christopher can dive down, see what is there, and overcome his fears. The experiment works so well that after lunch Christopher ventures out by himself. Fascinated with what he is seeing, he is unaware that he is drifting into deep water. When he tries to stand to clear his mask, he cannot touch bottom. He tries treading water, but then something brushes his foot, causing him to gasp. His mask and mouthpiece fill with water, and he panics. He calls for his father, but it is his dog Ben who comes to the rescue. Holding onto Ben's tail, Christopher makes it to shallow water. His father has come to the water's edge, where he reminds Christopher not to go out so far and makes certain that Christopher is not hurt. Once he has caught his breath, Christopher is again enthusiastic about the fish he has seen. He is also no longer afraid of the dark pond water, even though he cannot see into it from the surface.

As you think about a focus for your discussion you consider the theme of overcoming fear, the idea of where families go and what they do on vacations, and the topic of pond life. You decide to use the idea of fear because it is so central to the story, and because young children will be able to identify with that emotion. You decide to begin with two memory questions to establish the children's grasp of the facts of the story and then proceed to questions requiring other thinking skills. You plan to ask the following questions:

1. Why was Christopher afraid to swim in the pond?
2. What did his father do to help?
3. Do you think this was a good idea? Why? Why not?
4. What else might his father have done to help?
5. Later in the story Christopher is afraid again. How do the illustrations help you know how Christopher is feeling? (Show illustrations.)
6. How is this fear different from his fear of what might be in the pond?
7. Tell us about a time when you were afraid. What did you do? Did anyone help you?
8. When do you think it might be good to be afraid?
9. Do you think Christopher will go snorkeling again? What makes you think this?
10. Do you think there may be other times when Christopher will be afraid? Tell why you think this.

You will have guided children in a discussion about their own emotions, starting and ending with the story itself, and making your final question one that concludes the unit. In the process, children will have been asked memory (1,2,7), interpretation (6,9,10), analysis (5), synthesis (4), and evaluation (3,8) questions. After you have led several similar discussions, categorize the kinds of questions you have been asking. If there are types that you never seem to use naturally, work in a conscious manner to develop your questioning skills in the appropriate areas.

Try to state your questions as concisely as possible so that young children don't lose the thread of meaning or answer one part before you finish the entire question. Pace yourself to wait for answers. If the question requires thought, then you must give children time to think. Silence makes some teachers and day-care professionals nervous, so they answer the question themselves, or ask another question to fill the space. You can train yourself to give children time to think. Some teachers count to themselves until they establish the habit of allowing the children time to respond.

Not every book should be followed by questions. Discussion is only one means of exploring a book's ideas more fully. You will want a balance among discussion, activities, and no follow-up at all.

Planning for Divergent Responses

Another way of classifying questions and activities is to assess the number of *correct* responses that may be offered. Convergent questions have only one best, or right, answer. Divergent questions have more than one acceptable response. The question, "What did Christopher's father do to help?" is a convergent one because the book clearly shows what his father did, and thus there is only one correct answer. The question, "When do you think it might be good to be afraid?" is a divergent one because both the answer given and the rationale behind it would vary from child to child. Sometimes a question is convergent because it is on a literal level, but at other times it may be a higher level question for which the evidence is so strong that there appears to be only one reasonable answer.

Activities, like questions, may call for either convergent or divergent responses. The book *Jumanji* (1981) by Chris Van Allsburg captures children's imaginations and lends itself to many divergent activities. It is the story of Judy and Peter who are left home alone for the afternoon and get bored. They decide to take a walk in the park where they find a game titled *Jumanji: A Jungle Adventure Game*, with a notation on the box in what appears to be a child's handwriting that the game is free, and that the instructions should be read carefully. They take the game home, discovering during play that the events described on the gameboard really do happen. The lion actually does appear in their house and attack; the monkeys steal food; and the monsoon season arrives. When Judy finally reaches the Golden City, thus winning the game, the house is cleared of all its jungle inhabitants and order is restored. The children take the game back to the park leaving it just where they found it. The book closes with two other children picking up the box.

Children might write a new set of directions for the game, perhaps suggesting a different method of ending the game. (In the book the game could only be ended by someone winning.) They might create a story about a time when one of their board games became like *Jumanji*, or one about who would pick up the game next and what would happen. They might construct a board game using only events that they would like to see happen for each of the squares, or they might role-play Judy and Peter explaining to their parents what was going on as though the parents had returned in the middle of the game. All of these activities would encourage a variety of responses.

Divergent questions and activities stimulate children to consider a broad range of possibilities, both as they think through responses themselves and as they listen to the ideas and opinions of others. Many of the activities suggested throughout this book call for divergent responses. Look particularly at the section in chapter 9 entitled "Stimulating Creativity in Art, Music, and Movement."

Engaging in Problem Solving

You will be helping children regularly to define and solve their problems. How can Jim get a turn at jump rope? What can Susan do to keep Jill from teasing her? What could the class make as gifts for their parents?

Literature presents ample opportunities for children to define and suggest possible solutions to problems book characters have. Their solutions may not be the one or ones chosen by the book characters. It is important to help children realize that there may be many solutions to a problem, and that solutions may be evaluated according to their consequences. Some may be problems much like those the children themselves have; others may be totally in the realm of fantasy.

Three-year-olds can listen to *The Blanket* (Burningham, 1975), a very short story in which the boy cannot find the blanket he always takes to bed with him. His mother and father look for it, but finally he finds it under his pillow. Children can tell about any toy or object that they usually take to bed with them. Then present two problems for them to solve. First, if you could not find your toy at bedtime, where would you look? And second, if you did not find it, what could you do?

Five-year-olds could find another blanket problem more challenging. *Owen* (Henkes, 1993) has owned and loved his yellow blanket Fuzzy since he was a baby. Urged on by the rather nosey neighbor, Mrs. Tweezers, Owen's parents try several strategies to get rid of it, but Owen outsmarts them. The blanket fairy, for example, cannot take the blanket and leave something in its place because Owen stuffs the blanket into his pajamas when he goes to bed. When Owen must go to school, Owen's parents take a firm stand—Owen cannot take it with him. Owen's mother thinks of a solution—she cuts the blanket into many squares and hems the edges. Now Owen has many handkerchiefs that he can take with him wherever he goes.

Primary children might listen to "The Squad Car" (Neville, 1966). In this poem, the narrator buys his older brother Woody a windup Dick Tracy squad car for his birthday. The boys at the birthday party play with the car, but then the key gets knocked down a hole in the wall. They try fishing it out with a magnet, but that does not work. They write the toy company for another key, but the company does not answer. They try other keys, but none fit. The squad car sits on the shelf, still shiny.

Children can be asked to brainstorm ideas for what might be done about the squad car. In brainstorming they try to think of as many ideas as they can, not stopping to evaluate any of the ideas. The teacher lists their suggestions on the board or on chart paper. Once all their ideas are listed, the teacher leads a discussion in which they look at each suggestion and tell what might happen if that were done. As a group they decide on which solution they think has the most merit. Then the teacher reads "The Last Part of the Squad Car Story." This tells about the family's solution to the problem. A year later, when Woody is having another birthday party, they decide to get him another Dick Tracy squad car. Then he will have two cars and one key. When the car comes, the key is welded into the keyhole. So Woody keeps the new squad car and gives the old one to his brother. The poem ends when they make a new friend who trades his key to an old squad car for three marbles. You can point out to the children that none of the solutions in the poem worked. It was the unexpected arrival of someone new with a key that made the car usable again.

Because most stories involve some problem that must be solved, it is possible to stop in almost any story and ask children what the problem is and what solutions they might have for it. Doing this on a regular basis, however, is likely to lessen their enjoyment of the literature. You will want to select only one or two books each month to use for problem solving. Look for ones where the problem is fairly clear.

Thinking of solutions to problems of book characters can be gamelike. The idea is to present alternatives, not to guess what happened in the book. For this reason, you might well ask some of your problem-solving questions after a book has been completed. Questions would then ask what a character might have done other than what he or she actually did do.

SUMMARY

Young children come to school with a wealth of information. They are attempting to organize that information, to make sense of their world, to integrate their experiences. They are actively constructing concepts and engaging in the thought processes that are fundamental in concept formation. Until they are six or seven years of age, children tend to rely more on sensory data than on logic to reach conclusions regarding physical objects. They may also engage in transductive reasoning, going from particular to particular without reference to the general, resulting in faulty conclusions. They engage in intuitive and associative thought as well as the rational, and find enjoyment in imaginative thought and play.

The following long-term goals are appropriate for the intellectual growth of young children:

Children will continue to acquire new concepts and to refine those already held.

Children will develop skill in a variety of thinking processes.

Children will expand their powers of logical reasoning.

Children will utilize critical-thinking skills.

Children will engage successfully in problem solving.

Books offer opportunities to help children in the acquisition and refinement of concepts. Table 6–1 suggests appropriate teaching strategies. Often information that children could not discover on their own is presented in books. Other books, particularly concept books, are in themselves teaching aids, for they organize information logically and present it with illustrations that add to children's understanding. Literature can both stimulate children to explore a topic and provide reinforcement for knowledge they have acquired through direct experience.

Literature furnishes an opportunity for children to engage in many thinking processes. They may observe carefully as they look at the illustrations in picture books; they may make predictions about what will happen in a book; they may compare two books on similar topics or themes; they may classify objects portrayed in books, or classify the stories themselves; they may organize, using sequence as the organizing factor; and they may apply the information given in books, following directions that they have read themselves or that the teacher has read to them.

Much literature involves cause-and-effect relationships. Because of this, children are able to gain experience in predicting outcomes using an if . . . then approach to logic. There are also books that center on errors in logical reasoning or on trickery that give children the chance to show their grasp of the absurdity described.

Children can be encouraged to think critically and to engage in problem solving through carefully planned questions and activities. After establishing a firm base of literal understanding, the teacher guides the children to use higher levels of thinking, making inferences and judgments. He or she plans questions and activities that elicit divergent rather than convergent responses, praising children for new and thoughtful ideas.

Table 6–1. Supporting Children's Language Development

Developmental Goals	Teaching Suggestions	Recommended Literature	
Children will continue to acquire new concepts and to refine those already held.	Share concept and informational books. Have children compare experiential knowledge with information from books. Use books as visual teaching aids. Read several books on the same topic to provide more than one perspective. Let children use books themselves to reinforce concepts. Use books as a stimulus for further exploration. Present books that reinforce concepts already being acquired. Read books that may help clarify misconceptions.	**Ages 3–5:** Cole Crews Daughtry Hoban Hoban Rockwell Siomades Spier	*The New Baby at Your House* *Freight Train* *What's Inside?* *Of Colors and Things* *Under and Through* *The Toolbox* *My Box of Colors* *Crash! Bang! Boom!*
		Ages 5–8: Aliki Aliki Aliki Anno Arnosky Brown Carrick Friedman Harvey Kurelek London MacLachlan McCully Schertle Turner	*Digging Up Dinosaurs* *Dinosaur Bones* *How a Book Is Made* *Anno's Counting House* *Crinkleroot's Guide to Walking in Wild Places* *The Bionic Bunny Show* *Big Old Bones* *How My Parents Learned to Eat* *My Prairie Year* *A Prairie Boy's Winter* *Ali, Child of the Desert* *Sarah, Plain and Tall* *The Bobbin Girl* *Maisie* *Dakota Dugout*

Table 6–1.   *(continued)*

Developmental Goals	Teaching Suggestions	Recommended Literature	
Children will develop skill in a variety of thinking processes.	Have children observe and describe detail in illustrations. Have children play observational guessing games with book illustrations. Let children tell the story in wordless picture books. Encourage children to make predictions. Engage children in structural comparisons of books. Compare changes in illustrations within a single book. Share books that classify objects. Build classification activities based on books. Dramatize stories so that children must organize by sequencing events. Let children apply the information in "how to do it" books.	**Ages 3–5:** Ahlberg Ahlberg Chwast Dubanevich Galdone Hines Hoban Hutchins Lobel Rounds Schick Schick Spier Zemach	*Each Peach Pear Plum* *Peek-a-Boo!* *Tall City, Wide Country* *Pigs in Hiding* *The Little Red Hen* *It's Just Me, Emily* *Shapes and Things* *1 Hunter* *Frog and Toad Are Friends* *The Three Billy Goats Gruff* *City in the Summer* *City in the Winter* *Noah's Ark* *It Could Always Be Worse*
		Ages 5–8: Anno Babbit dePaola Gardner Goodall Handford Handford Hoban Isadora Jonas Martin Martin Mayer Roche San Souci Ziebel	*Anno's Journey* *Bub, or the Very Best Thing* *Charlie Needs a Cloak* *The Look Again . . . Book* *The Story of an English Village* *Find Waldo Now* *Where's Waldo?* *Look Book* *A South African Night* *Round Trip* *Island Winter* *Summer Business* *A Boy, A Dog, A Frog, and a Friend* *Loo-Loo, Boo, and Art You Can Do* *North Country Night* *Look Closer*

Table 6–1. *(continued)*

Developmental Goals	Teaching Suggestions	Recommended Literature	
Children will expand their powers of logical reasoning.	Let children predict what will happen next in a story. Have children discover errors in reasoning in books or trickery or humor.	**Ages 3–5:** Gage Lionni Zimelman **Ages 5–8:** Anno Hutchins Macaulay Wolkstein	*Cully Cully and the Bear* *An Extraordinary Egg* *Treed by a Pride of Irate Lions* *Topsy-Turvies* *Clocks and More Clocks* *Why the Chicken Crossed the Road* *Bouki Dances the Kokioki*
Children will utilize critical-thinking skills.	Ask questions about literature that are above the literal level. Plan questions and activities that will elicit divergent responses.	**Ages 5–8:** Carrick Van Allsburg	*Dark and Full of Secrets* *Jumanji*
Children will engage successfully in problem solving.	Let children define problems book characters have. Have children brainstorm possible solutions to problems. Encourage children to evaluate possible solutions in terms of consequences. Let children engage in imaginative and humorous problem solving.	**Ages 3–5:** Burningham Henkes **Ages 5–8:** Neville	*The Blanket* *Owen* "The Squad Car Story"

Extending Your Learning

1. Select a book by Anne and Harlow Rockwell or by an author of your choice. Tell how the book can contribute to children's concept development.

2. Read three picture books that are set in the same region of the United States. Describe the image of this part of the country that emerges.

3. Select five realistic picture books about animals. Make plans to use at least three of them with children.

4. Share with two or three children one of the books mentioned in chapter 5 that requires the children to observe closely. Compare their responses to the book.

5. Select a picture book appropriate for first- or second-graders. Develop a set of questions to use when discussing it. The majority of questions should be above the memory level and all should be sequenced logically.

6. For a single picture book, describe two activities that would evoke divergent responses.

7. Select three books from the list of recommended children's books at the end of this chapter. Tell how each of these might support a child's intellectual growth.

8. Read from any two of the recommended references at the end of this chapter. Identify three central concepts related to children's development that would be useful for you, as a day-care professional or teacher, to know.

RECOMMENDED REFERENCES

Bergen, D. Ed. (1987). *Play as a Medium for Learning and Development.* Portsmouth, NH: Heinemann.

Bredekamp, S., and Copple, C. Eds. (1997). *Developmentally Appropriate Practice in Early Childhood Programs.* Washington, DC: National Association for the Education of Young Children.

Bukatko, D., and Daehler, M. (1998). *Children's Development: A Thematic Approach.* 3rd ed. Boston: Houghton Mifflin.

Dixon-Krauss, L. (1996). *Vygotsky in the Classroom.* White Plains, NY: Longman.

Donaldson, M. (1978). *Children's Minds.* New York: Norton.

Furth, H., and Wachs, H. (1975) *Thinking Goes to School.* New York: Oxford University Press.

Gardner, H. (1993). Anniversary ed. *Frames of Mind: The Theory of Multiple Intelligences.* New York: Basic Books.

Healy, J. (1987). *Your Child's Growing Mind: A Guide to Brain Development and Learning.* Garden City, NY: Doubleday.

Mussen, P., Conger, J., Kagan, J., and Huston, A. (1990). 7th ed. *Child Development and Personality.* New York: Harper & Row.

Papalia, D., Olds, S., and Felman, R. (1998). *Human Development.* 7th ed. Boston: McGraw-Hill.

Siegler, R. (1998). *Children's Thinking.* 3rd ed. Upper Saddle River, NJ: Prentice-Hall.

Sousa, R. (1998). *Cognitive Psychology.* 5th ed. Boston: Allyn & Bacon.

Vygotsky, L. (1978). *Mind in Society: The Development of Higher Psychological Processes.* Cambridge, MA: Harvard University Press.

Wadsworth, B. (1989). 4th ed. *Piaget's Theory of Cognitive and Affective Development.* White Plains, NY: Longman.

Wood, D. (1988). *How Children Think and Learn.* New York: Basil Blackwell.

RECOMMENDED CHILDREN'S BOOKS

Alexander, Lloyd. (1992). *The Fortune-Tellers.* Ill. by Trina Schart Hyman. New York: Dutton.

Allard, Harry. (1977). *Miss Nelson is Missing.* Ill. James Marshall. Boston: Houghton Mifflin.

Anno, Mitsumasa. (1987). *Anno's Math Games.* New York: Philomel.

Carle, Eric. (1987). *A House for a Hermit Crab.* Natick, MA: Picture Book Studio.

Conrad, Pam. (1995). *Call me Ahnighito.* Ill. Richard Egielski. New York: HarperCollins.

Coucher, Helen. (1991). *Tigress.* New York: Farrar.

Demi. (1997). *One Grain of Rice.* New York: Scholastic.

Dorros, Arthur. (1993). *Radio Man, A Story in English and Spanish.* New York: HarperCollins.

Hopkinson, Deborah. (1993). *Sweet Clara and the Freedom Quilt.* Ill. by James Ransome. New York: Knopf.

McDermott, Gerald. (1992). *Zomo the Rabbit.* San Diego: Harcourt.

Mollel, Tololwa. (1997). *Anansi's Feast.* Ill. Andrew Glass. New York: Clarion.

Provensen, Alice and Martin. (1987). *Shaker Lane.* New York: Viking.

Rathman, Peggy. (1995). *Officer Buckle and Gloria.* New York: Putnam's.

Selsam, Millicent. (1995). *How to be a Nature Detective.* Ill. Marlene Hill Donnelly. New York: HarperCollins.

Shannon, George. (1997). *True Lies: 18 Tales for You to Judge.* Ill. John O'Brien. New York: Greenwillow.

Tafuri, Nancy. (1997). *What the Sun Sees/What the Moon Sees.* New York: Greenwillow.

Torres, Leyla. (1993). *Subway Sparrow.* New York: Farrar.

Tunnell, Michael. (1997). *Mailing May.* Ill. Ted Rand. New York: Greenwillow.

Van Allsburg, Chris. (1979). *The Garden of Abdul Gasazi.* Boston: Houghton Mifflin.

Van Laan, Nancy. (1998). *Little Fish Lost.* Ill. by Jane Conteh-Morgan. New York: Atheneum.

PROFESSIONAL REFERENCES CITED

Bloom, B. (1956). *Taxonomy of Educational Objectives.* New York: Longman.

Coon, D. (1989). *Introduction to Psychology.* 5th ed. St. Paul, MN: West Publishing Co.

Papalia, D., Olds, S., and Felman, R. (1998). *Human Development.* 7th ed. Boston: McGraw-Hill.

Piaget, J. and Inhelder, B. (1969). *The Psychology of the Child.* New York: Basic Books, Inc.

Robison, H. (1983). *Exploring Teaching in Early Childhood Education.* Boston: Allyn & Bacon.

Sanders, N. (1966). *Classroom Questions: What Kinds?* New York: Harper & Row.

Sousa, R. (1998). *Cognitive Psychology.* 5th ed. Boston: Allyn & Bacon.

Vygotsky, L. (1978). *Mind in Society: The Development of Higher Psychological Processes.* Cambridge, MA: Harvard University Press.

CHILDREN'S LITERATURE CITED

Ahlberg, Janet and Allan. (1978). *Each Peach Pear Plum.* New York: Viking.

Ahlberg, Janet and Allan. (1997). *Peek-A-Boo!* New York: Viking.

Aliki. (1981). *Digging Up Dinosaurs.* New York: Crowell.

Aliki. (1988). *Dinosur Bones.* New York: Crowell.

Aliki. (1986). *How a Book Is Made.* New York: Crowell.

Anderson, Joan. (1985). *Christmas on the Prairie.* Ill. George Ancona. New York: Clarion.

Anno, Mitsumasa. (1982). *Anno's Counting House.* New York: Philomel.

Anno, Mitsumasa. (1978). *Anno's Journey.* New York: Collins World.

Anno, Mitsumasa. (1970). *Topsy-Turvies.* New York: Weatherhill.

Arnosky, Jim. (1990). *Crinkleroot's Guide to Walking in Wild Places.* New York: Bradbury.

Babbitt, Natalie. (1994). *Bub, or the Very Best Thing.* New York: HarperCollins.

Brown, Marc and Laurene Krasny. (1984). *The Bionic Bunny Show.* Boston: Little, Brown.

Burningham, John. (1975). *The Blanket.* London: Jonathan Cape.

Carrick, Carol. (1989). *Big Old Bones: A Dinosaur Tale.* Ill. Donald Carrick. New York: Clarion.

Carrick, Carol. (1984). *Dark and Full of Secrets.* Ill. Donald Carrick. New York: Clarion.

Chwast, Seymour. (1983). *Tall City, Wide Country.* New York: Viking.

Cole, Joanna. (1998). *The New Baby at Your House.* Ill. Margaret Miller. New York: Morrow.

Crews, Donald. (1978). *Freight Train.* New York: Greenwillow.

Daughtry, Duanne. (1984). *What's Inside?* New York: Knopf.

dePaola, Tomie. (1973). *Charlie Needs a Cloak.* Englewood Cliffs, NJ: Prentice-Hall.

Dubanevich, Arlene. (1983). *Pigs in Hiding.* New York: Four Winds.

Ets, Marie Hall. (1944). *In the Forest.* New York: Viking.

Friedman, Ina R. (1984). *How My Parents Learned to Eat.* Ill. Allan Say. Boston: Houghton Mifflin.

Gage, Wilson. (1983). *Cully Cully and the Bear.* Ill. James Stevenson. New York: Greenwillow.

Galdone, Paul. (1973). *The Little Red Hen.* New York: Seabury.

Gardner, Beau. (1984). *The Look Again . . . and Again, and Again, Book.* New York: Lothrop.

Geisert, Bonnie and Arthur. (1998). *Prairie Town.* Boston: Houghton Mifflin.

Goodall, John. (1979). *The Story of an English Village.* New York: Atheneum.

Handford, Martin. (1987). *Where's Waldo?* Boston: Little, Brown.

Handford, Martin. (1988). *Find Waldo Now.* Boston: Little, Brown.

Harvey, Brett. (1986). *My Prairie Year.* Ill. Deborah Logan Ray. New York: Holiday.

Henkes, Kevin. (1993). *Owen.* New York: Greenwillow.

Hines, Anna Grossmickle. (1987). *It's Just Me, Emily.* New York: Clarion.

Hoban, Tana. (1997). *Look Book.* New York: Greenwillow.

Hoban, Tana. (1989). *Of Colors and Things.* New York: Greenwillow.

Hoban, Tana. (1973). *Over, Under & Through.* New York: Macmillan.

Hoban, Tana. (1970). *Shapes and Things.* New York: Macmillan.

Hutchins, Pat. (1970). *Clocks and More Clocks.* New York: Macmillan.

Hutchins, Pat. (1982). *1 Hunter.* New York: Greenwillow.

Hutchins, Pat. (1968). *Rosie's Walk.* New York: Macmillan.

Isadora, Rachel. (1998). *A South African Night.* New York: Greenwillow.

Jonas, Ann. (1983). *Round Trip.* New York: Greenwillow.

Kurelek, William. (1973). *A Prairie Boy's Winter.* Boston: Houghton Mifflin.

Lionni, Leo. (1994). *An Extraordinary Egg.* New York: Knopf.

Lionni, Leo. (1960). *Inch by Inch.* New York: Astor-Honor.

Lobel, Arnold. (1970). *Frog and Toad Are Friends.* New York: Harper & Row.

London, Jonathan. (1997). *Ali, Child of the Desert.* Ill. Ted Lewin. New York: Lothrop.

Macaulay, David. (1987). *Why the Chicken Crossed the Road.* Boston: Houghton Mifflin.

MacLachlan, Patricia. (1985). *Sarah, Plain and Tall.* New York: Harper.

McCully, Emily Arnold. (1996). *The Bobbin Girl.* New York: Dial.

Marshall, James. (1997). *George and Martha: The Complete Stories of Two Best Friends.* Boston: Houghton Mifflin.

Martin, Charles. (1984). *Island Winter.* New York: Greenwillow.

Martin, Charles. (1984). *Summer Business.* New York: Greenwillow.

Mayer, Mercer and Marianne. (1971). *A Boy, A Dog, A Frog, and a Friend.* New York: Dial.

Miles, Miska. (1976), *Chicken Forgets.* Ill. Jim Arnosky. Boston: Little, Brown.

Neville, Mary. (1966). "The Squad Car" in *Woody and Me.* Ill. Ronni Solbert. New York: Pantheon.

Otto, Carolyn. (1996). *What Color is Camouflage?* Ill. Megan Lloyd. New York: Harper.

Provensen, Alice and Martin. (1987). *Town & Country.* New York: Viking.

Raskin, Ellen. (1971). *Nothing Ever Happens on My Block.* New York: Atheneum.

Roche, Denis. (1996). *Loo-Loo, Boo, and Art You Can Do.* Boston: Houghton Mifflin.

Rockwell, Anne and Harlow. (1971). *The Toolbox.* New York: Macmillan.

Rounds, Glen. (1993). *The Three Billy Goats Gruff.* New York: Holiday.

San Souci, Daniel. (1990). *North Country Night.* New York: Doubleday.

Schertle, Alice. (1995). *Maisie.* Ill. Lydia Dabcovich. New York: Lothrop.

Schick, Eleanor. (1969). *City in the Summer.* New York: Macmillan.

Schick, Eleanor. (1970). *City in the Winter.* New York: Macmillan.

Simon, Norma. (1982). *Where Does My Cat Sleep?* Ill. Dora Leder. Chicago: Whitman.

Siomades, Lorianne. (1998). *My Box of Colors.* Honesdale, PA: Boyds Mills Press.

Spier, Peter. (1972). *Crash! Bang! Boom!* Garden City, NY: Doubleday.

Spier, Peter. (1977). *Noah's Ark.* Garden City, NY: Doubleday.

Turkle, Brinton. (1965). *Obadiah the Bold.* New York: Viking.

Turkle, Brinton. (1969). *Thy Friend, Obadiah.* New York: Viking.

Turner, Ann. (1985). *Dakota Dugout.* Ill. Ronald Himler. New York: Macmillan.

Van Allsburg, Chris. (1981). *Jumanji.* Boston: Houghton Mifflin.

Wolkstein, Diane. (1997). *Bouki Dances the Kokioko.* Ill. Jesse Sweetwater. San Diego: Harcourt.

Zemach, Margot. (1976). *It Could Always Be Worse.* New York: Farrar.

Ziebel, Peter. (1989). *Look Closer!* New York: Clarion.

Zimelman, Nathan. (1990). *Treed by a Pride of Irate Lions.* Ill. Toni Goffe. Boston: Little, Brown.

7

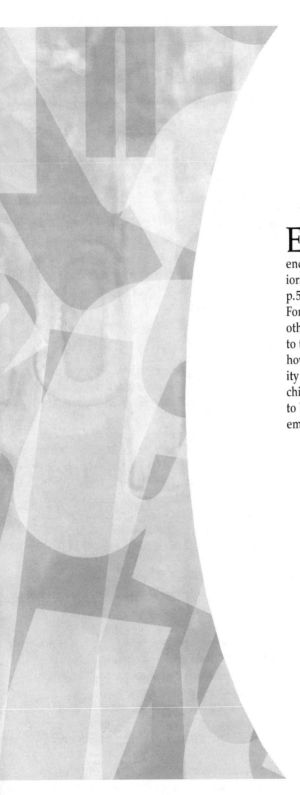

SUPPORTING CHILDREN'S PERSONALITY DEVELOPMENT

Emotions, values, ways of perceiving, and feelings about self are all a part of personality. Papelia defines personality as encompassing "a person's overall pattern of character, behavioral, temperamental, emotional, and mental traits" (1998, p.58). Some aspects of personality are genetically influenced. For example, children who are physically attractive often find others reacting to them in positive ways, and this helps them to think positively about themselves. The social environment, however, plays a greater role in the development of personality than does the biological inheritance of an individual. A child raised in a society that stresses competition is more likely to become competitive than is a child raised in a society that emphasizes sharing and cooperation.

PERSONALITY DEVELOPMENT IN YOUNG CHILDREN

Erikson (1986) seeks to explain personality growth by describing how human beings respond to potential conflicts at specific periods in their lives. He posits eight stages in a total lifespan, of which the first four are most applicable for young children. The first stage, the first year of life, is critical in that it is during this period that children develop trust, which leads to later feelings of security. The conflict is between trust and mistrust. Trust develops when the primary caregiver responds warmly and lovingly to the child.

During ages two and three, children struggle for autonomy. The conflict is between autonomy and doubt. Children want to explore, to do things for themselves, to be in control. Children who have been encouraged by their parents to be independent at this age are more highly motivated to achieve when they reach school than are children who were not rewarded for such behavior.

At ages four and five, children have a conflict between initiative, wanting to carry out activities on their own, and guilt over what they would like to do. For nursery school and kindergarten teachers, this is a time when children can be encouraged to make choices, to take action on their own.

From ages six to eleven, children struggle with industry versus inferiority. Productivity becomes important. They want to complete tasks, to learn what is expected of them, to gain recognition for their efforts. These are crucial years in the development of self-concept and self-esteem.

Self-concept refers to individuals' ideas of their own capabilities, what they see themselves as being able to do. *Self-esteem* is the value individuals put on themselves, how worthy they feel themselves to be. Both self-concept and self-esteem are influenced strongly by the way in which the others react to and treat the individual. Children who know that the important people in their lives value them think more highly of themselves. They become more confident, and this confidence leads them to attempt difficult tasks and to anticipate success. Teachers and day-care professionals can aid the development of positive self-concepts in children by suggesting tasks that are challenging yet attainable. They can show also that they value and support each child's efforts.

The development of the self-concept begins early at home. So too does another learning based on children's interactions with their parents. This is the process of identification, in which an individual accepts the characteristics and beliefs of another as his or her own. A boy may walk just like his father, or a girl use the mannerisms and voice inflection of her mother. This early identification with the parent of the same sex leads to sex typing, the adoption of the sex roles considered appropriate in a particular culture (Brewer, 1997). As sex roles become far less restricted, day-care professionals and teachers will want to provide children with ways of identifying their own sexuality while remaining free from sex role stereotypes.

Identification is a lifelong process. As children encounter a larger social world, they begin to identify with models other than their parents. Teachers, friends, and characters from books, movies, and television all may be emulated. Children thus acquire a complex system of beliefs and behaviors.

Children just coming to school are learning about themselves and their emotions as well as about their physical and social environments. One may learn that his temper tantrum, which effectively provided attention at home, is ignored at school. Katz notes that "Children's ability to regulate their emotions is a major contributor to the development of both peer status and friendships"(1997, p. 4). Another child may find that many of her classmates, like her, are afraid of the dark and fear being left alone. As children begin to learn ways of expressing and of managing their feelings, they learn what is acceptable behavior in a particular situation and what is not. In seeking to help children, the adult will want to provide experiences that will enhance each child's self-concept, that will help each child function as independently as possible, and that will help each child deal successfully with his or her emotions.

GOALS FOR TEACHING

Teaching goals for personality development can be categorized into long-term developmental goals, into general goals for each grade or age level, and into specific goals for individual children. Long-term goals describe behaviors or competencies that are developed over time and that are thought of as desired patterns of behavior. The long-term goal that children will attempt new tasks willingly is reflective of personality development because the willingness to attempt something new is related both to self-concept and to the need to achieve.

General goals for each grade level are often listed in curriculum guides. Personality goals and social goals may be combined under a heading of *affective goals,* distinguishing them from the *cognitive,* or intellectual, goals. One such goal for kindergarten is that children will function independently in several work areas within the classroom. It is more specific than a long-term goal and is keyed to the needs and abilities of children of this age. All, or nearly all, of the children in the group will be expected to reach this general goal.

Goals for individual children are even more specific. You will develop these goals as you work with a group and come to know each child. "Steven will overcome his fear of the coatroom and go in by himself to get his coat" is an individual goal, one developed by a teacher who saw Steve's need, a need that was not shared by other children in the classroom.

There are times when your use of books will help in the achievement of all three types of goals. This chapter focuses on long-term developmental goals, ones that are common to the preschool and primary years. Books offer opportunities for you to help children grow toward the following goals for personality development:

> Children will weigh evidence and make appropriate choices.
>
> Children will set tasks for themselves and will complete tasks they begin.
>
> Children will develop positive and realistic self-concepts.
>
> Children will develop feelings of self-worth and self-esteem.
>
> Children will begin to recognize their own values and to choose from among values.
>
> Children will understand their emotions and will express them in socially acceptable ways.

As with other areas, these goals can be correlated with national and regional standards. For example, the goal that children will develop positive and realistic self-concepts relates to

Theme IV, Individual Development and Identity, in the ten themes that provide the organizational framework for the social studies standards developed by the National Council for the Social Studies (1994). That standard focuses on the idea that "personal identity is shaped by one's culture, by groups, and by institutional influences" (1994, p. 25). It is suggested that in the early grades, activities such as observing brothers and sisters and older adults and engaging in "remembering past achievements and projecting oneself into the future" are useful because "young learners develop their personal identities in the context of families, peers, schools, and communities." As you look at national standards, or those for your region or school district, look for ways in which these goals and the specific standards mesh.

OPPORTUNITIES BOOKS OFFER
Involving Children in Choice-Making

"Would you like to hear a story?" is more often a rhetorical than a real question in a classroom or center. Children are not being asked for their preferences; they are being informed that it is story time and the adult is going to read to them. Listen to your own way of telling children about planned activities. If they have no choice, try to introduce the activity in statement rather than question form. "Today I am going to read a story about George and Martha," or "Please get ready for story time. I think you'll be surprised at how this story ends."

Presenting Options

Begin to think of ways that children can be encouraged to make choices. If you present children with a choice, you must be willing to accept their decision. This means that objectionable options should not be presented. As you share literature with children, there are many opportunities for them to make choices and ways for you to structure the choice-making so that all the alternatives are acceptable. Some are very simple ones. Children may be asked which story or poem they would like to hear read or reread. Narrow the choices to two or three and have all available. Poetry especially lends itself to this sort of choice-making, for poems become better liked as they become more familiar. One nursery school teacher constructed a poster board *poetry rabbit.* In its basket the rabbit had a collection of paper eggs of different sizes, colors, and designs. On each egg was a poem about spring. The three- and four-year-olds could select an egg and the teacher would read the poem on it. After several days, the children knew which egg had the poem they particularly liked. Rereading poems helps children find poetry pleasurable, as well as giving them a chance to choose.

Sometimes the choice will be one of sequence, of what will be done first. Would they like to hear the story before or after snack time? Would they like to have art first, or story time first? These choices are group ones, where each child's opinion counts, but which are decided by what the majority prefers. Many others can be individual choices, where one child makes the choice and where the decision involves only the child's behavior.

One area for choice is whether the child wants to listen to a story or not. It may be in the form of announcing that all who are ready for a story should come to the story circle, or should go in the corner where an aide is sitting with the book to be read. The principal of one elementary school reads to children during the lunch period each day. She announces as they come into the lunchroom what the book for that day will be. Children who wish to hear it go with her to another room, listening to the story as they eat their lunches. She reports that the number of listeners fluctuates, and that different children attend. The choice is theirs, each day, whether they would like to hear that story, or whether they would like to eat in the lunchroom, visiting with friends as they eat. They are responsible for their choices. Once made, they cannot change rooms that day. However, they are not asked to make a long commitment. In a classroom or day-care facility, children can be given a choice of listening or not by having a listening center set up in the room. Those who want to hear a story or poem may go to the center; those who do not can engage in other quiet activities.

Encouraging Book Selection

Young children can select which book they would like to take with them from the library to their room, or perhaps from the classroom or center to their homes. Some classes have periods for *sustained silent reading* or *Drop Everything and Read* (DEAR), a period when everyone, including the teacher, reads the books of his or her choice. The purpose for sustained silent reading is to show that recreational reading is valued by the school, as well as to give each child the opportunity to read in a quiet setting. In preschool and primary classes, where some children are reading and some are not, this might be a brief period of looking at books following a trip to the library. Their choices of books become important because the children know there is a special time for looking at them.

In schools or centers where book clubs are permitted or in those that have book fairs, children can select books not just to borrow but to keep. In these cases, they can purchase paperback books at moderate prices. The Reading Is Fundamental program also provides children with books of their own.

Planning Several Activities

If you have planned to have an activity following the reading of a book, think about having two or three independent activities and allowing each child to choose one of them. Suppose you have read *Officer Buckle and Gloria* (Rathmann, 1995) to a class of kindergarten children. In this story, Officer Buckle visits schools giving talks on safety to the children. When he brings his dog Gloria with him, he notices that the children really pay attention, and he is asked to give these talks quite often. What the children see is Gloria standing behind Officer Buckle and imitating him or enacting the rule he is stating. When he says that the children should not leave a thumbtack where someone might sit on it, Gloria is jumping high into the air with her paw on her bottom. Whenever Officer Buckle looks around, Gloria is sitting at attention. It is only when one of his talks is taped and shown on television that Officer Buckle learns the source of his popularity.

One activity would be for children to illustrate one of Officer Buckle's safety rules, or one of their own, by showing what Gloria might do on stage to dramatize it. They would write the safety tip under their drawings, or perhaps put the tip and the illustration on a star, as is done on the endpapers of the book.

Another activity might be for children to make a card for Officer Buckle to make him feel better after he has learned that it is Gloria whom the children enjoy. What could they say that would encourage him to continue his school safety presentations?

Children could choose one of the two activities or devise one of their own. The teacher's time would be spent talking with children as they worked and perhaps transcribing their invented spelling into standard orthography. All of the children would be engaged in discussions of their reactions to the story and to the illustrations.

Varying the Types of Choices

You can vary the sorts of choices you provide. The choice might be variety in art media; it might be variety in oral versus written work; it might be variety in level of difficulty of the activities. In a third-grade class, one activity might involve writing a paragraph. Another might be making a list. Both would engage the children in thinking about the literature that had been shared, but one would require more skill in composition than the other. This would allow children at differing skill levels to select an activity in which they could be successful.

Children can be encouraged to work together on projects for both the social and the language growth it promotes. For many children, working together makes a task more enjoyable. There are times, however, when children prefer to work alone. Some activities based on literature may be phrased so that children choose to "work with a friend or by yourself." Two children might easily work together on an album of drawings or making a chart. They might make feltboard stories and tell them to their class or other classes. Given two activities, one group and one individual, children may choose on the basis of the type of activity or on the basis of the number of people participating in it.

Children can decide whether or not they wish to share literature activities they have completed. Their work can be displayed or their activities described. They may tell the entire class or just a few children what they have done. Giving the opportunity to show their work demonstrates that you value it; giving the option of not sharing shows that you respect the feelings of the child.

Helping Children Make Responsible Choices

As you encourage children to make choices, try to make certain that they have the information necessary to make satisfactory choices. If they are to select their own book from the library, do they know where the picture books section is? Where they can find the poetry? How to get a librarian to help them if they cannot find what they want? Do readers know to open the book and try reading a page or two to see how difficult the reading is? Do prereaders know to look at some of the pictures as well as the cover before taking a book?

Once they have made their choice, encourage children to stay with it long enough to give it a good try. While it is unreasonable to force a child to keep looking at a book she is tired of, or to prohibit a child from sharing his project if he has had to hear three other children before getting the courage to speak, it is equally unproductive to allow children to change their choices capriciously. A part of learning to make choices is learning to accept responsibility for them. If a child has made a poor choice, this is the time for discussing the selection process he or she used and how it could be modified for better results.

Finally, keep notes on the activities and the types of books children choose, noting if any of your pupils are in a pattern that is limiting to their growth. You can then counteract their choices through planned activities. A child who always chooses to work alone can be assigned

Children can learn to make book selections carefully, looking at the illustrations and reading a page or two.

group experiences in other classroom or center projects. Another who never chooses a writing activity may be required to write at other times, or be given a choice between two writing activities. It is possible to balance children's choices with your perception of their needs by making all options you offer valid learning experiences and by structuring other activities to compensate for areas of neglect in those they may choose.

Encouraging Children to Set and Complete Tasks

Children in the primary grades can set tasks for themselves with some guidance from teachers and other adults. A group sharing special toys from home becomes curious about teddy bears and panda bears. Are there really animals that look like that?

Defining a Task

The teacher helps the children define the task so that the action they need to take to answer their question is clear. Two children from the group go to the library, or to classroom references if they are available, to look in dictionaries and encyclopedias under *teddy bear* and *panda*. If they have not used these references before, this would be an ideal time for the teacher to demonstrate their use. The children return quickly, reporting that there is indeed an animal called a giant panda, but that there is no listing under teddy bear.

At this point the teacher asks the group how they could find more about the panda and where else they might look to find out about teddy bears. Some of the children suggest library books, but not all know how to use the online catalogue. One who does goes to the library with two others to see what they can find on pandas. As they look, two of the three children will be learning ways of using the library.

Three other children are to look under the listing for teddy bear, to look in several dictionaries, and to ask the librarian for help. When the first group returns, they have found a book titled *Panda* by Susan Bonners (1978) and another titled *The Giant Panda* by Steele (1994). The other group has found that teddy bears are modeled after koalas and returns with *I Lost My Bear* by Jules Feiffer (1998), *Koalas* by Caroline Arnold (1987), and *High in the Trees* by Neecy Twinem (1996).

Keeping Children Task Oriented

The children then list, and the teacher records on chart paper, what they would like to know about these bears. "Where do they live? What do they eat? How big are they? Do they have lots of babies?" When the questions have been listed, the teacher asks for volunteers to listen especially for the answer to particular questions. One by one the questions are assigned. The teacher reads the book about pandas. Children go down the list and tell what they have learned about these bears. The question, "What did you think was especially interesting about pandas?" which the teacher adds at the end allows children to tell other information they have gleaned. "They can even eat splinters without hurting their stomachs," and "They get new teeth just like we do." There are also new questions as a result of the information they have heard. "What is a takin?" and "Are pandas found in other places besides China?"

In this case the children found appropriate books that are also excellent nonfiction. In the book by Bonners, the watercolor and gouache illustrations in shades of aqua capture the softness of the winter landscape where the pandas live. Children looking at the pictures can see what bamboo is, how pandas mate, and stages in a cub's growth. The text is clear and informative. The Steele book piques children's interest with its fold out flaps that reveal information about pandas and their habitat.

Helping Children Assess Their Efforts

Sometimes children will return with books that are not appropriate to the questions being asked. This is a time for teaching children to listen critically to the content and to make judgments themselves about its value for them. They can be guided to look at the content of a book in depth in the classroom and to check content briefly as they are selecting the book.

The teacher notes that two of the books the second group found about koalas are nonfiction, and one is fiction. She reads the nonfiction books first, with children listening for specific information as they did for pandas. When she has finished *Koalas,* the children answer their own questions. Again, more questions are raised. "What's special about eucalyptus leaves that koalas need them to eat?" "Where did the name 'teddy bear' come from?" "Why call it a teddy *bear* when it isn't a bear?" There are plans for further investigation. The teacher uses *High in the Trees* as a kind of observational game, having children look at the close-ups of the different parts of a koala.

She then reads *I Lost My Bear* to the class. "How is this book different from the other ones about koalas?" she asks. The children answer that it is a story, that it is about a toy teddy bear rather than a real animal. "Which book is better for learning about real koalas?" she asks. Then she continues by asking what they liked about each of the books.

As you talk with children about the appropriateness of particular books, try to make it clear that appropriateness is related to purpose. Rather than books being *good* or *bad,* there are some that answer their needs and others that do not. Be careful also not to overgeneralize. It is tempting to guide children to the conclusion that informational books give facts and that these are the books to read when information is needed. Many fiction books include accurate informational content, however, and certainly they are a prime source for information about how people act and feel. The insight gained from reading fiction should not be made to sound insignificant in comparison to the factual knowledge gained from nonfiction. Nor should the categories be labeled so that nonfiction becomes associated only with work, while fiction fits under fun. This contradicts the feelings of many readers who choose nonfiction for recreational reading. It also can make fiction appear less important than nonfiction.

Judging the Appropriateness of Tasks

You will need to judge the maturity and capabilities of your students as you help them set tasks. Some can go to the library themselves. Others may need your guidance. Some may be able to listen for answers to an entire list of questions, while others can concentrate on only one.

Both fiction and nonfiction offer opportunities for children to set tasks. The books may be needed in the completion of the task or may be the forerunner to the task of describing a response to literature. Children who have had experience in sharing their reactions to books can decide for themselves how they would like to present their thoughts and feelings. They could tell two friends how the story begins, trying to make it interesting enough that the friends will read the book. They could create a painting that they think the main character in a book would like. Then they can tell their classmates about their painting and its appeal to the book character. They could make clay models of characters from the book. Second- and third-graders may want to write comments about the book for display in the book corner.

Primary-grade children can be helped to set their own tasks by having a chart in the room that lists suggestions for sharing a book. They may use the ideas as stated or may build on the ideas to develop a new idea. Both preschool and primary children can set tasks in consultation with the teacher.

Whether the task is set by the child or chosen from a series of alternatives, you can urge that it be completed. Successfully finishing a project makes the child feel competent and enhances his or her self-concept. You can make this completion more likely to occur by ensuring that:

1. The task is on an appropriate level for the child.
2. The standards for successful completion are reasonable.
3. The materials needed are readily available.

4. The project is feasible in terms of teacher time; that is, it will not require an inordinate amount of explanation in relation to the time the project itself takes.

5. There is a classroom pattern of giving attention to completed projects.

Suppose that you were the teacher of the class learning about pandas and koalas. After reading the books discussed earlier, you decide to read *Corduroy (Freeman, 1968)*, a picture book about a teddy bear living in a department store. Corduroy overhears Lisa say that he is the bear she has always wanted. He also hears her mother say that they have spent too much money already and that the bear is missing a button on the strap of his overalls. That night, after the shoppers have gone, Corduroy begins searching for his lost button. He wanders around the store, finally discovering the bedding department. As he is pulling a button off a mattress, it gives way and he falls backward, knocking over a lamp. The watchman who hears the noise finds Corduroy and takes him back to his shelf in the toy department. The next morning Lisa is the first customer in the store. She has counted the money in her piggy bank and has come to buy Corduroy. When she gets him home, she sews a button on the strap and gives him a big hug.

You have decided to read this book because it goes back to the children's initial interest in their own toys and because it is good literature. You introduce it by saying, "Remember the story we heard about the little girl who couldn't find her bear?" After the children have responded to this question, you continue, "This is another story about a teddy bear, and it is called *Corduroy*." After reading the story, you ask the children to get their own toys and come back to the reading circle. Then you have them close their eyes and imagine what their toys might like to do in their houses at night, when everyone is asleep. They imagine what their toys like, what they might say if they could talk. Children then choose one of two activities. They can create a picture that shows what their toy might do at night, or they can use their toy as a puppet and have a conversation with another toy. Those who choose to draw should be able to get the paper and crayons or paint and chalk for themselves and begin. Those who choose the conversation may work in pairs simultaneously, or may listen as pairs take turns with the dialogue. This would depend on their experience with the use of puppets in spontaneous drama and their ability to work together on their own.

You would suggest the tasks knowing that the children can do them. You might need to give help midway, perhaps joining a conversation with a toy yourself, but children will feel good about what they have done. You will look at the thought that went into the pictures and conversations, not expecting mature artists or master puppeteers. You have planned so that the children think about the ideas before they begin work. When they get the materials, they begin quickly. You show your interest in their tasks by talking with the children as they work and by allowing them to share their work with their classmates if they wish. Your planning and follow-up are strong motivators for children to establish the habit of completing their work.

Building Self-Concept

Literature can help children develop positive self-concepts through content and theme, and also through activities which may follow the sharing of a book. One aspect of self-concept is recognizing one's strengths and weaknesses.

Recognizing Capabilities

There are books for young children that emphasize the many capabilities that they have. Jamaica Louise James, in the book of that name (Hest, 1996), uses the paints she is given for her eighth birthday to paint a series of pictures. Then, on her grandmother's birthday, Jamaica and her mother go to the subway station where Grammy sells tokens and post the pictures on the walls as a surprise for Grammy. It was Jamaica'a idea and it works. It even makes the harried and grouchy subway riders smile. Children not only have good ideas, they can make those ideas reality.

The concept book *My Hands Can* (Holzenthaler,1978) shows through clear illustrations and simple text many of the things that "my hands" can do, from zipping to clapping, to both building and breaking. Children listening to the book can be thinking of all the things they can do with their hands. After hearing it, they might take turns telling one thing they can do, or perhaps demonstrating or pantomiming the skill. They might play follow-the-leader using their hands for each action to be imitated. Both content and activities reinforce the concept that children are capable.

They might also follow the illustrations in the wordless picture books, *Sunshine* (Ormerod, 1981). They see the little girl getting up, having breakfast with her parents, but able to brush her teeth and get fully dressed without their help. They can describe or demonstrate those tasks they can do at their own homes and take pride in being independent at the center or nursery school.

Children can be encouraged to tell how they have solved problems after they listen to *Alfie's Feet* (Hughes, 1997). Alfie enjoys wearing his new rubber boots, but notices that they feel funny. By himself he discovers that the right boot is on his left foot and vice versa. Although his mother paints an "R" on the right boot and an "L" on the left to help him, he can tell right from left even after the letters wear off. Children need to know that they are capable of solving certain problems by themselves.

They may also need to recognize that some problems take time to solve, but that they can persevere and be successful. The boy in *Donald Says Thumbs Down* (Cooney, 1987) does manage to stop sucking his thumb, but it takes several weeks and several plans. And D.W., in *D.W. Flips* (Brown, 1987) learns to do a forward roll only through practice—every night and everywhere.

Seeing Oneself Realistically

Literature can help children see themselves realistically, yet with a focus on their strong points. *Tidy Titch* (Hutchins, 1991), for example, shows the very neat protagonist being the inspiration for his brother and sister to each clean their rooms. However, as they throw out toys and books and games, Titch rescues the cast-offs, and soon his room is a mess. How do children see themselves on the neat-to-messy scale? If they see themselves as either tidy or neat, are they always that way? Can they change?

As children come to see themselves in relation to others and to compare themselves with others, both in characteristics and in physical appearance, books can help them make realistic yet positive judgments.

You may want to present several books that describe opposing characteristics. An earlier book about Titch, titled *Titch* (Hutchins, 1971) shows him as smaller than his sister Mary and his brother Pete. They ride bicycles; he rides a tricycle. They fly kites but he has a pinwheel. In a triumph of poetic justice, they have the spade and the flowerpot, but Titch has the tiny seed that grows into a huge plant. Titch could be presented with *Daphne Eloise Slater, Who's Tall for Her Age* (Willner-Pardo, 1997) to encourage discussion and acceptance of physical differences.

Recognizing Growth and Change

These books lead into another aspect of self-concept, the realization that one is continually growing and changing. *It's My Birthday* (Watanabe, 1988), appropriate for preschoolers, makes the point clearly when Bear's grandparents give him a photo album for his birthday. It is filled with pictures of Bear as a baby and a toddler. *It's Going to Be Perfect* by Carlson (1998) shows a mother describing how she thought her daughter's life would be from birth through kindergarten, and contrasting that with how things really turned out—not quite as orderly as expected, but certainly loving. *Birthday Presents* (Rylant, 1987) appropriate for primary-grade children, has the parents recalling, with love and affection, each of their child's birthdays. They tell what happened, and the child's reaction, beginning with the day she was born—when they told her they loved her and she screamed. The pattern continues until the year the child is six. Then she makes cards for her parents' birthdays, and tells them that she loves them. Both books show the character growing and maturing.

After hearing either of them, children could ask their parents to tell them what they were like at age two or three. They could also collect photographs of themselves at various ages and use these to tell how they have changed. You might even develop your own book of photographs to share with the children, showing how you have changed.

Many children will enjoy and identify with the title character in *You'll Soon Grow Into Them, Titch* (Hutchins, 1983) because they have worn hand-me-down clothes that older children in the family have outgrown, and that may not be the perfect fit for the next in line. Titch inherits pants from his older brother, a sweater from his sister, and socks from both of them. All are too large, but his brother and sister assure him that he will soon grow into them. Titch's parents, however, decide that he should have some new clothes. Once he is outfitted, Titch presents his old clothes to the new baby; after all, he'll soon grow into them.

Children might also dictate a list of skills that they have acquired only recently to demonstrate that changes aren't related solely to physical appearance. They could create poems using one in the form suggested by Kenneth Koch. Children begin every odd line with "I used to _____," and every even line with "But now _____," resulting in a poem that tells about the changes in their lives (Koch, 1970). They might tell stories about times when they learned to do something special: cross the street by themselves, ride a bicycle, get out their own milk and cereal in the morning. They might even draw pictures in which they show what they hope to be able to do next year. After such sharing of experiences, try reading poems such as Hoberman's "A Year Later" or Margolis's "Two Wheels."

> A Year Later
>
> Last summer I couldn't swim at all
>
> I couldn't even float!
>
> I had to use a rubber tube

Or hang on to a boat;
I had to sit on shore
While everybody swam
But now it's this summer
And I can!
Mary Ann Hoberman

Two Wheels

I told you I won't. It's too hard.
I told you I can't. It's too hard.
Didn't I tell you?

My feet, they won't reach.
My hands, they won't steer.
It's too hard.

Watch out—I'm tipping.
Don't let go—I'm falling.
Please: I give up.

Not so fast, not so fast.
I don't like this.
Stop stop stop stop.

Hey, I can't stop.
Hey, I'm riding, I'm riding.
Hey, hey, hey, hey.

Did you see me?
What did I tell you?
It was easy.
Richard Margolis

Both poems relate the good feeling that comes from mastering a new skill, and both show that the skill did not come automatically. Growth takes time; not all skills are acquired the moment one wants.

Some, but probably not all, primary-grade children will understand the boy's feeling in *Someone New* (Zolotow, 1978). He thinks that something is strange, but he does not know what. He keeps feeling that someone is missing. The wallpaper he had chosen he no longer likes. His toys seem strange, and he packs them into a box along with the shells he found last summer at the beach. Then he realizes that he is becoming a new person.

Someone's gone.

Someone's missing

and I know who.

He's in that box

with all those things

and I—

I am someone new.

Charlotte Zolotow

The idea is a complex one, and not all children will comprehend the theme. For some, however, it may be an opening to talk about themselves and to think about the someone new they are becoming.

Becoming Confident

Children can be helped to see themselves as generally capable and as having within themselves the resources that will help them to meet difficult or unexpected demands. Of the four basic forms of literature, two, comedy and romance, show how the protagonist overcomes problems and goes onto achieve fulfillment and success. The mood is one of hope. Most literature for young children is either romance or comedy. Thus most of the stories you will share with children will be offering a picture of a book character who succeeds. These books show children who are able to cope with problems.

First- and second-grade students can see Jamila Jefferson in *Faraway Drums* (Kroll, 1998) as being somewhat like themselves. When Mama has to go to work, and thus leaves Jamila in charge of her little sister Zakiya after school, Jamila is uncomfortable. They have just moved and the noises in the apartment building are scary. Yet Jamila finds a way to cope. She describes to Zakiya how the sounds they hear are like sounds from Africa, remembering how Great-gramma had taught her to imagine the beating of her frightened heart as being a proud African drum within her. By the time Mrs. Harris, their neighbor, stops to check on them, they are calm and feeling safe. The story shows that young children can be independent, that they can cope with fear and uncertainty. It is not necessary to discuss the point with them. Simply by reading the book, they are being given a model of a capable individual.

Similarly, the books by Shigeo Watanabe, appropriate for three- and four-year-olds, show a bear cub engaged in various activities, and although he may have a few setbacks, he forges ahead confidently in stories such as *I Can Ride It!* (Watanabe, 1982), *I Can Build a House!* (Watanabe, 1983), *and I Can Take a Walk!* (Watanabe, 1976).

Identifying with One's Heritage

Self-concept involves an identification with one's heritage. There are books for young children that address this theme directly. *Journey Home* (McKay, 1998) does this as Mai travels to Vietnam with her mother in search of her mother's birth family. Her mother had been left in an orphanage in Saigon during the Vietnam War, eventually being raised in the United States by a foster family. The language and the country are new to Mai, but she is open to this key part of

John's grandfather tells him how the Navaho language was used as code in World War II, and that he must never forget his language. (Illustration from The Unbreakable Code *by Sara Hoagland Hunter. 1996. Reprinted by permission of Northland Publishing.)*

not just her mother's heritage, but hers as well. Young John, in *The Unbreakable Code* (Hunter, 1996), questions his Navaho grandfather directly about what life is like off the reservation because he is going to have to move with his mother and her new husband. Grandfather tells him that he will be all right because he has an unbreakable code to take with him, the Navaho language. He tells how during World War II the Navaho language provided an excellent code because it had never been written down and few people knew it.

Grandfather explains that in his own lifetime, he was taken off the reservation to be educated in government schools and punished for speaking Navaho, but that later during the war he was trained and served as a radioman, using Navaho. The language John speaks once helped save his country.

Books like Joseph Bruchac's *Fox Song* (1993) show children that knowledge of their heritage opens new worlds to them and helps them know who they are. Jamie remembers all the things her Abenaki grandmother taught her before her death, and it is not just the things they did and made together that will stay with her, but also the outlook on life.

Books that present characters of varying ethnic backgrounds are discussed also in chapter 8 on the social development of children. Learning about children who are different from themselves is part of children's social development. The book that for one student presents a model for ethnic identification is for another student an introduction to a new group of people or new customs. Suggested books in the social development chapter emphasize that teachers and day-care professionals should have a variety of peoples represented in the books they choose no matter what the ethnic makeup of their class. You will want to be certain, however, that you read some books whose major characters represent the ethnic backgrounds of the children in your class.

Developing Sex Role Expectations

Just as books present models for ethnic identification, so too do they present models for sex role identification. When you read books to children, be aware that you are showing them one perception of how the world is structured. If you read only books that show female characters as passive and male characters as active, you are saying to them that this is the behavior expected of females and of males.

There are many books for children that have broken away from sex role stereotypes. They include more female characters who are active, assertive, and competent. Women in some books are portrayed as career oriented and successful outside the home. Males are permitted to show tenderness, to cry. One second-grade girl, involved in a discussion of appropriate sex role behaviors, pondered the question of why it had been considered acceptable for girls to cry but not for boys to do so. Her solution was simple: "Girls had more to cry about." Those who have seen their horizons expanded in recent years may well agree with her assessment.

As you select books, eliminate those that present stereotyped characters, whether the character is sexist or not. Stereotyping means that all individuals within a group are described as though they were alike. Women work in the home and wear aprons; men work in offices and wear suits. Boys play baseball; girls play with dolls. Books whose characters are stereotyped are poor literature, for the author has not developed the individuality necessary for good characterization. Thus these books should be discarded on literary grounds.

Do not depend on the date of publication to tell you if a stereotype exists. Some recent books present stereotyped characters, and many old favorites do not. One could hardly ask for a more active and unique female than Madeline in the books by Ludwig Bemelmans, the first of which was published in 1939. In the list of professional references at the end of this chapter are several bibliographies of non-stereotyped books for children, which you may find useful.

A second problem exists, and that is to provide a balance of types of characters in the total body of literature you share with children. To present only books that show women working at exciting careers is to create as imbalanced a picture as to present only books that show women functioning as mothers or homemakers. Assess each book for its literary value, then make a list of role models presented. See if any gaps exist, and if so, look for books to rectify omissions.

There will be opportunities to discuss with the children their attitudes toward certain behaviors of characters. One teacher read *Max* (Isadora, 1976), *Ira Sleeps Over* (Waber, 1972), *Tough Eddie* (Winthrop, 1985) and *Crusher Is Coming* (Graham, 1988) to his class of first-graders.

In the first book, Max is on his way to a baseball game when he stops in at his sister's ballet lesson. Intrigued by the whole procedure, he joins the line of girls in doing exercises at the bar and particularly enjoys the leaps. He goes to the baseball game, play wells, and decides to warm up for each game with ballet.

Ira, in *Ira Sleeps Over,* is invited to spend the night with his friend Reggie. His sister begins needling him about his teddy bear, asking him if he plans to take it to Reggie's and reminding him that he has never slept without it. His parents reassure him that it is fine to take Tah Tah, but his sister insists that Reggie will laugh. When the time comes, Ira goes next door, leaving his teddy bear behind. As the two boys tell ghost stories in bed, Reggie gets up and gets something from a drawer—his teddy bear, named Foo Foo. Ira goes home to get Tah Tah, this time convinced that Reggie will not laugh.

In *Tough Eddie,* it is again the sister who makes life difficult. This time she tells Eddie's two friends, Andrew and Philip, about the dollhouse Eddie keeps in his closet. They are interested, and although they never show any negative reaction, Eddie assumes one and won't talk to them. He just keeps walking, feeling tough as he always does when he is wearing his cowboy boots and his thick leather belt. When their class takes a trip to the park, Eddie proves his bravery by not panicking when a bee lands on him. And when Philip considers bringing his cricket for show-and-tell, Eddie responds that he might bring his dollhouse.

In the last book, *Crusher Is Coming,* Pete prepares for a visit from Crusher, the school football hero, by giving his stuffed animals to his baby sister Claire and instructing his mother that she is not to kiss him when he and Crusher arrive, nor to let Claire into his room. The delightful irony of the book is that Crusher is smitten with Claire and pays far more attention to her than he does to the suggestions Pete makes about what they might do.

The teacher talked with one group of eight children. They readily described the toys they slept with. The names ranged from a bear called Fuz to a more elegant stuffed rabbit called Mr. O. Hare. None of the children had ever been to a ballet lesson. All, however, played with dolls, or "action figures," of some type, often those related to television cartoons. In the discussions they all agreed that boys did sleep with stuffed animals. They thought that playing with dolls was fine, particularly as they defined dolls. They weren't sure about the dollhouse, although one boy described the play stove and sink he had at home. They could readily understand the concerns of each of the characters who feared being laughed at by his friends. They did not, however, agree on Max's dancing. Some said that dancing was fun and that anyone could do it. Others said that boys should not take ballet, but that this was okay because Max was preparing for a ball game. And still others said that ballet was for girls, not boys. The teacher did not give an opinion but pointed out that they seemed to have different feelings about it, and asked them to think about how they knew what boys did and what girls did. This was a first step in urging children to question conventional stereotypes.

As you assess the role models in books that contribute to children's concept of their own sexual identity, plan to provide a variety of non-stereotyped characters and allow discussion of roles. If children are thinking in stereotypical terms, you may well want to introduce evidence that conflicts with their current beliefs. The teacher who read *Max* could later show news clippings of male dancers or have all the children engage in dancing themselves. Literature allows you to provide a great variety of possible behaviors and to broaden children's conceptions of possibilities for themselves.

Building Self-esteem

Self-esteem is influenced strongly by the reaction of others to the individual. Children gain an impression of their worth from their perception of the treatment they are given by the important people in their lives. Parents, teachers, and classmates all contribute to the total picture. You as teacher can influence this directly through your relations with the children and indirectly as you model behavior for children to use with others. You also can select curriculum materials and activities that build self-esteem.

Using Content That Reaffirms Self-worth

Look for literature whose content reaffirms self-worth. *Big Sister Tells Me That I'm Black* gives a catchy, cheerleader beat to a poem celebrating proud feelings:

> big sister tells me
>
> that i'm black
>
> she says she knows me
>
> front and back . . .
>
> hip hip
>
> hip hooray
>
> hip hip
>
> i'm black today
>
> *Arnold Adoff*

First Grade Takes a Test (Cohen, 1980) describes a situation that is very real for many primary-grade youngsters. The children are given a paper and pencil test by a lady who comes in especially for the task. On the basis of the test results, one child, Anna Maria, is chosen for a special class. The other children then begin calling each other "dummy." The teacher intervenes and explains forcefully that the test doesn't really tell all the things they *can* do, such as reading books, having good ideas, and helping others. Her point is strengthened when Jim figures out that they can settle an argument over which child has the larger cookie simply by weighing the cookies. Because there is typically so much emphasis on doing well in school, it is valuable to call children's attention to the many positive qualities each possesses that may not be related directly to school work.

Presenting Themes of Individuality

Look also for books with themes of individuality. Children need to both recognize and value their own uniqueness. *The Cousins* (Caseley, 1990) shows this by contrasting Jenny and Jessica, first cousins who are described by their parents as different as night and day, but who like each other and accept themselves, and each other, just as they are.

The theme that each of us is unique appears in books at all levels, for preschoolers there is *Elvira* (Shannon, 1993), the dragon who really doesn't like fighting or eating up princesses as the other dragons do. What she likes is sitting in the grass making daisy chains and dresses. When the teasing of the others gets to be too much, she packs up and leaves, finding that she gets along quite well with the princesses, who dress her in pretty clothes and curl her eyelashes. In the end her parents welcome her home, complete with her rather stunning wardrobe.

A similar theme is presented for kindergartners and first-graders in *Sloppy Kisses* (Winthrop, 1980). Emmy Lou comes from a family where everyone likes to kiss. One day Rosemary observes Emmy Lou being kissed good-bye by her father as he drops her off for school. Rosemary offers the opinion that kissing is for babies and is "yukky." Emmy Lou, in response to her friends' criticism, decides that she is now too old for kissing and informs her family of this decision. They comply with her request that they no longer kiss her but assure her that they still love her. Emmy Lou proudly tells Rosemary of her decision; but that night she cannot get to sleep. Finally her father says he knows what she needs, picks her up, and gives her a big sloppy kiss. She goes right to sleep. The next day, as father pats Emmy Lou on the shoulder in front of the school, she calls him back for a kiss. This time when Rosemary begins with more critical comments, Emmy Lou states that kissing is for everybody and gives Rosemary a kiss on the cheek. A theme within the story is that one should choose behaviors that are satisfying to oneself, rather than matching behavior to the expectations of others.

The need to be an individual is effectively presented in *The Other Emily* (Davis, 1984). Emily loves her name and is not prepared to find another child in her class with the same name. The other Emily is not bothered and even wants them to do Show and Tell together. Emily soon adjusts to the idea of sharing her name, but the importance of having one's own special identity comes through clearly.

For second- and third-graders, Jacqueline Wilson's *Double Act* (1998) shows that twins may look alike, but each is a person in his or her own right, with a unique personality and unique skills.

All of these books, on different levels of difficulty, present a theme of the value of one's own decisions, one's own special skills, one's own preferences. You can follow the reading of these books with activities that focus on the individuality of your students. You might try one or more of the following ideas:

1. Have the children make booklets about themselves, describing in words or pictures their special skills, what they might like to learn to do, what they enjoy, what they dislike.

2. Make a bulletin board that features pictures of each child, labeled with the child's name. The children can dictate a sentence to accompany each picture, a sentence in which they tell one unique feature about themselves. Parents can be encouraged to help their children with this.

3. Tape record the children individually as they tell about a pet, their home, or their favorite food. Then play the tape for the group. As the children guess who is speaking, they learn about that child. Each child becomes the center of attention for a brief period of time. All learn that each person has a unique voice, one that others recognize even when they cannot see the speaker.

Sharing Literature That Promotes Feelings of Security

Books can help give a feeling of security to very young children. The day-care child, held on the lap of an adult, associates reading with the warmth of human contact. The nursery school child sits beside an aide and the two share a moment of understanding as they laugh together over a humorous book. Focusing attention on children in this way helps them feel that they are valued. Books such as *When Mama Comes Home Tonight* (Spinelli, 1998), *Mama, Do You Love Me?* (Joosse, 1991), *and Grandfather's Love Song* (Lindbergh, 1993) have content that reinforces that feeling. In the first one, Mama comes home after a long day at work, but then cuddles and plays with her toddler, gives her a bath, and tucks her snuggly into bed. In the second, a young Innuit girl asks a series of questions to assure herself of her mother's love, much as the little bunny in *The Runaway Bunny* (Brown, 1942) did. And in the third, grandfather and grandson wander beside the ocean and through the fields during changing seasons, with grandfather telling in a short and lyric rhyme on each page how he loves the boy. The language patterns in all three books invite rereading, and the message that "you are important" helps build the young child's self-esteem.

Older children, particularly those from single parent families, may gain security from books that show the love of both parents, or of extended family, even though the child is not living with those particular individuals. In *Boundless Grace* (Hoffman, 1995), Grace learns to love two families, her mother and grandmother with whom she lives, and her father, who has gone back to Nigeria, and his new wife and family.

Suggesting Activities That Encourage Positive Feedback

Your behavior toward each child can show that each is valued. You can also arrange activities in which children will receive positive comments and treatment from their classmates and learn to give praise themselves. Some positive feedback will occur naturally as children take responsibility for care of classroom pets, plants, and materials. Others may be based on books read. One teacher read *Odd Velvet* (Whitcomb, 1998) to her class of second-graders. When the book opens, it is the first day of school, and already Velvet is different from the other children. They bring the teacher tea and potpourri; Velvet brings rocks and half a sparrow's egg. As the school year continues, the children are polite to Velvet, but they do not choose her as a playmate. Then Velvet wins the school drawing contest, and she does it without fancy paints, using only her box of eight crayons. Little by little, the children come to recognize the unique things about Velvet—and she teaches them to draw. The teacher used the idea of special talents, and that Velvet's winning drawing was an apple, and had each child draw and color an apple and put his or her name on it. She collected the apples and then had each child, without looking, pick one of the apples. The child wrote on the back three things that were special about the child who had drawn the apple. The teacher collected the apples again and read the three special talents or qualities as she handed each apple to its owner. She might have done a similar activity using *I Wish I Were a Butterfly* (Howe, 1987), discussed in chapter 4, for it also emphasizes the idea that each individual has skills and accomplishments.

The children thought about the special attributes of their friends, and each child received praise. The teacher had built in some checks, however, to ensure that the activity went well. She used two children as examples and asked what they did well, what the children liked about them, what they liked. Thus the class understood the sorts of comments that were expected. Then she collected the apples just before recess, glancing at the writing on each one. Had there been comments that were denigrating, she was in a position to have them changed without hurting a child's feelings and without making it common classroom knowledge. As you plan what is *right* about an activity, plan also for the *wrongs* that might occur. Those extra few minutes of thought may help children to feel a warm satisfaction about themselves.

Recognizing One's Own Values

Values are the belief system one holds about what is important. Children learn values from the people who are central to their lives. For preschool children, parents are of primary importance; for the school-age child, teachers and peers, as well as parents, have influence. Children in school are exposed to more than one set of values and are able to think about them in terms other than "Mommy is right" or "Mommy is wrong."

Literature, in its exploration of actions and motivations for actions, presents a panorama of value systems. Books that present value conflicts clearly lend themselves to discussion and to activities by which children can judge their own beliefs. One approach is to ask students which character they want to be more like when characters conflict over values. In *Nim and the War Effort* (Lee, 1997), Nim is collecting old newspapers for a school contest. The paper drive is in support of the American war effort in 1943. Nim has a chance to get a whole roomful of papers, and to show the boy who is teasing her that she is a real American. She gets the papers, but is late getting home. Her grandfather tells her she has shamed the family in her arguing with the boy and in being late. Children can be asked what they think is more important, showing one's patriotism and winning in a contest where your opponent is cheating, or honoring family rules, wishes, and traditions. They may think of a time when they had to make such a choice. They can share their responses through art, through writing, or through oral activities. As they explain their answers, they can be asked to tell whether they act that way often. This is one step in discovering what they value and how consistent they are in acting on that value.

Other times you can emphasize the reasons for holding a particular value, and the consequences of acting on it. In the book titled *Frederick* (Lionni, 1967), a group of mice are preparing for the winter. All but Frederick are gathering corn, nuts, and wheat and storing them for the winter. Frederick sits alone and explains that he is gathering sun rays for cold winter days, and colors, and words. When winter comes, the mice eat through their store of supplies. Then they call upon Frederick, who alleviates their discomfort by reciting a poem that makes them feel the sun and see the colors of summer.

Children can be asked to write down whether they think Frederick should have been permitted to share in the mice's food since he did not gather any of it. Having them write "yes" or "no" on a paper forces them to decide for themselves, not be swayed by what a friend says or by what the majority seem to feel. Those who said "yes" can be grouped together and those who said "no" together. Each group is to list all their reasons for feeling as they do. They could also be asked to select what the group thinks is the best reason.

Then you might lead a discussion in which you ask the groups to apply their beliefs to new situations. Do those children who hold that only people who work should share the food think that children who do not generally hold jobs should share in the family's food? Do those who hold that poets contribute something of value and should not have to work in the way others do also feel that a poetry-writing classmate should be excused from clean-up time in order to continue writing?

Preschool as well as primary children can identify the values a book character holds if they are asked what is important to that character. They might also be asked if they agree with the character. In *Miss Rumphius* (Cooney, 1982), the story begins with the title character as a small girl telling her artist grandfather about her dreams. She wants to go to distant places and to live in a house by the sea when she grows up. Her grandfather says that she must do a third thing—make the world more beautiful. She agrees, but doesn't know how she will do this. The story continues with her travels and her move to a house by the sea. As an old woman, she sees the lovely lupines she had planted in her garden, then others growing where the seeds had spread. She decides she can fulfill her commitment to make the world more beautiful by scattering lupine seeds along the country lanes and walks. The story concludes as Miss Rumphius talks with her great-niece and tells her that she must do something to make the world more beautiful? How could they accomplish this, either now or in the future?

In these examples, children are not told what to believe but only asked to think about their beliefs. You will find that literature often revolves around questions of values. The strategy of having students take a stand, think through their reasons for it, listen to the reasoning of those who differ, and discuss the consequences of acting on various value systems is one that can apply to many books. It opens the way for children to consider other positions and perhaps make more knowledgeable choices.

Helping Children Understand and Express Their Emotions

Literature highlights the role of emotions in human lives. It shows not only what happens to a character or what a character does but also how that character feels. Part of the reader's response to literature is usually a recognition of the emotions being expressed. Much of the discussion of books centers on how characters felt about one another and how their feelings influenced their actions. Reading every day to children cannot help but aid their understanding of people and of human emotions.

As you select books, it may be helpful for you to think of these four ways in which literature can contribute to young children's emotional growth. First, literature shows that many of the feelings they experience are experienced by others, and are both normal and natural. Second, it explores the feeling from several aspects, giving a fuller picture and providing the base for the naming of that emotion. Third, literature, through the actions of various characters, shows options for ways of dealing with particular emotions. And fourth, literature makes clear that one person experiences many emotions, sometimes conflicting ones.

Finding That Others Share Similar Feelings

To show children that others have felt as they do, look for books that describe common childhood experiences. *Will I Have a Friend?* (Cohen, 1967) describes Jim's first day in kindergarten. He wants a friend, and his father assures him that he will find one, but Jim is shy in his new environment. Children may know what it is like to enter a new classroom but may not have realized that others share their feelings. In the same way, children who have been lost or even momentarily separated from their parents will appreciate the openness with which Christopher, in *Left Behind* (Carrick, 1988), describes his feelings when he becomes lost in the subway during a class field trip. And those of us who have taken children on trips will appreciate his teacher's relief when she picks him up at the police station and knows that he is safe!

Many books show children that others have feelings similar to theirs. (From Gettin'
Through Thursday *by Melrose Cooper. 1998. Reprinted by permission of Lee & Low
Publishers.)*

In *Gettin' Through Thursday* (Cooper, 1998), Andre knows that Thursday, the day before
payday, is tight for his family. If they run out of something, be it food or toothpaste or birdseed
for the parakeet, they must make do until Friday when his mother gets paid. When he makes
the third-grade honor roll, grade cards are distributed on a Thursday, and he knows that the
celebration he was promised cannot be. He is angry and dejected, but finally succumbs to the
family's "pretend" celebration as a rehearsal for the real one—held on Friday. Children who
feel the pinch of hard economic times know the disappointment Andre feels. In like manner,
preschoolers understand the distress felt by D. W. (Brown, 1998) when she cannot find her blanket. The feelings are treated seriously in these books, a recognition that children care and that
their feelings matter.

A second-grader bending down to pick up a crayon bumped his head on his desk as he straightened up. The teacher knew that earlier in the day he had broken his thermos. Seeing the pain on his face, he commiserated by saying, "This is just a bad day for you, Tom." From the depths of his misery Tom answered, "All my days are bad days." The next day the teacher read *Alexander and the Terrible, Horrible, No Good, Very Bad Day* (Viorst, 1972) in which Alexander tells all the horrible, no good things that happened to him. There was no prize in his breakfast cereal, only he had a cavity, there were lima beans for supper, and there was kissing on TV. Tom thoroughly enjoyed the story, as did the rest of the class. It is quite probable, however, that it would not have been so funny to Tom on his bad day. You will need to make a judgment about children's reactions to a book, knowing when they may need time before they are ready to relive or talk about an emotion.

Books for preschoolers often concentrate on a single emotion. The narrator of *William and the Good Old Days* (Greenfield, 1993) is worried about his grandmother. He remembers her before she became ill, misses the "good old days," and tries to cheer her up with his telephone calls. He fantasizes how it will be when she is better, but the overriding emotion is worry. *The Summer My Father Was Ten* (Brisson, 1998) is more complicated and thus is more appropriate for primary-grade children than preschoolers. The narrator, planting a garden with her father, tells what he has told her about his tenth summer. He and several friends got into a tomato fight, throwing tomatoes from a neighbor's garden at each other and watching them splat. Wild and laughing, they uprooted the plants in the garden and completely destroyed it. Then he saw the neighbor watching. All the old man said was "Why?" and the next year he did not plant a garden. The other boys forgot the incident, but the girl's father was filled with guilt and shame, yet couldn't bring himself to apologize. Eventually he helps the neighbor plant and care for a new garden, and becomes friends with the neighbor. The emotions of both the father and the neighbor are portrayed, changing with the events and often overlapping.

For some books, you may want to discuss with the children times when they have felt the way the character does. At other times, you may want to focus entirely on the literature itself, drawing out how the character felt and how the author let the reader know these feelings.

Exploring Various Aspects of an Emotion

Reading several books in which characters have the same or similar feelings gives children data from which to generalize. It is also an opportunity for putting feelings into words. Suppose you have read two books about the arrival of a new baby, which you chose because several of the children in your group have new brothers or sisters. The two that you read, *A Baby Sister for Frances* (Hoban, 1964) and *Julius, the Baby of the World* (Henkes, 1990) both describe the feelings of jealousy experienced by the older child. To expand upon this theme, you choose two more books in which jealousy plays an important role. One, *A Birthday for Frances* (Hoban, 1995) has Frances suffering again but this time because it is her sister's birthday, not hers. And the other, *One Frog Too Many* (Mayer, 1975), shows the reactions of a boy, his turtle, his dog, and his frog when the boy is given another frog. The first three welcome it, but the frog is not pleased. He glares at their new companion and manages to bite it and kick it off a raft when the others are not looking. The children tell what was similar about these feelings. They may relate times when they have felt that way. If none of the children offers the term *jealous,* interject it into the discussion yourself. These children will begin to realize that a single emotion may be produced by many different circumstances, and will be building a vocabulary for telling others how they feel.

You might then introduce a book in which jealousy is only one of the emotions being experienced and give children the opportunity to describe it in a more complex context. In *Timothy Goes to School* (Wells, 1981), for example, Timothy heads out for his first day at school full of enthusiasm. The teacher seats him next to Claude, who immediately makes fun of the sunsuit Timothy is wearing. The next day Timothy wears a new jacket, and Claude again criticizes his clothes. Timothy hopes that Claude will make mistakes, or fall in a puddle, or have some other mishap, but he never does. Timothy is jealous of Claude's confidence and tries to dress to conform to what appear to be Claude's expectations. At the same time, he dislikes Claude's attitudes and actions. Finally he meets Violet, who has the same feelings toward Grace that Timothy has toward Claude. They become friends and go home together laughing about Claude and Grace. The feelings of the characters are multidimensional. Because all the characters are animals, the ideas, rather than the actual appearance of the characters, are primary.

Some teachers have used the form of "Happiness is . . ." to elicit examples of specific emotions. Children complete the sentence in as many ways as they can. The emotion may be whatever the teacher or children select: "Love is . . ." or "Grouchy is . . ." If you begin with this approach, you may want to read literature that approaches the emotion from this perspective. An example is Eloise Greenfield's poem entitled "Love Don't Mean" (1978) in which love is portrayed as a child keeping her mama company while her daddy is gone. Patricia McKissack's *Ma Dear's Aprons* (1997) shows the love between David Earl and his mother throughout the busy work week, as he helps her with her work and the two engage in gentle teasing. The book provides another opportunity to discuss emotions and how people express them.

Perceiving Options for Managing Emotions

As they see how emotions are expressed by book characters, children are given options for handling their emotions. Some may be methods they already use. Crying may not change the circumstances that produced the disappointment, but it does offer release.

Fantasizing is another way of managing feelings, from anger to longing. Christopher, in *Mommy Go Away* (Jonell, 1997), is tired of his parents telling him what to do, and imagines his mother on his toy boat, and tells her to go away as the boat floats in the bathtub. His anger assuaged, he rescues her when the boat capsizes. The title, *Next Year I'll Be Special* (Giff, 1993), expresses the little girl's state of mind as she thinks about what school will be like for her next year, when she has the lovely Miss Lark, who never yells, for her second-grade teacher. Unhappiness with "mean Miss Minch" is overshadowed by imaginings of being the best in the class, appreciated by all her classmates and honored by her teacher.

A book by Charlotte Zolotow, *A Father Like That* (1971), poetically tells about a boy's imaginings of what his father would be like. His father would play checkers with him. His father would understand if he were in trouble at school. His father would not call him a sissy when he cried. When he has finished, his mother tells him that she likes that kind of father.

And in case one like that never comes along, he should remember what he has been thinking, because he can be a father like that himself someday.

Fantasizing is not offered as a permanent escape but as one way of sorting through feelings and expressing them, if only to oneself. It is also a safe way of previewing possible actions.

Within stories that children are hearing every day, they will encounter characters who hide their feelings, who share them, who reveal them through their actions. They will see that some characters are misunderstood because they did not explain their feelings. They will experience, with the characters, a full range of feelings.

Exploring the Varied Emotions of a Single Character

Some of the books you read will show the many emotions of a single character. Consider also reading a series of books about one character. The books about Frances by Russell Hoban show this "human" badger in many different situations. Two other excellent groups of books can be read so that they form a chronological story. Lucille Clifton's books about Everett Anderson start with Everett's experiences for one week, *Some of the Days of Everett Anderson* (1970). Another book tells about his Christmas; another, about a new neighbor. Then comes *Everett Anderson's 1-2-3* (1977) when his mother decides to marry Mr. Perry. The next book is the self-explanatory *Everett Anderson's Nine Month Long* (1978). *Everett Anderson's Goodbye* (1983), the final book in the series, tells of Everett's adjustment to the death of his father.

In the second group of books, three can form a continuing story, with the fourth being an epilogue. *Lost in the Storm* (1974) by Carol and Donald Carrick shows Christopher and his dog Bodger, how they play together, how worried Christopher is when Bodger is out all night in a storm. Then, in *The Accident* (1976) Bodger is killed and Christopher must cope with his grief. In *The Foundling* (1977), Christopher is not ready to replace Bodger with a new dog from the pound, but a stray puppy that follows him changes his feelings about having another dog. In a later story, *Dark and Full of Secrets* (1984), the puppy has grown to full size and is now an integral part of the family, just as Bodger had been.

Frances, Everett Anderson, and Christopher become like friends as their adventures are shared. They show that one person may feel a variety of emotions, in a manner compatible with young children's ability to comprehend the situations.

Following the reading of books such as these, plan ways for children to verbalize emotions, either their own or those of the book characters. They may add words to wordless picture books, either in dialogue or narrative form. They could dramatize a story, following the plot but giving their own dialogue, thus expressing the feelings in their own words. Older children can role-play a situation. Look for times when the children can use puppets or masks as they engage in dialogue. Children often speak more freely when they are speaking through another personage.

Occasionally you will find books or poems with patterns children can use to express their own feelings. Karla Kuskin has something to say about her feelings in this poem:

> Okay everybody, listen to this:
>
> I am tired of being smaller
>
> Than you And them
>
> And him

And trees and buildings.

So watch out

All you gorillas and adults

Beginning tomorrow morning

Boy

Am I going to be taller.

Karla Kuskin

What might the children in your group say with an opening line like, "Okay everybody, listen to this"?

Overcoming Unfounded Fears

Common fears of childhood are the themes in some books and common occurrences in others. Characters will be frightened by animals or afraid of the dark. Sometimes children's fears are unfounded in reality, but at other times they are reflective of actual danger. The children in Donald Crews' book *Shortcut* (1992) have reason to be frightened when they find themselves on the train tacks with a train approaching rapidly. Children talking about their fears and the fears of characters in books are gathering information that will help them determine which fears are useful for providing an awareness of dangerous situations and which inhibit them in areas where the potential danger is minimal. They are also facing their fears, the first step in overcoming them.

Literature can help children cope with fears of the unknown by providing knowledge about common objects and events as well as new experiences they are about to undertake. *Holes and Peeks* (Jonas, 1984) for the three- or four-year-old, simply has a child looking in various holes around the house. Bathroom fixtures become less frightening when the child sees and talks about where the pipe leads.

A child who has never been to a hospital is given valuable information, and a large measure of reassurance, in Fred Roger's *Going to the Hospital* (1988). The photographs show just what to expect, and the text is clear. In the section describing x-rays, the child is told that the machine takes pictures of the inside of the body. It also explains that the x-ray table may feel hard and there will be a buzzing sound; that the child will have to stay still and others will have to stay outside the room; and, most importantly, that it does not hurt. This book, like others in this series of books that introduce children to new situations, gives insight into the uneasiness children may feel and arms them against it by making the experience understandable and less strange. As you learn what children in your group are facing, whether a trip to the dentist or a move to live with a new set of foster parents, you will be able to share literature with them that will make the experience less frightening.

Literature can give children the opportunity to talk about their fears. If they are responding to a book, they may say how they feel and put the fear in perspective. Children listening to *Jim Meets the Thing* (Hoban, 1981) will be encouraged to tell about times when television monsters or horror stories have frightened them. Other tricks of the imagination are humorously but understandingly portrayed in *What's Under My Bed?* (Stevenson, 1983). After laughing at all the terrible things Grandpa describes as having seen and heard when he once stayed with his grandparents long ago, children can talk about the things they imagine lurking in the dark when they are in a strange place. Jane, in *Swimming Lessons* (Jay, 1998), overcomes her fear of water with help from Jimmy. After days of insisting that she would not take swimming lessons, and resisting in every way she can, she jumps into the water to prove to Jimmy that his taunts that she is afraid are unfounded. Children can appreciate the conflicting feelings Jane experiences as she stands at the pool's edge.

Young children are often afraid of separation, of being left alone and having no one to care for them. Three- and four-year-olds listening to the concept book *You Go Away* (Corey, 1976) see many instances of the meanings of "going away" and "coming back." The early pages show "away" and "back" as games of peek-a-boo, or a father playfully tossing his child in the air. But as the book continues, the distances become greater. A mother leaves her child at school and comes back. Finally parents are shown leaving with suitcases, and the child is assured that they will come back. The book provides an opportunity for children to tell how they feel when their parents leave. The illustration showing a child crying when her mother is out of sight in a grocery store might be a good opening for discussion.

Children between five and nine are in a period of realizing that death, the ultimate separation, is permanent. Books about the death of a pet or a grandparent will give them an idea of how others feel when a death occurs. Just as adults have varied beliefs about death, so too is there a range of beliefs presented in literature. Children have a better chance of coping if adults are honest with them, admitting that separation is painful and that people have differing beliefs about death.

Over a year's time you could read several books in which a death occurs, each giving new information about people's responses to it. *Grandpa's Slide Show* (Gould, 1987) focuses on how much the family misses the grandfather after his death, and how they sit together once again looking at the family slides, just as they had done on many nights with him. *Annie and the Old One* (Miles, 1971) shows that Annie, no matter how much she wishes it, cannot prevent the death of her grandmother. She comes to accept her grandmother's teaching that death is a natural part of life. In *The New King* (Rappaport, 1995), a young boy becomes king when his father is killed in a hunting accident. He commands the doctor, the Imperial Wizard, the High Councilor, to bring his father back to life, but all insist it cannot be done. Then he talks with the Wise Woman. She tells him that God gave the first human couple the choice of dying like the moon or like the banana tree. The moon wanes but returns, dying but coming back to life. The banana tree dies but its shoots keep growing. The man wanted to die like the moon, but the woman convinced him that to die like the banana tree was better, for they could love their children during their lifetimes, and then live on by giving life to others. The Wise Woman assures the prince that his father will live on in him. All four books contribute to children's understanding of emotions after a loved one's death.

To encourage children to talk about their fears and to see ways they might lessen them, read several books that present fears children commonly have. Some of the children may volunteer to talk about fears they have; others may tell about them when asked. You will learn about areas where you may be able to help, and children may give valuable advice to one another.

SUMMARY

Emotions, values, ways of perceiving, and feelings about self are all a part of personality. Erikson seeks to explain personality growth by describing how human beings respond to conflicts at specific periods in their lives. Central to how children resolve such conflicts and to the development of self-esteem and a positive self-concept is the way in which adults and peers respond to them.

The following long-term goals are appropriate for the personality development of young children.

Children will weigh evidence and make appropriate choices.

Children will set tasks for themselves and complete the tasks they begin.

Children will develop positive and realistic self-concepts.

Children will develop feelings of self-worth and self-esteem.

Children will begin to recognize their own values and to choose from among values.

Children will understand their emotions and will express them in socially acceptable ways.

Books offer opportunities for helping children achieve these goals. Table 7-1 suggests appropriate teaching strategies. Children can be involved regularly in choice-making, deciding which books they would like to hear read, which activity they wish to complete, which book they will take from the library. They can learn, also, to be responsible for the choices they make. In many instances teachers can help children set tasks for themselves and assess their own efforts in completing the tasks.

Literature, through content and through activities based on content and theme, can strengthen the development of self-esteem. As children hear literature that shows the skills and abilities of others they discover they, too, have many skills and abilities. Comparisons aid in the ability to see oneself realistically and to recognize the process of growth and change. Books present models with which children identify. Thus teachers will want to avoid books that stereotype characters and look for those that present well-developed characters in a variety of roles and settings. Teachers will also share books that promote feelings of security and self-worth.

Because literature explores the actions and motivations of characters, it presents a panorama of value systems and of emotional reactions. Primary-grade children can clarify their own value positions as they assess the actions of book characters. Both primary and preschool children gain experience in recognizing and talking about emotions as they participate in literary experiences. Books provide particular support for helping children overcome unfounded fears, both through giving information about new experiences and through providing a stimulus for the discussion of common fears.

Table 7–1. Supporting Children's Personality Development

Developmental Goals	Teaching Suggestions	Recommended Literature	
Children will weigh evidence and make appropriate choices.	Give children real choices and abide by their decisions. Encourage children to choose their own books for independent perusal. Provide children with a choice of activities following the reading of a book. Vary the types of choices offered. Help children make responsible choices.	**Ages 3–5:** Rathmann	*Officer Buckle and Gloria*
Children will set tasks for themselves and will complete tasks they begin.	Teach children to define the task. Library projects (7–8 years). Keep children on task by having them list questions to be answered. Have children assess their own efforts. Let children decide how to share a story. Suggest tasks attainable but challenging for the children.	**Ages 3–5:** Feiffer Freeman **Ages 5–8:** Arnold Bonners Steele Twinem	*I Lost My Bear* *Corduroy* *Koalas* *Panda* *The Giant Panda* *High in the Trees*
Children will develop positive and realistic self-concepts.	Choose books that emphasize capabilities children have. Choose books that show characters seeing themselves positively and realistically. Choose literature that shows children growing and changing. Engage children in activities that demonstrate change. Read books that show children who can cope with problems. Choose books that provide models for ethnic and sex role identification.	**Ages 3–5:** Bemelmans Brown Cooney Graham Hoberman Hughes Hutchins Hutchins Ormerod Watanabe Watanabe Watanabe	*Madeline* *D. W. Flips* *Donald Says Thumbs Down* *Crusher is Coming* "A Year Later" *Alfie's Feet* *Tidy Titch* *You'll Soon Grow into Them, Titch* *Sunshine* *I Can Build a House!* *I Can Ride It!* *I Can Take a Walk!*

Table 7–1.   *(continued)*

Developmental Goals	Teaching Suggestions	Recommended Literature	
Children will develop positive and realistic self-concepts.	Discuss children's ideas of appropriate sex role behaviors.	**Ages 5–8:**	
		Bruchac	*Fox Song*
		Carlson	*It's Going to be Perfect*
		Hunter	*The Unbreakable Code*
		Isadora	*Max*
		Kroll	*Faraway Drums*
		Margolis	*"Two Wheels"*
		McKay	*Journey Home*
		Rylant	*Birthday Presents*
		Waber	*Ira Sleeps Over*
		Willner	*Daphne Eloise Slater*
		Winthrop	*Tough Eddie*
		Zolotow	*Someone New*
Children will develop feelings of self-worth and self-esteem.	Choose literature that reaffirms self-worth. Choose literature that supports individuality. Have children make booklets and tapes about themselves. Read books that give children a feeling of security. Plan activities that promote children complimenting one another.	**Ages 3–5:**	
		Adoff	*Big Sister Tells Me That I'm Black*
		Brown	*The Runaway Bunny*
		Davis	*The Other Emily*
		Joosse	*Whan Mama Comes Home Tonight*
		Lindbergh	*Grandfather's Love Song*
		Winthrop	*Sloppy Kisses*
		Ages 5–8:	
		Cohen	*First Grade Takes a Test*
		Howe	*I Wish I Were a Butterfly*
		Whitcomb	*Odd Velvet*
Children will begin to recognize their own values and to choose from among values.	Lead discussions about value conflicts in books. Have children decide which character they agree with when characters express differing values. Encourage children to evaluate the rationale for particular beliefs.	**Ages 5–8:**	
		Cooney	*Miss Rumphius*
		Lee	*Nim and the War Effort*
		Lionni	*Frederick*

Table 7–1.   *(continued)*

Developmental Goals	Teaching Suggestions	Recommended Literature	
Children will understand their emotions and express them in socially acceptable ways.	Share books that show emotions common to young children. Combine books to explore several facets of a single emotion. Present children with options for dealing with emotions. Show one character experiencing many emotions. Engage children in dialogue that expresses emotion through dramatic activities such as puppetry and role-play. Let children tell their feelings using the format of a specific book or poem. Provide children with knowledge about new experiences. Encourage children to talk about their fears.	**Ages 3–5:** Clifton Cohen Cohen Greenfield Hoban Jonas McKissack Stevenson Wells Zolotow	*Everett Anderson books* *Jim Meets the Thing* *Will I Have a Friend?* *William and the Good Old Days* *A Birthday for Frances* *Holes and Peeks* *Ma Dear's Aprons* *What's Under My Bed?* *Timothy Goes to School* *A Father Like That*
Children will understand their emotions and express them in socially acceptable ways.		**Ages 5–8:** Brisson Carrick Carrick Cooper Giff Gould Greenfield Jay Mayer Miles Rappaport Viorst	*The Summer My Father Was Ten* *Books about Christopher* *Left Behind* *Gettin' Through Thursday* *Next Year I'll Be Special* *Grandpa's Slide Show* "Love Don't Mean" *Swimming Lessons* *One Frog Too Many* *Annie and the Old One* *The New King* *Alexander and the Terrible, Horrible, No Good, Very Bad Day*

Extending Your Learning

1. Select a picture book and describe three possible activities based upon it.

2. Make a list of five choices children might reasonably be asked to make during one school day, or three during a half-day at preschool.

3. Look at any two of Shigeo Watanabe's books. How does each encourage a child to be independent?

4. Analyze sex role models presented in ten picture books. Identify any stereotypes that may be present. Do the same for five books from one of the bibliographies of nonsexist books listed in the recommended references.

5. Read at least one of the picture books recommended in *Building Bridges with Multicultural Picture Books for Children 3–5* by Beaty. Tell how it might contribute to a child's self-concept, and to appreciation of that child's culture by members of other cultures.

6. Identify the values underlying the actions of the main character in five different picture books.

7. Read several books about the same character, listing the situations and emotions they experience and assessing the range of emotions shown by the character. Recommended books include the books about Christopher by Carrick; the books about Everett Anderson by Clifton; the books about Jim and his classmates by Cohen; and the books about Frances by Hoban.

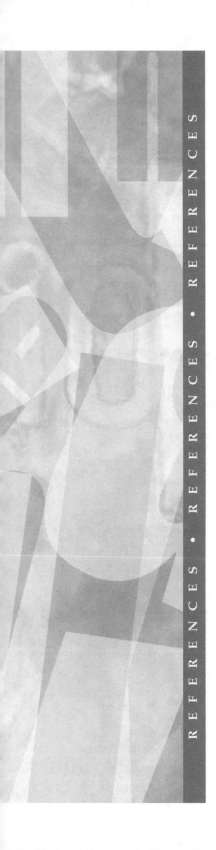

RECOMMENDED REFERENCES

Beaty, J. (1997). *Building Bridges with Multicultural Picture Books for Children 3–5.* Upper Saddle River, NJ: Prentice-Hall.

Beilke, P. and Sciara, F. (1986). *Selecting Materials for and about Hispanic and East Asian Children and Young People.* Hamden, CT: Shoestring Press.

Coopersmith, S. (1967). *The Antecedents of Self-Esteem.* San Francisco: W. H. Freeman.

Day, F. (1997). *Latina and Latino Voices in Literature for Children and Teenagers.* Portsmouth, NH: Heinemann.

Elkind, D. (1988). *The Hurried Child.* Rev. ed. Reading, MA: Addison-Wesley.

Erikson, E. (1993). *Childhood and Society.* (updated ed.) New York: Norton.

Goleman, D. (1995). *Emotional Intelligence.* New York: Bantam.

Glenn, H. S. (1988). *Raising Self-Reliant Children in a Self-Indulgent World.* Rocklin, CA: Prima Publishing.

Greenspan, S. (1985). *First Feelings.* New York: Viking.

Hyson, M. (1994). *The Emotional Development of Children.* New York: Teachers College Press.

Kagan, J. (1994). *The Nature of Emotion.* The Monographs of the Society for Research in Children's Development, Vol. 59., Nos. 2-3, serial no. 240. Chicago: University of Chicago Press.

Kübler-Ross, E. (1983). *On Children and Death.* New York: Macmillan.

Medeiros, D., Porter, B., and Welsh, I. (1983). *Children Under Stress.* Upper Saddle River, NJ: Prentice-Hall.

Mussen, P., Conger, J., Kagan, J. and Huston, A. (1990). *Child Development and Personality.* 7th ed. New York: Harper.

Odean, K. (1997). *Great Books for Girls.* New York: Ballantine.

Schacter, R. and McCauley, C. (1988). *When Your Child is Afraid.* New York: Simon.

Wright, M. (1998). *I'm Chocolate, You're Vanilla: Raising Healthy Black and Biracial Children in a Race-conscious World.* San Francisco: Jossey-Bass.

Youngs, B. (1985). *Stress in Children.* New York: Arbor House.

RECOMMENDED CHILDREN'S BOOKS

Bang, Molly. (1996). *Goose.* New York: Scholastic. (Discovering capabilities)

Bunting, Eve. (1987). *Ghost's Hour, Spook's Hour.* Ill. Donald Carrick. New York: Clarion. (Overcoming fear)

Carter, Dorothy. (1998). *Bye, Mis' Lela.* Ill. Harvey Stevenson. New York: Farrar. (Understand death)

Fox, Mem. (1994). *Tough Boris.* Ill. Kathryn Brown. San Diego: Harcourt. (Expressing emotion)

Frasier, Debra. (1991). *On the Day You Were Born.* San Diego: Harcourt. (Building self-esteem)

Goble, Paul. (1989). *Beyond the Ridge.* New York: Bradbury. (Understanding death)

Henkes, Kevin. (1995). *The Biggest Boy.* Ill. Nancy Tafuri. New York: Greenwillow. (Using imagination)

Henkes, Kevin. (1991). *Chrysanthemum.* New York: Greenwillow. (Maintaining self-esteem)

Hoffman, Mary. (1991). *Amazing Grace.* Ill. Caroline Binch. New York: Dial. (Overcoming stereotyping)

Jukes, Mavis. (1984). *Like Jake and Me.* Ill. Lloyd Bloom. New York: Knopf. (Relating to stepfather)

Little, Jean. (1992). *Revenge of the Small Small.* Ill. Janet Wilson. New York: Viking. (Experiencing revenge and forgiveness)

Molnar-Fenton, Stephan. (1998). *An Mei's Strange and Wondrous Journey.* Ill. Vivienne Flesher. New York: DK Ink. (Learning about self)

Park, Frances and Park, Ginger. (1998). *My Freedom Trip: A Child's Escape from North Korea.* Ill. Debra Reid Jenkins. Honesdale, PA: Boyds Mills. (Overcoming fear)

Raschka, Chris. (1996). *The Blushful Hippopotamus.* New York: Orchard. (Building self-esteem)

Rylant, Cynthia. (1996). *The Old Lady Who Named Things.* Ill. Kathryn Brown. San Diego: Harcourt. (Overcoming loneliness)

Say, Allen. (1993). *Grandfather's Journey.* Boston: Houghton Mifflin. (Experiencing homesickness)

Shea, Pegi Deitz. (1995). *The Whispering Cloth.* Ill. Anita Riggio. Honesdale, PA: Boyds Mills. (Overcoming adversity)

Wells, Rosemary. (1988). *Shy Charles.* New York: Dial. (Overcoming shyness)

Wells, Rosemary. (1998). *Yoko.* New York: Hyperion. (Gaining acceptance)

Wyeth, Sharon Dennis. (1998). *Something Beautiful.* Ill. Chris Soentpiet. New York: Bantam. (Recognizing beauty)

PROFESSIONAL REFERENCES CITED

Brewer, J. (1997). *Introduction to Early Childhood Education: Preschool through Primary Grades.* (3rd ed). Boston: Allyn & Bacon.

Erikson, E. (1986). *Childhood and Society.* (35th anniversary ed). New York: Norton.

Katz, L., and McClellan, D. (1997). *Fostering Children's Social Competence.* Washington, DC: National Association for the Education of Young Children.

Koch, K. (1970). *Wishes, Lies, and Dreams.* New York: Random House.

National Council for the Social Studies. (1994). *Expectations of Excellence: Curriculum Standards for Social Studies.* Wilmington, DE: National Council for the Social Studies.

Papelia, D., Olds, S., and Felman, R. (1998). *Human Development.* (7th ed). Boston: McGraw-Hill.

CHILDREN'S LITERATURE CITED

Adoff, Arnold. (1976). *Big Sister Tells Me That I'm Black.* New York: Holt. Reprinted by permission of Holt, Rinehart & Winston.

Arnold, Caroline. (1987). *Koalas.* Ill. Richard Hewitt. New York: Morrow.

Bonners, Susan. (1978). *Panda.* New York: Delacorte.

Brisson, Pat. (1998). *The Summer My Father Was Ten.* Ill. Andrea Shine. Honesdale, PA: Boyds Mills.

Brown, Marc. (1987). *D.W. Flips.* Boston: Little, Brown.

Brown, Marc. (1998). *D.W.'s Lost Blankie.* Boston: Little, Brown.

Brown, Margaret Wise. (1942). *The Runaway Bunny*. Ill. Clement Hurd. New York: Harper.

Bruchac, Joseph. (1993). *Fox Song*. Ill. Paul Morin. Boston: Little, Brown.

Carlson, Nancy. (1998). *It's Going to Be Perfect*. New York: Viking.

Carrick, Carol. (1976). *The Accident*. Ill. Donald Carrick. New York: Seabury.

Carrick, Carol. (1984). *Dark and Full of Secrets*. Ill. Donald Carrick. New York: Clarion.

Carrick, Carol. (1977). *The Foundling*. Ill. Donald Carrick. New York: Seabury.

Carrick, Carol. (1988). *Left Behind*. Ill. Donald Carrick. New York: Clarion.

Carrick, Carol. (1974). *Lost in the Storm*. Ill. Donald Carrick. New York: Clarion.

Caseley, Judith. (1990). *The Cousins*. New York: Greenwillow.

Clifton, Lucille. (1983). *Everett Anderson's Goodbye*. Ill. Ann Grifalcone. New York: Holt.

Clifton, Lucille. (1978). *Everett Anderson's Nine Month Long*. Ill. Ann Grifalcone. New York: Holt.

Clifton, Lucille. (1977). *Everett Anderson's 1-2-3*. Ill. Ann Grifalcone. New York: Holt.

Clifton, Lucille. (1970). *Some of the Days of Everett Anderson*. Ill. Evaline Ness. New York: Holt.

Cohen, Miriam. (1980). *First Grade Takes a Test*. Ill. Lillian Hoban. New York: Greenwillow.

Cohen, Miriam. (1981). *Jim Meets the Thing*. Ill. Lillian Hoban. New York: Greenwillow.

Cohen, Mirian. (1967). *Will I Have a Friend?* Ill. Lillian Hoban. New York: Macmillan.

Cooney, Barbara. (1982). *Miss Rumphius*. New York: Viking.

Cooney, Nancy Evans. (1987). *Donald Says Thumbs Down*. Ill. Maxie Chambliss. New York: Putnam's.

Cooper, Melrose. (1998). *Gettin' Through Thursday*. Ill. Nneka Bennett. New York: Lee & Low.

Corey, Dorothy. (1976). *You Go Away*. Ill. Lois Aceman. Chicago: Whitman.

Crews, Donald. (1992). *Shortcut*. New York: Greenwillow.

Davis, Gibbs. (1984). *The Other Emily*. Ill. Linda Shute. Boston: Houghton Mifflin.

Feiffer, Jules. (1998). *I Lost My Bear*. New York: Morrow.

Freeman, Don. (1968). *Corduroy*. New York: Viking.

Davis, Gibbs. (1984). Ill. by Linda Shute. Boston: Houghton Mifflin Co.

Giff, Patricia Reilly. (1993). *Next Year I'll Be Special*. Ill. Marylin Hafner. New York: Doubleday.

Gould, Deborah. (1987). *Grandpa's Slide Show*. Ill. Cheryl Harness. New York: Lothrop.

Graham, Bob. (1988). *Crusher Is Coming*. New York: Viking.

Greenfield, Eloise. (1978). "Love Don't Mean." in *Honey I Love*. Ill. Leo and Diane Dillon. New York: Crowell.

Greenfield, Eloise. (1993). *William and the Good Old Days*. Ill. Jan Spivey Gilchrist. New York: Harper.

Henkes, Kevin. (1990). *Julius, the Baby of the World*. New York: Greenwillow.

Hest, Amy. (1996). *Jamaica Louise James*. Ill. Sheila White Samton. Cambridge, MA: Candlewick.

Hoban, Russell. (1964). *A Baby Sister for Frances*. Ill. Lillian Hoban. New York: Harper & Row.

Hoban, Russell. (1995, 1968). *A Birthday for Frances*. Ill. Lillian Hoban. New York: Harper & Row.

Hoberman, Mary Ann. (1959). "A Year Later" in *Hello and Good-By*. Boston: Little, Brown. "A Year Later" reprinted by permission of Russell & Volkening, Inc. as agents for the author. Copyright © by Mary Ann Hoberman.

Hoffman, Mary. (1995). *Boundless Grace*. Ill. Caroline Binch. New York: Dial.

Holzenthaler, Jean. (1978) *My Hands Can*. Ill. Nancy Tafuri. New York: Dutton.

Howe, James. (1987). *I Wish I Were a Butterfly*. Ill. Ed Young. San Diego: Harcourt.

Hughes, Shirley. (1997). *All About Alfie*. Includes Alfie's Feet. New York: Lothrop.

Hunter, Sara Hoagland. (1996). *The Unbreakable Code*. Ill. Julia Miner. Flagstaff, AZ: Rising Moon.

Hutchins, Pat. (1991). *Tidy Titch*. New York: Greenwillow.

Hutchins, Pat. (1971). *Titch*. New York: Macmillan.

Hutchins, Pat. (1983). *You'll Soon Grow Into Them, Titch*. New York: Greenwillow.

Isadora, Rachel. (1976) *Max*. New York: Macmillan.

Jay, Betsy. (1998). *Swimming Lessons*. Ill. Lori Osiecki. Flagstaff, AZ: Rising Moon.

Jonas, Ann. (1984). *Holes and Peeks*. New York: Greenwillow.

Jonell, Lynn. (1997). *Mommy Go Away!* Ill. Petra Mathers. New York: Putnam.

Joosse, Barbara. (1991). *Mama, Do You Love Me?* Ill. Barbara Lavallee. San Francisco: Chronicle.

Kroll, Virginia. (1998). *Faraway Drums.* Ill. Floyd Cooper. Boston: Little, Brown.

Kuskin, Karla. (1975). "OK Everybody, Listen to This" in *Near the Window Tree.* New York: Harper. Copyright © by Karla Kuskin. Reprinted by permission of Scott Treimel, New York.

Lindbergh, Reeve. (1993). *Grandfather's Lovesong.* Ill. Rachel Isadora. New York: Viking.

Lee, Milly. (1997). *Nim and the War Effort.* Ill. Yangsook Choi. New York: Farrar.

Lionni, Leo. (1967). *Frederick.* New York: Pantheon.

Margolis, Richard. (1984). *Secrets of a Small Brother.* Ill. Donald Carrick. New York: Macmillan. Text copyright © by Richard J. Margolis. "Two Wheels" from *Secrets of a Small Brother* reprinted with the permission of Simon & Schuster Books for Young Readers, an imprint of Simon & Schuster Children's Publishing Division.

Mayer, Mercer and Marianna. (1975). *One Frog Too Many.* New York: Dial.

McKay, Lawrence. (1998). *Journey Home.* Ill. Dom and Keunhee Lee. New York: Lee & Low.

McKissack, Patricia. (1997). *Ma Dear's Aprons.* Ill. Floyd Cooper. New York: Atheneum.

Miles, Miska. (1971). *Annie and the Old One.* Ill. Peter Parnall. Boston: Little, Brown.

Ormerod, Jan. (1981). *Sunshine.* London: Kestrel.

Rappaport, Doreen. (1995). *The New King.* Ill. E.B. Lewis. New York: Dial.

Rathmann, Peggy. (1995). *Officer Buckle and Gloria.* New York: Putnam's.

Rogers, Fred. (1988). *Going to the Hospital.* Ill. Jim Judkis. New York: Putnam's.

Rylant, Cynthia. (1987). *Birthday Presents.* Ill. Sucie Stevenson. New York: Orchard/Watts.

Shannon, Margaret. (1993). *Elvira.* New York: Ticknor & Fields.

Spinelli, Eileen. (1998). *When Mama Comes Home Tonight.* Ill. Jane Dyer. New York: Simon & Schuster.

Steele, Philip. (1994). *The Giant Panda.* Ill. Joan Butler. New York: Kingfisher.

Stevenson, James. (1983). *What's Under My Bed?* New York: Greenwillow.

Twinem, Neecy. (1996). *High in the Trees.* New York: Charlesbridge.

Viorst, Judith. (1972). *Alexander and the Terrible, Horrible, No Good, Very Bad Day.* Ill. Ray Cruz. New York: Atheneum.

Waber, Bernard. (1972). *Ira Sleeps Over.* Boston: Houghton Mifflin.

Watanabe, Shigeo. (1983). *I Can Build a House!* Ill. Yasuo Ohtomo. New York: Philomel.

Watanabe, Shigeo. (1982). *I Can Ride It!* Ill. Yasuo Ohtomo. New York: Philomel.

Watanabe, Shigeo. (1976). *I Can Take a Walk!* Ill. Yasuo Ohtomo. New York: Macmillan.

Watanabe, Shigeo. (1988). *It's My Birthday!* Ill. Yasuo Ohtomo. New York: Philomel.

Wells, Rosemary. (1981). *Timothy Goes to School.* New York: Dial.

Whitcomb, Mary. (1998). *Odd Velvet.* Ill. Tara Calahan King. San Francisco: Chronicle.

Willner-Pardo, Gina. (1997). *Daphne Eloise Slater, Who's Tall for Her Age.* Ill. Glo Coalson. New York: Clarion.

Wilson, Jacqueline. (1998). *Double Act.* Ill. Nick Sharratt and Sue Heap. New York: Delacorte.

Winthrop, Elizabeth. (1985). *Tough Eddie.* Ill. Lillian Hoban. New York: Dutton.

Winthrop, Elizabeth. (1980). *Sloppy Kisses.* Ill. Anne Burgess. New York: Macmillan.

Zolotow, Charlotte. (1971). *A Father Like That.* Ill. Ben Schecter. New York: Harper & Row.

Zolotow, Charlotte. (1978). *Someone New.* Ill. Erik Blegvad. New York: Harper. Reprinted by permission of the author.

8

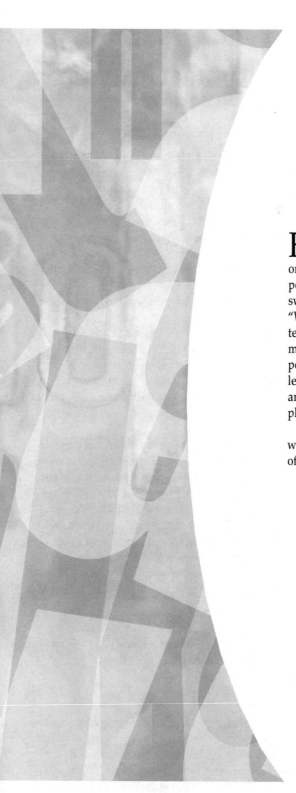

SUPPORTING CHILDREN'S SOCIAL AND MORAL DEVELOPMENT

Five-year-old Holly came running into the classroom, telling her teacher in indignant tones that Ralph kept chasing her on the playground. The teacher asked Holly what had happened. Holly explained that Ralph was standing near the swings, and that when she approached him he started after her. "What did you do when he started toward you?" asked the teacher. "I ran away," answered Holly. "What do you suppose might have happened if you had kept walking toward him or perhaps stood still?" probed the teacher. There was a long silence. Then Holly's face showed that she had grasped the idea and with a decisive "Oh" she turned and walked back to the playground.

Holly was just beginning to learn that her behavior toward others could affect their behavior toward her. It is but one of many social lessons that Holly will learn as she matures.

SOCIAL AND MORAL DEVELOPMENT IN YOUNG CHILDREN

Social Development

Much of children's social development, their ability to relate to other people, is correlated with their ability to see from the viewpoint of another (Shaffer, 1989). Piaget describes children who are in the preoperational stage of intellectual development, usually from about two to about six or seven years of age, as being egocentric. They are unable to consistently put themselves in someone else's place because they consider their own point of view the only possible one. Social workers and day-care professionals are finding that many preschool youngsters whose parents are divorced see themselves as the cause of the separation. They are not able to view the problems from their parents' perspectives, to comprehend that they may not be the center around which all actions revolve. They may also reason from one event to another, adding the element of causation. If Daddy left home, and if they had misbehaved, then Daddy must have left because they misbehaved.

The ability to take the perspective of another increases with age, most likely as a combination of cognitive development and the child's social experience. Thus there will be differences among children in this skill. And as children get older, they become better able to evaluate multiple attributes of a situation. A three-year-old may look at the situation another child is in and draw a conclusion, valid or not, about the child's feeling from that alone. A six-year-old will look at the expression on the child's face as well as the situation (Mussen, Conger, Kagan, & Huston, 1990).

Young children will often need help recognizing that other people have feelings that matter and that may differ from their own, as well as help learning to interpret the emotions of others. Being able to see from another's viewpoint and to interpret another person's response are developments central to the ability to interact successfully in social relationships.

Mussen and Eisenberg-Berg were concerned with conditions under which children exhibited prosocial behavior, actions that were intended to aid another person and for which no rewards were expected. When would a child volunteer to give her toy to someone who did not have one, or help a classmate who was injured or crying? After analyzing hundreds of studies, they concluded:

> To act in accordance with learned or internalized norms, the child must first perceive the other person's needs, interpret them accurately, and recognize that he or she can be helped. In addition, the child must feel competent in this situation, that is, capable of providing what is needed, and the cost or risk entailed in helping must not be prohibitive. Unless these preconditions are met, even the child who knows the norm of social responsibility is not likely to render aid.

Mussen & Eisenberg, pp. 5–6

Thus it requires more than simply telling children to help others in order for them actually to provide help when it is needed. The authors write that experiences such as seeing prosocial behavior modeled and having participated in role-playing will enhance prosocial behavior.

The models of behavior that children see are a powerful force in their learning. According to social learning theorists, children observe how behaviors are performed and in what situations. If they see a teacher treating children courteously and kindly, they are likely to adopt this behavior toward one another. They are also influenced by the rewards that follow behaviors, both when the reinforcement comes directly to them and when they observe its being given to someone else (Bandura, 1977). If one child is praised for completing a task, both that child and the observers learn that completing tasks is a behavior that will be rewarded. Likewise, negative reinforcement identifies behavior to be avoided.

Children observe a wide variety of models and use these, along with their perceptions of the reinforcement given, to determine acceptable behaviors for themselves. Sometimes they will make mistakes from an adult's perspective. Kelly knew from kindergarten that at snack time each child received an equal share of the food. She listened at home as her parents planned a dinner party, estimating the number of hors d'oeuvres needed for the guests. On the evening of the party, Kelly greeted the guests by explaining, "You each get five shrimp, three little sandwiches, and three meatballs." From her perception, that was acceptable behavior. The reaction of her parents, a look of distress, and that of the guests, amused laughter, indicated to Kelly that the behavior in a kindergarten setting was not appropriate in this setting. Much social learning involves determining when and where behaviors are likely to be condoned, as well as learning the behaviors themselves.

Children are influenced by observing adults interacting with other people of varying ethnic and national backgrounds. Parents and other significant adults who either denigrate those who differ from themselves or totally avoid them contribute to children's distrust of people of different races, religions, or nationalities. Parents and adults who model that they appreciate and value diversity contribute to a more open attitude among children. Including literature that supports a multicultural curriculum can help children see similarities as well as differences among people.

Many behaviors are culturally defined. Children are reared in a cultural context that shows them most aspects of social relationships and they may take these unwritten rules for granted. They learn when it is appropriate to touch, when not; if one looks directly at an authority figure or keeps ones eyes downcast; whether one competes or cooperates. Then, when they encounter others whose expectations and constraints are different from their own, they may be shocked and uncomfortable. While teachers and day-care providers cannot know the norms and expectations of all the cultures represented in their group of children, they can work toward understanding and respect for differing backgrounds, and model this for children. Katz writes that

> It is likely that teachers who understand and appreciate their own culture and the cultures of others can better help children bridge cultural differences. It is also likely that these teachers will be able to practice and facilitate a broader range of social skills than will teachers who rely solely on their own cultural background.

Katz & McClellan, p. 55.

Knowledge of children's social development results from both experimental studies and from simply observing children. Observational studies at the Bank Street College of Education have found that toddlers who were together on a consistent basis appeared to learn social skills of interaction earlier than those without that experience (Oppenheim, 1984).

Friendships are important for children for several reasons. First, they provide opportunities for children to learn and practice social skills. Adults will often interpret a child's unclear request or stop conflict the minute it begins; but children engage with one another as equals, which requires that communication be clear in order to be effective and that techniques of handling conflicts or making requests be learned. Second, friendships give children a context in which they can compare themselves with others. Who is the taller of the two? Who can run faster? This sort of social comparison helps children develop a valid sense of their own identity. Finally, friendships foster a feeling of group belonging, a security that differs from that achieved within the family. However, friendships may have undesirable as well as desirable effects. They may be the cause of jealousy, rejection of others, or antisocial behavior as well as security, self-acceptance, and trust. In writing about children's friendships, Rubin states, "The fact of the matter is that children's closest friendships manifest all of the prominent features of close relationships among adults, including their destructive as well as their constructive elements. Perhaps the biggest difference between children's and adults' interactions is that children tend to be more straight-forward" (Rubin, 1984, p. 11).

Friendships are not the same as popularity. A person can get along with others and have status in a peer group yet not be able to form caring and reciprocal relationships with a few peers. Katz notes that both aspects of social competence are important, but that "The capacity for friendship most likely has greater significance for long-term development than does popularity"(Katz and McClellan, 1997, p. 2).

As children mature, their concept of friendship changes. The three-year-old is likely to describe a friend in terms of physical attributes. He or she may say, for example, "Carlos is the same size as me." Children at this age will often consider those who are playing with them at the moment to be their friends. Two to three years later the description of a friend will include observations about behaviors and physical features, such as "Carlos wears a red coat. He can make people laugh whenever he wants." Friendship is determined by what that person does for the child and is generally tied to specific episodes. By age eight or nine, children describe the traits they like or dislike and are beginning to see friendship as a relationship that lasts over time. At this stage, a child might say, "Carlos is my friend because we like each other, and he will help me even when he's busy. He's my friend even when he's away visiting his grandmother." Thus the shift is from viewing people as physical entities to seeing them as both physical entities and psychological beings as well, and from thinking of friendship as a momentary encounter to seeing it as a lasting relationship (Rubin, 1984).

It is likely that children develop part of their concept of friendship from observing adult friendships. It appears, however, that the major portion of their understanding comes from their own encounters with others and the way they integrate what they have learned. Thus children need to have the experience of working with each other in both large and small groups. Adults must recognize, though, that children vary in their social needs and social styles, and to respect these differences.

Moral Development

Moral, as well as social, development is related to intellectual development. Jean Piaget and Lawrence Kohlberg see the growth of moral reasoning as developing in stages which coincide with stages of cognitive growth. Piaget (1955) describes two broad stages of moral development. In the first, children have difficulty seeing situations from another's point of view and perceive acts as either totally right or totally wrong. They tend to judge an act on the basis of consequences and not on intention. The child who broke the cookie jar into many pieces trying to dry it is guiltier than the child who only cracked the jar while trying to sneak a cookie. They follow rules set down by adults not because of a belief in the need for a particular rule, but because the adult who gave it wields authority.

In the second stage, children are more likely to be able to see another's point of view. They are less absolute in their judgments and will assess acts more by intentions than by consequences. They also begin to favor less punishment for wrongdoers. Piaget sees this shift in stages as occurring when the child is around eight or nine years old.

Kohlberg (1981) based his studies on Piaget's model of moral development. He describes a total of six stages of development, each keyed to the individual's sense of justice and to the reasoning used to solve moral dilemmas. Children ages four to ten reason at the first two stages, at the *preconventional* level. In stage 1, punishment and obedience orientation, they obey rules in order to avoid punishment. In stage 2, instrumental purpose and exchange, they conform to rules out of self-interest and do things for others in order to get things in return. As they mature, they will pass through further stages. Stage 3 is one of doing what "good boys" or "good girls" do, and stage 4 one of respecting the laws a way of maintaining society. In the last two stages, personally developed moral principles take precedence over concern with authority. Kohlberg believes that most Americans operate at about stage 4.

Children develop their ability in moral reasoning through consideration of moral problems and through contact with the moral reasoning of others. Reasoning just one stage above their own is more meaningful to them than reasoning that is several stages higher. And the stage at which children as well as adults reason about moral questions is not always a predictor of their actual behavior in a situation involving a moral question.

Kohlberg based his work entirely on the reactions of males. Carol Gilligan (1982), studying the responses of women, found that they based their reasoning on moral dilemmas on being considerate of others and on maintaining relationships. They were cognizant of how their actions might affect others. Gilligan notes that women are socialized to consider the effects of their actions on others more than to follow personal principles.

Social learning theorists emphasize the importance of models of moral behavior and the use of rewards and punishment in children's moral development. Children who have internalized the standards of their parents may feel guilty when they do not comply with the standards, even if the parent is not in a position to punish them. The theorists note also that children's responses to moral questions can be changed by their listening to or observing a model who holds the opposite opinion (Bandura, 1977). After being given directions for one set of behaviors, then observing other behaviors being modeled, children are likely to imitate the model. "Do as I say and not as I do," is often ignored.

Although the theories of moral reasoning and of social learning have different key elements, they are not contradictory when applied to young children. A child reasoning at Kohlberg's stage 1, that of behaving in a particular way to avoid punishment, will be greatly influenced by rewards and punishments as well as by the behavior he sees modeled and the consequences it brings.

But theories are useful in guiding young children's moral development. Piaget and Kohlberg illustrate the need for children to discuss the reasons behind moral decisions and help teachers understand the kinds of reasoning common among young children. Social learning theories remind teachers of the importance of the models of behavior they present, both through their own actions and through vicarious sources introduced into children's learning environments.

GOALS FOR TEACHING

Once again, the goals for teaching can be classified as long-term developmental goals, general goals for a particular age or grade level, and specific goals for individual children. A long-term goal for social and moral development is that children will become sensitive to the feelings and intentions of others. This ability to empathize with others and understand their motivations will help children interact successfully with both peers and adults. Teachers and day-care professionals will be helping children achieve this goal throughout the preschool and primary years.

A general social goal for preschoolers is that, in a small group, each child will tell about an experience or perhaps share an object, and will listen to others tell about their experiences. The children are learning the social skills of taking turns and of listening to others, as well as developing their own speaking skills. The amount of waiting time in relation to the amount of action time is kept low by limiting the number of children in the group.

A general social goal for second grade is that children will work in small groups on specific tasks for 10 to 15 minutes without the teacher's immediate presence and will make progress toward completing the task. It is expected that by the end of the year, nearly all of the children in each of these levels will have achieved the general goals set for them.

In addition, there will be goals for individual children that teachers develop as they come to know their classes. A social goal for a third-grader could be that Peter will volunteer to help Robin and Chris with their reading. The teacher knows that Peter is capable of the task, but wants him to recognize both his own competence and the needs of others and then engage in prosocial behavior.

Literature can contribute to the achievement of all three types of goals. This chapter focuses on long-term developmental goals. Books offer opportunities for you to help children grow toward the following goals for social and moral development:

> Children will make inferences about the feelings and intentions of others.
>
> Children will view a situation from more than one perspective, seeing the viewpoint of another person.
>
> Children will engage in prosocial behavior.
>
> Children will judge the appropriateness of specific behaviors and predict the possible consequences of particular behaviors.
>
> Children will learn about others who differ from themselves and value this diversity.
>
> Children will engage competently in group activities.
>
> Children will evaluate various solutions to moral problems and ethical questions.

As with other areas, these goals can be correlated with national and regional standards. For example, the goal that children will learn about others who differ from themselves and value this diversity fits with Theme 1, Culture, in the ten themes that provide the organizational framework for the social studies standards developed by the National Council for the Social Studies (1994). That standard states that "Social studies programs should include experiences that provide for the study of culture and cultural diversity" (1994, p. 21). As you look at national standards, or those for your region or school district, look for ways in which these goals and the specific standards mesh.

OPPORTUNITIES BOOKS OFFER
Giving Children Experience in Making Inferences About the Feelings and Intentions of Others

Books provide a rich source of data from which children can begin to gain information, make inferences, and check the validity of inferences they make. As stories unfold, characters reveal more and more of their feelings and more and more of their reasons for acting as they do. Children can make hypotheses at several points in a story and, as the story progresses, see if their hypotheses were accurate. The situation is nonthreatening—there is no penalty if their predictions are not what actually happens in the story. Children simply explore whether there was ample evidence to support their guesses or whether they missed some important clues to the feelings of the characters.

Interpreting Nonverbal Language in Illustrations

The illustrations in books give children experience in reading and interpreting body language and facial expressions. Because these illustrations are static, catching a moment in time, they give children a chance to study them and talk about specific aspects. The illustrations in *When Zaydeh Danced on Eldridge Street* (Rael, 1997) clearly show the fear and uncertainty Zeesie has as she talks with her Zaydeh Avrum, the grandfather who seems to her to dislike children. She stands looking downward, hands clasped tightly in front of her, toes turned inward. Once she has seen a different side of Zaydeh, has seen how important it was to him that she asked about the meaning of the Torah, has seen him dancing, her posture changes. She looks up, and moves with her arms swinging at her sides.

Marie Hall Ets's book *Talking Without Words* (1968) focuses on the use of body language to communicate. Sometimes actions take the place of words. Holding out a bag of cookies or candy to someone else is a way of offering the sweets to them. A finger in front of the lips means to be quiet. At other times the body expresses a reaction to an event, a mood, or an emotion. Holding the nose usually means the presence of an unpleasant odor—real or metaphoric—and sticking out the tongue expresses dislike for someone. Ets shows these actions and others in illustrations and uses a brief text to say what they mean. The fact that the illustrations portray children and their mother helps children relate to what is being communicated. The book provides an excellent point of departure for having children pantomime messages, with others telling what is being said. You could have the children take turns, demonstrating one of the gestures shown in the book. Then they could begin to think of other body messages that were not shown. Children in preschool through the primary grades can understand this book and enjoy using their bodies to show meanings.

Wordless picture books are an excellent source of material in which body language and facial expressions are emphasized. In *Frog Goes to Dinner* (Mayer, 1974) the expressions range from the pleasure of the parents as the family goes into a restaurant, to the surprise of one of the patrons when the boy's frog lands in her salad, to the haughtiness of the headwaiter as he expels the family, to the disdain and anger of parents and sister as they glare at the boy and his frog on the way home. The final surprise of the story happens as the boy and frog are sent away in disgrace. The boy, with head bowed, carries an unhappy frog to his room. But as soon as the door is closed, boy and frog convulse with laughter. The variety of emotions, as well as the changes in emotions, provide much material for drawing inferences. Children can tell the story in their own words, perhaps by one recalling just what happened and the next suggesting how the characters feel. Another technique is for the children to take the part of one of the characters and speak in appropriate dialogue. It is useful to give children a card with the name or the picture of their character on it. This avoids confusion about who has which part, and if you want to have different children play the parts, you can help them remember by simply changing the cards. It eliminates arguments about who was to do what.

Wordless picture books vary in difficulty just as other picture books do. *Frog Goes to Dinner* is most appropriate for children in the primary grades or higher. For kindergarten and younger children, look for books with fairly simple plots in which the action is straightforward. A book such as *Picnic* (McCully, 1984) is appropriate for young children because the plot is uncomplicated and easy to follow. The book shows a family of mice heading out for a picnic. As their red truck bounces along the dirt road, one of the nine mouse children falls from the back and is left behind. The pictures then alternately show the lost mouse and the rest of the family. When the family discovers that someone is missing, they begin calling for her; then all get back in the truck and head toward home, searching along the way. The lost mouse hears the truck, runs out to the road, and all are reunited. Before they can continue, however, the rescued one must retrieve her doll, also a mouse, which she had dropped in the excitement of hearing her family returning. Together again, they can at last settle down for the picnic lunch.

Books with text may have illustrations that are as explicit concerning the characters' actions and feelings as those in wordless picture books, but the listeners, or watchers, do not have to make the interpretations themselves. Children can still be given the opportunity to discuss the illustrations. They may be asked to tell what they can about a character from the early illustrations. The endpapers for *Sam* (Scott, 1992) show Sam stretched out on the floor, looking rather wistful, his head resting on his crossed arms. On the title page, Sam's back faces the readers, but his head is turned so that his facial expression can be seen. Once again, he is looking uncertain. Children can be shown these two pictures before the reading begins and asked to say how they think the boy feels. They should be encouraged to give their reasons for their judgments. Then the story can be shared. Sam wants to play, but all the other members of his family are busy. He tries to join them, picking up one of his brother's books, and then joining his sister as she cuts clothes for her paper dolls. Each person suggests that he do something else. Finally, in frustration, he sits down and cries. The family realizes how he feels and his mother asks him to help her in the kitchen. After the children have heard the story, let them look again at some of the illustrations. Ask the children to tell how Sam feels in selected pictures, and how they know. Have children sit or walk like one of the characters. Have them show with their bodies and faces what the characters were feeling.

In some instances, you will want to ask the children to interpret some of the illustrations and to make predictions about what may happen next as you read a story. At other times, you may want to complete an entire story before engaging the children in any discussion. You can decide how to approach the story and the discussion by remembering that enjoyment and understanding of the story are the central purposes for your reading. Thus, if interrupting the narrative would destroy the story, wait until it is completed before talking about illustrations. But if the children seem confused, or if discussion throughout the story heightens interest for them, then go ahead with discussions at various points in your reading.

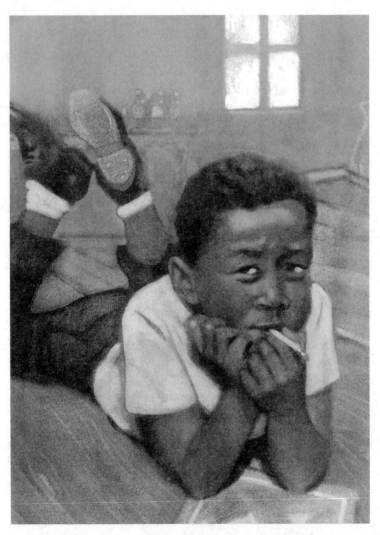

Children can be asked to describe a character's feelings as they look at an illustration. (From Coming Home: From the Life of Langston Hughes *by Floyd Cooper. Copyright © 1994 by Floyd Cooper. Used by permission of Philomel Books, a division of Penguin Putnam Inc.)*

Look for illustrators who are particularly adept at showing facial expressions and body language. Floyd Cooper, Trina Schart Hyman, James Ransome, Ted Lewin, Pat Cummings, Stephen Gammell, Symeon Shimin, Lillian Hoban, Mercer Mayer, and Donald Carrick are just a few whose work almost always captures easily recognizable emotions in physical expressions.

Relating Voice Inflection to Meaning

Children can gain experience in relating voice inflection to meaning and to the feelings of the speaker. The facets of language that linguists call *suprasegmentals* add meaning to speech. These are *pitch,* the high and low tones; *stress,* the emphasis with which a particular word or syllable is said; and *juncture,* the pause between syllables, words, or sentences. Variations in these tell the listener whether the sentence is a question or a statement; whether the phrase is "ice cream" or "I scream;" whether the speaker is being sincere or sarcastic.

Children do not need to know the terms or even know how to isolate pitch, stress, and juncture. They do need to hear expressive speech so that they can begin making generalizations for themselves about the speaker's meaning. You can provide many examples through your skillful reading. For example, your voice should reflect the change in Sam's father; from his angry statement of "SAM, get your hands off that typewriter. . . . How many times must I tell you—that typewriter is not a toy for children," to his concerned question, "What in the world is the matter with Sam?" (Scott, 1992, n.p.)

Children can use expression themselves in interpreting the dialogue in *Yo! Yes!* (Raschka, 1993). A more extroverted boy makes friends with a shy youngster, with the entire story told through one or two word utterances from each, and the illustrations showing the attendant emotions. The text is large enough for a group of children to see as a teacher holds the book. Children can read the dialogue, adding the expression in their voice so that the full meaning of the exchanges is conveyed.

Going Beyond a Literal Interpretation of Dialogue

Children can be given the opportunity to analyze when dialogue can be accepted at face value, and when a meaning other than a literal interpretation of the words is intended. Preschool children can recognize the hidden agenda in Frances' suggestion that perhaps a whole candy bar would be too much for her little sister Gloria to eat in *A Birthday for Frances,* (Hoban, 1995). Frances has already put two of the bubble gum balls intended for Gloria into her own mouth without "noticing" it.

Primary children will comprehend the more subtle nuances of the language used by Clancy and his friend Tippitt in *Clancy's Coat* (Bunting, 1984). The two have been angry with each other ever since Tippitt's cow trampled the vegetables in Clancy's garden. Tippitt looks out one day to see Clancy approaching, a package under his arm. He has brought a coat that needs turning, and tells Tippitt he has brought it to him "for the reason that you're the best tailor in Crossgar, and not for the sake of old friendships." Clancy rubs his hands together and comments on how cold it is outside, all the while eyeing the steaming teapot. Tippitt ignores him and the hints and informs Clancy that the coat will be ready the next Saturday.

During the week, Tippitt goes to the barn on an extra cold night and, looking for something to keep his cow warm, spies Clancy's coat. He forgets about using the coat as a blanket until Clancy arrives, then invites him in to soothe the expected annoyance. When Clancy asks for his coat, Tippitt replies, "It's not ready yet. It's been over my . . . over . . . overlooked." He assures Clancy it will be ready the next Saturday and gives him a cup of tea. For several weeks, Tippitt uses the coat for emergencies, telling Clancy things such as "There's good work being done on it, I'll promise you that" when his hen is laying eggs on it.

Little by little the two friends mend their differences, and when Tippitt remarks to Clancy that it was a lucky thing his coat needed turning, Clancy winks and says, "I told you there was a lot of use left in it." The meaning of the dialogue goes far beyond the literal.

Knowing the context in which dialogue occurs helps children interpret the meaning and whether the content should be taken literally. The persuasive language of sales permeates *Yard Sale* by James Stevenson (1996). The animals are selling things they'd like to get rid of, but make the objects sound attractive and the problems unimportant. Crocker explains that the alarm clock he is selling is "rare and special" because it is silent, not making those nasty noises. There is no key because the clock is pre-wound, and how could Henry ask about the lack of numbers on the clock face. Doesn't he remember where the numbers on a clock are? All ends well with the animals' sense of fairness prevailing. Children can discuss the accuracy of the sales pitches used by various animals and the purposes of persuasive language.

Following a Sequence of Action

The meaning behind some dialogue is related to an entire sequence of action. Only if the readers know what has happened earlier are they able to interpret the statements of various characters accurately. In *Could Be Worse* (Stevenson, 1977), Grandpa relates a dream at the breakfast table. He was pulled out of bed by a large bird, had an encounter with an abominable snowman, was chased across the desert by a huge blob of marmalade, met up with a squid and a giant sea turtle, and finally returned to his bed by getting a ride on a piece of toast and an airplane made out of newspaper. The readers know that Grandpa has not lost his mind but is reacting to his grandchildren's comments about him that he had overheard. They think the reason he never says anything interesting is because nothing interesting ever happens to him. Readers who have heard Grandpa respond to all the problems his grandchildren have by saying "Could be worse" are ready and waiting for the response that Grandpa gets when he asks the children what they think of his adventure: "Could be worse!"

Children who have had to defend their toys from being taken over by jealous younger brothers or sisters recognize the sequence of events in *Peabody* (Wells, 1983) as Annie opens her birthday present and finds a large teddy bear. Her younger brother Robert immediately announces that he wants it. Children recognize the cleverness, and the lack of accuracy, in Annie's response, "Peabody bites." After they have seen Robert gazing longingly at Peabody, they also can appreciate Annie's telling Robert that the red wool string that makes a fence around Peabody is an electric fence, something not to be touched.

A subtle change occurs in *The Scarebird* (Fleischman, 1988). Lonesome John lives by himself now that his family has gone and his dog has died. He builds a scarecrow and adds a head first, since a headless scarecrow is enough to "give a man the cold creeps." He paints eyes on the face and begins saying good morning and good night to his scarebird. He adds gloves, shoes, and a hat, each in response to changing weather conditions. Eventually he plays himself in checkers, sitting by the scarebird and talking as he plays. About that time Sam, a young farmhand looking for work, appears. John lets Sam stay, thinking of another task for him to do each day or two and, as the need arises, taking gloves, hat, and shoes from the scarebird and giving them to Sam. The book ends with John asking Sam if he plays checkers. Children who recognize the pattern of action and see John's need for companionship shifting its focus from the scarebird to Sam will understand the import of the question. The answer, shown in the final illustration, is yes, Sam does play checkers.

Following the sequence of action is as helpful in making inferences about characters' feeling and intentions as it is for fully understanding dialogue. Young children develop an understanding of action and reaction in human relationships when they see an entire drama played out in book form.

Observing Patterns of Behavior

Some youngsters, like Holly mentioned earlier, are just beginning to learn that their actions influence the actions of others. It was a new thought that Ralph may have chased her because she had been running herself. Other children, like six-year-old Rob, have learned how to control the behavior of others in certain situations. "Want to see my mommy get mad?" he asked his uncle and cousins who were visiting. Before they could answer, he opened a gate to the kitchen and put the cat in where his mother was working. Within seconds the angry words of his mother could be heard. "How did the cat get in here! I told you to keep the gate closed." Rob just grinned.

Children vary in their comprehension of the total situation in which action occurs. To help them see specific behaviors in a broader context, share books in which the action-reaction pattern is fairly clear and use these books as the basis for dramatization. One such book is *The Quarreling Book* (Zolotow, 1968). When the book opens, Mr. James has just left the house on a rainy morning and has forgotten to kiss his wife good-bye. She is then cross and becomes critical of Jonathan when he comes down for breakfast. He thinks her criticism unfair and so, when Sally appears, he asks why she cannot ever be on time. The pattern continues, with each character having his or her mood spoiled, becoming irritable, and managing to ruin someone else's day in turn. The chain is broken when Eddie shoves his dog off the bed but is licked into better humor by the dog, who has interpreted the action as an invitation to play. Once Eddie feels better, he reacts to his sister's search for her pencil by giving her his best one. The pattern then reverses, with each character cheering another and apologizing for earlier actions. By five o'clock the sun has come out, and all is complete when Mr. James returns home and kisses his wife hello.

If children are linked up in the order in which the characters appear, they can dramatize this story fairly easily. Each knows that first someone will say something sharp or unkind to them, and that feeling angry, they will then do the same thing to someone else. When the pattern is reversed, the action moves back up the line.

Another story that lends itself to dramatization is *Revenge of the Small Small* (Little, 1992). Patsy is the youngest child in the Small family. Her three older siblings tease her constantly. Because she hates being left out even more than being teased, she does kind things for each of them when they are ill with the chicken pox. However, when she gets sick, the favors are not returned. Seeing what is going on, her father brings her a large box filled with paper, crayons, and a variety of objects that can be used in construction, and tells her she need not share. Her brothers and sisters talk about what she might do, hinting rather broadly that they'd like to be included, and when she doesn't, they begin a series of derogatory comments about the village she is creating. When the village is nearly completed, they notice that Patsy has placed gravestones in the churchyard for each of them, with inscriptions describing them as mean and bad. They head for bed subdued, and in the morning offer things to Patsy that she can add to her village. She in turn tells her dad what she has done and then proceeds to change the inscriptions. The action/reaction is clear, with the behavior of each character having an impact on that of the others. The "cast" can be enlarged or limited by changing the number of siblings, and new suggestions for ways of teasing and of making up can be added. Dramatizing the story helps children comprehend how one person's behavior can affect another's.

Empathizing with a Book Character

As children learn to "read" another's feelings they also become more sensitive to those feelings. You can ask them to empathize with a character by having them think about how they would feel if something similar happened to them. They might each tell about a pet they have, or have had, prior to your reading of *My Dog, Trip* (Ray, 1987). Allie tells about her father bringing home a puppy whose mother had been hit by a car; about her caring for it, the search when it runs away, and her joy when they finally find it. They name the pup Trip because it is so often underfoot. Children who have described their own pets can tell about how they would feel if their pet disappeared. Others who do not have pets might tell how they would feel if they lost one of their favorite toys. From "How would *you* feel if . . ." to "How do you think Allie felt when . . ." is a transformation from a question that is centered on the child to a question that is centered on the book character, but both ask the child to imagine feelings.

For some discussions, you may want to return to several different places in a book and ask children how they think the character may have been feeling at that time and why they think so. Depending on the story, you may want to do this as you read. For example, if you were sharing *How Smudge Came* (Gregory, 1997), you might first ask how Cindy, a young woman with Down's syndrome, is feeling when she sneaks the puppy she has found past Mrs. Watson and up to her room or as she shows her puppy to one of the patients at the Hospice where she works. Other points to stop might be when the dog is sent to the SPCA, when Cindy gets help in locating the SPCA from the patients at the Hospice, when she goes after the puppy but finds it has been given away, or when she goes to the Hospice House and finds that they have retrieved the puppy for her and that she can keep it there.

One step further in the process of identifying and empathizing with a character is for children to be asked to tell about times when they have felt the way they think the character feels. Thus children who have heard *How Smudge Came* might tell about times they have not been allowed to keep something they wanted, or have been disappointed, or have had other people be very caring and helpful to them. The emotional contact can help children relate to a person who may be very different from themselves and to gain an appreciation of others. Cindy is a real person with real feelings, real capabilities, and real friends who care about her—not just a person with a handicapping condition.

Child-care professionals sometimes encourage self-reporting by young children by supplying incidents that they have observed. Thus the adult might say, "Remember how you felt when you showed your new kitten during sharing time?" as they discuss Cindy's showing the puppy to Jan at the Hospice. Both techniques help children make a connection with another person and increase their awareness of others' feelings.

You might also share literature in which one character shows empathy for another. In *My Dog, Trip,* Allie sees that the little girl who had found and fed Trip has been crying, and realizes that she had thought Trip would be her dog. Allie invites her to come visit Trip any time she wants.In *How Smudge Came,* the Hospice patients and doctor recognize Cindy's love for Smudge and find a way to both get the puppy back and for Cindy to keep it.

On occasion the child protagonist in a story may have the feelings and needs of others explained. This happens in *The Zebra Wall* (Henkes, 1988) when Adine's mother knows that Adine doesn't want her Aunt Irene to visit. Her mother tells Adine that she understands her feelings, but that Irene has been divorced recently and is having a difficult time. She needs to be with her family. Adine decides that she understands—"sort of." But she also remembers a time when her mother made changes because of the way she was feeling.

Children can be given the opportunity to empathize with a book character and to see characters within literature empathizing with one another.

Fostering Children's Ability to See from the Viewpoint of Others

When children de-center, that is, recognize that not everyone thinks as they do, they are ready to see from the viewpoint of another. The books and activities that help give children experience in recognizing how others feel provide a base for developing skill in taking various perspectives. Children can talk first about how the character may have felt or how they would have felt under the same circumstances and then begin to take the role of a character: reacting as that character would, telling what that character thinks, doing what they think that character would do in a new situation.

Sharing Books That Present Several Viewpoints

You can help children recognize different viewpoints by reading to them several books in which different points of view are clearly illustrated. One such book, *The Pain and the Great One* (Blume, 1984), is written in two parts. In one part, a boy of six describes life with The Great One, his older sister. In the other part, the sister describes life with her younger brother, The Pain. The same feelings of jealousy are described by both, and the reader sees several incidents told from two different viewpoints.

In another book with two narrators, *On The Day I Was Born* (Sharmat, 1980), Alexander and his brother take turns describing the day of Alexander's birth. Their memories of the event differ. Alexander says that his father and older brother went to a restaurant to celebrate his birth; the brother says that he and his father went out to eat because if they hadn't, they would have had to eat reheated creamed cauliflower. In both of these books, children can see that the story differs when the teller changes. These books with multiple narrators are unusual. Generally a story will have just one narrator, either a participant in the story who relates events from his or her point of view or an omniscient narrator who describes the thoughts and reactions of several characters.

An example of a book with an omniscient narrator is *The Sweetest Fig* (Van Allsburg, 1993). Bibot is a dentist who is harsh with both his dog and his patients. He doesn't allow the dog to bark at all, and when an old lady, in lieu of a monetary payment, gives him two figs that she says will make his dreams come true, he withholds her pain pills. He eats one

Bibot prepares to teach his dog Marcel to stay off the furniture. (Illustration from The Sweetest Fig *by Chris Van Allsburg. Copyright © by Chris Van Allsburg. Reprinted by permission of Houghton Mifflin Company. All rights reserved.)*

of the figs, and only when he finds himself in front of a cafe in his underwear, and sees the Eiffel Tower drooping, does he recall that this is exactly the dream he had the night before. He vows to make the second fig bring him the dreams he wants. Having prepared himself through self-hypnosis, he places the fig on a dish, but when he turns his back, his dog eats it. He goes to bed angry, awakening in the morning to find himself in his dog's place underneath the bed, and facing his own image, an image that reaches down and pulls him out for his morning walk.

Children might list all the specific things Bibot might wish for in his desire to be the richest man in the world, and the things the dog would see as useful in changing places with its master. They could role-play the two characters, telling each other why they acted as they did.

Observing Book Characters Whose Perspective Is Limited

In some books, one character's lack of understanding of the viewpoint of another is central to the story. In *The Happy Lion* (Fatio, 1954) the lion does not understand why all the people who greeted him so pleasantly when he was at the zoo run from him as he wanders down the street. After all, on all previous occasions on which they met, the people were polite and friendly.

The fish in *Fish Is Fish* (Lionni, 1970) cannot imagine the land creatures that his friend the frog describes to him. He sees everything as a sort of fish mutation: birds become fish with many-colored wings, two legs, and fins, and cows are fish with udders, horns, four legs, and fins.

The illustrations and the text in Van Allsburg's *Two Bad Ants* (1988) are from an ant's perspective. The ants go through the "woods" (grass) and climb the face of a "mountain" (the bricks on the side of a house). When the other ants take one of the marvelous crystals and head for home, the two bad ants eat until they fall asleep in the sugar bowl. They are awakened in the morning when a "giant silver scoop" lifts them into the air and drops them into a "boiling brown lake." Once children catch on to the point of view, you could read the text before showing the illustrations and let the children guess what the ants are seeing or where they are.

Children could take on the limited perspective of any of these characters, drawing cars, buildings, or various animals as they might appear to the fish, or drawing and describing how a place within the classroom might appear to the ants. After hearing *The Happy Lion,* they could dictate what the lion would write if he kept a diary. In each case, the children develop a broader perspective than the one they have been taking.

Taking the Viewpoint of Another

Children can be asked to take the viewpoint of someone who is far different from themselves if the literature gives some point of contact or if you as teacher can establish this contact. Young children can imagine what it is like to be much older than they are. They can share with each other what their grandmothers and grandfathers like and dislike, how they behave. They can listen to stories such as *The Piano Man* (Chocolate, 1998) in which a young girl describes her grandfather's life as a piano player, first for silent movies, then on Broadway, on to vaudeville, and finally working as a piano tuner. For his seventy-fifth birthday, his daughter buys him the old piano that had been stored in the theatre where he played. Now he turns the sound down on the television and accompanies old movies, remembering his days in the silent movie theatres.

One second-grader who had heard this story wrote his own story about his grandfather:

> I know why my grandfather paints. It is because he is old. He paints what he remembers.

Knowing that memories are important to many older people is one step in understanding a different perspective.

Engaging in Role-Play and Puppetry

Children can enjoy and benefit from taking the perspective of first one character and then another. Children who have listened to *Katharine's Doll* (Winthrop, 1983) could dramatize parts of the story with one child being Katharine and the other Molly, then dramatize it again with the roles reversed. In the story, the two girls are friends, playing together often, even wearing the same shoe size. Then Katharine gets a new doll named Charlotte. Both girls play with the doll, but Katharine finds it difficult to share and Molly feels left out. At one point Katharine is so busy with the doll that she forgets to say good-bye to Molly when she leaves. At another time, Katharine asks Molly whom she came to play with, her or Charlotte, and Molly replies Charlotte. Children could work in pairs, with several pairs dramatizing simultaneously. They could create situations of their own in which one has a new toy and the other comes to play with it. They might conclude by discussing how they felt in each role and times when they have played those roles in real life.

They can also engage in role-play where the roles are not ones that they themselves might play on different occasions. In *Eliza's Daddy* (Thomas, 1976) they might first be Eliza, waiting for the Saturday visit of her divorced father, wanting to see his new home and new wife, his new family. They could decide how they would ask to visit his new home if they were Eliza, and how they would feel. They could then play the role of Eliza's father, trying to imagine how he feels as he comes to pick her up. In the book, he agrees to take her to his house if she really wants to spend her Saturday there, but never says why he had not taken her there before. Children might extend the dialogue, with Eliza asking what his home is like or what he thinks of his new daughter and new baby. Her father can answer and also explain why he had not suggested that she come to visit.

Try using puppets or masks to stimulate children to take different roles. As they change puppets, they change characters. They must switch from one outlook to another, from one set of characteristics to another. You will also see whether children are able to de-center as you listen to their use of puppets. Some may never take the character's role but only hold the puppet and say what they think. Others may begin as a different character but midway revert to their own outlook, unable to sustain another perspective. This gives you valuable insight into the children's development.

As you plan your literature selections, and especially as you are developing language activities that extend the books, think about ways in which children can be given the opportunity to take the perspective of another person. Role-play and puppets provide natural situations for this to happen. You can also set up special activities. One child may be the book character and the others could be interviewers for a television station. The interviewers ask questions, and the child answers as the character would. What would Bibot say when asked about his dog, or the piano man when asked about the role of music in his life?

Or suppose that the book character kept a scrapbook or a photo album. The children can make pages for the book or album, then describe what is in it and why it is important to them as that book character. They might dictate captions for items in the books. What would the lion save as mementos of his trip away from the zoo; or, given snapshots of his stroll through the main street of town, how would he label the reactions of various people upon seeing him? Give children the opportunity to share their books, explaining to classmates what they have included and why it is important.

Providing Models of Prosocial Behavior

Literature that portrays characters engaged in social behavior shows children not only a way of acting but also the ingredients necessary for prosocial behavior to occur. That is, the character is able to recognize that another needs help or that there is something that could be done for him or her, feels confident that he or she can provide that help, and sees the risk as not too great to get involved. When you share stories that include prosocial behavior, you might call attention to these aspects individually as well as looking at the action as a whole.

Reading Books That Demonstrate Prosocial Behavior

Suppose you read *Nights of the Pufflings* (McMillan, 1995) to your class. This is a true story of children on Heimaey Island, Iceland, who each August rescue pufflings that have landed in town rather than making it all the way to the water when leaving their burrows. They are in danger of being caught by cats and dogs, and they are unable to take flight from level ground.

The children go out at night, gather any pufflings they find, and keep them in boxes until the next morning. Then they take them to the water's edge and release them. Children can tell about times they have helped animals, how they recognized the need and what they did. The assumption is made that children are capable of helping in such situations. Your seeing them as capable helps them to see themselves in that light.

After sharing and discussing one book on prosocial behavior, simply read another so that children view various models of such behavior. *David and Dog* (Hughes, 1977) also published under the title *Dogger,* would be an excellent choice. In this story, David's older sister Bella recognizes David's unhappiness at having lost his stuffed dog and his frustration when he finds it at a school sale, only to have a little girl purchase it before he can. Bella is quick to change her approach after the girl refuses to sell David's dog back to them. She offers to trade the huge teddy bear she has won in a raffle for David's toy. The ploy is successful, and David's hug for Bella says thank you. Bella even assures him that she will not miss the teddy bear, and that with all her other toys in bed, the teddy bear would have left no room for her.

Loop the Loop (Dugan, 1992) is more complex in that Anne knows that Mrs. Simpson is fun, makes funny comments, and has a nurse with her, but does not, nor will young readers, recognize what appears to be Alzheimer's disease. Mrs. Simpson has notes for herself to turn off the stove, does not remember what she has said earlier, and sometimes forgets who Anne is. Yet when Mrs. Simpson is hospitalized, Anne brings Mrs. Simpson's cat to visit, and leaves her favorite doll to keep Mrs. Simpson company.

Preschool children will identify with Alfie's feelings in *Alfie Gives a Hand* (Hughes, 1987). He attends a backyard birthday party and has to adjust to a rather obstreperous host. He is timid and wants to cling to his blanket. When he must choose between the blanket and giving a comforting hand to another child, however, he is willing—and able—to release the blanket. Helping others may not always be easy, but it is within the capabilities of even the youngest.

Discussing Ways of Providing Help

Once you have read several books that have instances of prosocial behavior, have children tell or role-play what they could do in specific problem situations. Give them the setting and the problem. For example:

You are walking home by yourself and you see a little boy standing on the sidewalk crying. He tells you he is lost. What would you do?

On the playground a friend of yours tells you that she feels sick. She is holding her stomach. What would you do?

Planning Prosocial Behavior

Consider also grouping books that show social behavior so that children can make some generalizations. One grouping would be to read books in which the child character does something for a family member. In *Evan's Corner* (Hill, 1990) Evan helps his younger brother Adam make a special corner for himself. In *Ask Mr. Bear* (Flack, 1932) Danny goes from animal to animal, looking for a gift for his mother's birthday. Mr. Bear has the answer—a bear hug. In *Happy Birthday, Grampie* (Pearson, 1987) Martha makes a birthday card for her grandfather who is in a nursing home—a special card with every part textured, so that he can "see" with his hands what he cannot see with his eyes. *Ask Mr. Bear* is particularly good for preschool children because of the highly appealing repetition of language and because the emotions are less subtle in these than in the other two books. Children can be led to generalize that there are many ways of giving to and helping others and that children can be helpful. After reading two, three, or all four of the books, ask children to select one member of their family. Then have them make a catalog of all the good things they could do for that person. Have them think of realistic actions. They might help a younger sister get dressed, share a toy with a brother, or help mother by making a bed. They can take their booklet home and let the family member choose one item that the child will then give. You might conclude by sharing Shirley Hughes' *Giving* (1993), having the children compare what they thought of giving with the many examples described in the book. Another time, have them think of imaginative things they would like to do for another person, things that they might not really be capable of doing. "I'll get him all the cotton candy he wants," or "I'll take her to the beach every day," or "I'll buy him a car that starts even on cold mornings."

Comparing Themes of Helping

This could lead into talking about how it feels to help someone without being asked. Children can give examples of their own. Follow the discussion by reading a book such as *Mrs. Katz and Tush* (Polacco, 1992). Larnel visits Mrs. Katz, an elderly neighbor, with his mother and, seeing how lonely she is, the next day goes to visit on his own. He even talks her into taking a kitten found in the basement of the building. Over the course of many years, Mrs. Katz shares her Jewish heritage with Larnel and he grows to love her. It is a give-and-take relationship.

Children can identify this theme of helping one another by comparing books. A book with a similar theme but very different characters is *Amos & Boris* (Steig, 1971). In this fantasy, Boris the whale befriends Amos the mouse when Amos falls off his boat. Years later, Boris is washed ashore, and it is Amos who gets two elephants to push him back into the ocean. The language of the book is so evocative that it is likely you will want to concentrate on this aspect of the book. However, asking, "How is this book like *Mrs. Katz and Tush?*" shows children that two very different books may express a common theme and focuses their attention on the idea of helping one another.

A book character is just one model among many to which children are exposed. Some books that you present will show behavior that you would not choose to have children emulate. Often the problem to be solved in the book results from the behavior of one of the characters, behavior that may not reflect values that you condone. However, you would not want to select only those books in which characters exhibit prosocial behavior. This would eliminate excellent literature that may portray humans in some of their very human but not-so-lovable thoughts and actions, and you would be exercising a kind of censorship, a screening of literature based on the values presented. Rather than eliminating these books, add them to the collection of books that show children engaged in prosocial behavior. Help children see that they, too, are capable of aiding others in given situations, and that there are internal rewards for such behavior.

Encouraging Children to Judge the Appropriateness of Particular Behaviors

Learning when a behavior is appropriate requires generalizing about types of situations and types of behaviors. A social encounter is not likely to be repeated in exact form. Children can be helped to generalize about the appropriateness of behaviors by seeing many examples of both behaviors and their consequences. Some examples will come from direct observation or participation, but others will come from vicarious experiences such as literature.

Preschoolers hearing John Burningham's *The Cupboard* (1975) see a young child taking pots and pans from a kitchen cupboard and playing with them. When his mother suggests that he think of something else to do, he does, but as he walks away she asks him to please come back and put the pots and pans away. The last illustration shows the two of them placing the utensils in the cupboard. Young children hearing the story can be asked to recall times when they are expected to put things away. It is probably a safe generalization for them to say that they should put away anything that they have finished playing with and are no longer using.

Not all situations are as easily assessed, however. Children who hear a story and know the full context of a situation can be asked to make judgments about a character's behavior, noting the circumstances that may have influenced it. Second- and third-graders who have heard *The Washout* (Carrick, 1978) can be asked what they think the boy in the story, Christopher, could have done when he saw that the logs and rocks he usually used to cross the brook were gone. Christopher and his mother had just come to the family's summer cottage. A storm during the night had washed away a part of the road, and at other places fallen trees had made it impassable. They had neither food nor telephone. Christopher's mother had told him he could explore but that he was to stay out of the brook. Christopher is by the brook when he discovers a new rowboat that has broken loose from its mooring. In a somewhat dangerous fashion he poles the boat around the lake and then walks to a small grocery store. Once there, the grocer gives him a food supply and a man at the store takes him home, cutting the trees out of the way as they go. Christopher's mother has been extremely worried about him. He apologizes, then asks her if she is glad he made the trip. She agrees that she is.

Children can describe what else he could have done and postulate consequences for each of the suggested behaviors. They might relate what their own parents' reaction would be if they behaved as Christopher did. Ask questions that will focus children's attention on the relationship between the situation and the behavior. For *The Washout,* such a question would be, "Do you think Christopher's mother would have said the same thing to him if he had taken the boat when nothing special had happened? What makes you think this?"

As children become more accustomed to viewing single incidents within broader contexts, and as they become more able to predict the reactions of others, they will be able to assess more accurately the sorts of behaviors that are most likely to be appropriate in any given situation.

Helping Children Learn About and Value Differences Among People

Basic to being open to others is feeling good about oneself. Thus many of the activities designed to enhance the self-concept of young children aid in their acceptance of others. As they explore what they can do, they see also what their classmates can do; as they tell what they like, they hear what their classmates like. Thus they are beginning to see the diversity within their own small group and to value both themselves and their friends. The differences add interest.

Selecting Literature That Values Diversity

Literature can focus attention on how individuals vary and emphasize the value of this variance. In *Liliana's Grandmothers* (Torres, 1998) Liliana interacts with Mima, who lives on the same street as Liliana in a town in the Northern United States, and Mama Gabina, who lives in another country and speaks only Spanish. Mima has a cat named Suzzy, does yoga, makes quilts to raise money for the church and is afraid of mice. Mama Gabina has a parrot named Roberto, grows flowers and vegetables in her garden, and is afraid of frogs. Liliana likes both her grandmothers, enjoying different things about each one, recognizing that each is special in certain ways. Children can compare people they know, telling what is special about each. It may be grandmothers, but it could just as well be neighbors or friends. The discussion can be focused on what is liked about each to emphasize positive feelings.

The theme of valuing others different from oneself or from the norm appears in literature at all levels. Young children hearing *Oliver Button Is a Sissy* (dePaola, 1979) see Oliver being teased because he takes tap dancing lessons and because he neither enjoys playing ball nor is good at it. When he loses a talent show he comes back to school doubly dejected, but is surprised to find that the graffiti on the wall proclaiming he's a sissy has been changed—sissy has been marked out and "star" written in. Children might think about what makes their friends "stars," what their special talents are. Some classrooms in the primary grades have graffiti walls, bulletin boards where youngsters can write messages. A wall such as this could be used to write positive comments about classmates, with the teacher providing several examples and making clear the nature of acceptable comments.

Read books to your students that reflect positive attitudes toward others. Preschool children listening to *Subway Sparrow* (Torres, 1993) see how a child speaking English, a man speaking Spanish, and a woman speaking Polish can work together to capture and then free a sparrow that has flown into a subway car. The book introduces the concept that people may speak different languages but that they are still able to get along with one another and work toward a common goal.

Focusing on Similarities

Share several books that picture a particular people, race, or religion so that one book does not become representative of that group in the minds of the children. You might look over your literature curriculum to see if you could be fostering any misconceptions. If, for instance, all the books you have selected that have African-American characters have urban settings, you should add several books with black characters that are set in suburban or rural areas. You might also select books that have characters with whom children can empathize but that have foreign settings. It is easy for children to understand the little girl's fear of the dark in *Darkness and the Butterfly* (Grifalconi, 1987) even though she is living in an African village.

To avoid a "we-they" approach, focus on similarities, and on individuals within groups rather than on the groups themselves. Thus you could assemble several books by themes or central idea in which the protagonists represent several different backgrounds and group classifications. You could, for example, read several books that feature a child living in a temporary home. The American father and son in Eve Bunting's *Fly Away Home* (1991) are living in an airport until the father earns enough money for them to rent an apartment. Sami and his family in *Sami and the Time of the Troubles* (Heide, 1992) are living in the basement of his uncle's house in Beirut, emerging only when there is a break in the fighting and gunfire. The boy who describes his life in *The Roses in My Carpets* (Khan, 1998) is living in a refugee camp in Afghanistan.

In each of the books, the protagonist is a member of a group that could be studied for itself. By grouping the stories according to the circumstances and feelings of the characters, children see the human qualities that they share and that they themselves understand. This helps them to see the similarities among people who may differ from them in some ways, but who share common emotions and needs.

Some books demonstrate similarities among cultures directly. *Now We Can Have a Wedding* (Cox, 1998) has neighbors from many different countries contributing to Sallie's wedding banquet, each preparing a dish that is special for weddings in their culture. *Dominoes Around the World* (Lankford, 1998) and *Hopscotch Around the World* (Lankford, 1992) show how these games are played in various countries. Children could learn one variation, then teach their classmates.

Reading Literature from Other Countries

Finally, share literature from other countries with children. Foreign folktales are especially plentiful. When you introduce one, tell the country where it originated. If you are going to read Demi's retelling of *One Grain of Rice* (1997), for example, you might begin by saying, "This story is titled *One Grain of Rice* and it is a tale that was first told in India." Young children have not yet developed clear concepts of distance nor the meaning of country, and learning where India is would add little to their literary experience. However, telling them that the story comes from another country introduces the idea that many countries have literature and that stories from many places can be enjoyed. Some books, such as *Look What We've Brought You from Vietnam* (Shalant, 1988) may include games and crafts as well as folktales and stories from a particular country. There is a list of recommended folktales at the end of this chapter.

Day-care centers and schools are natural places for children to develop social skills.

The same procedure can be used with books that were first published in another country. Tell children the title of the story and the name of the author, and then tell where the author lives or lived. For example, you might read *Snail Started It* by Katja Reider (1997), explaining that the author lives in Germany and has written a book about how some animals get along with one another. The book has been translated from German into English. It may remind them of stories they already know. They will be able to recognize the structure in which one animal makes a comment that irritates a second, then this animal irritates a third, and so on, until the snail, who started it, recognizes what he has done and reverses the pattern.

Some foreign authors whose work is appropriate for young children are Edward Ardizzone, Nicola Bayley, Raymond Briggs, John Burningham, Shirley Hughes, Pat Hutchins, Helen Oxenbury, Brian Wildsmith, Mitsumasa Anno, Jean de Brunhoff, Max Bollinger, Alois Carigiet, C. Hans Fischer, Astrid Lindgren, and Svend Otto. Activities can be based on the literary content of the stories, but also stress the idea that people of other countries write stories that American children enjoy.

Engaging Children in Group Activities

Children develop social skills only in a context where they have the opportunity to practice them. Day-care centers and schools are natural places for this to happen. As you plan the presentation of literature and related activities, capitalize on the opportunities to help children be a part of the group.

Children will feel like a part of the group in activities where all are working together, especially if an attitude of cooperation permeates the endeavor. This activity may be simply listening to a story, being quiet so others can hear, or laughing along with others at humorous passages. It might be a group response to the literature: participating as the book is read a second time, singing the words to the song illustrated as a picture book, engaging in choral speaking, or doing finger plays. The enjoyment of activities such as these is enhanced when each child feels secure in his or her own group membership.

As you plan ways of extending books, develop activities that require the children to work together. For those preschoolers who are working side-by-side but not *with* one another, suggest projects where they will need to share materials or space. They could make a collage of mushroom shapes after hearing *Mushroom in the Rain* (Ginsburg, 1974). The brightly colored mushrooms used in the book illustrations suggest to children the possibilities for various shapes, colors, and patterns. Paper, fabric, yarn, foil, magazines, and other materials should be placed in a central location. Children are grouped around the materials, thus encouraging conversation as they work. They can comment about each other's work or perhaps tell others about their collages. They become engaged in social interaction because of the way the activity is structured. Other activities that promote the development of social skills are those that require some joint planning. Creative dramatics, puppetry, pantomiming, writing group stories, dancing with partners, and making murals all require children to participate and to listen to the ideas of others in order to be successful.

Begin with small groups, only two or three children, and enlarge the groups as the children become more adept at handling the situation. Pairs of children could work together to create pictures showing some of Grandpa's adventures in *Could Be Worse!* (Stevenson, 1977). Those children who worked well in pairs could then be put in larger groups for other activities. Four could work together to create a mural showing how the fish in *Fish Is Fish* (Lionni, 1970) might imagine a highway filled with traffic. Vary group membership so that the children learn to cooperate with many different people, and so that you can better assess the causes of any difficulty groups may experience. Try to structure the activities and the groups so that the children will not only gain practice in social interaction but also feel successful about their participation.

Stimulating Children to Explore Moral Problems and Ethical Questions

Whether you plan to or not, it is likely that you will read stories to children that represent various levels of moral reasoning on the part of the characters.

Presenting Examples of Moral Reasoning

In some books, such as *Arnie and the Stolen Markers* (Carlson, 1987) the character reasons at Kohlberg's stage one, the avoidance of punishment. Arnie wants markers that he sees in Harvey's Candy and Toy Shop, but he has already spent all his money. He steals the markers, but his mother finds them and makes him return them to the store. Harvey has Arnie work at the store for a week to earn what the markers cost, then gives them to him along with some paper. Arnie had felt guilty about taking the markers and had thought he might be sent to jail. His future behavior will be governed by his fear of punishment.

In the folktale *Under the Shade of the Mulberry Tree* (Demi, 1979) the character reasons at stage two, where personal reward determines ethical decisions. A poor man asks to sit in the shade of a rich man's tree, but his request is refused. Then he offers to buy the shade, and the greedy rich man assents. Once the poor man owns the shade, however, he then has the right to follow it as the sun moves, so that eventually he moves into the rich man's house. Trickery is a common motif in folktales. In this particular tale, the trickery might be considered justified because it brings pleasure to the poor man and because the rich man was selfish in not sharing his shade.

Moral reasoning at stage three is widely represented in the decisions that book characters make. At this stage, right is determined by what "good girls" or "good boys" do. For example, Nim in *Nim and the War Effort* (Lee, 1997) is sorry for her actions that have angered her grandfather, but explains that she was trying to bring honor to the family by winning the contest. Her decision was based on trying to be good—she just did not interpret "good" in the same manner as her grandfather.

Children grow in their ability to reason about moral questions as they hear the reasoning of others. In general, they understand the reasoning at their own stage, the stages below their own, and one stage above theirs. Hearing various stages of reasoning expressed by book characters and classmates expands their own reasoning power and is instrumental in their movement from one stage to another.

Engaging Children in the Reasoning Process

With preschool children, a first step is to read stories in which characters are faced with a decision to be made and in which there is no clear-cut answer. Read half of *Finders Keepers* (Lipkind, 1951) and ask the children who should get to keep the bone: Nap, the dog who saw it first, or Winkle, the dog who touched it first. As in many questions of justice, there is reasoning for more than one decision. What makes some ethical decisions so difficult is that the conflict is between two values, both of which seem to represent morality. Should people tell their friends the truth if the truth will be hurtful? Should people lie if in so doing they could save a friend's life? Even young children can be asked to suggest and defend a solution to a problem in which the right answer is debatable.

At other times children may be asked to tell about instances when they act in accordance with the reasoning a book character is using. Are there things they would do if they weren't afraid of getting caught and being punished, for instance.

Read some books that present questions about behavior and ask students to decide which behavior they think is right and why. If you read the story about split pea soup in *George and Martha* (Marshall, 1972) you could discuss the theme of the story, that friends should always tell each other the truth. Martha has made an enormous quantity of split pea soup, which she serves to George. He does not care for it but does not want to hurt her feelings. When he has eaten all he can, he pours what is left in his bowl into his loafer. Martha sees him from the kitchen and wants to know why he did not tell her that he did not like the soup. When he has explained his reason, Martha responds that friends should always tell each other the truth—and that he will not have to eat split pea soup again.

You might read another book that presents the same question. In *Towser and Sadie's Birthday* (Ross, 1989) Sadie the cat is crying because she has not gotten birthday presents for the last few years. Towser, a terrier, offers to get her whatever she wants, and she says she wants the moon. When he cannot get it for her, Towser blows up a large white balloon and tells her it is the moon. She is delighted and takes her present everywhere with her. She even listens to Towser's explanation that what appears to be the moon in the sky is simply the hole where the moon was. The next day the wizard asks Sadie why she is holding an old balloon. She tells him to speak quietly because Towser might hear. After all, he thinks it's the moon, and he'd be upset to find out it's only a balloon. The wizard leaves thinking how nice Sadie is.

Primary-grade children can write their opinions on slips of paper to answer the question of whether friends should *always* tell each other the truth. Have them share their responses and their reasons for agreeing or disagreeing with Martha's position that friends should always tell one another the truth. Ask the group to decide which reasons they think are the best. The emphasis is on the reasoning given, and there is no attempt to reach a consensus on a final "yes" or "no" to the question.

Looking at the Same Issue in Several Books

Children might look at a single moral question, such as honesty, through a comparison of several books. After reading *George and Martha,* read *A Bargain for Frances* (Hoban, 1970). When Frances starts over to visit Thelma, her mother tells her to be careful, reminding her that on previous occasions when she played with Thelma, she got the worst of things. Frances says it will be safe because they are just going to have a tea party. Once at Thelma's, Frances explains her plan to buy a new blue china tea set. Thelma convinces her that those sets are not made anymore and offers to sell her red plastic set to Frances. When the deal is completed, Thelma insists on "no backsies." After she returns home, Frances learns from her sister that blue china sets are still made, that they are in the stores, and that Thelma was shown one a day earlier in the candy store. Frances runs to the candy store in time to see Thelma buying a new blue tea set and returns home without being seen. After some thought, Frances puts a penny in the sugar bowl of the set she bought from Thelma and calls her.

"Remember," said Thelma, "no backsies."

"I remember," said Frances. "But are you sure you really want no backsies?"

"Sure I'm sure," said Thelma.

"You mean I never have to give back the tea set?" said Frances.

"That's right," said Thelma. "You can keep the tea set."

"Can I keep what is in the sugar bowl too?" said Frances.

"What is in the sugar bowl?" said Thelma.

"Never mind," said Frances. "No backsies. Good-bye."

Frances hung up. Frances waited for the telephone to ring, and when it rang she said, "Hello."

"Hello," said Thelma. "This is Thelma."

"I know," said Frances.

"I just remembered," said Thelma, "I think I had something in the sugar bowl. I think it was a ring. Did you find a ring?"

"No," said Frances. "And I don't have to tell you what is in the sugar bowl because you said no backsies."

"Well," said Thelma, "I just remembered that I put some money in the sugar bowl one time, I think it was some birthday money. I think it was two dollars, or maybe it was five dollars. Did you find money?"

"You said no backsies," said Frances. "So I don't have to tell you. I don't have to say how much money is in the sugar bowl." (Hoban, 1970, pp. 41–47)

With Thelma now eager to make a deal, Frances offers to return the tea set for the money. Thelma must explain that she has purchased another tea set and then offers to trade her new tea set plus a dime for her old one. When the exchange is made and Thelma discovers the penny, and consequently the trick, she says it was not nice, and now she will have to be careful when she plays with Frances. The two decide that it is better to be friends than to be careful, and Frances shares the dime with Thelma.

After the children have enjoyed the story, catching on to the trick in time to relish Thelma's entrapment, ask if Frances told a lie to Thelma. Reread parts of the dialogue as the discussion progresses so that the children can listen with this purpose clearly in mind. They might offer opinions about whether deliberately misleading someone is lying. Then ask them if they think it was all right for Frances to trick Thelma. Did she deserve what she got? Did Thelma's behavior justify Frances's?

Next read *Sam, Bangs & Moonshine* (Ness, 1966). Sam makes up tales, "moonshine" her father calls them. Moonshine is not real. But when she tells her friend Thomas, who goes wherever she tells him, that her baby kangaroo is visiting her mermaid mother in a cave behind Blue Rock, her moonshine causes trouble. The tide comes up, covering the road to the Blue Rock. Sam tells her father in time for him to go after Thomas in a boat. When he returns, Sam's father tells her that there is good moonshine and bad moonshine, and that she must learn to tell the difference. Children can draw what for them is good moonshine, the use of their imaginations. Then they can explain what the terms "good moonshine" and "bad moonshine" mean to them. Ask whether they think there is any difference between "bad moonshine" and "lying" and "fibbing."

By reading several books concerning the issue, added dimensions are given. Children begin to look at situations in which the answer to what is right requires them to weigh possible actions themselves, to use their own reasoning power. The purpose is not to recommend specific actions, but to encourage children to reason about moral questions.

SUMMARY

Much of children's social development, their ability to relate to other people, is correlated with their ability to see from the viewpoint of another. Realizing how another feels and understanding the intent of another person's response are central to the ability to interact successfully in social relationships. These are also key elements in determining whether children will engage in prosocial behavior.

Children learn socially acceptable behavior through observing a wide variety of models, and through positive and negative reinforcement. Children develop their ability to reason about moral questions partially in relation to their stage of intellectual development, and partially as a result of rewards and punishment that have been given for particular actions.

The following long-term goals are appropriate for the social and moral development of young children.

> Children will make inferences about the feelings and intentions of others.
>
> Children will view a situation from more than one perspective, seeing the viewpoint of another person.
>
> Children will engage in prosocial behavior.
>
> Children will judge the appropriateness of specific behaviors and predict the possible consequences of particular behaviors.
>
> Children will learn about others who differ from themselves and value this diversity.
>
> Children will engage competently in group activities.
>
> Children will evaluate various solutions to moral problems and ethical questions.

Books offer opportunities to give children experience in making inferences about the feelings and intentions of others. Table 8–1 suggests appropriate teaching strategies. Children can interpret nonverbal language as shown in illustrations in picture books; they can relate voice inflection to meaning as they listen to the dialogue from books; they can go beyond a literal interpretation of dialogue, inferring what is really meant; and they can follow sequences of action and observe patterns of behavior in stories.

Table 8–1. Supporting Children's Social and Moral Development

Developmental Goals	Teaching Suggestions	Recommended Literature	
Children will make inferences about the feelings and intentions of others.	Have children interpret the body language of characters in illustrations. Let children interpret the meaning of voice inflections in portions of dialogue you have read. Encourage interpretation of dialogue beyond the literal level. Help children relate sequences of action of feelings and intentions of book characters. Encourage children to relate their own feelings to those of book characters.	**Ages 3–5:** Ets Gregory Hoban Raschka Ray Scott Zolotow	*Talking Without Words* *How Smudge Came* *A Birthday for Frances* *Yo! Yes!* *My Dog, Trip* *Sam* *The Quarreling Book*
		Ages 5–8: Bunting Fleischman Henkes Little Mayer McCully Rael Stevenson Stevenson	*Clancy's Coat* *The Scarebird* *The Zebra Wall* *Revenge of the Small Small* *Frog Goes to Dinner* *Picnic* *When Zaydeh Danced on Eldridge Street* *Could Be Worse!* *Yard Sale*
Children will view a situation from more than one perspective, seeing the viewpoint of another person.	Read books that present several viewpoints. Let children analyze the limited perspective of certain characters. Have children imagine being someone else. Let children role-play more than one role in a single situation.	**Ages 3–5:** Chocolate Fatio Thomas Winthrop	*The Piano Man* *The Happy Lion* *Eliza's Daddy* *Katharine's Doll*
		Ages 5–8: Blume Lionni Sharmat Van Allsburg Van Allsburg	*The Pain and the Great One* *Fish Is Fish* *On The Day I Was Born* *The Sweetest Fig* *Two Bad Ants*

Table 8–1. *(continued)*

Developmental Goals	Teaching Suggestions	Recommended Literature	
Children will engage in prosocial behavior.	Share books that present models of prosocial behavior. Discuss the kinds of help children can provide others. Compare themes of helping.	**Ages 3–5:** Flack Hughes Hughes	*Ask Mr. Bear* *Alfie Gives a Hand* *David and Dog*
		Ages 5–8: Dugan Hill McMillan Pearson Polacco Steig	*Loop the Loop* *Evan's Corner* *Nights of the Pufflings* *Happy Birthday, Grampie* *Mrs. Katz and Tush* *Amos & Boris*
Children will judge the appropriateness of specific behaviors and predict possible consequences of such behaviors.	Ask children to evaluate the behaviors of book characters. Have children suggest other possible behaviors for book characters.	**Ages 3–5:** Burningham **Ages 5–8:** Carrick	*The Cupboard* *The Washout*
Children will learn about others who differ from themselves and value this diversity.	Present literature in which diversity among people is valued. Focus on the similarities rather than the differences among peoples. Read more than one book about a particular group of people. Focus on individuals within groups rather than on the groups themselves. Share literature from other countries.	**Ages 3–5:** Grifalconi Reider Torres **Ages 5–8:** Bunting dePaola Demi Cox Heide Khan Lankford	*Darkness and the Butterfly* *Snail Started It* *Liliana's Grandmothers* *Fly Away Home* *Oliver Button Is a Sissy* *One Grain of Rice* *Now We Can Have a Wedding* *Sami and the Time of the Troubles* *The Roses in My Carpets* *Dominoes Around the World*

Table 8–1.   *(continued)*

Developmental Goals	Teaching Suggestions	Recommended Literature	
		Lankford	*Hopscotch Around the World*
		Shalant	*Look What We've Brought You from Vietnam*
Children will engage competently in group activities.	Engage children in choral speaking. Structure activities so that children must work together. Begin with groups of two or three, enlarging the membership as children become more adept in group work.	**Ages 3–5:** Ginsburg	*Mushroom in the Rain*
		Ages 5–8: Lionni Stevenson	*Fish Is Fish* *Could Be Worse!*
Children will evaluate various solutions to moral problems and ethical questions.		**Ages 3–5:** Lee Lipkind Marshall Ross	*Nim and the War Effort* *Finders Keepers* *George and Martha* *Towser and Sadie's Birthday*
	Read books in which characters engage in various stages of moral reasoning. Invite children to suggest and defend solutions to moral or ethical problems presented in books. Have children select the "best" reason for particular solutions to problems. Let children compare the presentation of a single moral issue in several books.	**Ages 5–8:** Carlson Demi Hoban Ness	*Arnie and the Stolen Markers* *Under the Shade of the Mulberry Tree* *A Bargain for Frances* *Sam, Bangs & Moonshine*

Literature fosters children's ability to see from the viewpoint of others. Some books will describe an event from several perspectives; others will present a story with a character who has a more limited viewpoint than does the reader. Children can be encouraged to take the perspective of another in discussions and in dramatic activities such as role-play or puppetry. Children can begin to assess behavior and the consequences that may follow by discussing what happens to book characters in particular situations. Sometimes that character may provide a model for prosocial behavior, with the children seeing that they too would be capable of helping someone else. At other times, the children may generalize about what behaviors are appropriate in specific situations.

Literature provides children with information about people who differ from themselves, and by emphasizing the humanity of individual members of a group, helps children develop positive attitudes toward others and value diversity. Teachers will read books about many ethnic and cultural groups, including folktales from many regions.

Finally, literature can stimulate children to explore moral problems and ethical questions. Characters in books will demonstrate various levels of moral reasoning and will be faced with more dilemmas. Children can reason themselves about the questions facing the characters and may compare how different characters have reacted to the same question.

Extending Your Learning

1. Find ten specific illustrations in picture books that show a character's feelings. See if your colleagues can identify the emotion from looking at the illustration without knowing the story line.

2. Find a book in which the meaning of the dialogue extends beyond the literal level. Then share the book with a child to see if he or she can interpret the meaning.

3. Read a picture book to a small group of primary children. After you have finished, ask them to retell the story from the viewpoint of a particular character.

4. Select five books that would lend themselves to role-play or puppetry. Tell why each is appropriate for this type of activity.

5. Make a list of at least ten activities in which children could take the perspective of another person.

6. Suppose you had read several books to children in which the characters exhibited prosocial behavior. Write five situations you now could share with the children in which you give a setting and a problem and ask the children what they could or would do to help.

7. Select three books from those by any of the foreign authors listed in the section "Reading Literature From Other Countries" or from the Tomlinson book listed under Recommended References that you think the children you know would enjoy.

8. For each of five books, plan one activity that could be done by an individual child and one that would require group cooperation.

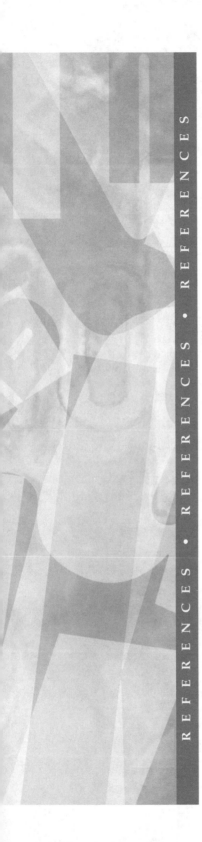

RECOMMENDED REFERENCES

Bandura, A. (1977). *Social Learning Theory.* Upper Saddle River, NJ: Prentice-Hall.

Banks, J. and Banks, C. Eds. (1997). *Multicultural Education: Issues and Perspectives.* Boston: Allyn & Bacon.

Berman, S. (1997). *Children's Social Consciousness and the Development of Social Responsibility.* Albany, NY: SUNY.

Charney, R. (1997). *Habits of Goodness.* Greenfield, MA: Northeast Foundation for Children.

Charney, R. (1991). *Teaching Children to Care: Management in the Responsive Classroom.* Greenfield, MA: Northeast Foundation for Children.

Coles, R. (1986). *The Political Life of Children.* Boston: Atlantic Monthly Press.

Corsaro, W. (1985). *Friendship and Peer Culture in the Early Years.* Norwood, NJ: Ablex.

DeVries, R. and San, B. (1994). *Moral Classrooms, Moral Children: Creating a Constractvist Atmosphere in Early Education.* New York: Teachers College Press.

Dunn, J. (1988). *The Beginnings of Social Understanding.* Cambridge, MA: Harvard University Press.

Eisenberg, N. Ed. (1982). *The Development of Prosocial Behavior.* New York: Academic Press.

Gilligan, C. (1982). *In a Different Voice.* Cambridge, MA: Harvard University Press.

Gordon, A., and Browne, K. (1996). *Guiding Young Children in a Diverse Society.* Boston: Allyn & Bacon.

Hart, C., Burts, D., and Charlesworth, R. Eds. (1997). *Integrated Curriculum and Developmentally Appropriate Practice: Birth to Age Eight.* Albany, NY: SUNY.

Johnson, D. (1991). *Learning Together and Alone: Cooperative, Competitive, and Individualistic Learning.* Upper Saddle River, NJ: Prentice-Hall.

Kagan, M. and Lamb, S. Eds. (1987). *The Emergence of Morality in Young Children.* Chicago: University of Chicago Press.

Kohlberg, L. (1981). *The Philosophy of Moral Development.* Vol. 1, Moral Stages and the Idea of Justice. New York: Harper.

Kostelnik, M., Stein, L., Whiren, and Soderman, A. (1993). *Guiding Children's Social Development.* 2nd ed. Albany, NY: Delmar.

McCracken, J. (1993). *Valuing Diversity: The Primary Years.* Washington, DC: National Association for the Education of Young Children.

Mussen, P., and Eisenberg-Berg, N. (1977). *Roots of Caring, Sharing, and Helping.* San Francisco: W.H. Freeman.

Piaget, J. (1932, 1955). *The Moral Judgment of the Child.* New York: Macmillan.

Ramsey, P. (1991). *Making Friends in School: Promoting Peer Relationships in Early Childhood.* New York: Teachers College Press.

Tomlinson, Carl. Ed. (1998). *Children's Books from Other Countries.* Lanham, MD: Scarecrow Press.

Whitmore, K., and Crowell, C. (1994). *Inventing a Classroom: Life in a Bilingual, Whole Language Learning Community.* York, ME: Stenhouse.

RECOMMENDED CHILDREN'S BOOKS

Bang, Molly. (1997). *Common Ground.* New York: Scholastic.

Blos, Joan. (1987). *Old Henry.* Ill. Stephen Gammell. New York: Morrow.

Borden, Louise. (1997). *The Little Ships.* Ill. Michael Foreman. New York: McElderry.

Bunting, Eve. (1998). *So Far From the Sea.* Ill. Chris Soentpiet. New York: Clarion.

Castenada, Omar. (1993). *Abuela's Weave.* Ill. Enrique Sanchez. New York: Lee & Low.

Cohen, Miriam. (1983). *See You Tomorrow, Charles.* Ill. Lillian Hoban. New York: Greenwillow.

Hausherr, Rosemarie. (1997). *Celebrating Families.* New York: Scholastic.

Hughes, Shirley. (1998). *Alfie and the Birthday Surprise.* New York: Lothrop.

Lionni, Leo. (1988). *Six Crows.* New York: Knopf.

Luenn, Nancy. (1998). *Celebrations of Light.* Ill. Mark Bender. New York: Atheneum.

Mochizuki, Ken. (1997). *Passage to Freedom: The Suhihara Story.* Ill. Dom Lee. New York: Lee & Low.

Polacco, Patricia. (1994). *Tikvah Means Hope.* New York: Doubleday.

Raffi. (1988). *One Light, One Sun.* Ill. Eugenei Fernandes. New York: Crown.

Rahaman, Vashanti. (1997). *A Little Salmon for Witness: A Story from Trinidad.* Ill. Sandra Speidel. New York: Lodestar.

Rockwell, Anne and Harlow. (1982). *Can I Help?* New York: Macmillan.

Rosa-Casanova, Sylvia. (1997). *Mama Provi and the Pot of Rice.* Ill. Robert Roth. New York: Atheneum.

Russell, Ching Yeung. (1997). *Moon Festival.* Ill. Christopher Zhong-yuan Zhang. Honesdale, PA: Boyds Mills.

Shannon, George. (1997). *True Lies.* Ill. John O'Brien. New York: Greenwillow.

Stewart, Sarah. (1991). *The Money Tree.* Ill. David Small. New York: Farrar.

Wood, Douglas. (1998). *Making the World.* Ill. Yoshi and Hibiki Miyazaki. New York: Simon.

RECOMMENDED FOLKTALES

Aardema, Verna. (1989). *Rabbit Makes a Monkey Out of Lion: A Swahili Tale.* Ill. Jerry Pinkney. New York: Dial. (Africa)

Adler, David. (1997). *Chanukah in Chelm.* Ill. Kevin O'Malley. New York: Lothrop. (Poland—Jewish)

Alexander, Ellen. (1989). *Llama and the Great Flood.* New York: Harper. (Peru)

Aylesworth, Jim. (1998). *The Gingerbread Man.* Ill. Barbara McClintock. New York: Scholastic. (England)

Bruchac, Joseph and Ross, Gayle. (1995). *The Story of the Milky Way: A Cherokee Tale.* Ill. Virginia Stroud. New York: Dial. (US—Native American)

de Paola, Tomie. (1975). *Strega Nona.* Upper Saddle River, NJ: Prentice-Hall. (Italy)

Farley, Carol. (1997). *Mr. Pak Buys a Story.* Ill. Benrei Huang. Chicago: Whitman. (Korea)

Ginsburg, Mirra. (1997). *Clay Boy.* New York: Greenwillow. (Russia)

Gonzalez, Lucia M. (1997). *Señor Cat's Romance: And Other Favorite Stories from Latin America.* New York: Scholastic. (Latin America)

Hickox, Rebecca. (1998). *The Golden Sandal: A Middle Eastern Cinderella Story.* Ill. Will Hildenbrand. New York: Holiday. (Iraq)

Ho, Minfong and Ros, Saphan. (1997). *Brother Rabbit: A Cambodian Tale.* New York: Lothrop. (Cambodia)

Hogrogian, Nonny. (1988). *The Cat Who Loved to Sing.* New York: Knopf. (Armenia)

Huck, Charlotte. (1995). *Toads and Diamonds*. Ill. Anita Lobel. New York: Greenwillow. (France)

Lattimore, Deborah Nourse. (1987). *The Flame of Peace: A Tale of the Aztecs*. New York: Harper. (Mexico)

Oram, Hiawyn. (1998). *Baba Yaga and the Wise Doll: A Traditional Russian Folktale*. Ill. Ruth Brown. New York: Dutton. (Russia)

San Souci, Robert. (1997). *The Hired Hand: An African-American Folktale*. New York: Dial. (US—Virginia)

Shute, Linda. (1988). *Clever Tom and the Leprechaun*. New York: Lothrop. (Ireland)

Steptoe, John. (1987). *Mufaro's Beautiful Daughters: An African Tale*. New York: Lothrop. (Africa)

Zelinsky, Paul O. (1997). *Rapunzel*. New York: Dutton. (Germany)

Zemach, Harve. (1973). *Duffy and the Devil: A Cornish Tale*. Ill. Margot Zemach. New York: Farrar. (England)

PROFESSIONAL REFERENCES CITED

Bandura, A. (1977). *Social Learning Theory*. Upper Saddle River, NJ: Prentice-Hall.

Gilligan, C. (1982). *In a Different Voice*. Cambridge, MA: Harvard University Press.

Katz, L., and McClellan, D. (1997). *Fostering Children's Social Competence*. Washington, DC: National Association for the Education of Young Children.

Kohlberg, L. (1981). *The Philosophy of Moral Development*. Vol. 1. New York: Harper.

Mussen, P., and Eisenberg-Berg, N. (1977). *Roots of Caring, Sharing, and Helping*. San Francisco: W.H. Freeman.

Mussen, P., Conger, J., Kagan, J., and Huston, A. (1990). *Child Development and Personality*. 7th ed. New York: Harper.

National Council for the Social Studies. (1994). *Expectations of Excellence: Curriculum Standards for Social Studies*. Wilmington, DE: National Council for the Social Studies.

Oppenheim, J. (1984). *Kids and Play*. New York: The Bank Street College of Education.

Piaget, J. (1955, 1935). *The Moral Judgment of the Child*. New York: Macmillan.

Rubin, Z. (1984). *Children's Friendships*. Cambridge, MA: Harvard University Press.

Shaffer, D. (1989). *Developmental Psychology*. 2nd ed. Pacific Grove, CA: Brooks/Cole Publishing Company.

CHILDREN'S LITERATURE CITED

Blume, Judy. (1984). *The Pain and the Great One*. Ill. Irene Trivas. New York: Bradbury.

Bunting, Eve. (1984). *Clancey's Coat*. Ill. Lorinda Bryan Cauley. New York: Warne.

Bunting, Eve. (1991). *Fly Away Home*. Ill. Ronald Himler. New York: Clarion. Copyright © by Eve Bunting. Text used by permission of Viking Penguin, a division of Penguin Putnam, Inc.

Burningham, John. (1975). *The Cupboard*. London: Jonathan Cape.

Carlson, Nancy. (1987). *Arnie and the Stolen Markers*. New York: Viking.

Carrick, Carol. (1978). *The Washout*. Ill. Donald Carrick. New York: Seabury.

Chocolate, Debbi. (1998). *The Piano Man*. Ill. Eric Velasquez. New York: Walker.

Cox, Judy. (1998). *Now We Can Have a Wedding*. Ill. DyAnne DiSalvo-Ryan. New York: Holiday.

Demi. (1997). *One Grain of Rice*. New York: Scholastic.

Demi. (1979). *Under the Shade of the Mulberry Tree*. Upper Saddle River, NJ: Prentice-Hall.

dePaola, Tomie. (1979). *Oliver Button Is a Sissy*. New York: Harcourt.

Dugan, Barbara. (1992). *Loop the Loop*. Ill. James Stevenson. New York: Greenwillow.

Ets, Marie Hall. (1968). *Talking Without Words*. New York: Viking.

Fatio, Louise. (1954). *The Happy Lion*. Ill. Roger Duvoisin. New York: McGraw-Hill.

Flack, Marjorie. (1932). *Ask Mr. Bear*. New York: Macmillan.

Fleischman, Sid. (1988). *The Scarebird*. Ill. Peter Sis. New York: Greenwillow.

Ginsburg, Mirra. (1974). *Mushroom in the Rain.* Ill. Jose Aruego and Ariane Dewey. New York: Macmillan.

Gregory, Nan. (1997). *How Smudge Came.* Ill. Ron Lightburn. New York: Walker.

Grifalconi, Ann. (1987). *Darkness and the Butterfly.* Boston: Little, Brown.

Heide, Florence Parry and Gilliland, Judith Heide. (1992). *Sami and the Time of the Troubles.* Ill. Ted Lewin. New York: Clarion.

Henkes, Kevin. (1988). *The Zebra Wall.* New York: Greenwillow.

Hill, Elizabeth Starr. (1990, 1967). *Evan's Corner.* Ill. Sandra Speidel. New York: Holt.

Hoban, Russell. (1970). *A Bargain for Frances.* Ill. Lillian Hoban. New York: Harper & Row. Text copyright © 1970 by Russell Hoban. Copyright renewed 1992 by Russell Hoban. Used by permission of HarperCollins Publishers.

Hoban, Russell. (1995, 1968). *A Birthday for Frances.* Ill. Lillian Hoban. New York: HarperCollins.

Hughes, Shirley. (1987). "Alfie Gives a Hand." in *All About Alfie.* New York: Lothrop.

Hughes, Shirley. (1977). *David and Dog.* Upper Saddle River, NJ: Prentice-Hall.

Hughes, Shirley. (1993). *Giving.* Cambridge, MA: Candlewick.

Khan, Rukhsana. (1998). *The Roses in My Carpets.* Ill. Ronald Himler. New York: Holiday.

Lankford, Mary. (1998). *Dominoes Around the World.* Ill. Karen Dugan. New York: Morrow.

Lankford, Mary. (1992). *Hopscotch Around the World.* Ill. Karen Milone. New York: Morrow.

Lee, Milly. (1997). *Nim and the War Effort.* Ill. Yangsook Choi. New York: Farrar.

Lionni, Leo. (1970). *Fish Is Fish.* New York: Pantheon.

Lipkind, William and Mordvinoff, Micolas. (1951). *Finders Keepers.* New York: Harcourt.

Little, Jean. (1992). *Revenge of the Small Small.* Ill. Janet Wilson. New York: Viking.

Marshall, James. (1972). *George and Martha.* Boston: Houghton Mifflin.

Mayer, Mercer. (1974). *Frog Goes to Dinner.* New York: Dial.

McCully, Emily Arnold. (1984). *Picnic.* New York: Harper.

McMillan, Bruce. (1995). *Nights of the Pufflings.* Boston: Houghton Mifflin.

Ness, Evaline. (1966). *Sam, Bangs and Moonshine.* New York: Holt.

Pearson, Susan. (1987). *Happy Birthday, Grampie.* Ill. Ronald Himler. New York: Dial.

Rael, Elsa Okon. (1997). *When Zaydeh Danced on Eldridge Street.* Ill. Marjorie Priceman. New York: Simon.

Raschka, Chris. (1993). *Yo! Yes!* New York: Orchard.

Ray, Deborah. (1987). *My Dog, Trip.* New York: Holiday.

Reider, Katja. (1997). *Snail Started It.* Ill. Angela von Roehl. New York: North-South.

Ross, Tony. (1989). *Towser and Sadie's Birthday.* New York: Pantheon.

Scott, Ann Herbert. (1992, 1967). *Sam.* Ill. Symean Shimin. New York: Philomel.

Shalant, Phyllis. (1988). *Look What We've Brought You from Vietnam.* Ill. Joanna Roy. New York: Messner.

Sharmat, Marjorie and Sharmat, Mitchell. (1980). *On the Day I Was Born.* Ill. Diane Dawson. New York: Dutton.

Steig, William. (1971). *Amos & Boris.* New York: Farrar.

Stevenson, James. (1977). *Could Be Worse!* New York: Greenwillow.

Stevenson, James. (1996). *Yard Sale.* New York: Greenwillow.

Thomas, Ianthe. (1976). *Eliza's Daddy.* Ill. Moneta Barnett. New York: Harcourt.

Torres, Leyla. (1998). *Liliana's Grandmothers.* New York: Farrar.

Torres, Leyla. (1993). *Subway Sparrow.* New York: Farrar.

Van Allsburg, Chris. (1993). *The Sweetest Fig.* Boston: Houghton Mifflin.

Van Allsburg, Chris. (1988). *Two Bad Ants.* Boston: Houghton Mifflin.

Wells, Rosemary. (1983). *Peabody.* New York: Dial.

Winthrop, Elizabeth. (1983). *Katharine's Doll.* Ill. Marylin Hafner. New York: Dutton.

Zolotow, Charlotte. (1968). *The Quarreling Book.* Ill. Arnold Lobel. New York: Harper.

SUPPORTING CHILDREN'S AESTHETIC AND CREATIVE DEVELOPMENT

Aesthetic development denotes a person's increasing sensitivity to and appreciation of beauty in art and in nature. This ability to respond to the beautiful is sometimes termed a skill of *impression.* It is paired with the skill of *expression,* the ability to create. Broudy, in an article supporting the need for aesthetic education, writes that "performance activity in various media is probably a necessary condition for acquiring the skills of impression, because so much of proper aesthetic perception depends on familiarity with the expressive potentialities of paint, clay, sound, gesture, etc." (1977, p. 635). Performance, or creative activity, thus provides a base for children's aesthetic development as well as being a valid educational experience itself.

AESTHETIC AND CREATIVE DEVELOPMENT IN YOUNG CHILDREN

Art and music, including dance and movement, are indispensable elements of any curriculum for young children. The arts give children a choice of ways in which they can express their thoughts and feelings. Children may also find that they can understand an idea expressed through music, art, or drama that they might not have understood through words alone (Efland, 1984). For many children, experiences with art parallel experiences with text. Alejandro writes that "When we read and write, we use the same critical thinking and decision-making brain power that we use when we paint or respond to paintings" (1994, p. 13). In addition, the arts provide a means of expression for what Krogh terms "the widest possible diversity." She notes that "Children can move in response to the same music whether they are in a wheelchair or are totally mobile. Or they can use the same art materials to create objects or pictures that portray their own or others' cultures" (Krogh, 1994, p. 522). As teacher, you judge whether there is enough freedom in an activity to meet various needs or whether you must make adjustments so that all can take part.

Day-care professionals and teachers should work to help children enjoy participating in the arts, use their imaginations and creative potential, and progress toward more complexity in aesthetic values. A successful arts program introduces new forms of art to children, expanding their skills of both expression and impression, but does so gradually, allowing the children to accommodate the new information and gain control over new techniques. It also encourages children to use their creative potential.

Creative Potential

Torrance has defined creativity as "a special kind of problem solving" (1970, p. 2). Sousa agrees, writing that creativity is "a cognitive activity that results in a new or novel way of viewing a problem or situation" (1998, p. 468). It is a process in which the learners first become aware of personal gaps in knowledge, problems, or disharmonies, and then set about resolving inconsistencies. They look for new relationships among existing information. They make, test, modify, and perfect hypotheses and, finally, communicate their results to others. Torrance believes that a sensitivity to problems may be aroused either through self-initiated activities or through a structured sequence of activities. Creative learning can take place in any subject area.

In the arts, creative learning is exhibited as a four-year-old attempts to make a snake from modeling clay, only to have it separate in segments as he rolls it out. He has encountered a problem. The teacher helps, not through telling him what to do or through doing it for him, but by asking questions that stimulate his thinking. "Where is it breaking? Why do you suppose that's the place it breaks? What could you do differently?" The child then hypothesizes that keeping the clay thicker, not rolling it so rapidly, using both hands to roll, or moving his hands along the snake as he works might help. He tries his ideas and reports to the teacher when his snake is finished.

Creativity has been characterized by Guilford (1965) and others as involving divergent thinking, fluency in the production of ideas, flexibility, originality of ideas, and elaboration. Teachers and day-care professionals can encourage creative thinking by establishing an atmosphere of acceptance in the classroom and by asking questions and structuring activities that permit a variety of responses. Creativity is viewed as a process as well as a product, and as a quality that all people have to some degree. As you plan activities in the arts, you will need to provide opportunities for children to use creative thinking. You will also need to know the general capabilities of the children you are teaching.

Development in Art

There is a sequence of development in art that is fairly predictable; although, as with other developmental sequences, the age levels that correspond with each stage are approximations. Most children first begin scribbling at about two years of age, although some may start a few months earlier. Their activities with crayon on paper are basically a physical activity. Lowenfeld (1987) divides the scribbling stage into three segments. The first is *disordered scribbling.* Children simply move the crayon or pencil in wide sweeps across the paper. About six months after they have begun scribbling they move into *controlled scribbling.* Now they are beginning to gain some control over their markings and to experience the outcome visually. They may repeat motions resulting in patterns of lines or circles and often become engrossed in the activity. At about three-and-a-half years of age, they move into *naming of scribbling.* As the title implies, they begin telling what the scribble signifies—"This is my mommy," or "I'm eating lunch." This is an important step in their development because they have begun to think in terms of pictures rather than motions. The drawings themselves, however, may differ little from earlier scribbles.

By age four, most children can create shapes which resemble round or rectangular objects. Size relationships are more likely to be determined by the order in which children created each object and the medium they are using than by any attempt for accurate representation. They may also exaggerate size to show what is important to them. Color, also, is not chosen for accuracy. It may be determined by preference or simply the colors available for use (Chapman, 1978).

Around four-and-a-half or five, children reach the *early expressive* stage. They begin to develop their ideas for drawings or paintings before they begin the actual work. They may look to adults for guidance and use their own previous work or that of peers as models. They may practice a skill to gain mastery over it, sometimes repeating a picture or sculpture. They are generally able to tell about their work and may include more detail in the work if they are encouraged to reenact an experience or discuss a theme.

In the early elementary grades children begin to develop more complexity in their work. In pictures, they frequently place all figures along a baseline, but by the end of third grade are beginning to use overlapping shapes to show distance. They begin to be aware of relative size, being dissatisfied now if their flowers are as tall as their houses. They often use the stereotyped notion of proper colors—green leaves, brown tree trunks—although they will respond to structured observations and opportunities to mix colors. They enjoy art activities based on imaginative themes (Brewer, 1997).

Teachers and day-care professionals can help children develop artistic ability in several ways. They can provide a variety of media and give children ample time to experiment. Children need to see how paint runs together before they can begin to master its use. They need to try several ways to put legs on their clay figures or to use the sides as well as the points of their crayons.

Adults can give suggestions that encourage children to solve their own problems. This means refusing to draw the dog for the child who complains of being unable to do it and asking instead what elements make up the dog, or what is special about the dog that the child might want to emphasize.

As children show their work, teachers and day-care professionals can comment objectively upon what has been done. "You've used thick, straight lines and then wavy ones that contrast one another," or "You've mixed several interesting new shades of color." This introduces vocabulary for talking about art and allows the adult to show that all efforts are valued. Differences in style of art are to be expected and are desirable.

Adult art can be shared with children. Seeing different styles reinforces the idea that one style is not better than another and introduces children to art they might not see otherwise. Professional art can be used for talking about the process employed, but should not be used as a model for children to copy.

Development in Music

In music and movement, as in art, some abilities and responses are governed by the children's physical and motor development. Young children sing between middle C and G or A, the middle range on a piano. Gradually they add a tone or two below C, and by age eight will have added a tone or two above G. From initial stages of not matching melodic tones at all, children move to a stage where they engage in directional singing. They approximate the tones, moving in the direction of the melody. Then with practice they become more accurate in singing tunes within a range of four or five notes. McDonald writes that "Not surprisingly, the most tuneful young singers come from home and/or caregiving environments that have provided many experiences and opportunities for singing and listening to music" (1979, p. 25).

Children respond to music from very early ages and seem to respond most markedly to music with strong rhythm or melody. At ages three and four, children can respond to music through walking, running, clapping, and other physical movements. At first they may repeat the same movement throughout the rhythmic experience, but gradually will begin to experiment. Often a day-care professional or teacher will use a drum or other instrument to follow the rhythm of the children's actions rather than as the impetus for rhythmic movements (McDonald and Simons, 1989).

Children of four and five are developing in coordination and can add hopping and skipping to their repertoire of movement. They enjoy using rhythm instruments such as triangles, bells, blocks, and rhythm sticks. They can use these instruments in response to music and may also use them to illustrate stories, making judgments about appropriate pitch, rhythm, and tempo.

As children mature and engage in musical experiences, they move more accurately with the rhythm and develop more self-control in the use of rhythm instruments. With instructions that help them explore body movements, they use space, time, and weight variations in their response to music and in dramatizations. Teachers and day-care professionals help children gain these concepts by engaging them in directed movement activities. For example, to explore space, children can be instructed to find a space where they will not touch anyone else when arms are outstretched. Then they make themselves use as little of the space as possible, then as much as possible. Adding the element of time, they can move slowly, using all their space; move rapidly, using the lower half of their space; be a frightened mouse moving in their space; be an angry bear moving in their space.

Many of the teaching strategies that support development in art apply to development in music and movement also. Just as children need time to experiment with a variety of media, they also need time to experiment with singing, instruments, and movement. There should be an area where children can use rhythm instruments and tone bars in an unstructured setting;

where they can listen to the sounds, try different rhythms or melodies, or sing. Some teachers provide such an area for use during times when other "sound-producing" activities will be in progress. Others have special rooms for musical experimentation. There also should be times when children use rhythm instruments in a group response to music or literature.

Children should have the opportunity to sing often, both for enjoyment and to learn to reproduce a melody. Songs to be taught should be within the vocal range of the children. The most easily learned songs have repetition of melodic lines or refrains. Teachers can help children recognize the directionality of the music and introduce the concept of musical notation by moving their hands to indicate the movement of the melody, or by showing the movement with lines on the chalkboard. Duration of notes can be shown by hand movements or written symbols, with a long motion or line indicating a note to be held, and short motions or lines indicating eighth or quarter notes.

There should be a variety of musical selections for listening activities. Interest in listening to music can be maintained by having children respond rhythmically as they listen and by sharing selections several times so that children become familiar with them.

Day-care professionals and teachers can give children the vocabulary to talk about music and movement just as they can with art. They may comment objectively on children's responses—"You are marching in a steady rhythm," or "The tones you are using all have a high pitch." They may also use the vocabulary as they share adult music. Many vocabulary items are appropriate for use in several of the arts; therefore, as children hear them used in more than one context, they gain a clearer conception of the meaning of the terms.

Teachers of young children have the opportunity to engage pupils in activities that will foster their aesthetic and creative development, and build self-confidence in both expression and impression. The satisfaction that children experience as they participate in such activities is a reward for the teacher as well as the pupils.

GOALS FOR TEACHING

As in other areas, teaching goals for aesthetic and creative development can be categorized as long-term developmental goals, general goals for an age or grade level, and specific goals for individual children. The long-term goals are those behaviors or competencies that are developed over time and considered desired patterns of behavior. A long-term goal for aesthetic and creative development is that children will use, experiment with, and gain control over a variety of art media. It is a goal that will take several years to be achieved.

A general goal for second grade is that children will identify at least three different musical instruments by engaging in a special pattern of movement for each of the instruments as they listen to selections such as "Peter and the Wolf." School-wide curriculum guides may well suggest specific materials. In the absence of curriculum guides, or in addition to them, teachers develop their own general goals for their classes.

A specific goal is one for an individual child. "Raoul will use sand blocks to match the rhythm of John's movement." At age five, Raoul is becoming aware of the rhythms around him. He is beginning to explore the use of rhythm instruments, though he still needs to develop self-control in using them. Experiences in matching the rhythm of another child's movement will develop his awareness of rhythm and will give him reason to control his use of rhythm instruments such as sand blocks.

Literature contributes to the achievement of all three types of goals. This chapter focuses on selected long-term developmental goals common to the preschool and primary years. Literature offers opportunities for you to help children grow toward the following goals for aesthetic and creative development.

Children will respond favorably to diverse styles of art and music.

Children will exhibit a sensory awareness of their environment.

Children will use, experiment with, and gain control over a variety of art media. Children will sing in tune within their vocal range and will respond to music and literature with movement and rhythm instruments.

Children will use their imaginations as they participate in art, music, and movement.

Children will enjoy experiencing the work of others and participating in the arts themselves.

The first two goals are for skills of impression, the next three are for skills of expression, and the last combines the two.

As with other areas, these goals can be correlated with national and regional standards. For example, the goal that children will enjoy experiencing the work of others and participating in the arts themselves fits with Standard 1 in the Rhode Island K-12 Arts Framework (1997). That standard, Creation/Performance, is that "All students will engage in self or group expression by creating original or interpreting works of art." Specific descriptors are then given for dance, the visual arts, theatre, and music. As you look at standards for your region or school district, look for ways in which these goals and the specific standards mesh.

OPPORTUNITIES BOOKS OFFER

Helping Children Develop Favorable Attitudes Toward Diverse Styles of Art

For children of preschool and primary school age, art appreciation is basically a favorable attitude toward various art forms and various styles in art. It is not expected that children, any more than adults, will like all forms equally. It is important, however, that they be open to art that is new to them and that they recognize the validity of different modes of expression. You can help children achieve this openness by presenting the idea that art is a personal form of expression, by exposing children to a wide range of art, and by involving children with art in ways that give them a basis for relating to it.

Presenting Art as Personal Expression

One way to show art as personal expression is to share books that demonstrate the concept directly. Cynthia Rylant's *All I See* (1988) opens as a young boy named Charlie watches Gregory, an artist who has set up his easel beside a lake. When Gregory tires of his painting and goes out in his canoe, Charlie sneaks a look at Gregory's picture and is surprised. After several such visits, Charlie realizes that Gregory always paints the same thing—a blue whale. Charlie and

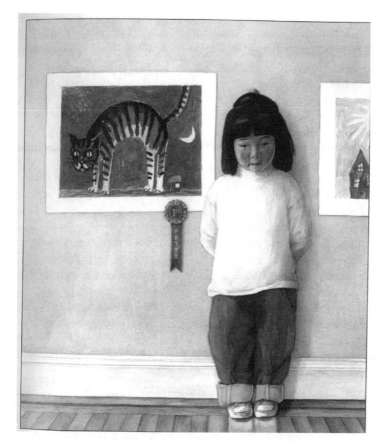

Emma learns that she can visualize images and draw them even without her special rug. (Illustration from Emma's Rug. *Copyright © 1996 by Allen Say. Reprinted by permission of Houghton Mifflin Company. All rights reserved.)*

Gregory become friends after Charlie paints a picture that shows Gregory painting and his cat sleeping. Charlie paints what he sees. Finally he asks Gregory why he always paints whales, and Gregory responds that it is all he sees.

This book might be combined with Allen Say's *Emma's Rug* (1996) because it too presents the artist as creating based on individual vision. Emma carries a small shaggy rug that was given to her when she was born and says that she sees the pictures she later draws and paints by staring at the rug. When her mother washes the rug, Emma thinks she can no longer create, but soon realizes that she can visualize images all around her. Both books show the artist as creating what he or she "sees," whether it is seen in that fashion or at all by other people. Have children look back over some of their own paintings and drawings to see if what they drew was important to them. Then let them look at one or two paintings by well-known artists and tell what they think might have been important to that artist at that time.

There are many books that show children as capable, developing artists. Ti Marie in *Painted Dreams* (Williams, 1998) uses paints she has taken from the trash and whatever other materials she can find to draw on the wall behind the stall where her mother sells vegetables in this story set in Haiti. Her picture, which includes the tomatoes and onions they are selling, draws the attention of people passing by and helps convert them into customers. Ali, in *Cool*

Ali (Poydar, 1996), brings relief from the heat to her neighbors with her chalk pictures on the sidewalk—pictures of a lake, and shade, and a snowstorm.

In *The Art Lesson* (1989) by Tomie dePaola, the young protagonist, named Tommy, is distressed when his first-grade teacher tells the children that they are to copy the Pilgrim she has drawn on the board, and that they are permitted only one sheet of paper. Tommy has been told by his cousins that artists do not copy and that they must "practice, practice, practice." Tommy goes on strike, but eventually manages to reach a compromise. The last illustration shows a gray-haired Tommy, still drawing. Do they think they will still be drawing when they have gray hair? And is the author/illustrator writing about and illustrating something that is important to him?

A week or two later you could share *Paint All Kinds of Pictures* (1964) by Arnold Spilka. This is a picture book about painting that shows contrasts between pictures: a large picture or a small one; one in color or black-and-white; a scary one or a funny one or an exciting one. It shows a difference in the mood of a painting by contrasting a painting of a city done in bright colors with a muted scene of islands surrounded by water. It shows different styles in several pictures of houses and of fish, and in designs. The books' dual theme is that pictures reflect how the artist feels, and that the readers can paint any kind of pictures they want. It is an excellent book for introducing vocabulary that will help children talk about painting and other arts. Children might look at the "quiet" illustrations in the book and try to find other quiet pictures from their own work, or look at designs and find designs on objects in their homes or classroom. While *All I See* can be used successfully with children from four or five on (when they have begun to decide what they will draw before beginning), *Paint All Kinds of Pictures* is more appropriate for second- and third-graders who are gaining more control over their use of media.

A second way of showing art as personal expression is to compare the work of two or more artists when they are using the same or similar subject matter. Songs and folktales often have several illustrated versions. *Hush, Little Baby,* for example, has been illustrated by Aliki (1968), by Jeanette Winter (1984), by Shari Halpern (1997), and by Sylvia Long (1997) among others. After children have participated in the telling or singing of the rhyme or song, let them look at the pictures in the books, holding the books side-by-side so that the text matches. Children can see how each of the illustrators chooses to portray the characters and the action. They would see Halpern's cut-paper collage forming a quilt-like pattern encircling the subject of each verse, for example, contrasting with Long's soft pen-and-ink illustrations of rabbit mother and baby. Having children tell which they prefer will demonstrate that not only do artists portray subjects differently, but others react to their work differently.

Occasionally let children make images of book characters in their own minds before showing the illustrations in the book. Have them describe what they imagined, then show how the illustrator portrayed those same characters. If you did this with the Everett Anderson books, you could show how two illustrators portrayed the same character. In *Some of the Days of Everett Anderson* (Clifton, 1970) and in *Everett Anderson's Christmas Coming* (Clifton, 1971), the illustrations were done by Evaline Ness. In *Everett Anderson's Year* (Clifton, 1974), *Everett Anderson's Friend* (Clifton, 1976), *Everett Anderson's 1-2-3* (Clifton, 1977), *Everett Anderson's Nine Month Long* (Clifton, 1978), and *Everett Anderson's Goodbye* (Clifton, 1983), the illustrations were done by Ann Grifalconi. The books about Frances by Russell Hoban also have two illustrators: *Bedtime for Frances* (1995) was illustrated by Garth Williams, the others by Lillian Hoban. Second-

and third-graders could compare the two Arthurs in the books by Russell Hoban, the one drawn by James Marshall in *Dinner at Alberta's* (1973) with the one drawn by Byron Barton for *Arthur's New Power* (1978).

You and the children could select one animal and then see how that animal is shown in several books of fiction. If you choose pigs, you might look at the familiar pig of William Steig in a book such as *Zeke Pippin* (1994). See how Steig's illustrations compare with the line drawings of Arthur Geisert in *Oink* (1991), the pencil sketches with vivid watercolors of Colin Mc-Naughton in *Oops!* (1997) and the pen-and-ink outlines with watercolor washes of Felicia Bond in *If You Give a Pig a Pancake* (Numeroff, 1998). All the books you choose should be appropriate to the age level of the children. With young children it is generally better to compare only two books at a time. A third, fourth, and fifth may be added later, one at a time. Children can see that artists use different media and different styles to show these different pig characters. Let the children use a variety of media themselves to create pigs of their own, perhaps placing them on a mural.

Exposing Children to a Wide Range of Art

Helping children see the diversity in the art in picture books and encouraging them to select different media and different styles in their own art demonstrates that differences are expected and valued. It also introduces the children to a range of two-dimensional art forms. As you select literature to share, keep a record of the methods of illustration that children are seeing. You may want to select several books from this list for comparison. If there are some forms that have not been presented, you will want to find good literature that fills the gap. Some illustrators are known for their work with certain media or with certain styles. Others vary considerably according to the text they are illustrating. As a beginning, look at some of the following books to familiarize yourself with media and styles of art found in books for young children.

Media:

Collage—

Fleming, Denise. (1994). *Barnyard Banter.* New York: Holt.

Keats, Ezra Jack. (1962). *The Snowy Day.* New York: Viking.

Pencil drawings—

Macaulay, David. (1993). *Ship.* Boston: Houghton Mifflin.

Van Allsburg, Chris. (1981). *Jumanji.* Boston: Houghton Mifflin.

Crayon—

Collington, Peter. (1993). *The Midnight Circus.* New York: Knopf.

Lionni, Leo. (1987). *Fish Is Fish.* New York: Pantheon Books.

Woodcut—

Emberley, Barbara. (1967). Ill., Ed Emberley. *Drummer Hoff.* Upper Saddle River, NJ: Prentice-Hall.

Tejima, Keizaburo. (1987). *Owl Lake.* New York: Philomel.

CHAPTER 9

Cardboard cut—

Hodges, Margaret. (1964). Ill., Blair Lent. *The Wave*. Boston: Houghton Mifflin.

Lent, Blair. (1987). *Bayberry Bluff*. Boston: Houghton Mifflin.

Scratchboard—

Cooney, Barbara. (1958). *Chanticleer and the Fox*. New York: Crowell.

San Souci, Robert S. (1995). Ill., Brian Pinkney. *The Faithful Friend*. New York: Simon.

Photography—

Ancona, George. (1998). *Fiesta Fireworks!*. New York: Lothrop.

McMillan, Bruce. (1998). *Salmon Summer*. Boston: Houghton Mifflin.

Pastels—

Coerr, Eleanor. (1993). Ill., Ed Young. *Sadako*. New York: Putnam.

Van Allsburg, Chris. (1985). *The Polar Express*. Boston: Houghton Mifflin.

Gouache—

Johnston, Tony. (1985). Ill., Tomie dePaola. *The Quilt Story*. New York: Putnam's.

Wildsmith, Brian. (1964). *Brian Wildsmith's Mother Goose*. New York: Franklin Watts.

Watercolor—

Potter, Beatrix. (1902). *The Tale of Peter Rabbit.* London: Frederick Warne.

Yolen, Jane. (1987). Ill., John Schoenherr. *Owl Moon*. New York: Philomel.

Oil Paint—

Locker, Thomas. (1998). *Home*. New York: Harcourt.

Zelinsky, Paul O. (1986). *Rumpelstiltskin*. New York: Dutton.

Style of Art:

Representation—

Bunting, Eve. (1989). *The Wednesday Surprise.* Ill., Donald Carrick. Boston: Clarion.

Cooper, Floyd. (1998). *Cumbayah.* New York: Morrow.

Impressionistic—

Burningham, John. (1975). *Mr. Grumpy's Motorcar.* New York: Macmillan.

McCully, Emily. (1992). *Mirette on the High Wire.* New York: Putnam.

Expressionistic—

Ehrlich, Amy. (1972). Ill., Robert Andrew Parker. *Zeek Silver Moon*. New York: Dial.

Grimm Brothers. (1980). Ill., Janina Domanska. *The Bremen Town Musicians*. New York: Greenwillow.

Cartoon—

Geisel, Theodore. (1940). *Horton Hears a Who.* New York: Random House.

Stevenson, James. (1996). *Yard Sale.* New York: Greenwillow.

Abstract—

Delaunay, Sonia. (1972). *Sonia Delaunay's Alphabet.* New York: Crowell.

Stone, Harris. (1967). Ill., Sheila Heins. *The Last Free Bird.* Upper Saddle River, NJ: Prentice-Hall.

Stylized—

Aardema, Verna. (1975). Ill., Leo and Diane Dillon. *Why Mosquitoes Buzz in People's Ears.* New York: Dial.

Goble, Paul. (1994). *Adopted by the Eagles: A Plains Indian Story of Friendship and Treachery.* New York: Bradbury.

Surrealistic—

Bang, Molly. (1988). *Delphine.* New York: Morrow.

Browne, Anthony. (1990). *The Tunnel.* New York: Knopf.

Let children react to the art in picture books. As they look at the illustrations in *From the Hills of Georgia* (O'Kelley, 1983) or *Circus!* (O'Kelley, 1986) tell them that the illustrator, Mattie Lou O'Kelley, is a self-taught artist who began painting late in her life. Let them express their opinions about the stylized, folk-art quality of her paintings. Share some illustrations that you anticipate the children will like immediately, then share some examples of more complex styles of art. The illustrations for *Ben's Trumpet* (Isadora, 1979) are almost art deco, more abstract than most art for children. The story line is slight; a little boy hears the music from a nearby club and longs to play the trumpet himself. Children could be asked to tell whether or not seeing the illustrations made the story better for them than just listening to it. They might look at specific pictures as they respond, calling attention to what they liked or telling why the illustrations were not helpful to them. They should be guided to look at the illustrations carefully, but not guided into saying they like whatever is presented.

Involving Children with Art

Make a practice of involving children with art in ways that will enable them to relate to it personally. As they look at a painting, drawing, or illustration in a book, have them imagine themselves someplace in the picture. What can they see from where they are standing? Do you hear any sounds? If so, what do they hear? If they could move around inside the painting, where would they go?

You might, for the fun of it, talk about what might happen if they really could enter a painting—or if the contents of a painting entered our world. *The Incredible Painting of Felix*

Clousseau (Agee, 1988) is about an artist whose paintings become real. It concludes with Clousseau returning to his studio—and walking back into a painting. *Eyes of the Dragon* (Leaf, 1987) has a similar motif—the artist's rendition of a dragon flies away after the artist has been forced to add eyes to it. Children might look at paintings, deciding which they might want to be like Felix Clousseau's.

Children might create stories about a painting or about a single illustration from a book. An example of how this might be done is *Little Girl in a Red Dress with Cat and Dog* (Nicholson, 1998) in which the author imagines a story that might be behind a painting.

Another technique for encouraging careful observation and personal involvement is to show a picture for a brief period of time. Then let children tell about what they saw and record their descriptions or reactions. Show the pictures as you play back the tape. You might use this technique with the illustration in the books by Shirley Glubok. The text in these books about the art of different countries and cultures is for intermediate-grade children. However, the photographs of actual art objects can be observed and discussed by primary grade children.

Showing videos about illustrators of children's books can help primary-grade children see the artists as real people. Weston Woods Studio has videos about many illustrators, including Steven Kellogg, Eric Carle, Gerald McDermott, Jerry Pinkney, Mem Fox, Patricia Polacco, Tomie dePaola, and Rosemary Wells. Children often want to explore the process of illustration that these illustrators describe.

Consider involving children in an art project before showing them a book that uses certain ideas or techniques. For example, let children decorate a plain white paper cup and paper plate, dishes that they may use at lunch or snack time if they choose. Talk with them about what they might do, whether making designs or drawing pictures. When the project is complete, share with them *When Clay Sings* (1972) by Byrd Baylor. Her poetic description of the art on prehistoric Indian pottery is illustrated to Tom Bahti. He based his illustrations on designs found on the pottery of the Anasazi, Mogollon, Hohokam, and Mimbres cultures. The children will find that other peoples also drew animals, birds, fish, all sorts of designs—even monsters. They have a point of reference for looking at the art of another person, another culture.

As children see and become involved with a variety of artistic styles and media, both through their own work and through observations and discussion of the work of others, they are learning that diversity in art is to be both valued and enjoyed.

Sharpening Children's Awareness

Much of literature, especially poetry, provides readers with a verbal description of authors' perceptions of their environments. Jim Arnosky, for example, writes vivid descriptions of the scenes he illustrates. In *Near the Sea* (Arnosky, 1990), his oil paintings show what he sees on an island off the coast of Maine, the tidal pools, the gulls, the ocean cliffs and salt marshes. Individuals who are sensitive to the world around them share their insights and reactions in evocative language. Reading such literature to children fosters a sharpened awareness. Children see a model of keen observation. They hear a detailed description, or a mood captured in metaphor. As a teacher, you can select books which present the sensory awareness of the author. You can also select books which describe activities the children can repeat, and others that can be a stimulus for activities which will enhance sensory awareness.

Sharing in the Awareness of Others

Look at both prose and poetry to find books in which authors write in sensory terms and illustrators convey the beauty they observe. An example of a book in which an author has shown the wonder and beauty of a commonplace event is *On a Starry Night* by Natalie Kinsey-Warnock (1994). A young girl and her mother climb to the top of a hill to look at the stars. The woods "rattle" with the sounds of crickets and frogs; owls hoot and there are the "snuffles and snorts" of an animal nearby. She smells the spruce trees, "sharp and spicy." She sees the eyes of the raccoons shining in the dark, "bright as beads." Papa joins them and they lie on a blanket, watching the sky and counting shooting stars. The text is sparse yet poetic, the very simplicity of the words focusing attention on the wonder of nighttime sights and sounds and smells. Sharing this book with children brings them to an appreciation of the various senses in experiencing and describing a place or an event.

Look for literature that highlights the various senses. *The Cloud* (Ray, 1984) tells about Nina and her mother as they hike to the top of a mountain, so high that they may walk into a cloud, her mother says. Nina thinks it will be fun and that clouds should feel soft. Once they are walking through the low-lying clouds, she finds that it is cold and damp, relieved only when they descend to the tree line and the air is warmer. Uri Shulevitz captures the beauty of daybreak in *Dawn* (1974) and the power of a snowstorm to transform an entire village in *Snow* (1998). In both books he emphasizes the visual.

Eve Merriam's "A Matter of Taste" asks questions that children will answer even before *you* ask.

What does your tongue like the most?
Chewy meat or crunchy toast?

A lumpy bump pickle or tickly pop?
A soft marshmallow or a hard lime drop?

Hot pancakes or a sherbet freeze?
Celery noise or quiet cheese?

Or do you like pizza?
More than any of these?

Eve Merriam

The onomatopoeia in the following two poems, "Mud" and "Poem to Mud," adds to children's delight in the message as two poets explore the feel of mud.

Mud

Mud is very nice to feel
All squishy–squash between the toes!
I'd rather wade in wiggly mud
Than smell a yellow rose.

Nobody else but the rosebush knows

How nice mud feels

Between the toes.

Polly Chase Boyden (1983)

Poem to Mud

Poem to mud—

Poem to ooze—

Patted in pies, or coating your shoes.

Poem to slooze—

Poem to crud—

Fed by a leak, or spread by a flood.

Wherever, whenever, whyever it goes,

Stirred by your finger, or strained by your toes,

There's nothing sloppier, slippier, floppier,
There's nothing slickier, stikier, thickier,

There's nothing quickier to make grown-ups sickier,

Trulier coolier

Than a wonderful mud.

Zilpha Keatley Snyder

Often poems about the weather or seasons will include sensory descriptions, and certain poets use such descriptions regularly. The work of Aileen Fisher is filled with portrayals of and reactions to the natural world. The following selections by Fisher are appropriate for young children:

Always Wondering. (1991). Ill. Joan Sandin. New York: Harper.

Cricket in a Thicket. (1976). Ill. Feodor Rojankovsky. New York: Scribner's.

Feathered Ones and Furry. (1971). Ill. Eric Carle. New York: Crowell.

Going Barefoot. (1960). Ill. Adrienne Adams. New York: Crowell.

I Like Weather. (1963). Ill. Janina Domanska. New York: Crowell.

In the Middle of the Night. (1965). Ill. Adrienne Adams. New York: Crowell.

In the Woods, In the Meadow, In the Sky. (1965). Ill. Margot Tomes. New York: Scribner's.

Out in the Dark and Daylight. (1983). Ill. Gail Owens. New York: Harper & Row.

Rabbits. Rabbits. (1983). Ill. Gail Newman. New York: Harper & Row.

When It Comes to Bugs. (1986). Ill. Chris and Bruce Degan. New York: Harper & Row.

Look also for Shirley Hughes's *Out and About* (1988), a collection of poems about the seasons that is fresh, cheery, and appropriate for preschool as well as primary children.

Experiencing One's Own Environment

Some books describe how artists have captu
red experiences that the children may have had themselves. Colleen Carroll presents sixteen pieces of art from a variety of places and times centered on the theme of weather in *How Artists See the Weather: Sun, Wind, Snow, Rain* (1996). Thomas Locker combines careful scientific observation with aesthetic observation in *Sky Tree: Seeing Science Through Art* (1995). Children can see how the elements they experience every day have been portrayed by different artists, and how they change both daily and seasonally. Look around the environment where you are teaching. What is there that you and the children can observe, perhaps over a period of time, in different conditions, to see the colors and the moods? Perhaps you are close to a pond or stream; or want to watch a grassy field, or pavement, in bright sunlight, on a gloomy day, or glistening wet from rainwater. Help children record what they have seen. List their reactions after each observation; then, after several entries, read over what they have dictated and help them put their thoughts together into a single experience chart. What would they want to capture in a painting?

After reading *I Took a Walk* (Cole, 1998) take the children on a walk of their own. See how many different things they see and sounds they hear, perhaps emphasizing the sounds. A listening walk can be taken indoors as well as outdoors, and in both large and small groups. Preschool children going in guided groups can stop and all listen to the different sounds together, discussing each sound as it is heard. Older children might go in pairs around the school, each pair noting either with words or pictures what they hear. When all have returned to the classroom, the groups compare their experiences. You will know how much responsibility your students can handle, whether they can go unaccompanied by an adult within limits or whether the experience is more likely to be successful if you or an aide go along.

Adapt the experiences to fit your environment. *We Walk in Sandy Places* (Baylor, 1976) describes tracks of various animals in the desert sand. You do not need to be living in a desert to use the idea of the book. Think about where tracks can be found near your school or center. It may be in sand, but in beach sand. It may be in the dust, or in mud, or in snow. All will suffice for children to observe the markings left by birds and insects, dogs or chipmunks, and to see the patterns and perhaps make some guesses about who was there and what was happening.

Using Books as Stimuli for Sensory Activities

Many books and poems provide stimuli for activities that require children to use their senses in discovery or exploration. As you select books, think about any possibilities there may be for using sight, sound, touch, taste, and smell. Here are some examples:

Sight.   Read *Goggles* (Keats, 1969), in which Peter and Archie look through an old pipe as they search for the dog Willie while hiding from some older boys. Then let children make spyglasses of their own by rolling paper into a tube. Have them look around the room through the tube, perhaps viewing it from the floor, or standing on a chair to look down. They can draw what they see in this limited field of vision from several perspectives.

Share *My Back Yard* (Rockwell, 1984) and have children observe their own backyards or the center or school play area, and describe what they see, just as Rockwell has done in the book. Then read *All Upon a Sidewalk* (George, 1974) an ant's eye view of a city sidewalk as Lasius Flavus searches for food for her queen. The illustrations show the ants' world as though seen through a magnifying glass. What do children discover as they explore with a magnifying glass? Let them tell about it, dictate a story, or record it with crayon or paint.

Sound.   Read poems that describe sounds with strong use of onomatopoeia, such as "Our Washing Machine" by Patricia Hubbell (1963). After they hear the clicks and whirrs of this machine, have them describe the sounds of other machines. Or, after looking at Peter Spier's *Gobble, Growl, Grunt* (1971) have them tell how they would make the sound of various animals. This is an excellent time for children to use a tape recorder, capturing a sound and listening to it several times, perhaps having others guess what it is.

Read *The Tiniest Sound* (Evans, 1969) poetic descriptions of quiet happenings that conclude with the question of whether there could be a tinier sound than the one described. Have children draw what for them is the tiniest sound.

Touch.   After preschoolers have played with *Pat the Bunny* (Kunhardt, 1962), make a class booklet of materials to be felt and decide together what words they will use to describe each one.

Use just one quotation from Marcia Brown's *Touch Will Tell* (1979) in which she asks if they have hugged a tree lately and felt its coat. Let children "hug" several trees, seeing if they all feel alike. Using crayons and medium-weight paper, let the children make rubbings of some of the bark. Let them see how the rubbings differ. Perhaps they will want to continue the project by making rubbings of other surfaces.

Read *The Seeing Stick* (Yolen, 1977) to primary-grade children. In this modern literary folktale, the emperor promises a fortune in jewels to anyone who can help his blind daughter see. An old man hears of this and sets out with his walking stick and whittling knife. He carves a stick and shows the princess how to trace likenesses with her fingers, feeling her own face and then his carving of it. He stays, carving and telling stories for the princess and helping her grow "eyes on the tips of her fingers." The story says that this is as true as the idea of a seeing stick. It is not until the conclusion of the story that readers learn that the old man is blind too. Let children see what they can recognize through touch. Can they identify objects? Can they touch a classmate's face and recognize the person?

Taste.   Read *Bread and Jam for Frances* (Hoban, 1969) in which Frances refuses to eat anything but her favorite food, bread and jam. Let children talk about their favorite foods. Then have a taste festival, encouraging children to try several kinds of fruit, two or three kinds of cheese, perhaps white bread, rye bread, and raisin bread. Let each child record his or her favorite food in each of the categories in a booklet. See if any class favorites emerge.

Smell.   Leave two or three "scratch-and-sniff" books in the book area where children can experience them individually. Then have the children list odors by categories: those they like or dislike, odors from school, or smells associated with particular holidays. Let children begin their own sniff area, bringing in substances whose smells they like. The substances can be kept in baby food jars with the lids on them but not screwed on or pressed down tightly. This will help preserve the odor while still allowing easy access.

In these activities, the children are using their senses to explore their own environments. Literature helps heighten sensory awareness both through providing an impetus for such exploration and through showing children how another person has experienced a part of the world.

Giving Children Experience with a Variety of Art Media

Children who are familiar with a variety of media are in a position to choose the medium that will best express their ideas, and to select media that they enjoy or feel most successful in using. As well as experimenting with many forms of two- and three-dimensional art materials, children need time to use each form repeatedly so that they can gain mastery in, and explore variations for, its use.

Experimenting with Media Used by Illustrators

Allowing children to experiment with art materials does not mean that the teacher never gives assistance. One child may need help learning how to hold scissors. Another may benefit from the teacher's suggestion that the pieces of a collage be arranged before the child begins pasting any of them onto the paper. Help is given in technique, but the work is not done for the child.

One way that picture books can stimulate children to explore various media is for you to call attention to the medium used by the illustrator and to have materials available for any children who would like to try using them. Lionni's *Let's Make Rabbits* (1982) calls attention itself to the media in use, for the story is of two rabbits, one made with a pencil and the other with scissors. The tools and the actual construction processes are shown as the pencil and scissors first decide to make rabbits and then later make carrots for the rabbits they have created.

In her biographies of artists, Jeanette Winter illustrates in the style the artist used. (Illustration from My Name Is Georgia: A Biography in Pictures and Words, *copyright © 1998 by Jeanette Winter. Reproduced by permission of Harcourt, Inc.)*

Primary-grade children may want to try folding paper to make objects, as is done in the story of *Paper John* (Small, 1987) or cutting silhouettes, as is done for the shadow life in Mitsumasa Anno's *In Shadowland* (1988). With other books, you may turn to certain pages and ask the children how they think the artist made the picture. In *Swimmy* (Lionni, 1963), for example, children looking closely at the illustration of the "forest of seaweeds" will see that the seaweeds are constructed of imprints made by covering lace doilies with paint and then pressing them on the paper. Children can make their own object imprints by painting one side of an object, then pressing it onto paper, or by using an ink or tempera paint pad or brayer to coat the object with paint. They can begin collecting objects themselves to add to the objects provided by the teacher. There is no attempt to copy the *work* of the illustrator, only the *method.*

Getting to Know Artists and Illustrators

Children might learn about an artist while they are enjoying the literature and exploring techniques, particularly if you select several books in which the same illustrator has used a different medium for different books. After *Swimmy,* share several other books by Leo Lionni. *Little Blue and Little Yellow* (1959) would lead to explorations in mixing paints; *Inch by Inch* (1962) or *An Extraordinary Egg* (1994) to collage made from cutting images out of paper that has been colored with crayon or paint, allowing patterns to be created before the shapes are cut. Children can see that some artists use a variety of techniques, just as they do.

Media in picture books that are appropriate for young children to use include crayon, colored pencil, chalk, pastels, scratchboard (use crayon resist with children), paints (tempera for all children, watercolor for primary children), pencil, photography (for primary children), torn paper, collage, and combinations of these.

Children might also come to know artists through books by them or about them. They could see how artists have portrayed their own experiences in *This Land Is My Land* (1993) where George Littlechild explains his painting and tells about his life as a contemporary Native American artist. They could compare the art in *Tar Beach* (Ringgold, 1991) with the paintings in *Talking to Faith Ringgold* (Ringgold, 1996). They could listen as a teacher read some of the interviews of illustrators of children's books in Pat Cummings' *Talking with Artists* (1992). They could see how Jeanette Winter paints in the style of the artist in the biographies of Georgia O'Keeffe (Winter, 1998) and Diego Rivera (Winter, 1991). They might also want to explore the home pages of children's book illustrators on the Internet.

Illustrating One's Own Work

As children explore various media, they can be encouraged to illustrate stories that they are writing or dictating. They see the patterns of picture and text in the books they hear read to them. They also see the endpapers, the first and last pages in a book that are attached to the cover. As they see how illustrators have prepared endpapers, they can make their own for booklets they write.

Some endpapers are simply designs. In *The Old Cotton Blues* (England, 1998), the endpapers are covered with musical notes showing the musical theme of this book. Lois Ehlert's *Snowballs* (1995) have endpapers with small white balls. Children can make such designs with crayons or paint, or might use cardboard cutouts or vegetable prints to make repetitive patterns.

Some books have endpapers that relate to the story by showing a scene from it. *A Gift for Abuelita* (Luenn, 1998) shows the church and graveyard where Rosita and her family go to celebrate The Day of the Dead and to honor her grandmother. *The Storytellers* (Lewin, 1998) shows the city of Fez in Morocco, the setting for the story.

Still other endpapers symbolize the story or picture things related to it. *Crow Boy* (Yashima, 1955) in which Chibi goes from frightened first-grader ignored by classmates to confident sixth-grader imitating crows in a talent show, features a butterfly and a blossom on the endpapers. *The Little House* (Burton, 1942), in which the house experiences a city growing up around it, shows a cartoon sequence in which the mode of transportation undergoes changes; from the first small picture of a horse and rider passing the little house, to the last of a horse van going by. *A Band of Angels* (Hopkinson, 1999), has sketches and a one- or two-sentence description of the members of the original Jubilee Singers, whose musical tour earned enough money to save Fisk School, later Fisk University, from closing.

Children will need to decide which type of endpaper they want to make. They might also create endpapers for books that do not have illustrated endpapers. The activity entails deciding what is essential about a story or what would symbolize it, as well as the actual creation of a picture. The design of book jackets can involve the same kind of thought process, and these jackets can often be used on paper booklets that are not going to be bound in cardboard covers.

Listening to Descriptions of Techniques

Share books with children that describe techniques they might try themselves. Some are casual in approach, giving the idea and telling the child to try it and see what happens. One such book is *Splodges* by Malcolm Carrick (1976). Written in first person, the text tells what the author did and the illustrations show the results. Suggestions include blowing paint on wet paper with a straw; painting with the edge of a ruler; using two crayons or two brushes tied together; making leaf prints; and folding paper over dabs of paint. After hearing it read aloud, preschool or primary children, individually or in small groups, could decide which idea they would like to try. It is not necessary to read the entire book at once, and choice-making might be easier if only two or three ideas are presented at a time. The choice would be what they wanted to try first, not a choice that would eliminate the ideas not immediately selected.

Other "how-to" books are more direct in their presentation of techniques. *Art Around the World: Loo-Loo, Boo, and More Art You Can Do* (Roche, 1998) suggests projects from various countries, giving a very brief history of the art, then showing and telling, step-by-step, how to use the technique. A child might choose to make an art project based on a burial mask from Peru, stained glass from France, a mosaic from Italy, or a block print from India. A section on things to know before beginning gives helpful information for preparing, cleaning up, and reading about the whole project before beginning.

Gail Gibbons' *Click!: A Book about Cameras and Taking Pictures* (1997) could be shared for the tips it gives about taking both indoor and outdoor photographs before children take photographs of their own. It would provide a strong base for appreciating the photographs in *All Around Town: The Photographs of Richard Samuel Roberts* (Johnson, 1998). Children could compare their own pictures with the ones taken by Roberts of the African-American community in Columbia, South Carolina, in the early twentieth century. They can explore what pictures can show about people's daily lives and the things they value.

Representing Stories Through Art

Books and book characters can be the subject of art activities. Children can be encouraged to respond to books through art. They may translate the images of the words into pictures, or two-dimensional art into three-dimensional art. Characters can be made from clay, Play-doh, wire, pipe cleaners, styrofoam, or boxes. Shadow boxes or dioramas can be constructed. Mobiles can be made using coat hangers or sticks as suspension rods.

Children are most likely to use and gain mastery over many media in art if they have the opportunity to work in art as one of their own choices, and if the materials are readily available. It is useful to have a storage area for materials that children can use, getting the materials they need and being responsible for returning materials when they are finished. Many teachers label the storage containers so that children are soon reading words such as *scissors* and *paste* and, in the process, seeing functional reading demonstrated. You will need to introduce new materials and their care either to the class as a whole, or to the children in a series of small groups, before you put them out for general use. New materials and techniques should be introduced gradually so that children are not overwhelmed, and so that the art area is constantly changing. If children know what materials are needed, they can bring many of them from home. String, yarn, ribbon, sticks, toothpicks, straws, milk cartons, boxes, old wrapping paper, and a variety of other "beautiful junk" can be brought to school for art projects rather than being thrown away. It is one way children contribute to their classroom and make it theirs.

Giving Children a Variety of Musical Experiences

Literature can give added dimension to children's musical experiences in the early years, contributing to their participation in singing, listening, using rhythm instruments, and movement. Many songs that are commonly taught to and enjoyed by young children are available in picture book format and on CDs, sound filmstrips, and videos. You have the option of sharing these songs as books, videos, or filmstrips; or simply as a listening experience if you play a CD or the cassette without showing the accompanying filmstrip. Teachers who are somewhat nervous about their own singing or piano playing often begin musical experiences for the children with tapes rather than singing themselves. The cassettes are especially useful for placing in listening centers so that children can hear the words and tune again to learn it themselves, or to sing along with the tape and gain practice in matching tones while engaged in an activity that, for them, is just fun.

Sharing Picture Books of Songs

In selecting picture books of songs that you plan to teach the children, use the same criteria you would use for selecting other songs. Look for songs that are within the range of the children's voices, have some repetition of words or melody, and do not have large melodic intervals. "Go Tell Aunt Rhody" fits these criteria. Then judge the quality of the illustrations. The version of *Go Tell Aunt Rhody* (Aliki, 1974) has full double-page spreads showing the events of this song. You might use the music at the back of the book as you play the song on piano or autoharp and sing it for the children. You can point out to them that the book tells you what notes to play and sing. Present the song as a whole, not line by line. It is often helpful to show the direction of the notes with your hand, or by drawing lines on the board; for example,

– – –

–

– –

for the first phrase of "Go Tell Aunt Rhody." One first-grader showed that she had grasped the concept of notation when she looked at six window blinds, all raised to a slightly different level, and reported, "We can sing the shades." As well as giving an introduction to notation, hand movements or lines drawn help children visualize the direction of the melody.

　　After you have taught the song, sing it with the children as you show the illustrations in one of the books. Children will see the words to the song on each page as they sing and will see that they are singing about the pictures also. If both books are shared, they will see that different artists can interpret a song differently, and perhaps will want to illustrate other songs themselves. Four artists or editors who have each produced several picture books of songs are Robert Quackenbush, Aliki, Peter Spier, and John Langstaff. You may want to look for their work.

　　You might also want to purchase a book or two of collections of songs for regular use with the children. *Singing Bee!* (Hart, 1982) has songs for young children with simple guitar chords and piano accompaniments provided. *Music for Ones and Twos: Songs and Games for the Very Young Child* (Glazer, 1983) has finger plays and games as well as songs. *Go In and Out the Window* (Fox, 1987) has the words and music to classic childhood songs, illustrated with reproductions of works in the Metropolitan Museum of Art. This book should be left where children can browse through it. Popular lullabies appear in *The Lullaby Songbook* (1986) by Jane Yolen, another book with illustrations that should be made available for the children's careful observation. *Father Fox's Feast of Songs* (Watson, 1983) adds music to selections from earlier verses by Clyde Watson, and *Early in the Morning* (1986) has new poems by Charles Causley, many of which are set to music. *Tortillas and Lullabies/Tortillas y Cancioncitas* (Reiser, 1998) combines family traditions with the singing of lullabies. All of these combine music and art in a way that will increase children's appreciation of both.

Sharing Literature in Audiovisual/CD-ROM Format

Literature in audiovisual format can provide musical listening experiences for children. They often enjoy listening to songs that may be too complex for them to sing. Preschoolers can listen to *The Fox Went Out on a Chilly Night* and *Clementine* in video format. After listening to the story of "Peter and the Wolf" (Prokofiev, 1982) in picture book format, they might attempt to follow the story in pictures as it unfolds in the music and as the various instruments indicate the character and the action. Some stories transferred to film have musical accompaniments. *Where the Wild Things Are* is available in video format, with a musical score and narration by Peter Schickele. *No Mirrors in my Nana's House* (Barnwell, 1998) includes a CD with the lyrics being sung by Sweet Honey in the Rock. Each of these combines literary and musical experiences.

Using Rhythm Instruments with Literature

Rhythm instruments can be used in conjunction with literature, with the children using drums, triangles, sand blocks, or rhythm sticks. Children can add rhythmic accompaniment to nursery rhymes that have a strong beat, such as "Ride a Cock Horse" and "A Bear Went Over a Mountain"; use tone bars with others such as "Rain, Rain Go Away"; or make an ostinato, a background of steady pitch and rhythm, for rhymes such as "Hickory Dickory Dock." Children may use instruments to capture the rhythm of the *17 Kings and 42 Elephants* (Mahy, 1987) bouncing along in the moonlight, going on their journey through the "wild wet night."

There are opportunities for varied rhythms and sounds that children might create to accompany *Rum-a-Tum-Tum* (Medearis, 1997). A young girl describes the streets of the French Quarter in New Orleans, filled with action and sound, with the rhythms of the vendors shouting and the jazz of a marching band on parade. Children could work in small groups to develop their own interpretation of particular pages.

Moving in Response to Literature

Movement is a natural response to music and to poetry and prose that has a strong rhythmic beat. Three-year-olds, still responding to their own rhythms, might move to stories or songs by adding motions rather than keeping time. Listening to *Drummer Hoff* (Emberley, 1967), for example, they might show what each of the soldiers carried as they prepared to fire the cannon. Four- and five-year-olds can keep the rhythm with soft drumming, marching, or by striking their thighs with their hands.

Teach children several action games played while singing. *London Bridge Is Falling Down* (Emberley, 1967), *Skip to My Lou* (Quackenbush, 1975), and *This Old Man* (Jonas, 1990) can all be learned quickly by children. After they play the games or do the actions, let children look through the books.

Help children explore contrasts in music. After reading *Mama Don't Allow* (Hurd, 1984), in which Miles, an opossum, gets a saxophone from Uncle Waylon for a birthday present and eventually starts his own band, teach children the song "Mama Don't Allow." The words and music are in the book. Play it in the loud and rollicking way the Swamp Band plays it. Let the children dance to the music. In the book, Miles and his band get a job playing for a group of alligators on a riverboat trip. At last they have found an audience that appreciates their playing. After an evening of music and dance, however, both the band and the alligators are ready for dinner. It is then that the band discovers that *it* is the dinner as well as the entertainment. The band offers to play one more song before dinner. They play a soft Lullaby of Swampland; the alligators all fall asleep and the band escapes. When Miles returns home, still playing the lullaby softly on his sax, his mother is pleased with the music she hears. Play some soft music or lullabies for the children. Let them move to this music and respond to the different rhythms and varying intensities of the songs. Encourage them to talk about the differences.

Think of all the books you have read that could provide a stimulus for children to move to music. They could be *Little Toot* (Gramatky, 1939) devising their own motions as the little tug boat who disliked hard work, preferring instead to glide around the harbor making fancy figure eights in the water. They could make up their own dance as Tanya does in *Tanya and the Magic Wardrobe* (Gauch, 1997). They could be Sam of *Sam the Zamboni Man* (Stevenson, 1998), skating around the ice rink with his hockey stick. Each activity allows the children to create their own

Tanya and the wardrobe lady create their own dance. (From Tanya and the Magic Wardrobe *by Patricia Lee Gauch, illus. by Satomi Ichikawa. Copyright © 1997 by Satomi Ichikawa, illustrations. Used by permission of Philomel Books, a division of Penguin Putnam Inc.)*

movements for a familiar character and each can be matched to appropriate music. As you share literature with children, make notes for yourself about the musical possibilities of stories and poems, including possibilities for singing, listening, rhythmic response, and movement.

Stimulating Creativity in Art, Music, and Movement

If creativity does indeed involve the ability to restructure information in new ways, to see inconsistencies or gaps in knowledge and generate and test hypotheses to fill these gaps, to engage in divergent thinking to be open and flexible, and to be able to elaborate on ideas, then certain approaches to teaching, and certain materials, are more likely than others to foster such behavior. Three that apply to literature as a stimulus for creativity in the arts are the use of questions and activities that lead to divergent responses; the use of books that are inventive; and the practice of encouraging children to give more than one response.

Evoking Divergent Responses

When you make suggestions for activities to expand on literature, or when you pose questions about literature, structure these so that they lead to many different responses on the part of the children. For example, questions that ask children "What would happen if . . .?" or "Tell us one thing you would do if . . .?" or "What else could this character have done . . .?" can be answered in a variety of ways. There is no one right answer, though you will require that the children be able to support their ideas.

Activities too, should have more than one acceptable response. Several children may show their answers about where an elephant could hide after hearing how Morris the elephant solved that problem in the book *Where Can an Elephant Hide?* (McPhail, 1979). Their answers will reflect their own thinking, however, and may well draw on the book's information about protective coloration. Some may show in drawing or painting the places that they recommend; others may use three-dimensional materials. The object is to develop a unique idea, not to remember an answer from a book.

If you are engaging the children in movement, allow them to choose the motions themselves. *Seven Little Monsters* (1975) is a brief book by Maurice Sendak with monsters reminiscent of those in *Where the Wild Things Are* (Sendak, 1963). Each monster has a movement, such as going up, or creeping, or eating, or sleeping, and the seven are lined up in a row "making trouble." Children dramatizing this brief text can add their own interpretations to the movements. They can decide on a rhythmic accompaniment to the text and to their movements. Your reading of the text gives a structure to their responses, but you do not tell them how to move.

The criterion of providing for divergent responses is one that can be applied to any activity designed to extend a child's understanding of a book or poem. This does not mean an excuse for a child to do whatever he or she pleases, disrupting everyone else. It does mean your acceptance of their ideas, even if they are not ideas you had thought of or expected. Children using rhythm instruments to make the sounds of the Wild Things can decide which instruments give the sounds they think fit, how they should be put together, when they should be loud and when soft, and how fast they should be played. It is their interpretation that is important, their feel for the book, for the mood of the "rumpus" that is the climax of the book. Allowing children to continue to play the instruments when the group is beginning a new activity, or to damage the instruments from using them inappropriately, is neither developing their creativity nor helping them to accept responsibility.

Presenting Books That Are Inventive

Select books in which the authors and illustrators have been inventive themselves and use these to suggest inventiveness on the children's parts. Some of these books are told in the first person, with the lead character describing his or her actions. *Sometimes I Dance Mountains* (Baylor, 1973) combines poetry and dance. The girl tells of her love of dancing and the illustrations show her whirling and rhythmic movements. She talks of her thoughts as she dances and presents dance as a mode of free expression, not one of learned steps or routines. How do children dance? Some third-graders talked about enjoying moving to "fast" music; others looked at the movements and told about classes in gymnastics. Some wanted to demonstrate how they could dance when they felt happy. None attempted to copy the movements caught in the illustrations. After their own experiences, they looked at the photographs in George Ancona's *Let's Dance!* (1998) and broadened even further their concept of dance.

Preschoolers can add their own fantastic stories of what they might see on the way to school after they hear what Marco saw on the way home in *And to Think That I Saw It on Mulberry Street* (Geisel, 1937). Each adds a new element, just as Marco's story became more and more elaborate as he retold it.

Children can explore making words look like the ideas they represent after seeing *Carousel* (1982) by Donald Crews. In this book, the carousel is empty at first; then riders get on, the music starts, and all go around faster and faster. Then the music ends; the carousel slows and stops; the ride is over. The text is sparse, with concise phrases rather than sentences. The illustrations show the increased blurring of colors to capture the increased speed of the carousel. The music, shown by words such as "toot" and "boom," also becomes blurred as the description changes from music "playing" to music "blaring."

Look for books that help children see things in new ways. *It Looked Like Spilt Milk* (Shaw, 1947) and *Dreams* (Spier, 1986) talk about the shapes cloud formations may take, prompting children to look at the clouds themselves. What do they see? Children can use chalk to record the formations, then describe them. Jonas, in *The Trek* (1985), has her young protagonist use her imagination to create jungle animals of the objects she sees between home and school. What can children imagine by using just the outline or coloration of a particular object?

Let children expand ideas that authors and illustrators have begun. *The Biggest House in the World* (Lionni, 1968) begs to be emulated. Lois Ehlert has illustrated a Mayan Indian tale from Mexico, *Cuckoo/Cucu* (1997), with brightly colored figures. Some figures have arms and legs attached with brads, so that they appear movable. Children could explore making such characters and placing them in various ways to indicate motion. Jan Ormerod's *Ms. MacDonald Has a Class* (1996) varies the lyrics to "Old MacDonald Had a Farm" as the class visits a farm and then makes plans for a play. The children might work together to write new lyrics to this, or other familiar tunes, making it fit their own lives.

Encouraging Multiple Responses

Finally, encourage children to give several responses. They might create several animals after hearing *Cuckoo,* or replay *Seven Little Monsters,* each time adding new movements, or make the biggest house for a bird, the biggest house for a snake, or the biggest house for themselves. Changing ideas, adding new elements, being flexible in approach—all encourage children to use their creative abilities.

Making Aesthetic and Creative Experiences Enjoyable for Children

If you enjoy aesthetic and creative activities and show that you do, this will influence children to enjoy such activities, for your behavior provides a model for them. You show that you value aesthetic experiences when you give projects such as listening to a composition your full attention, listening to the cassette or CD with the children and responding to the music yourself.

Planning for Enjoyable Creative Experiences

You can also plan so that the experiences will be enjoyable for you. For example, you know that if you are to teach a song to young children, you will need to sing it (or play it) many times, and you will probably sing it with the children throughout the year. Therefore it makes sense to select songs you like and that you don't think you will tire of readily. Most teachers find that they vary the songs they teach if they have taught for several years, and also select different themes or topics to explore in depth or to use in learning centers.

Organize art projects so that they operate smoothly both for you and for the children. Teach children to clean up after themselves, washing out brushes, and storing scissors and paste in their specified places. Children learn responsibility when they must care for the equipment they use, and develop independence as they become more and more able to get what they need and to replace it when they are finished.

Show your enjoyment of the products children produce. Display them, with the children's consent, on a regular basis. Comment on what they have done, and are doing, however, in a way that emphasizes the process rather than the product. "I see you found a way to make all the pieces lay flat," or "How did you feel while you were the troll waiting for the Billy Goats Gruff to start across the bridge?" Let children talk about their work when they seem eager to share.

Helping Children Feel Successful

Help children gain satisfaction from their experiences by selecting books and suggesting activities that match the children's developmental level. The song "Yankee Doodle" is one you could use with children of various ages. It appears in a book illustrated with woodcuts by Ed Emberley (Shackburg, 1965) that contains both a history of the song and the music for it, and in one with humorous illustrations by Steven Kellogg (Bangs, 1980), also available as a sound filmstrip from Weston Woods. The music is performed by The Colonial Williamsburg Fife and Drum Corps.

If you were working with three-year-olds, you might sing just the first verse and the chorus for the children rather than all the verses. They could listen to it several times and join in on any phrases they remembered. You would not expect them to match the tones accurately, nor to learn all the words. You might have them follow actions for the song, or walk to the rhythm of the music on the cassette that accompanies the filmstrip. Again, it is likely that, while most of them will be keeping a steady rhythm, their movement will not synchronize exactly with the music.

If you were teaching five- and six-year-olds, you could present an entire song. Most of these children would be able to learn the first verse and chorus. They could be drummers, with their hands keeping time as they sing, or they could use rhythm instruments. They could march like soldiers, using arm motions as well as leg movements. After looking at the Emberley illustrations, they could use a similar printing technique of their own, perhaps making a cardboard cut with a masking-tape loop on the back. They could then repeat the print of their figure, lifting it from the paper by the loop. They might talk about how Emberley used the print to show many soldiers and decide what they could show.

If you were teaching eight-year-olds, you might read the history of the song to them, and what some of the words in the lyrics mean. They too would enjoy singing and moving to the song. If they made prints, they could use overlapping cuts as Emberley did. They might make up new lyrics to the tune, trying out each suggestion to make certain that it fit the rhythm. For this age level, you might include activities from earlier stages. Eight-year-olds enjoy marching, even though they were able to do it when they were six.

The essential factor is that children be able to feel themselves successful in the activity. Thus, the three-year-old singing two phrases off tune will enjoy it and will be learning about matching tones as long as you let him or her know that this is acceptable behavior. If, however, you expect all tones to be matched and all of the words to be learned, the child may well become frustrated and decide that singing is an activity to be avoided. One parent cleverly maintained her son's good feelings about his own art when a teacher might have damaged both his interest in drawing and his self-confidence. The teacher, dissatisfied with the kindergartner's crayoning, had written "POOR" across the paper. He came home and showed the paper to his mother, beaming. She looked at it, looked at him, and asked him to tell her about the picture. "My teacher thought it was great," he said. "How do you know?" his mother asked. "Because she put a one hundred on it, and that means it's perfect. See the 0's." The mother decided that such a good paper should go on the refrigerator door for the family to enjoy for that week. The teacher's written comment was inappropriate, both for its implication that art should be graded and for the damage it could have done to that child's image of himself and his artistic ability.

Presenting Books That Promote Understanding and Appreciation of the Arts

Some books you may choose to present will have children as protagonists engaged in the arts; others will focus on adults. Both types are useful to present to children, for together they show that creative and aesthetic endeavors are not limited to any one age group. Rosa, in *Music, Music for Everyone* (Williams, 1984), has found that music brings her pleasure. She plays the accordion and is able to bring musical entertainment to others while making money for herself by performing with three friends at a party. Sugar, in *Papa's Lucky Shadow* (Daly, 1992), learns to tap dance from her grandfather, and the two present a winning rendition of "Me and my Shadow" at the Pensioner's Club party. Both girls are supported in their love of music or dance by at least one close family member.

   Begin at the Beginning (Schwartz, 1983) explores difficulties one may encounter in creating a work of art. Amy has been chosen to paint a picture to represent the second-grade class in a school art show. She is excited as she plans to create a painting that will have *everything* in it. She finds that it is not an easy task, however, and that the advice she is given by various members of her family is not helpful. Finally her mother talks with her, saying that she should begin with what she knows. So she begins with the tree outside her window. Books such as these provide excellent starting points for children to discuss their own artwork, their own reactions to the creative process.

   Stories with adults engaged in artistic pursuits often, but not always, show a more philosophical attitude toward the arts than do those that feature children as central characters. Two by M. B. Goffstein discuss the importance and purpose. In *Goldie the Dollmaker* (1969), Goldie, the artist who makes wooden dolls, is contrasted with Omus, the practical one who makes wooden crates. The value of both engaging in and appreciating art is presented clearly. In *An Artist* (1980), Goffstein begins her thesis with the opening statement, "An artist is like God, but small." In concise and poetic language she describes how an artist creates with his paints, trying to bring order to what he sees, trying to capture his own thoughts and feelings. Both books are for quiet and thoughtful times.

   Kuskin takes a more lighthearted approach in *The Philharmonic Gets Dressed* (1982). Just as the title implies, this book describes how the members of the orchestra begin to prepare for a concert, starting as they get dressed at home and concluding as they begin to play. In the course of the story the reader learns about an orchestra. Share books such as these with children to show that many people gain deep satisfaction from participation in and observation of the arts.

Sustaining an Atmosphere of Acceptance _____

Give children a wide variety of media from which to choose and allow children to decide for themselves on many occasions what materials they wish to use in art, or which movements they wish to use in response to music. Variety maintains interest and allows children to find activities that they particularly enjoy. The choice builds independence and allows for preferences and creative responses.

Finally, let children work together in response to music or literature. Many like to work with their friends, especially in the primary grades. They might make a mural of cats in stories they have heard, with each child contributing one character. They talk about their contribution and also plan how the mural will look when finished. At other times, working together is simply sharing materials or being in the same vicinity, but feeling free to converse with their neighbors if they like. An atmosphere of trust and friendship transfers positive reactions to the activity being undertaken. If you can help children enjoy their aesthetic and creative activities, you will be giving them the necessary attitude for continuing to develop their skills of impression and their skills of expression.

SUMMARY

Children's growth in creative expression through art, music, and movement is in part developmental as they gain more physical and motor control, and in part environmental as they have opportunities to engage in artistic and musical experiences. Performance skills of singing, using rhythm instruments, drawing, painting, and dramatizing appear to provide a base for aesthetic appreciation by helping children become familiar with the techniques involved.

The following long-term goals are appropriate for the aesthetic and creative growth of young children.

> Children will respond favorably to diverse styles of art and music.
>
> Children will exhibit a sensory awareness of their environment.
>
> Children will use, experiment with, and gain control over a variety of media.
>
> Children will sing in tune within their vocal range and will respond to music and literature with movement and with rhythm instruments. Children will use their imaginations as they participate in art, music, and movement.
>
> Children will enjoy experiencing the work of others and participating in the arts themselves.

Books offer opportunities for helping children achieve these goals. Table 9–1 suggests appropriate teaching strategies. Children are likely to develop favorable attitudes toward diverse styles of art if they recognize that art is personal expression; if they see a wide range of styles of art in picture books; and if they relate personally to the art they are viewing. Children

Table 9–1.   **Supporting Children's Aesthetic and Creative Growth**

Developmental Goals	Teaching Suggestions	Recommended Literature	
Children will respond favorably to diverse styles of art.	Show children that art is one form of personal expression. Show how more than one artist has interpreted the same song, tale, or character. Let children compare how one animal appears in several books of fiction. Help children see the diversity in artistic styles in picture book illustrations. Encourage careful observation of illustrations. Involve children in art projects related to techniques used or portrayed in books.	**Ages 3–5:** Aliki Clifton Hoban Say Winter	*Hush, Little Baby* Books about Everett Anderson Books about Frances *Emma's Rug* *Hush, Little Baby*
		Ages 5–8: Agee Baylor de Paola Geisert Hoban Hoban Leaf McNaughton Nicholson Numeroff O'Kelley O'Kelley Rylant Spilka Steig Williams	*The Incredible Painting of Felix Clousseau* *When Clay Sings* *The Art Lesson* *Oink* *Arthur's New Power* *Dinner at Alberta's* *Eyes of the Dragon* *Oops!* *Little Girl in a Red Dress with Cat and Dog* *If You Give a Pig a Pancake* *Circus!* *From the Hills of Georgia* *All I See* *Paint All Kinds of Pictures* *Zeke Pippin* *Painted Dreams*

Table 9–1.   *(continued)*

Developmental Goals	Teaching Suggestions	Recommended Literature	
Children will exhibit a sensory awareness of their environment.	Read prose and poetry by authors who write in sensory terms. Let children try sensory experiences described in books. Use literature as a stimulus for activities that require children to use their senses in discovery or exploration.	**Ages 3–5:** Boyden Fisher Hoban Hughes Keats Kinsey-Warnock Kunhardt Merriam Rockwell Shulevitz Snyder Spier	"Mud" *In the Middle of the Night* *Bread and Jam for Frances* *Out and About* *Goggles* *On a Starry Night* *Pat the Bunny* "A Matter of Taste" *My Back Yard* *Dawn* "Poem to Mud" *Gobble, Growl, Grunt*
		Ages 5–8: Arnosky Baylor Brown Carroll Locker Ray Yolen	*Near the Sea* *We Walk in Sandy Places* *Touch Will Tell* *How Artists See the Weather* *Sky Trees: Seeing Science Through Art* *The Cloud* *The Seeing Stick*
Children will use, experiment with, and gain control over a variety of art media.	Let children experiment with selected media used by illustrators of children's books. Encourage children to illustrate stories and poems they dictate or write. Help children try artistic techniques described in books. Have children respond to books through art, both two and three dimensional.	**Ages 3–5:** Ehlert Lionni Lionni Lionni Lionni Lionni Spier Tresselt	*Snowballs* *An Extraordinary Egg* *Inch by Inch* *Let's Make Rabbits* *Little Blue and Little Yellow* *Swimmy* *Noah's Art* *Hide and Seek Fog*

Table 9–1. *(continued)*

Developmental Goals	Teaching Suggestions	Recommended Literature	
		Ages 5–8:	
		Anno	*In Shadowland*
		Cummings	*Talking with Artists*
		England	*The Old Cotton Blues*
		Gibbons	*Click! A Book About Cameras and Taking Pictures*
		Johnson	*All Around Town*
		Littlechild	*This Land Is My Land*
		Ringgold	*Tar Beach*
Children will sing in tune within their vocal range and will respond to music and rhythm instruments.	Share picture-book editions of songs. Present literature in audiovisual format for children to hear musical accompaniment and songs too complex for them to sing. Let children use rhythm instruments in conjunction with literature. Encourage children to move in response to poems or stories, either adding motions or moving to the rhythm.	**Ages 3–5:** Aliki Emberley Emberley Gramatky Jonas Quackenbush Quackenbush Barnwell Ehlert Jonas Ormerod	*Go Tell Aunt Rhody* *Drummer Hoff* *London Bridge is Falling Down* *Little Toot* *This Old Man* *Go Tell Aunt Rhody* *Skip to My Lou* *No Mirrors in My Nana's House* *Cuckoo/Cucu* *The Trek* *Ms. MacDonald Has a Class*
		Ages 5–8: Daly Causley Fox Grifalconi Hurd Lionni Mahy	*Papa's Lucky Shadow* *Early in the Morning* *Go In and Out the Window* *City Rhythms* *Mama Don't Allow* *Alexander and the Wind-up Mouse* *17 Kings and 42 Elephants*

Table 9–1.   *(continued)*

Developmental Goals	Teaching Suggestions	Recommended Literature	
Children will use their imaginations as they participate in art, music, and movement.	Plan activities that will lead to divergent responses. Present books that are inventive. Encourage children to give more than one response.	**Ages 3–5:** Geisel	*And to Think That I Saw It on Mulberry Street*
		Hutchins	*Changes, Changes*
		Johnson	*All in Free But Janey*
		McPhail	*Where Can an Elephant Hide?*
		Sendak	*Seven Little Monsters*
		Sendak	*Where the Wild Things Are*
		Shaw	*It Looked Like Spilt Milk*
		Ages 5–8: Ancona	*Let's Dance!*
		Baylor	*Sometimes I Dance Mountains*
		Crews	*Carousel*
		Gauch	*Tanya and the Magic Wardrobe*
		Hurd	*Mama Don't Allow*
		Lionni	*The Biggest House in the World*
		Reiser	*Tortillas and Lullabies*
		Spier	*Dreams*
		Stevenson	*Sam the Zamboni Man*
Children will enjoy experiencing the work of others and participating in the arts themselves.	Organize art projects so that they operate smoothly. Show your own enjoyment of the work children produce. Talk with children while they work, emphasizing the artistic process in your comments. Suggest activities that match the children's developmental level. Give children frequent opportunities to choose the media or type of response they wish to use. Present books that promote understanding and appreciation of the arts. Let children work together on music and art projects.	**Ages 3–5:** Kellogg Shackburg **Ages 5–8:**	*Yankee Doodle* *Yankee Doodle*

become aware of the sensory qualities of their environment when they hear literature in which authors give descriptions written in sensory terms and in which illustrators re-create the beauty they observe. Books also may provide the stimulus for children to explore their environment, taking special note of sensory qualities.

Children become familiar with a variety of media when they are given the opportunity to experiment with art materials. They may explore techniques used by illustrators of picture books; they may make illustrations for their own writing; they may try artistic techniques or projects described in books. Children need both initial help in learning about the media available in their classroom and time on their own to use the media.

Literature can give added dimension to children's musical experiences in the early years, contributing to their participation in singing, listening, using rhythm instruments, and movement. Children listen to songs illustrated in picture books either read or sung; they enjoy hearing, in audiovisual format, songs too complex for them to sing themselves; they use rhythm instruments in conjunction with literature; and they move in response to poetry and prose that has a strong rhythmic beat or actions that can be dramatized.

Finally, children's creativity and their appreciation of the creativity of others can be fostered through literature. Questions and activities that are based on books should evoke divergent responses, be enjoyable for the child, and allow the child to be successful. An atmosphere of acceptance and a general pattern of encouragement for multiple reactions and responses to a single book or questions are key elements in developing children's creativity and aesthetic appreciation.

Extending Your Learning

1. Select one animal and compare how at least three illustrators have drawn it.

2. Select five picture books and identify as best you can the different media and styles of illustration.

3. Preview two of the videos about illustrators produced by Weston Woods Studios. Tell what primary children might learn from each of them.

4. Start a section of your poetry collection for children in which poets use sensory descriptions.

5. Plan a field trip in your area that would encourage children to observe their environment carefully.

6. Select three picture books in which the illustrator has used media that children could try themselves.

7. Design endpapers for any three picture books that have unillustrated endpapers.

8. Find three songs in picture-book format that are appropriate for young children.

9. Select three picture books that lend themselves to interpretation through music or movement. Describe how you would engage children in the activity.

10. Select a video or filmstrip of a song. Tell how you might share this with three-year-olds, six-year-olds, and eight-year-olds.

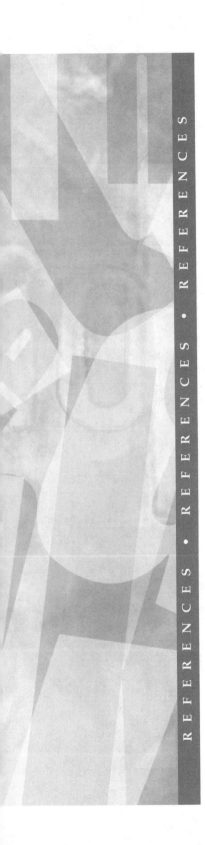

RECOMMENDED REFERENCES

Baer, J. (1997). *Creative Teachers, Creative Students.* Needham Heights, MA: Allyn & Bacon.

Barnes, R. (1987). *Teaching Art to Young Children Four to Nine.* Winchester, MS: Unwin Hyman.

Bayless, K, and Ransey, M. (1991). *Music as a Way of Life for the Young Child.* 4th ed. Columbus, OH: Merrill.

Blecher, S., and Jaffee, K. (1998). *Weaving in the Arts: Widening the Learning Circle.* Portsmouth, NH: Heinemann.

Burtnett, N., and Wiggins, P. (1983). *Today's Children Sing, Play, and Move.* Dubuque: IA: Kendall Hunt.

Cohen, E. and Gainer, R. (1995). *Art: Another Language for Learning.* Portsmouth, NH: Heinemann.

Edwards, L. (1990). *Affective Development and the Creative Arts: A Process Approach to Early Childhood Education.* Columbus, OH: Merrill.

Eisner, E. (1978). *Reading, the Arts, and the Creation of Meaning.* Reston, VA: National Art Education Association.

Engle. B. (1990). *Considering Children's Art: Why and How to Value Their Works.* Washington, DC: National Association for the Education of Young Children.

Goldberg, M., and Phillips, A., Eds. (1992). *Arts as Education.* Cambridge, MA: Harvard Publishing Group.

Haines, B., and Gerber, L. (1988). *Leading Young Children to Music.* 3rd ed. Columbus, OH: Merrill.

Hoffman, S. and Lamme, L. Eds. (1989). *Learning from the Inside Out: The Expressive Arts.* Wheaton, MD: Association for Childhood Education.

Jalongo, M. and Stamp, L. (1997). *The Arts in Children's Lives: Aesthetic Education in Early Childhood.* Needham Heights, MA: Allyn & Bacon.

Lowenfeld, V. and Brittain, W. (1987). *Creative and Mental Growth.* 8th ed. New York: Macmillan.

Lynch-Fraser, D. (1983). *Danceplay: Creative Movement for Very Young Children.* New York: Plume.

McDonald, D. (1979). *Music in Our Lives: The Early Years.* Washington, DC: National Association for the Education of Young Children.

McDonald, D., and Simons, G. (1989). *Musical Growth and Development: Birth Through Six.* New York: Schirmer.

Moline, S. (1995). *I See What You Mean: Children at Work with Visual Information.* York, ME: Stenhouse.

Newman, G. (1989). *Teaching Children Music.* Dubuque, IA: Wm. C. Brown.

Romen, B. (1982). *Learning Through Movement.* New York: Teachers College Press.

Russell, J. (1985). *Creative Movement and Dance for Children.* New York: Praeger.

Smith, N., Fucigna, C., Kennedy, M. and Lord, L. (1993). *Experience and Art: Teaching Children to Paint.* New York: Teachers College Press.

Szekely, G. (1988). *Encouraging Creativity in Art Lessons.* New York: Teachers College Press.

Torrance, E. P. (1970). *Encouraging Creativity in the Classroom.* Dubuque, IA: Wm. C. Brown.

RECOMMENDED CHILDREN'S BOOKS

A Is for Artist: A Getty Museum Alphabet. (1997). Los Angeles, CA: Getty.

Bartlett, T. C. (1997). *Tuba Lessons.* Ill. Monique. Mankato, MN: Creative.

Brown, Laurene and Brown, Marc. (1986). *Visiting the Art Museum.* New York: Dutton.

Bryan, Ashley. (1977). *The Dancing Granny.* New York: Atheneum.

Buffett, James, and Buffett, Savannah Jane. (1988). *The Jolly Mon.* Ill. Lambert Davis. San Diego: Harcourt.

Clement, Claude. (1986). *The Painter and the Wild Swans.* Ill. Frederic Clement. New York: Dial.

Cohen, Mirian. (1980). *No Good in Art.* Ill. Lillian Hoban. New York: Greenwillow.

Curtis, Gavin. (1998). *The Bat Boy and His Violin.* Ill. E. B. Lewis. New York: Simon.

dePaola, Tomie. (1979). *Flicks.* New York: Harcourt.

Ehlert, Lois. (1997). *Hands.* San Diego: Harcourt.

Hest, Amy. (1996). *Jamaica Louise James.* Ill. Sheila White Samton. Cambridge, MA: Candlewick.

Kellogg, Steven. (1996). *I Was Born about 10,000 Years Ago: A Tall Tale.* New York: Morrow.

Kinsey-Warnock, Natalie. (1996). *The Fiddler of the Northern Lights.* Ill. Leslie Bowman. New York: Cobblehill.

Levine, Arthur. (1993). *The Boy Who Drew Cats.* Ill. Frederic Clement. New York: Dial.

McDermott, Gerald. (1997). *Musicians of the Sun.* New York: Simon.

Pinkney, Andrea Davis. (1998). *Duke Ellington.* Ill. Brian Pinkney. New York: Hyperion.

Rohmer, Harriet. Ed. (1997). *Just Like Me: Stories and Self-Portraits by Fourteen Artists.* Mankato, MN: Children's.

Schroeder, Alan. (1996). *Satchmo's Blues.* Ill. Floyd Cooper. New York: Doubleday.

Shannon, George. (1982). *Dance Away.* Ill. Jose Aruego and Ariane Dewey. New York: Greenwillow.

Yenawine, Philip. (1991). *Stories.* New York: Museum of Modern Art and Delacorte Press.

PROFESSIONAL REFERENCES CITED

Alejandro, A. (1994). Like Happy Dreams—Integrating Visual Arts, Writing, and Reading. *Language Arts,* 71 (1), 12–21.

Brewer, J. (1997). *Introduction to Early Childhood Education.* 3rd ed. Boston: Allyn and Bacon.

Broudy, H. (1977). How Basic is Aesthetic Education? or Is ART the Fourth R? *Language Arts,* 54(7), 635.

Chapman, L. (1978). *Approaches to Art in Education.* New York: Harcourt.

Efland, A. (1984). Excellence in Education: The Role of the Arts. *Theory into Practice,* 23(4), 267–272.

Guilford, J. P. (1965). A Psychometric Approach to Creativity. In Anderson, H. (ed.) *Creativity in Childhood Adolescence,* pp. 1–19. Palo Alto, CA: Science and Behavior Books.

Krogh, S. (1994). *Educating Young Children: Infancy to Grade Three.* New York: McGraw-Hill.

Lowenfeld, V. and Brittain, L. (1987). *Creative and Mental Growth.* (8th ed) New York: Macmillan.

McDonald, D. (1979). *Music in Our Lives: The Early Years.* Washington, DC: National Association for the Education of Young Children.

McDonald, D. and Simons, G. (1989). *Musical Growth and Development: Birth Through Six.* New York: Schirmer.

Rhode Island K–12 Arts Framework. (1997). (Working copy) Providence, RI: RI Department of Education.

Solso, D. (1998). *Cognitive Psychology*. 5th ed. Boston: Allyn and Bacon.

Torrance, E. P. (1970). *Encouraging Creativity in the Classroom*. Dubuque, IA: Wm C. Brown.

CHILDREN'S LITERATURE CITED

Agee, Jon. (1988). *The Incredible Painting of Felix Clousseau*. New York: Farrar.

Aliki. (1974). *Go Tell Aunt Rhody*. New York: Macmillan.

Aliki. (1968). *Hush, Little Baby*. Upper Saddle River, NJ: Prentice-Hall.

Ancona, George. (1998). *Let's Dance!* New York: Morrow.

Anno, Mitsumasa. (1988). *In Shadowland*. New York: Orchard.

Arnosky, Jim. (1990). *Near the Sea*. New York: Lothrop.

Bangs, Edward. (1980). *Yankee Doodle*. Ill. Steven Kellogg. New York: Four Winds.

Barnwell, Ysaye. (1998). *No Mirrors in My Nana's House*. Ill. Synthia Saint James. San Diego: Harcourt.

Baylor, Byrd. (1973). *Sometimes I Dance Mountains*. Ill. Kenneth Longtemps. New York: Scribner's.

Baylor, Byrd. (1976). *We Walk in Sandy Places*. Ill. Marilyn Schwartz. New York: Scribner's.

Baylor, Byrd. (1972). *When Clay Sings*. Ill. Tom Bahti. New York: Scribner's.

Boyden, Polly Chase. (1983). "Mud" in Prelutsky, Jack. *The Random House Book of Poetry for Children*. New York: Random House.

Brown, Marcia. (1979). *Touch Will Tell*. New York: Watts.

Burton, Virginia. (1942). *The Little House*. Boston: Houghton Mifflin.

Carrick, Malcolm. (1976). *Splodges*. New York: Viking.

Carroll, Colleen. (1996). *How Artists See the Weather: Sun, Wind, Snow, Rain*. New York: Abbeville.

Causley, Charles. (1986). *Early in the Morning*. Ill. Michael Foreman. New York: Viking.

Clifton, Lucille. (1971). *Everett Anderson's Christmas Coming*. Ill. Evaline Ness. New York: Holt.

Clifton, Lucille. (1976). *Everett Anderson's Friend*. Ill. Ann Grifalconi. New York: Holt.

Clifton, Lucille. (1983). *Everett Anderson's Goodbye*. Ill. Ann Grifalconi. New York: Holt.

Clifton, Lucille. (1978). *Everett Anderson's Nine Month Long*. Ill. Ann Grifalconi. New York: Holt.

Clifton, Lucille. (1977). *Everett Anderson's 1–2–3*. Ill. Ann Grifalconi. New York: Holt.

Clifton, Lucille. (1974). *Everett Anderson's Year*. Ill. Ann Grifalconi. New York: Holt.

Clifton, Lucille. (1970). *Some of the Days of Everett Anderson*. Ill. Evaline Ness. New York: Holt.

Cole, Henry. (1998). *I Took a Walk*. New York: Greenwillow.

Crews, Donald. (1982). *Carousel*. New York: Greenwillow.

Cummings, Pat. (1992). *Talking with Artists*. New York: Bradbury.

Daly, Niki. (1992). *Papa's Lucky Shadow*. New York: Simon.

dePaola, Tomie. (1989). *The Art Lesson*. New York: Putnam.

Ehlert, Lois. (1997). *Cuckoo/Cucu*. San Diego: Harcourt.

Ehlert, Lois. (1995). *Snowballs*. San Diego: Harcourt.

Emberley, Barbara. (1967). *Drummer Hoff*. Ill. Ed Emberley. Upper Saddle River, NJ: Prentice-Hall.

Emberley, Ed. (1967). *London Bridge Is Falling Down*. Boston: Little, Brown.

England, Linda. (1998). *The Old Cotton Blues*. Ill. Teresa Flavin. New York: McElderry.

Evans, Mel. (1969). *The Tiniest Sound*. Ill. Ed Young. New York: Doubleday.

Fox, Dan and Marks, Claude. (1987). *Go In and Out the Window*. New York: Metropolitan Museum of Art.

Gauch, Patricia Lee. (1997). *Tanya and the Magic Wardrobe*. Ill. Satomi Ichikawa. New York: Philomel.

Geisel, Theodore. (1937). *And to Think That I Saw It on Mulberry Street*. New York: Vanguard.

Geisert, Arthur. (1991). *Oink*. Boston: Houghton Mifflin .

George, Jean. (1974). *All Upon a Sidewalk*. Ill. Don Bolognese. New York: Dutton.

Gibbons, Gail. (1997). *Click!: A Book about Cameras and Taking Pictures*. Boston: Little.

Glazer, Tom. (1983). *Music for Ones and Twos: Songs and Games for the Very Young Child*. Ill. Karen Ann Weinhaus. Garden City, NY: Doubleday.

Goffstein, M. B. (1980). *An Artist*. New York: Harper & Row.

Goffstein, M. B. (1969). *Goldie the Dollmaker*. New York: Farrar.

Gramatky, Hardy. (1939). *Little Toot*. New York: Putnam.

Halpern, Shari. (1997). *Hush, Little Baby.* New York: North-South.

Hart, Jane. (1982). *Singing Bee!* Ill. Anita Lobel. New York: Lothrop.

Hoban, Russell. (1978). *Arthur's New Power.* Ill. Byron Barton. New York: Crowell.

Hoban, Russell. (1995, 1962). *Bedtime for Frances.* Ill. Garth Williams. New York: Harper.

Hoban, Russell. (1969). *Bread and Jam for Frances.* Ill. Lillian Hoban. New York: Harper & Row.

Hoban, Russell. (1973). *Dinner at Alberta's.* Ill. James Marshall. New York: Crowell.

Hopkinson, Deborah. (1999). *A Band of Angels.* Ill. Raul Colon. New York: Atheneum.

Hubbell, Patricia. (1963)."Our Washing Machine"in *The Apple Vendor's Fair.* Ill. Julia Mass. New York: Atheneum.

Hughes, Shirley. (1988). *Out and About.* New York: Lothrop.

Hurd, Thacher. (1984). *Mama Don't Allow.* New York: Harper.

Isadora, Rachel. (1979). *Ben's Trumpet.* New York: Greenwillow.

Johnson, Dinah. (1998). *All Around Town: The Photographs of Richard Samuel Roberts.* New York: Holt.

Jonas, Ann. (1985). *The Trek.* New York: Greenwillow.

Jonas, Carol. (1990). *This Old Man.* Boston: Houghton Mifflin.

Keats, Ezra Jack. (1969). *Goggles.* New York: Macmillan.

Kinsey-Warnock, Natalie. (1994). *On a Starry Night.* Ill. David McPhail. New York: Orchard.

Kunhardt, Dorothy. (1962). *Pat the Bunny.* Racine, WI: Western.

Kuskin, Karla. (1982). *The Philharmonic Gets Dressed.* Ill. Marc Simont. New York: Harper & Row.

Leaf, Margaret. (1987). *Eyes of the Dragon.* Ill. Ed Young. New York: Lothrop.

Luenn, Nancy. (1998). *A Gift for Abuelita/Un Regalo para Abuelita.* Ill. Robert Chapman. Phoenix, AZ: Rising Moon.

Lewin, Ted. (1998). *The Storytellers.* New York: Lothrop.

Lionni, Leo. (1968). *The Biggest House in the World.* New York: Pantheon.

Lionni, Leo. (1994). *An Extraordinary Egg.* New York: Knopf.

Lionni, Leo. (1962). *Inch by Inch.* New York: Astor-Honor.

Lionni, Leo. (1982). *Let's Make Rabbits.* New York: Pantheon.

Lionni, Leo. (1959). *Little Blue and Little Yellow.* New York: Astor-Honor.

Lionni, Leo. (1963). *Swimmy.* New York: Pantheon.

Littlechild, George. (1993). *This Land Is My Land.* Emeryville, CA: Children's Book Press.

Locker, Thomas. (1995). *Sky Tree: Seeing Science Through Art.* New York: HarperCollins.

Long, Sylvia. (1997). *Hush, Little Baby.* Berkeley, CA: Chronicle.

McNaughton, Colin. (1997). *Oops!* San Diego: Harcourt.

McPhail, David. (1979*). Where Can an Elephant Hide?* New York: Doubleday.

Mahy, Margaret. (1987). *17 Kings and 42 Elephants.* Ill. Patricia MacCarthy. New York: Dial.

Medearis, Angela Shelf. (1997). *Rum-a-Tum-Tum.* Ill. James Ransome. New York: Holiday.

Merriam, Eve. (1962)."A Matter of Taste" in *There Is No Rhyme for Silver.* New York: Atheneum. Copyright © 1962, 1990 by Eve Merriam. Used by permission of Eve Merriam.

Nicholson, Nicholas. (1998). *Little Girl in a Red Dress with Cat and Dog.* Ill. Cynthia von Bahler. New York: Viking.

Numeroff, Laura. (1998). *If You Give a Pig a Pancake.* Ill. Felicia Bond. New York: HarperCollins.

O'Kelley, Mattie Lou. (1986). *Circus!* Boston: Atlantic.

O'Kelley, Mattie Lou. (1983). *From the Hills of Georgia.* Boston: Atlantic.

Ormerod, Jan. (1996). *Ms. MacDonald Has a Class.* New York: Clarion.

Poydar, Nancy. (1996). *Cool Ali.* New York: McElderry.

Prokofiev, Serge. (1982). *Peter and the Wolf.* Ill. Charles Mikolaycak. New York: Viking.

Quackenbush, Robert. (1975). *Skip to My Lou.* Philadelphia: Lippincott.

Ray, Deborah Kogan. (1984). *The Cloud.* New York: Harper & Row.

Reiser, Lynn. (1998). *Tortillas and Lullabies/Tortillas y Cancioncitas.* New York: Greenwillow.

Ringgold, Faith. (1991). *Tar Beach.* New York: Crown.

Ringgold, Faith, Freeman, Linda, and Roucher, Nancy. (1996). *Talking to Faith Ringgold.* New York: Crown.

Roche, Denis. (1998). *Art Around the World: Loo-Loo, Boo, and More Art You Can Do.* Boston: Houghton.

Rockwell, Anne and Harlow. (1984). *My Back Yard.* New York: Macmillan.

Rylant, Cynthia. (1988). *All I See.* Ill. Peter Catalanotto. New York: Orchard.

Say, Allen. (1996). *Emma's Rug*. Boston: Houghton Mifflin.

Schwartz, Amy. (1983). *Begin at the Beginning*. New York: Harper.

Sendak, Maurice. (1975). *Seven Little Monsters*. New York: Harper.

Sendak, Maurice. (1963). *Where the Wild Things Are*. New York: Harper.

Shackburg, Richard. (1965). *Yankee Doodle*. Ill. Ed Emberly. Upper Saddle River, NJ: Prentice Hall.

Shaw, Charles. (1947). *It Looked Like Spilt Milk*. New York: Harper.

Shulevitz, Uri. (1974). *Dawn*. New York: Farrar.

Shulevitz, Uri. (1998). *Snow*. New York: Farrar.

Small, David. (1987). *Paper John*. New York: Farrar.

Snyder, Zilpha Keatley. (1969). "Poem to Mud" in *Today is Saturday*. New York: Atheneum. Copyright © 1969. Used by permission of the author.

Spier, Peter. (1986). *Dreams*. Garden City, NY: Doubleday.

Spier, Peter. (1971). *Gobble, Growl, Grunt*. New York: Doubleday.

Spilka, Arnold. (1964). *Paint All Kinds of Pictures*. New York: Walck.

Steig, William. (1994). *Zeke Pippin*. New York: HarperCollins.

Stevenson, James. (1998). *Sam the Zamboni Man*. New York: Greenwillow.

Watson, Clyde. (1983). *Father Fox's Feast of Songs*. Ill. Wendy Watson. New York: Philomel.

Williams, Karen Lynn. (1998). *Painted Dreams*. Ill. Catherine Stock. New York: Lothrop.

Williams, Vera. (1984). *Music, Music for Everyone*. New York: Greenwillow.

Winter, Jeanette. (1998). *My Name Is Georgia*. San Diego: Harcourt.

Winter, Jonah. (1991). *Diego*. Ill. Jeanette Winter. New York: Knopf.

Winter, Jeanette. (1984). *Hush, Little Baby*. New York: Pantheon.

Yashima, Taro. (1955). *Crow Boy*. New York: Viking.

Yolen, Jane. (1986). *The Lullaby Song Book*. Ill. Charles Mikolaycak. San Diego: Harcourt.

Yolen, Jane. (1977). *The Seeing Stick*. Ill. Remy Charlip and Demetra Maraslis. New York: Crowell.

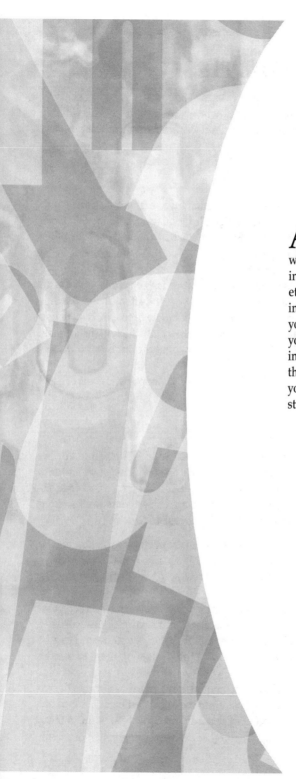

PLANNING YOUR PROGRAM

As you begin to plan the literature program for your class or group of children, you will first need to familiarize yourself with the actual literature. Spend several afternoons or evenings in the library reading picture books and browsing through poetry for children. Look up and read any of the books mentioned in this text or that you have found in other sources that seem to you to have promise for your students. Make notes about those you plan to use. Some teachers and day-care professionals use index cards; others use loose-leaf notebooks. The important thing, whatever method you choose, is to select one that allows you to find the books again easily and to remember what strengths you saw in them.

SEEING THE POSSIBILITIES

Choose books for their literary value and for the quality of the text and the illustrations. Then think about the ways in which the literature itself, or extensions of it, support goals of early childhood education and of your curriculum in particular. You will often find that one book has many possibilities. Here are some examples.

A Book for Preschoolers

Hattie and the Fox (Fox, 1986), for example, is selected by many day-care professionals and kindergarten teachers because of its patterned and predictable language. Hattie the hen looks out one morning and sees something in the bushes. She immediately announces to the other barnyard animals that she can see a nose. The goose, the pig, the sheep, the horse, and the cow each give their two-word responses to this information.

Hattie continues to announce what she sees, in cumulative fashion, adding a nose to the two eyes, then two ears to the two eyes and the nose. Each time the animals answer with the same phrases. Hattie gets more and more agitated as more and more of the fox is revealed. Finally she announces that it is a fox and flies up into a nearby tree. Only then do the animals really pay attention. The cow's loud "moo" frightens the fox away, and the animals stand quietly, too startled to speak.

Following are some examples of how this book can be used to support the goals of early childhood education.

Language Development

Goal.   "Children will enjoy the creative and aesthetic use of language." The patterned language, alliteration, and just plain fun of "Goodness gracious me!" makes this a story children enjoy hearing over and over. They should have the opportunity to hear it more than once, either through its selection by them as an "old favorite," through an aide or other adult sharing it with small groups, or by listening to a tape as they turn the pages of the book.

Goal.   "Children will become skilled listeners." Adults can enhance children's attentive listening by having them say the words they know as the book is being read. A variation is to have a child or small group of children take the part of the pig, the cow, or the horse, and say just what the animal says.

As children hear this story they quickly gain control over the story structure. As it is repeated, they then can match the words they are hearing and saying to the words in print. A big book format facilitates this with a group of children, but the same end can be achieved by sharing the book with one or two children at a time, allowing them to see the print clearly.

This is a fine story for dramatization. Children who portray the animals might decide upon their own stock responses rather than using those from the book, particularly if new animals are being added to accommodate the number of children to be involved in the activity. They might decide to have a different animal approaching, or to have different parts of the animal appearing first.

Intellectual Development

Goal.   "Children will become skilled in a variety of thinking processes." This book encourages observation as more and more of the fox is revealed. You could begin by reading the text and showing the illustrations, having skipped the title and covered the back cover, which shows the fox. Then children could see what Hattie sees and predict with each illustration what the animal might be.

The children could find and cut out animal pictures in magazines. They could then cover all but a small part of the animal and let others guess what is there.

The children also might demonstrate their grasp of the sequence of the story, and thus gain experience in organizing, by telling or helping to tell the story using feltboard figures. Have the pieces displayed in random order. Let the children select what one will be needed next as you tell the story, or let them arrange the pieces and tell the story themselves.

Goal.   "Children will engage successfully in problem solving." You might ask children why they think the other animals didn't seem to pay much attention to what Hattie was saying. What else might she have done to have gotten their help in identifying the animal in the bushes?

Personality Development

Goal.   "Children will weigh evidence and make appropriate choices." After reading the book, you might suggest that the children to decide what they would like to do in relation to the book. It might be a group decision, between activities such as making feltboard characters in order to retell it or making puppets. They may make individual decisions, with some choosing to make pictures using collage techniques or cut out and partially cover a picture of an animal and others creating an observational riddle. Children might decide whether they wanted to work by themselves or with others on the project.

Social and Moral Development

Goal.   "Children will view a situation from more than one perspective." If children are dramatizing the story or retelling it with puppets or feltboard characters, they should have the opportunity to play several roles. They might then tell the incident as the fox would or perhaps use Hattie's point of view.

Goal.   "Children will engage competently in group activities." You can help children work successfully in groups by making certain that the task is clear. Perhaps each child could identify what animal his or her puppet will be. For very young children, the task for "group" work may be to share materials, and to engage in friendly talk as they work.

Aesthetic and Creative Development

Goal.   "Children will use, experiment with, and gain control over a variety of art media." *Hattie and the Fox* is illustrated with a technique using tissue paper collage and conte crayon. Young children could explore making a collage picture. With preschoolers, however, this

Children will hear language used effectively as they listen to the description of these children in their attic bedroom. (From Island Boy *by Barbara Cooney. Copyright © 1988 by Barbara Cooney Porter. Used by permission of Penguin USA.)*

activity is likely to be more successful if you use construction paper rather than tissue paper, because its stiffness makes it easier to cut and paste.

Goal.   "Children will respond favorably to diverse styles of art and music." Children could be asked what they notice about the illustrations and encouraged to give a variety of responses. The book might be compared with *Rosie's Walk* (Hutchins, 1968), in which Rosie the hen goes for a walk, oblivious to the fact that she is being stalked by a fox. Rosie is safe in her naiveté as one misfortune after another befalls the fox, and she continues merrily on her way. Thus children would see one hen noticing danger and another totally unaware of it, but both being safe in the end. They might tell how the illustrations in the two books differ, describing the different styles of art and the media used.

A Book for Primary Grades

Just as there are many possibilities for preschool children to enjoy and respond to *Hattie and the Fox,* so too are there opportunities for second- or third-graders to enjoy and respond to *Island Boy* (Cooney, 1988). The story is of Matthias, whose father and mother moved to an island, cleared the land, and there raised twelve children. Eventually all the children grew up and left the island, even Matthias, the youngest, who sailed as a cabin boy on the ship *Six Brothers*. Fifteen years later, having seen much of the world and become master of the *Six Brothers*, Matthias decides to return to the island. His parents have moved to the mainland, so he and his new wife are alone. They have three daughters, all of whom marry and leave the island. Several years later, after the death of both Matthias's wife and the husband of one of his daughters, his widowed daughter and her son, young Matthias, decide to live with Matthias on the island. Young Matthias plans to be a sea captain when he grows up, then come back to the island. One rough and windy day the elder Matthias's dory capsizes and he is drowned. People come to the island for the funeral, and young Matthias hears them paying their respects to this steadfast man who was his grandfather, and recalling the good life he led. The book ends with Matthias's burial beneath the apple tree his mother had planted so long ago.

Language Development

Goal.   "Children will understand the mature syntax of their language." Simply listening to the story, children will hear the flow and the variation of effective writing. For example, the description of the twelve children in their attic bedroom contains specific vocabulary, attention to the sound of the words, and an inverted word order. "In the soft salt air wafting up from the cove, they slept, the girls on one side, the boys on the other. (n.p.)"

Goal.   "Children will communicate effectively, both orally and in writing." Children might interview an older relative or neighbor. They could then write a life story, including something about that person's childhood, life as a young adult, and life at present. They would be using both oral and written language skills.

Intellectual Development

Goal.   "Children will continue to acquire new concepts and refine old ones." As children read or listen to this story, they are presented with ideas about the passage of time and the changes that can occur in one lifetime. They see the connection of the generations; the constancy of the land; what life was and is like on an island in the northeast; how a map can be read (endpapers); and illustrations that show many things about life in an earlier period, from the individual slates the children used as their mother taught them to the trundle bed Matthias slept in when he was a child.

Goal.   "Children will develop skill in a variety of thinking processes." If you have read this to children, you might want to share *Yonder* (Johnston, 1988), another book that shows an individual settling, raising a family, dying and being buried on the family land. It also shows life in an earlier period, this time with an inland setting. Children could compare the relationships among the generations of relatives in each book, the importance of trees—indeed, special trees—and offer their ideas about why both authors include these aspects. They might also compare the lives of the children in the books with their own lives, the homes they live in, the ways they play, the objects in their homes, and the people who are important in their lives.

Personality Development

Goal. "Children will develop positive and realistic self-concepts." When little Matthias says he wants to be a sea captain and then come back and live on the island, old Matthias says it is better to see the world before deciding where one's "heart lies." Young Matthias says he already knows. Children might write in their journals where their hearts "lie" right now. If they had to decide where they would live and what they would do, what would they say? They might share their journals with a friend and discuss the entries each has made.

Goal. "Children will begin to recognize values and choose from among values." Children could be engaged in a discussion focusing on what was important to Matthias, using questions like the following.

1. When Matthias died, people said he had had a good life. Do you agree? Why or why not?
2. What would you consider to be a good life?
3. Matthias would not sell his house on the island. What do you have right now that you would be unwilling to sell? Why?
4. What would you want people to remember about you? Why is this important to you?

Social and Moral Development

Goal. "Children will view a situation from more than one perspective, seeing the viewpoint of another person." Children might role-play Matthias and a person who wants him to sell the island, after his wife's death and before his daughter and grandson come to live with him. Each would try to convince the other of his or her point of view. They might then repeat the role-play, changing both roles and partners. When they had played it twice, they could discuss as a group the reasons various people gave for their positions.

Goal. "Children will engage competently in group activities." In groups of three, children could plan and complete a series of four pictures that would show someone what they would need to know to live comfortably on the island. They would have to agree on what needed to be in the pictures and be able to explain their choices when they shared the pictures with others in the class.

Aesthetic and Creative Development

Goal. "Children will exhibit a sensory awareness of their environment." You could ask children to write a description of how it feels to slide down a snow-covered hill, wade knee-deep in water, climb over rocks, sit by a warm stove when it is cold and damp outside; all experiences shown in the book.

Goal. "Children will enjoy experiencing the work of others and participating in the arts themselves." Display the work the children have done, and give them a choice of media when they do their series of illustrations. They might want to experiment with dabbing paint on the paper after seeing *Yonder.*

SELECTING ACTIVITIES

Many of these goals and activities, though not all, are compatible with one another for each of the books. Given these possibilities, far more than you would actually do with any one group of children, your task becomes that of deciding which you wish to pursue. Here are three general suggestions for determining the merit of specific activities for extending books.

First, the activity should enhance the literature, not detract from it. Kindergartners or preschoolers dramatizing *Hattie and the Fox* take an active part in the story, help build the suspense, and work together in developing their understanding of it. They enjoy the predictability of the language and the plot. They are likely to want to hear the book again and to want to dramatize it in various ways, and to think positively about literature as a result. If, however, you require the children to practice individually with flash cards until they have learned the words each animal says, it is likely that many of the children will see literature as a source of frustrating work. They will not be eager to have you read more books, let alone repeat *Hattie and the Fox*. They will not have gained any deeper understanding of, or appreciation for, the literature.

Second, the activity should emerge naturally from the book. Because *Island Boy* gives such a full description of life on the island, in both text and illustrations, it lends itself to a comparison of Matthias's lifestyle with that of the children. What experiences did he have? What was his daily life like? What did he value? Why did he make the decisions he did? How might the children answer these questions for themselves, and what are the similarities and differences between the two? The children might construct a chart to visually display their responses and make the comparison easier. On the other hand, suppose you look at the page on which Matthias heads for the mainland in his dory even though the weather looks bad. He does not return alive. You initiate a study of water safety. The children relate experiences and make charts about safe swimming conditions, safe boating practices, and general safety rules around water. The experiences themselves are valid, but they are not central to the meaning of the story. You find that you have to strain to tie the idea back to the book once you have finished, and that rereading the book to the children has no new meaning resulting from your endeavors.

Third, the activities should match both the needs and the abilities of the children. Making collage illustrations with construction paper rather than tissue paper after sharing *Hattie and the Fox* allows preschoolers to explore the artistic technique using materials they can manipulate successfully. Having second- or third-graders interview an adult about his or her childhood memories after hearing *Island Boy* gives the children experience in planning an interview, using oral language and listening skills, and reporting accurately what another has said and in writing. The activities for both books relate to goals for early childhood education. Deciding which are most appropriate means knowing your children well, being able to assess and rank their needs, and knowing which needs will be met in other ways. It also means recognizing that there will be a range of needs and abilities in any group of children and that you will be planning activities for small groups or individuals much of the time. Some preschoolers are able to cut pictures from magazines; others still need practice controlling scissors and benefit more from cutting large, less detailed shapes. Some of your children may need help learning to work cooperatively with others. Some may need to work alone before they are ready to contribute to a group project. Being able to determine which activities should be suggested to which children is a professional skill of teaching and day-care work.

RECOGNIZING THE LARGER CONTEXT

The sharing of a single book fits within the context of all the literature the children are experiencing, and the literature fits within the context of their lives both at home and at school. Your planning will be more effective if you think of the larger picture as you make decisions about literature and literature-based activities.

The Literature Curriculum

As you select individual books and as you plan your curriculum, group some of the books into units or webs. Ideas for grouping may emerge as you look at the literature, a particular author or illustrator's work, or several books expressing a similar theme. Sometimes you may need to use reference guides to children's literature to help you find books that fit the topics you intend to develop. With *Hattie and the Fox* you might look for other stories about foxes and hens, particularly ones in which the fox presents a danger to the hen. Your grouping might be *Hattie, Rosie's Walk* (Hutchins, 1968), and *Red Hen and Sly Fox* (French, 1995).

You might focus on books with repetition, in which case *Hattie* could be combined with *When I First Came to This Land* (Ziefert, 1998), *The Little Old Lady Who Was Not Afraid of Anything* (Williams, 1986), and *Mr. Gumpy's Outing* (Burningham, 1971). You might even decide to engage children in games of careful observation and, after having shared *Hattie,* have them guess what they are seeing in *Just Look* (Hoban, 1996), then find the mouse in each of the illustrations of Waber's humorous *Do You See a Mouse?* (1995).

Can you find the mouse in this illustration? (Illustration from Do You See a Mouse? *Copyright © 1995 by Bernard Waber. Reprinted by permission of Houghton Mifflin Company. All rights reserved.)*

With *Island Boy,* you might look at other works by Barbara Cooney, perhaps narrowing the representation of this very prolific author/illustrator to her Caldecott Award books *Chanticleer and the Fox* (1958) and *Ox-Cart Man* (Hall, 1979), or selecting ones, such as *Emily* (Bedard, 1992), *Miss Rumphius* (1982) and *Eleanor* (1996) that depict the lives of strong protagonists. You might combine books on the theme of changes over time, particularly within the life of an individual, and have students compare *Uncle Jed's Barbershop* (Mitchell, 1993), *Maisie* (Schertle, 1995), and *Grandfather's Journey* (Say, 1993) with *Island Boy.* This would provide diversity in both the gender and the ethnic background of the characters, another strength.

You will sequence some units throughout the school year, and the placement of these units may be a determining factor in their success. You will have other units and books in mind, but will be flexible in your planning of when they will be presented. The units mentioned above might come at any convenient time, whereas holiday books obviously need to be scheduled to coincide with the event. You will check your general plan to make certain that you are developing a balanced literature curriculum that has both prose and poetry, fantasy and realism, classic and modern stories.

The Child's World

Plans for bringing children and books together must always revolve around the specific children with whom you are working. The children must be able to create meaning from the books you share because they are touched by them—through the topic, the language, the emotion expressed, and the intellectual stimulation they provide. You will want to have books that depict a diverse set of characters, so that children both see themselves and the people they know in books and come to know and appreciate others who are different from them. You will want children to see literature in various formats—hardcover and paperback books, videos, CD-ROM retellings—and come to appreciate the strengths of each of them. And you will think not just of the world in which the child finds himself or herself at the moment, but the world the child will live in for the future. Most of all, you will want children to find literature a source of joy and knowledge, and this will guide not only your selection of books but also the way in which you share them with children.

EVALUATING YOUR LITERATURE PROGRAM

You will evaluate your literature curriculum on a daily basis and at the close of the year. Daily evaluation will be based on the specific goals and objectives of each lesson. Did the children find at least three hidden objects in each picture? Could each child think of at least two activities Curious George might do if he were in the classroom? Did the children state two ways in which two books were alike, and two ways in which they were different? Did the children repeat the refrain with you as you read a book for the second time?

Evaluation at the close of the year will involve an assessment of the program and the children's development. Was the program balanced? Were the books and activities appropriate for the children? Were you using the best literature available? As you look at the children's behavior, you will discern changes that have occurred over the year and will find patterns of behavior that indicate the children's response to literature. A successful literature program should result in some or all of these behaviors: Children will reread or look at the illustrations in books you have read to them.

Children will choose to read or look at books in their free time or as work choices.

Children will recommend books and book-related activities to one another.

Children will choose to respond to literature through art, music, movement, and drama.

Children will talk about book characters and happenings in new situations.

Children will ask you to read to them.

You will also be evaluating goals for your students in their language, intellectual, personal, social, moral, aesthetic, and creative development. Your literature program will have supported growth in all of these areas.

Extending Your Learning

1. Select one book. List the goals of early childhood education that it supports, stating your rationale for why it supports each one. Then suggest several possible units for use of the book.
2. Evaluate a literature experience you have had with children. List specific criteria and describe how well each was met.

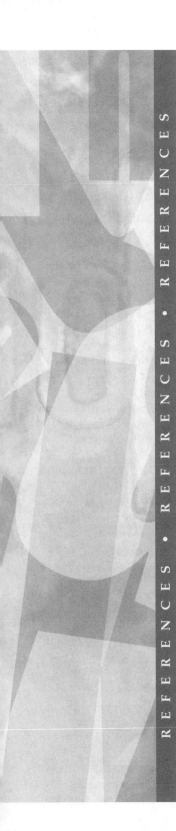

CHILDREN'S LITERATURE CITED

Burningham, John. (1971). *Mr. Gumpy's Outing*. New York: Holt.

Cooney, Barbara. (1988). *Island Boy*. New York: Viking.

Cooney, Barbara. (1982). *Miss Rumphius*. New York: Viking.

Fox, Mem. (1986). *Hattie and the Fox*. Ill. Patricia Mullins. New York: Macmillan.

French, Vivian. (1995). *Red Hen and Sly Fox*. Ill. Sally Hobson. New York: Simon & Schuster.

Hall, Donald. (1979). *Ox-Cart Man*. Ill. Barbara Cooney. New York: Viking.

Hoban, Tana. (1996). *Just Look*. New York: Greenwillow.

Hutchins, Pat. (1968). *Rosie's Walk*. New York: Collier.

Johnston, Tony. (1988). *Yonder*. Ill. Lloyd Bloom. New York: Dial.

Mitchell, Margaree King. (1993). *Uncle Jed's Barbershop*. Ill. by James Ransome. New York: Simon.

Say, Allen. (1993). *Grandfather's Journey*. Boston: Houghton Mifflin.

Schertle, Alice. (1995). *Maisie*. Ill. Lydie Dabcovich. New York: Lothrop.

Waber, Bernard. (1995). *Do You See a Mouse?* Boston: Houghton Mifflin.

Williams, Linda. (1986). *The Little Old Lady Who Was Not Afraid of Anything*. Ill. by Megan Lloyd. New York: Crowell.

Ziefert, Harriet. (1998). *When I First Came to This Land*. Ill. Simms Taback. New York: Putnam.

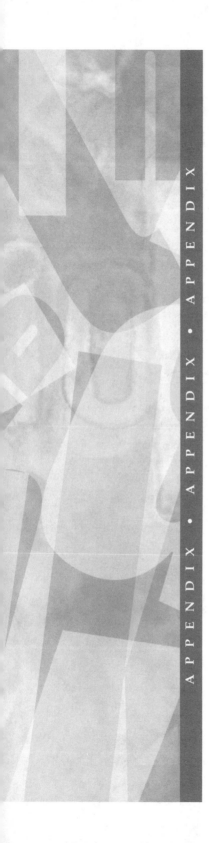

APPENDIX

The Caldecott Medal

The Caldecott Medal is awarded annually to the illustrator of the most distinguished American picture book for children. The winner is selected by a committee of the Association for Library Service to Children of the American Library Association.

1938. *Animals of the Bible* by Helen Dean Fish, ill. by Dorothy P. Lathrop, Lippincott. *Honor Books: Seven Simeons* by Boris Artzvbasheff, Viking; *Four and Twenty Blackbirds* by Helen Dean Fish, ill. by Robert Lawson, Stokes.

1939. *Mel Li* by Thomas Handforth, Doubleday. *Honor Books: The Forest Pool* by Laura Adams Armet, Longmans; *Wee Gillis* by Munro Leat, ill. by Robert Lawson, Viking; *Snow White and the Seven Dwarfs* by Wanda Gag, Coward-McCann; *Barkis* by Clare Newberry, Harper & Row; *Andy and the Lion* by James Daugherty, Viking.

1940. *Abraham Lincoln* by Ingra and Edgar Parin D'Aulaire, Doubleday. *Honor Books: Cock-A-Doodle-Doo* by Berta and Elmer Hader, Macmillan; *Madeline* by Ludwig Bemelmans, Viking Press; *The Ageless Story,* ill. by Lauren Ford, Dodd, Mead.

1941. *They Were Strong and Good* by Robert Lawson, Viking Press. *Honor Book: April's Kittens* by Clare Newberry, Harper & Row.

1942. *Make Way For Ducklings* by Robert McCloskey, Viking. *Honor Books: An American ABC* by Maud and Miska Petersham, Macmillan; *In My Mother's House* by Ann Nolan Clark, ill. by Velino Herrera, Viking Press; *Paddle-to-the-Sea* by Holling C. Holling, Houghton Mifflin; *Nothing at All* by Wanda Gag, Coward-McCann.

1943. *The Little House* by Virginia Lee Burton, Houghton Mifflin. *Honor Books: Dash and Dart* by Mary and Conrad Buff, Viking Press; *Marshmallow* by Clare Newberry, Harper & Row.

1944. *Many Moons* by James Thurber, ill. by Louis Slobodkin, Harcourt. *Honor Books: Small Rain: Verses from the Bible* selected by Jessie Orton Jones, ill. by Elizabeth Orton Jones, Viking; *Pierre Pigeon* by Lee Kingman, ill. by Arnold E. Bare, Houghton Mifflin; *The Mighty Hunter* by Berta and Elmer Hadar, Macmillan; *A Child's Good Night Book* by Margaret Wise Brown, ill. by Jean Charlot, W. R. Scott; *Good Luck Horse* by Chih-Yi Chan, ill. by Piao Chan, Whittlesey.

1945. *Prayer for a Child* by Rachel Field, ill. by Elizabeth Orton Jones, Macmillan. *Honor Books: Mother Goose,* ill. by Tasha Tudor, Walck; *In the Forest* by Marie Hall Ets, Viking; *Yonie Wondernose* by Marguerite de Angeli, Doubleday; *The Christmas Anna Angel* by Ruth Sawyer, ill. by Kate Seredy, Viking.

1946. *The Rooster Crows* (traditional Mother Goose), ill. by Maud and Miska Petersham, Macmillan. *Honor Books: Little Lost Lamb* by Golden MacDonald, ill. by Leonard Weisgard, Doubleday; *Sing Mother Goose* by Opal Wheeler, ill. by Marjorie Torrey, Dutton; *My Mother Is the Most Beautiful Woman in the World* by Becky Reyher, ill. by Ruth Gannet, Lothrop.

1947. *The Little Island* by Golden MacDonald, ill. by Lenord Weisgard, Doubleday. *Honor Books: Rain Drop Splash* by Alvin Tresselt, ill. by Leonard Weisgard, Lothrop; *Boats on the River* by Marjorie Flack, ill. by Jay Hyde Barnum, Viking; *Timothy Turtle* by Al Graham, ill. by Tony Palazzo, Viking; *Pedro, the Angel of Olivera Street* by Leo Politi, Scribner's; *Sing in Praise; A Collection of the Best Loved Hymns* by Opal Wheeler, ill. by Marjorie Torrey, Dutton.

1948. *White Snow, Bright Snow* by Alvin Tresselt, ill. by Roger Duvoisin, Lothrop. *Honor Books: Stone Soup* by Marcia Brown, Scribner's; *McElligot's Pool* by Dr. Seuss, Random House; *Bambino the Clown* by George Schreiber, Viking; *Roger and the Fox* by Lavinia Davis, ill. by Hildegard Woodward, Doubleday; *Song of Robin Hood* ed. by Anne Malcolmson, ill. by Virginia Lee Burton, Houghton Mifflin.

1949. *The Big Snow* by Betta and Elmer Hader, Macmillan. *Honor Books: Blueberries for Sal* by Robert McCloskey, Viking Press; *All Around the Town* by Phyllis McGinley, ill. by Helen Stone, Lippincott; *Juanita* by Leo Politi, Scribner's; *Fish in the Air* by Kurt Wiese, Viking.

1950. *Song of the Swallows* by Leo Politi, Scribner's. *Honor Books: America's Ethan Allen* by Stewart Holbrook, ill. by Lynd Ward, Houghton Mifflin; *The Wild Birthday Cake* by Lavinia Davis, ill. by Hildegard Woodward, Doubleday; *The Happy Day* by Ruth Krauss, ill. by Marc Simont, Harper & Row; *Bartholomew and the Oobleck* by Dr. Seuss, Random House; *Henry Fisherman* by Marcia Brown, Scribner's.

1951. *The Egg Tree* by Katherine Milhous, Scribner's. *Honor Books: Dick Whittington and His Cat* by Marcia Brown, Scribner's; *The Two Reds* by Will, ill. by Nicolas, Harcourt; *If I Ran the Zoo* by Dr. Seuss, Random House; *The Most Wonderful Doll in the World* by Phyllis McGinley, ill. by Helen Stone, Lippincott; *T-Bone, the Baby Sitter* by Clare Newberry, Harper & Row.

1952. *Finders Keepers* by Will, ill. by Nicolas, Harcourt. *Honor Books: Mr. T.W. Anthony Woo* by Marie Hall Ets, Viking; *Skipper John's Cook* by Marcia Brown, Scribner's; *All Falling Down* by Gene Zion, ill. by Margaret Bloy Graham, Harper & Row; *Bear Party* by William Pene du Bois, Viking; *Feather Mountain* by Elizabeth Olds, Houghton Mifflin.

1953. *The Biggest Bear* by Lynd Ward, Houghton Mifflin. *Honor Books: Puss in Boots* by Charles Perrault, ill. and tr. by Marcia Brown, Scribner's; *One Morning in Maine* by Robert McCloskey, Viking; *Ape in a Cape* by Fritz Eichen-

berg, Harcourt; *The Storm Book* by Charlotte Zolotow, ill. by Margaret Bloy Graham, Harper & Row; *Five Little Monkeys* by Juliet Kepes, Houghton Mifflin.

1954. *Madeline's Rescue* by Ludwig Bemelmans, Viking Press. *Honor Books: Journey Cake, HO!* by Ruth Sawyer, ill. by Robert McCloskey, Viking; *When Will the World Be Mine?* by Miriam Schlein, ill. by Jean Charlot, W.R. Scott; *The Steadfast Tin Soldier* by Hans Christian Andersen, ill. by Marcia Brown, Scribner's; *A Very Special House* by Ruth Krauss, ill. by Maurice Sendak, Harper & Row; *Green Eyes* by A. Birnbaum, Capitol.

1955. *Cinderella, or the Little Glass Slipper* by Charles Perrault, tr. and ill. by Marcia Brown, Scribner's. *Honor Books: Book of Nursery and Mother Goose Rhymes,* ill. by Marguerite de Angeli, Doubleday; *Wheel on the Chimney* by Margaret Wise Brown, ill. by Tibor Gergely, Lippincott; *The Thanksgiving Story* by Alice Dalgliesh, ill. by Helen Sewell, Scribner's.

1956. *Frog Went A-Courtin'* ed. by John Langstaff, ill. by Feodor Rojankovsky, Harcourt. *Honor Books: Play with Me* by Marie Hall Ets, Viking; *Crow Boy* by Taro Yashima, Viking.

1957. *A Tree Is Nice* by Janice May Udry, ill. by Marc Simont, Harper & Row. *Honor Books: Mr. Penny's Race Horse* by Marie Hall Ets, Viking; *1 Is One* by Tasha Tudor, Walck; *Anatole* by Eve Titus, ill. by Paul Galdone, McGraw-Hill; *Gillespie and the Guards* by Benjamin Elkin, ill. by James Daugherty, Viking; *Lion* by William Pene du Bois, Viking.

1958. *Time of Wonder* by Robert McCloskey, Viking. *Honor Books: Fly High, Fly Low* by Don Freeman, Viking. *Anatole and the Cat* by Eve Titus, ill. by Paul Galdone, McGraw-Hill.

1959. *Chanticleer and the Fox* adapted from Chaucer and ill. by Barbara Cooney, Crowell. *Honor Books: The House That Jack Built* by Antonio Frasconi, Harcourt; *What Do You Say, Dear?* by Sesyle Joslin, ill. by Maurice Sendak, W. R. Scott; *Umbrella* by Taro Yashima, Viking.

1960. *Nine Days to Christmas* by Marie Hall Ets and Aurora Labastida, ill. by Marie Hall Ets, Viking. *Honor Books: Houses from the Sea* by Alice E. Goudey, ill. by Adrienne Adams, Scribner's; *The Moon Jumpers* by Janice May Udry, ill. by Maurice Sendak, Harper & Row.

1961. *Baboushka and the Three Kings* by Ruth Robbins, ill. by Nicolas Sidjakov, Parnassus Imprints. *Honor Book: Inch by Inch* by Leo Lionni, Obolensky.

1962. *Once a Mouse . . .* by Marcia Brown, Scribner's. *Honor Books: The Fox Went Out on a Chilly Night* by Peter Spier,

Doubleday; *Little Bear's Visit* by Else Holmelund Minarik, ill. by Maurice Sendak, Harper & Row, *The Day We Saw the Sun Come Up* by Alice E. Goudey, ill. by Adrienne Adams, Scribner's.

1963. *The Snowy Day* by Ezra Jack Keats, Viking Press. *Honor Books: The Sun Is a Golden Earring* by Natalia M. Belting, ill. by Bernarda Bryson, Holt, Rinehart & Winston; *Mr. Rabbit and the Lovely Present* by Charlotte Zolotow, ill. by Maurice Sendak, Harper & Row.

1964. *Where the Wild Things Are* by Maurice Sendak, Harper & Row. *Honor Books: Swimmy* by Leo Lionni, Pantheon; *All in the Morning Early* by Sorche Nic Leodhas, ill. by Evaline Ness, Holt, Rinehart & Winston; *Mother Goose and Nursery Rhymes*, ill. by Philip Reed, Atheneum.

1965. *May I Bring A Friend?* by Beatrice Schenk de Regniers, ill. by Beni Montresor, Atheneum. *Honor Books: Rain Makes Applesauce* by Julian Scheer, ill. by Marvin Bileck, Holiday; *The Wave* by Margaret Hodges, ill. by Blair Lent, Houghton Mifflin; *A Pocketful of Cricket* by Rebecca Caudill, ill. by Evaline Ness, Holt, Rinehart & Winston.

1966. *Always Room for One More* by Sorche Nic Leodhas, ill. by Nonny Hogrogian, Holt, Rinehart & Winston. *Honor Books: Hide and Seek Fog* by Alvin Tresselt, ill. by Roger Duvoisin, Lothrop; *Just Me* by Marie Hall Ets, Viking Press; *Tom Tit Tot* by Evaline Ness, Scribner's.

1967. *Sam, Bangs & Moonshine* by Evaline Ness, Holt, Rinehart & Winston. *Honor Book: One Wide River to Cross* by Barbara Emberley, ill. by Ed Emberley, Prentice-Hall.

1968. *Drummer Hoff* by Barbara Emberley, ill. by Ed Emberley, Prentice-Hall. *Honor Books: Frederick* by Leo Lionni, Pantheon; *Seashore Story* by Taro Yashima, Viking; *The Emperor and the Kite* by Jane Yolen, ill. by Ed Young, World.

1969. *The Fool of the World and the Flying Ship* by Arthur Ransom, ill. by Uri Shulevitz, Farrar. *Honor Book: Why the Sun and Moon Live in the Sky* by Elphinstone Dayrell, ill. by Blair Lent, Houghton Mifflin.

1970. *Sylvester and the Magic Pebble* by William Steig, Windmill. *Honor Books: Goggles!* by Ezra Jack Keats, Macmillan; *Alexander and the Wind-Up Mouse* by Leo Lionni, Pantheon; *Pop Corn & Ma Goodness* by Edna Mitchell Preston, ill. by Robert Andrew Parker, Viking Press; *Thy Friend, Obadiah* by Brinton Turkle, Viking Press; *The Judge* by Harve Zemach, ill. by Margot Zemach, Farrar.

1971. *A Story, A Story* by Gail E. Haley, Atheneum. *Honor Books: The Angry Moon* by William Sleator, ill. by Blair Lent, Atlantic Little; *Frog and Toad Are Friends* by Arnold Lobel, Harper & Row; *In the Night Kitchen* by Maurice Sendak, Harper & Row.

1972. *One Fine Day* by Nonny Hogrogian, Macmillan. *Honor Books: If All the Seas Were One Sea* by Janina Domanska, Macmillan; *Moja Means One: Swahili Counting Book* by Muriel Feelings, ill. by Tom Feelings, Dial; *Hildild's Night* by Cheli Duran Ryan, ill. by Arnold Lobel, Macmillan.

1973. *The Funny Little Woman* retold by Arlene Mosel, ill. by Blair Lent, Dutton. *Honor Books: Anansi the Spider* adapted and ill. by Gerald McDermott, Holt, Rinehart & Winston; *Hosie's Alphabet* by Hosea, Tobias and Lisa Baskin, ill. by Leonard Baskin, Viking; *Snow White and the Seven Dwarfs* translated by Randall Jarrell, ill. by Nancy Ekholm Burkert, Farrar; *When Clay Sings* by Byrd Baylor, ill. by Tom Bahti, Scribner's.

1974. *Duffy and the Devil* by Harve Zemach, ill. by Margot Zemach, Farrar. *Honor Books Three Jovial Huntsmen* by Susan Jeffers, Bradbury; *Cathedral: The Story of Its Construction* by David Macaulay, Houghton Mifflin.

1975. *Arrow to the Sun* adapted and ill. by Gerald McDermott, Viking. *Honor Book: Jambo Means Hello* by Muriel Feelings, ill. by Tom Feelings, Dial.

1976. *Why Mosquitoes Buzz in People's Ears* retold by Verna Aardema, ill. by Leo and Diane Dillon, Dial. *Honor Books: The Desert Is Theirs* by Byrd Baylor, ill. by Peter Parnall, Scribner's; *Strega Nona* retold and ill. by Tomie dePaola, Prentice-Hall.

1977. *Ashanti to Zulu: African Traditions* by Margaret Musgrove, ill. by Leo and Dianne Dillon, Dial. *Honor Books: The Amazing Bone* by William Steig, Farrar; *The Contest* retold and ill. by Nonny Hogrogian, Greenwillow; *Fish for Supper* by M. B. Goffstein, Dial Press; *The Golem* by Beverly Brodsky McDermott, Lippincott; *Hawk, I'm Your Brother* by Byrd Baylor, ill. by Peter Parnall, Scribner's.

1978. *Noah's Ark* by Peter Spier, Doubleday. *Honor Books: Castle* by David Macaulay, Houghton Mifflin; *It Could Always Be Worse* by Margot Zemach, Farrar.

1979. *The Girl Who Loved Wild Horses* by Paul Goble, Bradbury. *Honor Books: Freight Train* by Donald Crews, Greenwillow; *The Way to Start a Day* by Byrd Baylor, ill. by Peter Parnall, Scribner's.

1980. *Ox-Cart Man* by Donald Hall, ill. by Barbara Cooney, Viking. *Honor Books: Ben's Trumpet* by Rachel Isadora, Greenwillow; *The Treasure* by Uri Shulevitz, Farrar; *The Garden of Abdul Gasazi* by Chris Van Allsburg, Houghton Mifflin.

1981. *Fables* by Arnold Lobel, Harper & Row. *Honor Books: The Bremen-Town Musicians* by Ilse Plume, Doubleday; *The Grey Lady and the Strawberry Snatcher* by Molly Bang, Four Winds; *Mice Twice* by Joseph Low, Atheneum; *Truck* by Donald Crews, Greenwillow.

1982. *Jumanji* by Chris Van Allsburg, Houghton Mifflin. *Honor Books: A Visit to William Blake's Inn: Poems for Innocent and Experienced Travelers* by Nancy Willard, ill. by Alice and Martin Provensen, Harcourt; *Where the Buffaloes Begin* by Olaf Baker, ill. by Stephen Gammell, Frederick Warne; *On Market Street* by Anita Lobel, Greenwillow; *Outside Over There* by Maurice Sendak, Harper & Row.

1983. *Shadow* by Blaise Cendrars, ill. by Marcia Brown, Scribner's. *Honor Books: When I Was Young in the Mountains* by Cynthia Rylant, ill. by Diane Goode, Dutton; *A Chair for My Mother* by Vera Williams, Morrow.

1984. *The Glorious Flight: Across the Channel with Louis Bleriot* by Alice and Martin Provensen, Viking. *Honor Books: Little Red Riding Hood* by Trina Schart Hyman, Holiday; *Ten, Nine, Eight* by Molly Bang, Greenwillow.

1985. *St. George and the Dragon* retold by Margaret Hodges, ill. by Trina Schart Hyman, Little, Brown. *Honor Books: Hansel and Gretel* retold by Rika Lesser, ill. by Paul Zelinsky, Dodd; *Have You Seen My Duckling?* by Nancy Tafuri, Greenwillow; *The Story of Jumping Mouse* by John Steptoe, Lothrop.

1986. *The Polar Express* by Chris Van Allsburg, Houghton Mifflin. *Honor Books: The Relatives Came* by Cynthia Rylant, ill. by Stephen Gammell, Bradbury; *King Bidgood's in the Bathtub* by Audrey Wood, ill. by Don Wood, Harcourt.

1987. *Hey, Al* by Arthur Yorinks, ill. by Richard Egielski, Farrar, Straus & Giroux. *Honor Books: The Village of Round and Square Houses* by Ann Grifalconi, Little, Brown; *Alphabatics* by Suse MacDonald, Bradbury; *Rumpelstiltskin* by Paul Zelinsky, Dutton.

1988. *Owl Moon* by Jane Yolen, ill. by John Schoenherr, Philomel. *Honor Book: Mufaro's Beautiful Daughters* by John Steptoe, Lothrop.

1989. *Song and Dance Man* by Karen Ackerman, ill. by Stephen Gammell, Knopf. *Honor Books: Goldilocks* by James Marshall, Dial; *The Boy of the Three-Year Nap* by Dianne Snyder, ill. by Allen Say, Houghton; *Mirandy and Brother Wind* by Patricia McKissack, ill. by Jerry Pinkney, Knopf.

1990. *Lon Po Po: A Red Riding Hood Story From China* by Ed Young, Philomel. *Honor Books: Hershel and the Hanukkah Goblins* by Eric Kimmell, ill. by Trina Schart Hyman, Holiday; *Bill Peet: An Autobiography* by Bill Peet, Houghton Mifflin; *Color Zoo* by Lois Ehlert, Lippincott; *The Talking Eggs* by Robert San Souci, ill. by Jerry Pinkney, Dial.

1991. *Black and White* by David Macaulay, Houghton. *Honor Books: "More More More," Said the Baby; Three Love Stories* by Vera B. Williams, Greenwillow; *Puss in Boots* by Charles Perrault, ill. by Fred Marcellino, Farrar/Michael di Capua.

1992. *Tuesday* by David Wiesner, Clarion. *Honor Book: Tar Beach* by Faith Ringgold, Crown.

1993. *Mirette on the High Wire* by Emily Arnold McCully, Putnam. *Honor Books: The Stinky Cheese Man* by John Scieszka, ill. by Lane Smith, Viking; *Working Cotton* by Sherley Williams, ill. by Carole Byard, Harcourt; *Seven Blind Mice* by Ed Young, Philomel.

1994. *Grandfather's Journey* by Allen Say, Houghton Mifflin. *Honor Books: In the Small, Small Pond* by Denise Fleming, Holt; *Owen* by Kevin Henkes, Greenwillow; *Peppe the Lamplighter* by Elisa Bartone, ill. by Ted Lewis, Lothrop; *Raven: A Trickster Tale from the Pacific Northwest* by Gerald McDermott; Harcourt; *Yo! Yes!* by Chris Raschka, Orchard.

1995. *Smoky Night* by Eve Bunting, ill. by David Diaz, Harcourt. *Honor Books: John Henry* by Julius Lester, ill. by Jerry Pinkney, Dial; *Swamp Angel* by Anne Isaacs, ill. by Paul O. Zelinsky, Dutton; *Time Flies* by Eric Rohmann, Crown.

1996. *Officer Buckle and Gloria* by Peggy Rathmann, Putnam. *Honor Books: Alphabet City* by Stephen T. Johnson, Viking; *The Faithful Friend* by Robert San Souci, ill. by Brian Pinkney, Simon & Schuster; *Tops and Bottoms* by Janet Stevens, Harcourt; *Zin! Zin! Zin! A Violin!* by Lloyd Moss, ill. by Marjorie Priceman, Simon & Schuster.

1997. *Golem* by David Wisniewski, Clarion. *Honor Books: Hush! A Thai Lullaby* by Minfong Ho, ill. by Holly Meade, Orchard; *The Graphic Alphabet* by David Pelletier, Orchard; *The Paperboy* by Dav Pilkey, Jackson/Orchard; *Starry Messenger* by Peter Sis, Farrar.

1998. *Snowflake Bentley* by Mary Azarian, Houghton Mifflin. *Honor Books: No, David!* by David Shannon, Scholastic; *Tibet Through the Red Box* by Peter Sis, Farrar; *Snow* by Uri Shulevitz, Farrar; *Duke Ellington: The Piano Prince and His Orchestra* by Andrea Davis Pinkney, ill. Brian Pinkney, Hyperion.

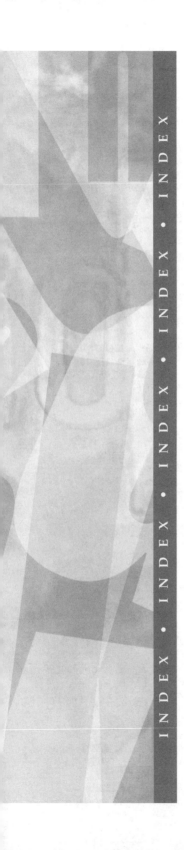

Author / Illustrator / Title Index

SUBJECT INDEX

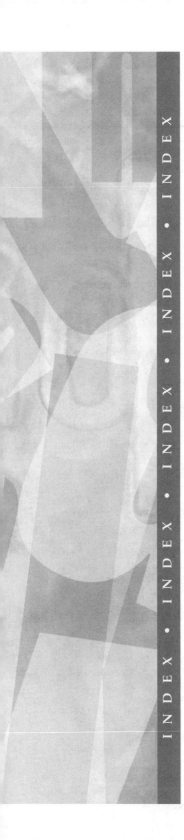

ABOUT THE AUTHOR

Joan I. Glazer is a Professor of Education at Rhode Island College, where she teaches courses in children's literature, language arts, and teacher research. She is co-director of the Ph.D. in Education program offered jointly by Rhode Island College and the University of Rhode Island. She has taught at the elementary school level, served as a Head Start supervisor, and worked as an educational consultant for numerous school districts. She is a past president of the United States Board on Books for Young People and is currently on the Executive Committee of the International Board on Books for Young People. Dr. Glazer was honored with the Distinguished Teacher Award from the School of Education and Human Development at Rhode Island College in 1982, was the first holder of the Thorp Professorship in 1979, and was presented the Award for Service in 1987.